I have never before read anything as positive, and at the same time as foreboding as this story. I feel that we have another Moses whose hand was guided by God. When I started reading this work, I thought I was going to be informed that there was no God. Now I'm not so sure! I have never suffered from anything bad to sink to the bottom and then be saved…

This story can be told to the minions of people who are aboard the *Titanic* and ready to hit the iceberg. It is a fine story which needs to be imprinted on the minds of the world. It is extremely well-written… It reads as smoothly as the proverbial mountain stream.

—Charles Roberts
Perth, Australia

Reading Mino Pavlic's memoir, I felt like a voyeur watching a man's life unfold. The story begins with his childhood and adolescence, moving across countries and between continents, then continuing through his adult years spent in and out of prison, and his struggles with addiction. It finally finishes with his recent struggles to turn his life around.

Mino gives the reader a sense of his history through detailed vignettes. For those of us who are unfamiliar with the world of crime, incarceration, and hardcore drug addiction, his story provides a poignant picture of a life very different from our own. The memoir reveals a man moving from living in the moment to contemplating his past, present, and future. The content is compelling, but so too is the writing; how amazing that someone who has gone through so much pain could write so freely about it.

The book is a window through which the process of one man's change and development is revealed. It allows the reader a glimpse into the author's life and a world many of us choose to ignore, and into how life can be lived more fully through reflection and connection.

—Nicole Bermbach, M.A., C.C.C.
Vancouver, British Columbia

In the spring of 2005, Mr. Pavlic addressed my criminology class at Mission Secondary. For an hour, Mino wound through his personal story of choices and consequences, drug addiction and crime, failure and success, and then answered difficult questions with candor and sincerity. I was pleased my students had the opportunity to share his experiences and hear his message.

Mino puts a face to the dark stranger, the East End addict, the HIV-infected patient struggling with and facing the results of his choices. He offers himself as an example and speaks with passion against substance abuse of all kinds. He does not minimize the small steps in the beginning, but links each step, each choice, to outcomes and possible tragedy. He is an effective anti-drug spokesperson.

Mino's message is also about hope, the will to succeed, and the ability to meet challenges. This book contains an important message about what can be achieved if one has the will and confidence.

The writing of the book stands as an example to young adults facing graduation and wondering if they are capable of fulfilling their dreams. I am pleased to support Mino's quest to tell his story. He is passionate about helping others and I believe he has a significant contribution to make.

—Joseph Abrams
Mission, British Columbia

Today I have read the first twenty-nine chapters of your book, and all I can say is "Wow." This has movie written all over it. What an amazing road you've travelled, and what interesting characters you've come across. At times your story is terrifying, at times ugly, but it's always compelling. There is betrayal, loyalty, and treachery. And the good guys aren't always good.

—Robert Cullen
Camden, Australia

I would never have believed that any normal man could have endured such hardship in his life and yet make such a turn around.

—Rebecca Cadger
New Westminster, British Columbia

I don't know how the author survived, but he did and I'm grateful that this book came out of all his trials and tribulations. Anyone who believes they are struggling against the odds in whatever circumstances can gain inspiration from this story.

—Chris Gibson
New Westminster, British Columbia

As I read, I knew I was reading about someone for whom God's word is not theory but an application. I am not surprised. We now live in challenging and exciting times. I believe you have been chosen to warn others. It is more believable when coming from a survivor!

—Jean Lutz
Ponchatoula, Louisiana

This wonderful story ought to be told to the whole world. He writes well and the story is truly compelling.

—*Adora Bayles*
Esperance, New York

Whether you have met Mino Pavlic personally, or read his book, without a doubt you have been in contact with a miracle. What social services, reform programs, experienced counsellors, and scientific medical discoveries could not do, the Lord Jesus Christ did in a moment's time.

I cannot comprehend the unimaginable depths of depravation a human like Mino could sink to. That's because I didn't know *that* Mino. The Mino I know now is a considerate, kind, sensitive, caring man whose lifestyle defines the word "Christian." He is certainly counted among one of the best saints at our church. What power could so drastically transform a man of Mino's caliber? There's only one answer. Who could it be but Jesus? God gave Mino his first breath, and Mino has committed to giving Him his last breath.

This book will inspire anyone who is beyond hope to again believe in hope (Romans 4:18) and walk into the extraordinary. It's no wonder that Brother Mino, as he is affectionately called, is so deeply involved in prison ministry. His story says it all, and captures the hearts of those listening. The spark of hope is once again lit in the hearts of unimaginable lives that can be changed into the extraordinary. Guaranteed, you will enjoy the read!

—*Beth Reynolds*
Surrey, British Columbia

What a great testimony! It is the signature of the powerful hand of God in Mino's life. Indeed, there is no obstacle when God decides to move His hand in our lives. It is a journey from Egypt to the Promised Land under the eyes of the Almighty God. We just have to accept His will for His glory and for the salvation of thousands of souls who are going to get encouragement, salvation, healing, and restoration through this testimony.

I pray the Lord bless Mino and all the people helping him to make this book possible for people around the world to read.

—*Corneliu Sandru*
New Westminster, British Columbia

Seema, many have read books & received nothing more than the kind words of encouragement, this book was written for those who are looking for something far greater than a mere encouragement...

Since the birthplace of the miraculous has always found itself within the pregnancy of expectation, then without doubt HOPE is the very fuel which ignites them, & that's the purpose of this book, as it offers a hope from within a life where absolutely none existed

3rd Print Run #31   Nov 5/2017

minopavlic@shaw.ca

(Christian testimony of transforming from the queer) on YouTube

FROM THE UNIMAGINABLE TO THE EXTRAORDINARY

To Seema, my hair stylist;

Thanks for your interest, but most of all thank you for your kind words.

I hope you enjoy the book

MIODRAG MINO PAVLIC

FROM THE UNIMAGINABLE TO THE EXTRAORDINARY
Copyright © 2015 by Mino Pavlic

All rights reserved. Neither this publication nor any part of this publication may be reproduced or transmitted in any form or by any means, electronic or mechanical, including photocopying, recording or any information storage and retrieval system, without permission in writing from the author.

Scripture quotations taken from the Holy Bible, King James Version, which is in the public domain.

ISBN: 978-1-4866-0584-2

Word Alive Press
131 Cordite Road, Winnipeg, MB R3W 1S1
www.wordalivepress.ca

WORD ALIVE
—PRESS—

Cataloguing in Publication information may be obtained from Library and Archives Canada.

DEDICATION

I now know without the slightest doubt that throughout the severest trials and greatest storms of my weathered life, the majesty of God has been my life preserver. Envision, even if only momentarily, that the night-and-day differences throughout the course of our sometimes broken lives can be those crossroads where the physical and spiritual worlds meet. Within this interpretation, everything about this book is truly dedicated to the everlasting glory of God.

I also wish to extend my deepest prayers of eternal gratitude to my best friend Bonnie Wilson, who by the grace of God has been one of the greatest night-and-day differences in my life. Without her influential encouragement and spiritual guidance, I would still be walking about aimlessly lost. At times, it felt as if she called in her own excavation crew, as together we sat for countless hours in reflection of my tragic life and searched the depths of my tortured soul. I'm still not sure how it happened, but she somehow melted the coldness that for so long imprisoned my heart. Once she peeled away all the calloused layers, one day while at the altar, like on the wings of a dove, she gave that heart to God. She has truly left an everlasting trail of footprints deep within my heart. If there were no tomorrow, I would want her to always know that after our Lord Jesus, I consider her friendship to be the greatest gift of my life.

Also a great thanks to Pastor David Jobson. He made it perfectly clear that church membership was never meant to be, nor should it ever be, a prerequisite in the path of baptism. His passion drove my desire to be baptized in the name of Jesus. In those whose hearts have opened and expressing a desire for baptism, which may have arisen from within a moment of divine revelation, all ministers should then clearly understand the importance and careful attention that is now necessary. Any hesitation, unwillingness, inattention, or neglect of the significance of baptism will weigh heavily on the balancing scale towards one's successful conversion.

Lastly, my deepest respect and appreciation is given to the widely recognized Pastor Paul Reynolds, bishop of the Emmanuel Pentecostal Church in New Westminster, British Columbia. Also, for her special gift of inspiration, encouragement, and continuing influence, I'd like to acknowledge the pastor's wife, truly a mother to the church, Sister Beth Reynolds.

These precious saints of God, within their own instrumental spheres of patience, wisdom, and spiritual enrichment, entered my life in what can only be described as a sweet-smelling gentle mist, and their presence continues to embrace the depths of my soul.

CONTENTS

INTRODUCTION — xi

PART 1: NO OBSTACLE TOO GREAT

1: Reality Beyond Comprehension — 3
2: In the Beginning — 7
3: Our Private Playground, the World — 12
4: Vancouver, Canada, and Yugoslavia — 18
5: Descent Into Hell — 24
6: Back In Society — 31
7: Oakalla Prison Farm and Beyond — 34
8: Tough Guy at Wilkinson Road Prison — 42
9: A Taste of Freedom — 52
10: Drumheller Penitentiary — 55
11: Bowden Penitentiary — 60
12: Puzzles of Treachery — 63
13: Going to the Supreme Court of Canada — 71
14: The Treachery Plays Itself Out — 78
15: Eight Months of Freedom — 83
16: Fort Saskatchewan Provincial Prison — 86
17: My Brother Mike, The Gentleman Conman — 92
18: Reunion in Vancouver — 94
19: On the Run Again — 97
20: Return to Edmonton — 101
21: A Change in Direction, Tree-Planting — 105
22: My Last Prison Sentence — 109
23: My Friend Brad — 113
24: HIV Confirmed — 116
25: Twenty-Five-Year Reunion — 119
26: Running Wild — 120
27: The Process of Change — 123
28: Hitting Rock Bottom — 125
29: Separation and Faith — 129
30: Miracles of Restoration — 132
31: Frightening HIV Decisions — 136
32: Positive Transformations — 138
33: Our Farm in Langley — 142
34: Disaster on the Horizon — 146
35: Close Calls and the Sasquatch — 148
36: The Coquihalla Cliff — 153
37: Trials and Tribulations — 156

PART 2: IN MEMORY OF AN ANGEL

38:	Shattered Dreams	161
39:	The Nightmare Begins	165
40:	Illness Beyond Comprehension	168
41:	Escaping Death Once Again	170
42:	Criminal Negligence	174
43:	Progressive Blindness	178
44:	Debby's World of Make-Believe	182
45:	Cancer and Isolation	186
46:	Deceptions and Unpardonable Sins	190
47:	Indescribable Heartaches	193
48:	Debby Moves Into the Blue Room	199
49:	Wedding in Armstrong, B.C.	202
50:	Final Moments in Sight	206
51:	Inescapable Heartache	210
52:	Surviving the Aftermath	217
53:	HIV Shows its Ugly Teeth Once Again	221
54:	Escaping Certain Death in Chilliwack	223
55:	Divine Restoration	226

PART 3: LEAVES IN THE WIND

56:	The Telephone Call	233
57:	Steps of Deception	236
58:	Lisa's Arrival	242
59:	Lisa Departs and Goes for the Jugular	247
60:	Escaping the Madness	254

PART 4: JOURNEY INTO GOD'S PRESENCE

61:	An Appointment With God	259
62:	God Turns Up the Heat	262
63:	A True Testimony Is Making A Difference	267
64:	A Proven Statistic and New Inroads	274
65:	Thirty-Three Years of Alcoholism Erased	278
66:	Finally, the Acknowledgement of God	282
67:	God Moves In for the Baptism Checkmate	285
68:	Baptism At Emmanuel Pentecostal Church	290
69:	The Moment of Truth	293
70:	The Footprints of God	296
conclusion		301

Introduction

As a first-time writer, especially when writing words of a non-fictional nature, I find myself assuming a great measure of accountability. From the moment I began writing, I quickly realized that the truths, convictions, and beauty of my powerful testimony, in one form or another, can only be measured by the extent of their influence upon the lives they deeply touched. Being able to capture and express my experiences in a book has without a doubt been a challenging accomplishment. Through it all, I've come to understand and accept one undeniable fact: I have truly been given a gift which is not of this world. I consider these writings to be an invaluable source of insight, an extraordinary journey of self-discovery. Without being aware of it, my destination has always been towards a spiritual awakening such as I never thought possible.

First and foremost, this is not just another religious book about God. Up until my fiftieth year, I never believed in God, nor did such things interest me in any way. This book is all about the hopelessness of a ruined life and its supernatural transformations, which could only have come from a sovereign and merciful God.

From its conception, the writing of this book has been an extremely difficult undertaking. Not a day has gone by when I haven't found myself wrestling with an unknown force seeking the book's failure, and my very destruction. It took ten long years before I came to understand what I was up against. If Jesus Christ has ever performed a miracle in your life and you're willing to share that testimony with others, rest assured that all hell is hot on your trail, wanting to put your lights out, since many could come to believe in Jesus through your testimony. Still not convinced? Just ask Lazarus. He was dead four days before Jesus brought him back to life. It's recorded in the book of Acts that the high priests then conspired to put him back to death.

You could read the Bible ten times from cover to cover and still not know the nature of God. The Bible is a doctrine of fundamental principles inspired by God Himself. Before one can begin to grasp such a doctrine, one first needs to have a personal relationship with God. In order to have such a relationship, regardless of what anyone tries to tell you, you must have a genuine experience of Jesus Christ coming into your life. Without the spirit of Jesus in your life, you will never know the true nature of God, nor will you ever hear from God.

The gospel of John tells us that no one comes to the Father except through the son, Jesus. He is the door by which we must enter. Most of the unbelieving world today laughs at Christianity, and those who believe do so within a casual indifference. Almost all of the thirty-three thousand denominational churches found around the planet believe in a God and preach about a certain supernatural reality, yet sadly, there exists no physical evidence of such a God in many of those churches. Don't let anyone deceive you: there's a huge distinction between believing *in* God and actually believing God!

To believe God is to be obedient to His instructions found throughout the Bible—which means, interpreted, "Basic Instructions Before Leaving Earth." When we're obedient to God's word, transformations follows. If there are no evident transformations, it's because there is no obedience, which is a direct result of having no fear towards a sovereign and supreme God. Most self-proclaimed Christians repeatedly ignore the Word of God, thinking themselves exceptions to God's instructions. When it comes to God, there are no exceptions!

Before he became the greatest champion the church ever knew, the Apostle Paul was its greatest persecutor. His goal had been to wipe Christianity off the face of the planet. Yet after his conversion, while addressing a congregation of believing Christians, he said, *"Examine yourselves, whether ye be in the faith; prove your own selves. Know ye not your own selves, how that Jesus Christ is in you, except ye be reprobates?"* (2 Corinthians 13:5) Just a few chapters earlier, it became crystal clear what he was getting at: *"Therefore if any man be in Christ, he is a new creature: old things are passed away; behold, all things are become new"* (2 Corinthians 5:17).

To truly be in Christ, separation from your old nature is an essential requirement. Anytime you come into contact with someone who claims to have had a personal encounter with Jesus Christ, expect to see physical evidences of divine intervention, deliverance, healing, restoration, and above all else, transformation. Believe me, anything less is a smokescreen of deception! Anytime Jesus Christ stepped into someone's life, signs, wonders, and miracles followed. We are no longer what we used to be; we are set apart. As to what the power of Jesus has done in my life, I am beyond a satisfied customer.

In the physical world, we can argue and debate over just about anything. However, there is one thing no man can ever debate: our own personal experiences. There is no greater influence or impact than that of a personal testimony, and this book is full of them. My life has played itself out in three different stages: testing, brokenness, and divine transformations.

The first part of this book, *No Obstacle Too Great*, as it was first written and self-published in 2004, was but the tip of the iceberg. It outlined the first forty years of my life. Make no mistake about it: there's nothing glamorous about the first part of this story, and I make no excuses. *No Obstacle Too Great* invites you on a riveting roller coaster ride. It's a journey through a shattered and tormented life.

In 2005, I rewrote the book, adding about ten thousand words. I still felt unsatisfied. Only now in the third revision, having combined all four manuscripts of my life into one, do I truly feel I have accomplished my intended purpose. In doing so, I changed the book's original title. What lies beyond the first part of this book gives God's majestic grace its breathlessness; there you will witness how my life began its transformational journey… *from the unimaginable to the extraordinary.*

Many are quick to argue the Bible's validity yet themselves have never read it. As a sad result, their hearts continue to remain cold. I challenge anyone who harbors doubt as to the existence of God, or the supremacy of Jesus, to read this book. It will unshackle your indifference. If you need to experience a modern parting of the Red Sea, believe me, within the pages of this book you'll find yourself walking through it.

If there was anything I ever believed in with strong conviction, it was "bad luck." I've definitely had more than my share of it. However, if you're looking for a miracle in your life, what you'll discover here may change its direction forever. That would be my greatest reward. The testimonies of my night-and-day transformations should be enough to convince anyone, if they're truly sincere, that there's a way out. It's all about Jesus! At fifty-seven years of age, you could never in a million years have convinced me just seven years ago that this was true. The Bible was just another book to me, and the reality of Jesus was just the fantasy of a colorful imagination. Now they're my sustaining lifelines. I'll never forget the crippling impossibilities of my life, nor of Jesus's divine intervention in it. Only His anointed touch could have brought deliverance and healing to a life that was literally drenched in human suffering.

For most of my life, I've felt deserted in the middle of a raging sea, left alone to defend myself in its cold, unknown darkness. With terrifying ferociousness, each year seemed to bring its own thundering wave of suffocating trials. Somehow, I always managed to keep my head above water.

It has never been my intention to lay the burden of blame at anyone's feet. Rather, my primary objective is to expose an enemy we all share. A presence of darkness surrounds us, and it's very real. In its simplest form, it's the wickedness of Satan. Once this darkness enters your life, it becomes like an inescapable electric current. It has taken many of us to unimaginable limits of desperation.

There really is an invisible spiritual battle being fought in the world today, and it's speeding towards a final climax. It's as clear as the reflection in your mirror, yet so many people fail to acknowledge it. Turn on any radio or television station and you'll hear about once beautiful cities around the globe now blanketed in wickedness and moral corruption. Entire nations are immersed in poverty, sickness, and suffering. Every week, disaster upon disaster hammers away at humanity. What will it really take to awaken a sleeping civilization?

When facing insurmountable obstacles without the reality of God in our lives, it's easy to reach a breaking point, where everything becomes as meaningless as scattered leaves blowing in the wind. In moments of weakness such as these, we give up all hope of anything positive in our lives. At sixteen years old, I began my thirty-two-year battle with chronic alcoholism and embarked on a life of criminality, prison survival, and violence. Fourteen of the next twenty-five years were spent in various prisons across Canada. At twenty-nine years of age, I became a narcotic drug addict, battling that addiction for twelve years.

When you see nothing but darkness and emptiness in front of you, and the world has taken that last glimmer of hope, when it seems as though you're out of options, please don't give up! Call upon the mighty name of Jesus and ask for His healing touch. In that moment of faith, He will enter your life.

However, as with anything in life, there's a price to pay. The only question you need to answer is, are you willing to go the distance? When God steps in with that amazing glue He calls grace, all the once-broken pieces of your life will slowly begin the process of being put back together. Changes will happen, but don't expect them to occur overnight, or without sweat. Some of my toughest battles were fought while in the midst of God's miraculous transformations. I'm a living testimony that when God steps in, He will reshape your life beyond your wildest expectations.

The Bible is full of mind-boggling accounts, where God has taken complete nobodies and used them as blessings beyond belief. I was definitely one of those nobodies. What appeared as a life beyond repair was in reality a journey towards the glory of God. Always be on the lookout for what God's chosen messengers have personally seen and endured. What insurmountable obstacles have they overcome? The signs and wonders which manifested themselves in my life speak volumes of my predetermined calling.

Before closing, I'd like to share a revelation which no one can deny. If someone had come to me seventeen years ago and quoted Genesis 12:2—*"And I will make of thee a great nation and I will bless thee, and make thy name great; and thou shalt be a blessing"*—while trying to convince me that such a promise was available to any of us right now, I would have shaken my head and laughed in their face. Not in a million years could you have convinced me that my name could be great, unless it was on a Ten Most Wanted list. That I could be a blessing to anyone would have seemed the fantasy of a deranged mind. No one but God could make such promises. No one but God Almighty could deliver such promises. More importantly, no one but God Himself could enforce such promises.

Whether I was in search of faith or inadvertently running from it, ten years had to pass before I grasped the significance of divine intervention and the role it's played in my life. Make no mistake about it: this supernatural yet mystical force is God on His throne. He never abandoned me, but instead embraced me in His merciful tenderness, and continued in His majestic grace to transform a life that was anything but lost.

PART 1

NO OBSTACLE TOO GREAT

Reality Beyond Comprehension   1

The date was April 24, 1997, and I would never forget it. How could you possibly forget the first time you ever seriously entertained suicide? I really had no idea as to the urgency in my doctor's request to see me, nor did I really care. All I knew for sure while sitting in the little examination room is that if he didn't get around to seeing me soon, I was leaving. My state of mind was that of a chronic alcoholic, and I also had a drug addiction that just wouldn't let go. In reality, I was only in the room for two minutes, but when your body is slowly going into withdrawals, two minutes can easily seem like an hour.

Before we go any further, I'd like to backpedal about two years. I was feeling under the weather, and my kid brother Tomo had talked me into getting a checkup by his doctor. In this very office in December 1995, after my bloodwork results were completed, I was officially diagnosed as HIV-positive. I was also told that as a result of my unpredictability as a drug addict, my life was to be very short-lived. Two years had passed, and I was now in rough shape.

At forty years of age, I was a pitiful sight. Everything I owned could easily fit in a couple of suitcases and any money I had was spent on drugs and staying drunk. During the last six months, my addictions had escalated to unmanageable limits. Somehow I had managed to crawl into a pit so deep that I would have never recovered, had it not been for the grace of God. I was on that speeding train for some time, headed towards its final destination. In many ways, I welcomed the brick wall at the end of the line. Believe me, no one but God could have rolled the dice in my favor. My life was about to enter a stage beyond repair.

Even though the doctor looked uneasy when he walked into the room, I was happy to see him, as I would shortly be heading across the street to the liquor store. While looking everywhere but at me, he stated that unfortunately my HIV infection was progressing into its final stages. Regrettably, I was in the process of slowly dying.

His words embraced me in a feeling of complete emptiness; actually, loneliness would be a better way to describe how I felt. I didn't hear any of the doctor's further comments, nor was I aware of my surroundings. Although no more than a few seconds had passed, it seemed as though my whole life flashed before me. You would have never known by looking at me, but a volcanic rage swept over me, and it definitely wasn't born of anger, but rather total helplessness. I just couldn't find any rational justification for all the suffering

I had thus far endured. I had even silently pleaded to God for a miracle to end this madness, which for the past twenty-five years had daily drained the very life from me. I figured even this feeble attempt to save myself would remain unanswered, as I needed something beyond a miracle.

In a nutshell, my life has been one of great instability. My existence has been a shattered and tormented one. My lifestyle was one of crime, prison survival, and violence, along with drug and alcohol addiction. The price I paid for this goes far beyond any of those things. As a direct result of sharing needles, I contracted the incurable and devastating HIV illness, which now threatened to extinguish my life. If I was in fact dying, I knew that it wasn't going to be from AIDS. There was no other alternative for me at this point, except a quick fix.

Before leaving the doctor's office, he gave me the telephone number of an HIV specialist who urgently wanted to see me. In receiving this crippling news, my immediate thought was, *What can anyone do for me at this point?* I assured him I would call, all the while knowing I wouldn't. It seemed as though my fate had been predetermined. I used the payphone before going into the liquor store and called my buddy Ross, letting him know that the party was on; I'd be there in a few hours. I first needed a few stiff drinks and some time alone to collect my thoughts.

I grabbed a couple of bottles of whisky and headed for the nearest park, just a few short blocks away. After several drinks, I found myself angry at everyone but myself. I looked everywhere but within myself for reasons to justify what was happening. The worst of my problem was my inability to even find a glimmer of hope to somehow lessen the harshness of what little existence I had remaining. I had about eight hundred dollars, and it was going to buy my farewell party. I didn't like the cards life had dealt me, and I desperately wanted out of the game.

Boarding the bus, I headed towards Ross's place, not caring if that's where it was all going to end. Little did I know that God was already at work in my life, and the events which were about to take place would change it forever. For the next three days, I had one foot in the grave. All I really needed was a little push and for someone to close the lid on the coffin in order to contain the smell. It's often said that you must first hit rock bottom before you can start to put the pieces back together. I was beyond rock bottom. Had the good Lord not sent me my own personal angels, in answer to my plea for help, I wouldn't have survived the week.

Before I get into the how spirituality has impacted my life, I wish to make it perfectly clear that at no time in my life, in or out of prison, have I ever professed or proclaimed myself to be a born-again Christian. After thirty years of surviving cold deceptions and calculated manipulations, some would easily conclude that I was an expert in the complicated art of treachery. This is true, to a degree. In fourteen years of incarceration, I had seen it all.

All too often, especially in prison, it's amazing how quick the cons find God. Once their release is secured, however, they suddenly seem to have lost Him again! There are many carrots between the gates of freedom, so common sense indicates prisoners would assume whatever role was necessary to establish an early release. Create a false appearance and tell them exactly what they want to hear! It works great, and it will continue to work. I've played the game countless times with the best—and fooled many.

You may be asking yourself how it was even possible for someone with such a twisted life to change. We'll come back to the process of change and its unique challenges. Firstly, I'd like to focus on what brought me to this point in my life.

This book is about more than choices, or the consequences involved. No one is to blame for the course of my life, as ultimately we all have the freedom of choice. However, where is that line really drawn? There's a huge gap between the period in our lives of being responsible for making our own choices and that earlier period when those choices were influenced. Without any argument, most of our choices and beliefs have greatly been influenced and enforced by our parents during the first five years of our lives. Those beliefs become ingrained in our very nature as we grow up, shaping us into the people we become.

Choices. What a powerful word, and it's one we often take for granted. Every day in our lives, we are governed by the choices we make. Since there are always consequences involved, we should place critical importance on how and why we make those choices. In most instances, we reach our decisions in a rational manner, but make no mistake about it, many things can strongly influence the choices we make. Throughout the process of any change, we all go through a period of deep reflection. In the full understanding of our motivations, we are able to completely accept and come to terms with our past. Only then can we comfortably let go of the binding chains that for so long have imprisoned us.

This is a crucial step in the process of change. Within the complicated paradox between our past and present lies the key to a more successful future. In my case, three major factors contributed: instability, environment, and associations. We all look for stability and acceptance, and in this we'd like for our environment and friendships to be of a positive nature. If we allow them, these very influences will cloud our judgment and leave lasting and destructive consequences in our lives. In the same breath, these same factors can at times be so deceptive, controlling, and manipulative when it comes to making our choices.

The greatest hardship I ever had to endure and come to terms with—a hardship which still haunts me to this very day—is the calculated coldness by which both my parents abandoned their children. This is incomprehensible, and at times inexcusable, for the damage and anguish caused by their actions remains irreversible. Their callousness crushed all possibilities of trust. This lack of structure was to be the governing, if not controlling force in all my insecurities.

"Oh, I'll never be like that!" These are famous last words, and believe me, I hear them all the time. Don't ever fool yourself in this false and deceptive perception. I never imagined myself going to prison, let alone spending a third of my life there. I definitely considered myself drug-free, yet I became an intravenous drug addict. HIV couldn't possibly have ever happened to me, but in the twinkling of an eye, my life was changed forever.

At some point in our lives, we've all faced what we thought was an overwhelming hardship. As my story unravels, it will become evident that most of my life has been nothing short of a shattered and tormented existence. Many times in its bitter course, I wished I had the courage to die, rather than face those hardships. It takes a tremendous amount of courage to live your life regardless of its obstacles. Imagine the sheer strength and determination it takes to pick up the broken pieces of a wasted life and slowly put it all back together again. By being able to stand fast and do this, without giving in to the destructive patterns of thought and behavior, you can possess courage and strength of the highest order.

I firmly believe that regardless of our circumstances in life, no matter how impossible things may appear to be, as long as we hold on to a belief and remain persistent and determined, then one day even an impossibility can and will become reality. My incredible story is a testament to this. However, before we begin exploring the extraordinary transformations of my life, we should first deal with the journey through the unimaginable.

In The Beginning   2

In 1972, my mother went into hiding in fear of her life, and only briefly resurfaced some twenty-five years later. Now and then, I can still faintly hear my mother's voice echoing from within those all but forgotten corridors of my mind. Even now, her words leave me speechless. She once said to me, "Mino, I can't believe what you've done with your life!" I still vividly remember deadpanning her with that classic Clint Eastwood stare, "I can, for I never had much to work with." I haven't heard from her since. As it is said, the truth will either set you free or continue to keep you in bondage.

In many ways, we inherit the characteristics of our parents, which in themselves become a very real part of our genetic make-up. It only stands to reason that before we can begin to put the pieces of our shattered lives back together, we must first start with a search of theirs. As will become evident, I got a little more than I bargained for.

I offer fair warning: some of the things I say may come across as a spear piercing your heart. In uncovering the mysteries of my life, as with any non-fictional account, certain realities deliver an impact of personal conviction to anyone offering an honest reflection of their own lives. Throughout this memoir, especially in delicate issues concerning my parents, all my interpretations of events are from my own personal accounts. I have respectfully tried to remain blameless, and above all have taken no one's side but my own.

My father, Milan Pavlich, was born on September 18, 1921, in the small village of Polenje, some fifteen miles from the town of Sisak, in Croatia, the former Yugoslavia. He had two younger sisters, Ankica and Paula. For most of his life, he proved to be a very elusive man, as he chose to keep his distant past hidden from view. There were definitely haunting fears within his life. For twenty years, he tried to stay one step ahead of them. He studied at a prestigious university in Zagreb for a number of years and received an architectural degree with high honors. With these skills, he entered the building and remodeling industry. Throughout his many accomplishments, he proved to be very successful in his chosen career. After trade school he joined the army for two years, which was mandatory. Also during this time he married his first wife, who gave birth to two beautiful daughters.

In order to understand the complexities of my life, I needed to first grasp the significance of both my parents. In order to comprehend what my father endured through the harshness of World War II, and how it affected his life, I needed to do my own research. The more I learned, the easier it was to understand my father's reluctance in talking about the war.

Predominately there existed two main ethic groups—the Serbs and the Croats. Long before Germany's invasion, Yugoslavia had been dealing with its own band of terrorist cutthroats, known as the Ustasha. They began as a revolutionary movement in 1929, when Yugoslavia was placed under a dictatorship. Since their birth, the main goal of the Ustasha was rebellion and overthrowing the government. Germany's invasion greatly profited as a result of the existing tension between the three factions. What took place during the next four years was easily declared one of the most barbaric episodes of World War II. In 1941, when German forces invaded Yugoslavia, the country was propelled into a war created from within its own borders, including unfathomable atrocities of savagery and butchery.

The Germans, receiving absolutely no cooperation, decided to divide the country up. Through this decision, Croatia became a state. The Germans needed someone to run it for them, and so they enlisted the help of the Ustasha. Can you even begin to imagine the consequences? Suddenly, a vicious terrorist group was given free rein over a state. Almost immediately came the purification of Croatia, unquestionably the greatest genocide of World War II in proportion to a nation's population. The occupation of Yugoslavia brought with it insurmountable hardships for its inhabitants, as Ustasha bands terrorized the countryside, initiating a bloody ordeal of mass murder. Resistant forces quickly emerged, and as a direct result Yugoslavia suddenly found itself embroiled in a volcanic and brutal anti-partisan war.

The resistant forces were divided into two groups, the Chetniks and the Partisans. The hearts of these groups were Serbs, who had evaded capture during the invasion by fleeing into the hills of Bosnia. Many of these bands simply wanted to protect their small villages from the brutalities of the Ustashe, whose tactics had become so horrific that they even drew protests from the Germans. These protests were not made on humanitarian grounds, as you might think, but rather on the grounds that their ethnic cleansing was rapidly fueling the resistance groups. Most of the Chetnik groups were anti-German, while others saw the emerging Partisans as a greater threat. The main goal of the Partisans was to create an independent socialist Yugoslavia by freeing the country of its occupation. My father joined this resistance and quickly rose in the ranks to become a major player in President Tito's Partisans.

At some point, he was given leave to go home and see his family. When he stepped from the train, someone he knew greeted him and begged him to get back on the train and not look back. He was informed that his wife and sister Ankica had been raped and brutally murdered, along with his children. I can only pretend to understand the emptiness and rage my father must have felt. Imagine receiving the news that his new family, along with his sister, had just recently been slaughtered and left lying in a pool of blood with their throats slit. Something inside him must have snapped, as he went back to the war with a vengeance. He formed an elite search and destroy team that wreaked havoc across the Balkans.

The Chetniks, who wanted to avoid further onslaught from the Germans suggested not only a truce, but a collaboration with the Germans and offered to fight against the Partisans, an offer which surprisingly was declined. By all appearances, the Partisans were now locked in a three-sided war; they found themselves fighting the tough Ustashe, the Chetniks, and the Germans. However, in spite of tremendous opposition, they proved to be the most effective band of resistance fighters against the invading Germans and their collaborators. In 1944, the Partisans finally liberated Belgrade, Yugoslavia's capital.

In the aftermath of German withdrawal, sizable Partisan forces controlled great portions of the country. The days following the end of the war led to one final round of bloodshed, in which the Partisans executed some thirty thousand Croat Ustashe troops. Tito's secret police also hunted down the Chetnik bands in Serbia, and in 1946 executed their leader as a war criminal. The violent struggles that took place in Yugoslavia between 1941–1946 resulted in over 1.7 million dead. Sadly, all war is barbaric. The bitterness and hatred that existed between these factions would be forever cemented by their own actions, as witnessed by the Balkan uprising some fifty years later.

My father went on to become a hero and was well-respected in the Tito camp. As a result of political positioning, he went on to become the mayor of a small town called Kostinjce, which had a population of around five thousand people. During 1946–47, he met and married his second wife, who gave birth to two sons, Danny (Danko) and Miljenko (Mickey).

One would think that my father had everything going for him now—success, recognition, and a family—but it just wasn't meant to be. From what I understand, he was part of a European delegation sent to Sweden to investigate and compare their standard of living. Apparently, he was so impressed by what he discovered, and how simple life was there, that when he returned to Yugoslavia he voiced his opinions and openly tried to implement some positive changes. Yugoslavia was firmly a communist country at that time and the governing body didn't want any kind of change. He was quickly stripped of his position. Shortly thereafter, for personal reasons, he separated and divorced his wife.

Having an uncanny ability for adaptability, he quickly re-established himself in business. As a result of his acquisitions, he became not only very successful, but wealthy as well. He owned two pig farms, which were a lucrative source of income. However, the big moneymaker was a company that built roads; this, too, was to be short-lived. Sometime in 1954, at thirty-two years of age, while road building in upper Mokrice, he met my mother.

My mother was born on January 13, 1938, and her given name was Katica Rokich. She had two sisters, Jelica and Maca, along with an older brother named Ivica. Before I go any further, I want to point out that my mother was almost seventeen years younger than my father. Obviously this fact should have raised many issues that speak of forbidden boundaries which never should have been crossed. Drawing upon my own conclusions in piecing the story together, my father crossed a deadly line. There really can be no other explanation; she was a kid, infatuated with a wealthy businessman who acted upon dark and hidden desires which found their origins in the brutal realities of war. The reasons behind his divorce of his second wife were his explosive temper, and continuing womanizing. His deviant nature was always there, but nobody seemed to care. My mother's father, somewhat wealthy in his own right, owned and operated a beer parlor located on the main floor of his house. My father and his workers used to frequent there, often during breaks. No one in their right mind would allow any such relationship to develop, yet it did, with everyone's blessing.

Sometime in 1954, a story was fabricated around my father that not only stripped him of all his businesses, but sent him to prison with an eighteen-year sentence. One day while blasting with dynamite, one of his workers was killed in the explosion. A story was concocted that implicated my father in premeditated murder. My next comments are pure speculation. In the aftermath of the war, in fear of reprisals which undoubtedly resulted in executions, the higher echelon of the Ustashe and Chetniks groups, which had no means of escape, lived in a shadow existence. Was it possible that evidence was uncovered linking this dead worker to the higher echelon of either faction? I would think my father was beyond bitter. After losing his wife, his children, and one sister in the brutal treacheries of war, he must have been incensed with hatred.

In 1955, after escaping from prison, he and my mother fled on foot across the Austrian border, where ten months later I would be born. They crossed the border close to the Austrian Alps, so you can imagine how treacherous the crossing was at night on foot. Once across the border, they turned themselves in to the local police, who in turn placed them in an internment camp, where they waited to see if their refugee status would be granted. Finally allowed to stay in Austria, they settled down in a small rooming house, but not for long; my father once again adapted, even though he didn't know the language.

Although fifty-seven years have gone by, one particular image remains vividly clear in my brother Danny's mind. It goes to show the extent of the hatred which to this day still exists between those who supported and proudly served as Partisans and those who were in opposition. Until my parents situated themselves in Austria, and while arrangements for his safe passage were being made, Danny lived with my dad's parents. One day, a group of men showed up, as they had many times since my father fled the country. They were always different men, but rest assured they were cut of the same cloth, with only one purpose in mind: they wanted to gain any insight as to my father's whereabouts. No longer was it the aftermath of the Second World War, where torture and murder were the endorsed methods of gaining information. Somewhat civilized now, they instead relied heavily on intimidation and fear.

They were cold but calculating in their pursuit. They would ransack the farm in search of any document that might disclose my father's sanctuary. They found nothing, except his war medals. One in particular proclaimed him to be a Partisan. A medal that should have been recognized and held in high honor was now viewed in complete mockery. Danny, even though he was only eight years of age, understood the importance of remaining silent. To do otherwise would just invite more contempt. It's sad how the ravages of a war-torn country can so quickly educate even the smallest of children. It shows absolutely no favoritism and no mercy. The men pinned this medal on Danny and joked about how he looked like a great Partisan, all the while spitting on him. Danny stood still, not in fear or tears but rather in immense pride and respect for the man who was his father. Needless to say, the men left no wiser than when they had arrived, but rest assured, they would always return.

In Austria, my father met someone he had known in Yugoslavia who helped to place him in a line of employment that was made to order. Having architectural skills, it was his job to remodel and build custom-made furniture for the many ancient and medieval castles scattered across the countryside. By then, secure precautions were taken and Danny finally arrived in Austria.

I was born on July 20, 1956, on a Friday night around 10:00 p.m. in the city of Graz. I weighed in at three pounds. My given name was Miodrag, which meant "sweet and dear." It would be tough living up to that name, as I was anything but sweet and dear.

My next comments aren't intended as an attempt at humor, but rather as an omen to the crippling reality that would be my life. While in my mother's womb, if I could have had a premonition of what life had in store for me, I would have reached up and grabbed hold of a rib, and held on with paralyzing fear! It would seem that right from birth, the curse of hardships was to be my only birthright. Not only was my arrival of a premature nature, but being underweight caused many complications within the first three years of my life. For the next fifty years, bad luck would continue to plague me.

My father tried to get this whole mess about him in straightened out on his own. So the story goes, one day he went to the small Yugoslavian embassy, but there was no possibility of reason. At one point, they tried to literally bag him; they wanted to send him back to Yugoslavia. A fight broke out and he managed to escape by jumping out a second-story window. Whether this story is accurate, the facts of the following twenty years give it considerable credibility, for after I was born we crisscrossed Europe and continued into Canada, Australia, Tasmania, and New Zealand. In all appearances, it would seem my father wasn't only running from something, but possibly from *someone*.

As I mentioned, my father was so successful in his occupation that we were given the opportunity to travel through most of Europe. We lived in Switzerland, Sweden, Norway, and Holland all within a two-year period. Years of participating in and witnessing the atrocities of mayhem, murder, and torture throughout the war left its barbarity forever engraved in my father's thoughts. As all factions were equally guilty of the same barbarism, no one was excusable. If for no other reason than accountability, their actions would continually haunt the darkest corridors of their minds.

Participation in such acts instilled within him a calculated, detached coldness which wrapped itself around his personality like an ill-fitting coat. Like a band of gypsies, we roamed from city to city, country to country, from continent to continent. In reality, we weren't living, but running. Regardless of our extensive travels over the next twenty years, the reality of those nightmarish memories continuously haunted my father. By far, the toughest prison to escape from was the one created within the depths of his own mind.

Our Private Playground, the World   3

In 1957, we were leaving Europe and immigrating to Canada. From Sweden, we traveled by small ship to Copenhagen where we boarded an ocean liner named *The Seven Seas*. After sailing for twenty-six days, we docked in Montreal harbor. We didn't stay in Montreal, as we immediately moved to Toronto.

When we first arrived in Canada, we adopted the name Pavlic. My father opened a cabinet shop in which he built custom-made furniture. It wasn't long before he landed a lucrative contract with two of Canada's department stores, the Hudson's Bay Company and Eaton's. This afforded us the opportunity to travel and live in many cities across Canada.

We briefly lived in Edmonton, where again my father had a shop, and this time he was building furniture and boats. My brother Mike (Milan) was born on April 12, 1958. Things weren't going as expected and we quickly moved to Calgary; it wasn't long before we relocated to Toronto. In 1960, we moved to Ottawa and owned about five or six houses, which my dad rented out. On December 14, 1960, my youngest brother, Tomo, was born. As far back as I can remember, I was nicknamed Mino, not only because I couldn't pronounce or spell Miodrag, but because I was a mean kid.

We lived in a modest house on St. Catherine Street. I remember wanting to build a tree fort in the front yard, but we had no lumber. My dad was away in another city, but I had a plan and enlisted the help of my younger brother Mike to get the building materials. There was a lumberyard just down the block, and being a Sunday, they weren't open. I didn't think they'd miss a couple of boards. I told Mike to wait for me by the front entrance. Outside the gate, between the fence posts, there was an opening I could squeeze through. I was back in about ten minutes with all the lumber I could carry and no Mike in sight. Instead, a policeman was waving me over. I dropped the wood and surrendered myself. He took me home and explained to my uncle what had happened. Needless to say, once the policeman left I got a terrible beating.

Trouble for some reason always had a way of finding me. One time I actually stuck a pair of scissors in the electrical wall outlet, and the force of the current sent me flying across the room. Since all the power in the house dimmed, my mother and uncle came to investigate. By the time the power was shut off, a good part of the scissors were burnt.

By 1962, my dad was living with us again. He had by all appearances settled down. We moved to an Ottawa suburb known as City View and lived in a beautiful house on Largo Crescent, which my dad had bought and remodeled. Life from my perspective was good.

I remember one night in particular, how within a moment of innocent horseplay I could have again easily lost my life. My brother Mike was lying in the doorway to the kitchen. As I went by him, he tripped me. I cracked my head wide open on the corner of the doorjamb. There was so much blood; it just wouldn't stop gushing out of my head, even though my mother packed about six towels to my forehead. Luckily, my dad reacted quickly in getting me to the hospital, where they stitched me up. I still have a nasty scar. It goes without saying that Mike and I got a beating for goofing around. My dad was very strict and believed in tough discipline. We liked to stay out of his way, but sometimes he'd catch us and there'd be hell to pay.

As far back as I can remember, there was no solid direction or control in our family structure. These governing factors could be considered the backbone to building a family. Without stability, there can be no direction, and without the impact of direction, you lose the authority of control. Any child growing up in these conditions would develop deep insecurities, allowing for dysfunctional behavioral patterns. I could be wrong about this if I were the only black sheep of the family. However, my four brothers have also had their share of similar hardships.

For the most part, my dad was always on the move, and my poor mother, having her hands full with me, Mike, and Tomo, lost control of Danny. In 1963, at fifteen years of age, he dropped out of school and drifted with a bad crowd. I knew he carried a loaded gun and craved not the attention it brought, but rather the recognition and respect. It wasn't long before he found himself in trouble with the police. Not long afterwards, he ended up in Guelph Reformatory, which had infamously become known as a gladiator school for young hoodlums. However, nothing in this experience was to prepare him for what was to come just a few short years later.

In the early part of 1964, while the whole family was out one night, we returned to discover our house had burnt to the ground. I'm still not sure whether it was before or after the fire that my dad decided we were going to move to Australia. As always, he left ahead of us and made preparations for our arrival. In December of that year, my mom, my brothers, and I boarded the *S.S. Orsova*, a huge ocean liner docked in Vancouver. Danny, at age sixteen, had found himself in prison and he wouldn't join us there until his release in the summer of 1965.

The trip took three weeks to complete, as we took many colorful stops along the way. I was eight years old, and to me the ship represented one big adventure, which I fully planned to explore. I'm sure I wasn't the only kid who gave the staff and crew a headache; many times, I would wander off without letting my mom know and she'd go into a panic trying to find me. My days on board were mostly spent exploring and trying to stay out of trouble.

Our first stop was Hawaii. When we docked and off-loaded, we were greeted by pretty Hawaiian girls in hula dresses. Each passenger was welcomed to the island by one of the girls placing a flower lei around their necks. For two days, we roamed Waikiki Beach. Once back aboard the ship, our next destination was Fiji. Along the way, we celebrated Tomo's fourth birthday. The staff even put together a little surprise party, with a cake and all.

During this next leg of our voyage, as a result of stupidity I almost lost my life again. This kid I hung around with exploring the ship was a couple of years older than me. One night, he talked me into going swimming in the big outdoor adult swimming pool. I didn't have a clue how to swim, but as it sounded adventurous, I went along. I jumped in and, you guessed it, I sunk to the bottom like a rock. I kept pushing myself up from the bottom of the pool with my feet, but would only break water long enough to let out a feeble cry and get some air before returning to the bottom of the pool. Luckily for me, there was a cocktail banquet taking place on the upper deck that night. This deck partially overlapped the pool. Someone jumped in and pulled me out. After they pumped all the water out of me, I looked for the kid who had been with me, but he was nowhere in sight. I guess he couldn't swim, either? As a result of that incident, one of the staff took it upon themselves to teach me how to swim. By the time we reached Australia, I could swim like a fish.

As we neared Fiji, we could tell we were definitely in an exotic part of the world. It was nearly Christmas and almost everyone on the ship wore shorts. The weather was just incredible. While docked at the Fiji harbor, we didn't get to leave the ship. From the back of the ship, we would throw coins into the ocean, and the Fijian kids would dive in after them. Each and every time, they'd surface with the coin.

These memories, along with countless others, I will treasure fondly for the remainder of my life. Being aboard the *S.S. Orsova* was truly a wonderful experience for me. We briefly stopped in Auckland, New Zealand, before continuing on with the last leg of our journey.

Just like our adventures in Europe and Canada, Australia would prove to be no less exciting. Once again, we crisscrossed the continent, visiting and living in so many exotic places. Arriving in Sydney was truly astonishing; it is a spectacular city. We lived there for a while before moving to Belgrade, a suburb of Melbourne. We had a beautiful house located high on the side of a mountain, situated on a couple of acres of land.

Here, my dad was captivated by the local birds that flew around the garden, especially the beautiful cockatoos. He would rig up a wire cage propped up by a stick with a rope attached to it to try and trap them. He'd hide for hours in the bushes, waiting for the birds to come eat the birdseed. After he had the birds ensnared, he would attempt to get them out of the trap. More times than not, he ended up bitten by the escaping bird. He never was successful in catching one for himself. Eventually, he just went down to the local market place, where on the weekends they'd have all kinds of things for sale. He bought a cockatoo. He named the bird Cocky, and I'd swear by the way he used to treat it that he liked that bird better than he did me.

I often played around with a boomerang, but I could never get the hang of it. They just didn't want to come back for me.

In the summer of 1965, Danny arrived in Australia, and he immediately fell in love with everything about this amazing country. He was truly captivated. Even when talking about Australia today, you'd think he was describing heaven. It wasn't long before he and my dad were off to Perth, on the other side of the continent, where they would start up a lucrative business.

We had moved to another suburb called Tacoma, where we stayed for a couple of months while we waited for my dad to send for us. My mom had a part-time job in the local hospital. Instead of getting a babysitter, she'd ask us if we wanted to go see a movie, which we certainly did. I remember one particular movie vividly; it was called *The Great Race*, starring Tony Curtis and Jack Lemon. We must have seen it at least a dozen times.

My mother was having her own problems in getting used to the extreme low humidity. Australia has a hot and dry climate. As a result, not only did she get migraine headaches all the time, she would literally pass out.

Once everything was in place, we boarded a bus for our journey to Perth, which is said to be one of the loneliest cities in the world. Its closest neighboring city is Adelaide, some twelve hundred miles to the east. To get there, you have to cross the treeless, waterless expanse known as the Nullarbor Desert, more famously known as the Australian Outback. Only by traveling this void by bus could you truly begin to understand and appreciate the enormous distance between Perth and the rest of the world.

When Perth suddenly appeared on the horizon, nothing could have prepared me. This beautiful city is amongst one of the most unforgettable of my childhood memories. It's the capital of Western Australia and finds itself situated on the Swan River, which winds its way through the city. Perth has some of the best beaches. The sand is pure white and the ocean a crystal clear blue. In the summer, you can expect the temperature to remain at a blistering 110 degrees.

The business my dad put together was not only inventive, but insightful as well. They were now mass-producing twenty-five to thirty-five foot "caravans" from the ground up. We know them as travel trailers. They had a huge warehouse where they constructed these caravans. One day, my mom wanted to check out the new design, and while trying to climb out she lost her footing and slipped. She wickedly sliced her arm just above the wrist on the rough unfinished aluminum edge around the doorframe and nearly cut her hand off. Luckily, they got her to the hospital in time.

We lived in Perth for about nine months. My most beautiful recollections have always found themselves in the fact that we lived in a thirty-five-foot trailer right on the edge of one of the most beautiful beaches I've ever known. Scarborough Beach was breathtaking. Words alone couldn't begin to explain the feeling of having an entire ocean as our backyard.

By nine or ten in the morning, it was so hot that you couldn't walk unprotected on the sand. I fancied myself somewhat of a surfer, but then again, how much of a surfer could you be at ten years old, especially with a Styrofoam surfboard? I had fun trying, though. Danny was very good at it. Only one thing really paralyzed me in absolute fear: sharks. There had been a number of shark attacks in the area. As a result, during the day there would always be a helicopter in the air watching out for sharks. Now and then, you'd hear someone say, "Get out of the water now!" through the loud bullhorn. Many times after falling off my surfboard, my feet would brush against some seaweed and I'd panic, thinking it was a shark.

As the business slowed down, my dad decided it was time to move on. This time, his choice of destination was Darwin, the capital of the northern territory. It was the only fair-sized city on the northern coast, and it wasn't unusual to see saltwater crocodiles. Swimming on the beaches was banned, as the water was heavily infested with deadly jellyfish. Not that it really mattered, as we didn't stay long. We were soon moving again. The plan was to take the two remaining caravans and travel the Nullabor Desert and coastline, some thirty-two hundred miles back to Melbourne.

Off we went again, with everything we owned crammed inside the trailers. The trip was spectacular. Traveling in this manner, we really appreciated the size and flatness of the Nullabor Desert. With the breathtaking shoreline views of stunning cliffs and gorges of red rock, we were captivated by the sheer beauty. The cliffs dropped straight into the clear sea hundreds of yards below, along with endless expanses of golden beaches. In these waters along the Nullabor Plain, you'll find the world's biggest white pointer sharks. These spectacular sights have truly helped me to capture Australia's incredible uniqueness.

We would just drive, and when my dad came across a spot, whether it was in the vast desert or on the shoreline, we would stop and set up camp, staying for as long as we wished.

However, not everything went smoothly. We had one serious incident. As the distance between civilized rest stops was often quite long, we carried three forty-five-gallon drums full of gasoline. You definitely wouldn't want to run out of gas in the middle of the desert. While traveling through the desert, one of the trailers got a flat tire and the trailer, after breaking free from the car, flipped over on its side. No one was hurt, and unbelievably the drums of gas didn't break open or spill. We set up camp while Danny drove to the closest town to get a big enough tow truck with a winch so we could upright the trailer.

Once we got settled in Melbourne, my dad sold both trailers for a fraction of their worth. After a couple months, we were off on yet another adventure, this time in Brisbane, in Queensland. The Great Barrier Reef is the world's greatest natural wonder and Australia's most spectacular treasure. Beginning at Lady Elliot Island, the reef stretches over a thousand miles along the coast, displaying brilliantly colored coral, white sandbars, and hundreds of green tropical islands. After enjoying this tropical paradise through the summer, we went back to Melbourne to make arrangements for our move to Tasmania.

Before we were scheduled to leave, however, a tragedy of great proportions took place.

When Danny arrived in Australia, he straightened out his life. He was working for my dad full-time and doing very well. His newfound peace suddenly shattered in a million pieces as the world came crashing down, taking away everything he had worked for in one swift blow. For the rest of his life, this incident was to govern how he lived. In 1967, at the age of nineteen, he was drafted to go to Vietnam. His immediate response was to refuse, as it wasn't his war. He had already experienced the aftereffects of war in Yugoslavia. Because of his refusal, he was sentenced to a two-year prison term in Sydney's infamous Long Bay Prison. During his incarceration, arrangements were made so we could visit with him before we left to join my dad.

My last memory of Australia was a very sad one. You would think that the prison administration would have at least grant us more than a ten-minute visit, as we were set to leave the country, never to return. We showed up at the entrance to the prison and were paraded through the main doors to a courtyard surrounded by huge stone walls. We stood in front of some metal doors that opened inwards towards the prison yard. What I saw has remained as clear in my mind as if it had taken place yesterday; Danny stood shackled hand and foot with two guards holding shotguns about ten feet behind him, one on either side. I cannot begin to describe the emptiness and indignity on Danny's face. I'm sure he felt totally alone in that moment, about to be abandoned by his family in a strange land. I wouldn't see him again until 1970 in Vancouver, Canada.

He has told the nightmare to me many times. Knowing the nature of the man, as he is today, it's easy to believe him when he says that each and every day he had to fight to survive. It wasn't just your everyday kind of fighting, but barbaric attacks. He had to act like an animal and attack with whatever he had at hand, swiftly and almost always violently, as the other prisoners were intent on trying to kill him. Not only was he a foreigner, they classified him as a deserter who wouldn't serve their country. I can't even begin to entertain what he must have gone through. However, heartache and struggle were to be a part of the Pavlic history.

Tasmania's capital city, Hobart, is about a four- to six-hour ferry ride from Melbourne. Like an apparition, the island slowly took shape out of the rainy mist. Forbidding rocky spires and cliffs projected straight up from the waves along the coast. Beyond them lay mountains cloaked in dense rainforests.

Tasmania has a very interesting history. Located on the rugged west coast is Sarah Island, the oldest convict settlement, which was in operation from 1822–1833. It had a reputation for being a place of banishment for the worst description of convicts, but it was also one of the most severe penal settlements. Sarah Island was a very successful center of industry, and shipbuilding was among the trades carried out by the convicts. In its day, Sarah Island was the largest shipbuilding yard in all of Australia.

We only stayed four months, as my dad didn't like it there and decided we were going to move to Auckland, on the North Island of New Zealand. We were left alone for two months while my dad arranged for our visas.

I remember a little more about Auckland, as we actually stayed in one place without moving for eight months. We lived in a small house on Balmoral Street. There was a big park at the end of the street where my brothers and I spent most of our free time.

I went to Mungawell School, and I'll never forget how much I hated it. The school system had in place a program to provide free dental care. Every two weeks, one class would go to the school of dentistry, where there were thirty dental chairs. For some reason, it seemed as though I'd always get the worst chair in the place; there was always extensive work being done on my teeth. After a while, I got smart. When it was our turn to go, I wouldn't show up at school. Realistically, I should have had the best-looking teeth on the island. I'd had enough of the torture and would let someone else have my chair.

At the age of twelve years old, I began my first bad habit: smoking. I did quit, but it took me thirty-eight years to do it.

My brother Mike had found his own form of escape; he immersed himself in the game of soccer. The only thing he loved more than the game was his ball. He was extremely athletic and had an unbelievable talent.

In June 1969, our exotic adventure came to an end. We were getting ready to move back to Canada. Up to this point, we could easily have been considered more of a traveling circus than a family. Would Canada now remain our permanent base, where we would finally have some form of stability? Only time would tell.

Vancouver, Canada, and Yugoslavia   4

Seeing as our pet cockatoo had now become a welcome addition to the family, in order to bring him with us to Canada, we had to put him in quarantine before leaving Australia. It took six months for him to catch up with us.

We settled briefly in the east end of Vancouver, and moved three times within the first four months. I was enrolled in Grade Five at Charles Dickens School, but the damage caused by our extensive traveling had firmly taken hold. For the next three years, as each of my report cards would sadly indicate, I was a chronic underachiever in school. Had it not been for highly paid tutors and summer school, I would have never made it to the next grade.

My dad bought an old three-story, six-bedroom home and almost immediately began remodeling the whole house. He even built a huge two-story addition to the back. The address was 1735 East 28th Avenue; the only reason I remember the address is because for the next five years we never moved.

It didn't take us long to make new friends in the neighborhood. One of my best friends was Raymond, and he came from a large family. His dad, Paul, worked in the demolition industry and often received work through my dad. His mother, Bunty. had a heart of gold. At one end of the block lived a nice Italian family. I remember John, Connie, Grace, and Peter. Peter, being the youngest, was one of my best friends as well. At the other end of the street were the Balarinni brothers, with whom we used to fight all the time.

As always, things seemed to be going really well for us. My dad had formed the first of many construction companies he would have throughout his life. He called himself a city general contractor. At the time, he had a very rewarding contract building and remodeling the Toronto Dominion banks throughout British Columbia. For the first time in a very long time, we were actually a whole family. Almost every weekend, weather permitting, we would take the hour-long drive to White Rock, where we would spend the day at the beach and have a big barbecue.

We were all signed up for soccer at Kensington Park. However, it was Mike who excelled in this sport. As a result of his athletic abilities in track and field, at age twelve he received a written note of achievement from Premier Bill Bennett. Mike was so talented in soccer that he was fast becoming a local celebrity. He was quite often mentioned in the sports section of the local newspaper. I still remember how we would all go watch his games whenever he played. My dad would be quite the sight. He would have the movie camera going as he ran up and down the field. When Mike was in scoring range of the net, you would often hear my dad shouting, "Shoot, Mike, shoot!" Knowing he was being filmed, Mike would do something outstanding, like score a goal with a flying back kick. At one point, an opportunity presented itself for Mike to go to Europe and play at the professional level.

In 1970, Danny had come back from Australia, bringing his future wife Sandra with him. They had a son named Michael, but the marriage didn't last very long and my dad ended up paying for her plane fare back to Australia.

In the fall of that year, my brothers and I were enrolled at Selkirk Elementary, which was only three blocks away from where we lived. No matter how hard I tried, I never did well in school. For one reason or another, I always found myself in the principal's office. My best friends then were Ross, Paul, and Bob. There was also Rick and his sister Lanny, who in the 80s became heavily involved with outlaw bikers. Eventually, probably as a result of my inability to stay focused, the staff didn't want me at Selkirk anymore. Seeing as it was halfway through the school term, my parents enrolled me in a private Catholic school, St. Patrick's, with the hope that this might help straighten me out. It did for a while. I somehow managed to pass to the next grade without much trouble. In the next year, however, I switched high schools twice, going first to Vancouver Technical and then to Gladstone.

Finally, my dad came to the stark realization that there simply was no point in me continuing high school. I just wasn't getting anywhere. He decided that at the end of the year, I would be sent to live with his sister Paula in Sisak, Yugoslavia, with the intention that I would go to trade school and study to be an electrical engineer. This was only possible because in Yugoslavia, once someone finishes Grade Eight, they go to trade school, then from there to a mandatory two years in the army. I don't really think my dad fully thought this out, or maybe he had. Right from the beginning, I was at a major disadvantage. Grade Eight in Yugoslavia was like Grade Twelve in Canada. I knew how to speak and understand Yugoslavian, but I didn't have a clue how to read or write.

This adventure took me away from home for a year and a half. In the summer of 1971, my mother and I flew over, as she was going to get me settled in. When arriving, my aunt and uncle strongly suggested that I start immediately learning to read and write. My mom, however, had a different idea; she decided that we should take two weeks to see all our relatives and then end with a fun-filled week on the Adriatic coast, near the world-famous resort city of Dubrovnik. Sadly, most of the former Yugoslavia has now been bombarded from land, sea, and air as a result of the recent wars in the Balkans.

Meeting all of my relatives for the very first time was a memorable experience. The love and attention I was continually showered with left its beautiful impression forever engraved on my heart. It spoke volumes of how being separated by an ocean didn't necessarily cut our family ties. We first stopped in Petrinja, where I met my mom's sister Jelica, her husband Ivo, and my cousins Pepo and Marian. Also, I got to meet my half-brother Miljenko, my dad's son from a previous marriage.

Our next stop was the village of Mokrice, where my mother had been born and raised. I met her parents and older brother Ivica. Our arrival turned into a two-day celebration. For the very first time, I got to see how a pig was roasted on an open spit. This was a learning experience.

It was agreed that I would go with my brother Miljenko to Kostinjce, where I would meet his and Danny's mother. Meeting their mother was a pleasure, as she was really a very sweet woman. That first night, we stayed up until three in the morning; she had a million and one questions about her son Danny, whom she hadn't heard from or seen in almost twenty years. I told her all about him as I smoked her cigarettes. Three days later, my mother showed up and together we made our way to the coast, where my aunt and uncle and their two sons, Kreso and Ivica, had already rented a cabana.

Cradled in Dubrovnik's walls is a mystical city that has always been a popular tourist destination. The eventual bombing of this elegant and adored city seemed to strengthen the fact that Yugoslavia was finished as an independent nation, which is rather ironic as it was along this stretch of coast that Yugoslavia had been conceived and named.

The next five days could only be described as spectacular. As in Australia, the water was crystal clear and from the canoe we rented we could see all sorts of exotic and intriguing marine life swimming in the water.

Finally, it was time to return to Sisak. But before I went crazy studying, I saw something very interesting. My dad's father owned a huge vineyard, and everyone pitched in the harvest. All the relatives got together in horse-drawn wagons and made the two-hour trip. From the moment we arrived, everything seemed to run like a well-oiled machine; everyone knew exactly what they were supposed to do. The grapes were picked and placed in a huge wooden barrel, which had a lid that wound itself down when someone turned the grinding wheel, thus crushing the grapes. From the juice, my grandfather made wine that everyone shared in equally.

Once my mom returned to Canada, I only had a month left before school started. I spent five hours every day reading and writing, and found that it wasn't as hard as everybody thought it would be. However, in many ways I was still at a tremendous disadvantage. I guess my dad really had thought of everything; once I started school, I had private tutor, a Mr. Bussdar. Every day after school, I'd go see him and he would teach me the heavy-duty algebra I was expected to know, along with whatever else I needed help in, which was practically everything. He was a very good teacher and had a lot of patience with me. He had a remarkable way of making everything seem easy.

Despite my difficulties, I enjoyed school that year. No heavy pressure was placed upon me from teachers or at home, which made it even more enjoyable. Everyone concerned showed a great deal of patience and support.

My mom had bought me a really expensive bicycle, and I used to like going to my dad's parents' place, which was about a forty-minute bike ride. They owned a modest-sized farm and for the most part were self-sufficient, needing only the most basic supplies from the store. I went with my cousin Kreso the first few times, but after that I'd go on my own. To get there, I had to travel down an old dirt road that passed behind a huge metals factory. The factory was surrounded by a scary, ten-foot brick wall. Looking back on it now, I'm sure my uncle was just trying to scare me. He'd say, "Mino, be careful when riding your bike down that back road, and whatever you do, never stop until you get to your grandparents' house. From time to time, gypsies have been known to kidnap kids."

With these thoughts in mind, I'd be pedaling down the road when I'd see a group of gypsies. I'd start pedaling like there was no tomorrow, leaving them in a cloud of dust as I flew past them. A couple of times, I even came close to running into a few of them.

Being new in a strange country, and for the most part unfamiliar with the culture and language, was always good for a laugh. One day I was sitting around talking with my uncle, aunt and two cousins when the topic of supper came up. Thinking nothing of it, I said, *I wouldn't mind eating some pizza.* Suddenly, my aunt flew to her feet and gave me a slap, which knocked me clean off my chair. Apparently, pizza in the Croatian language is a slang term referring to the privates of a young girl! How was I to know? After explaining what I was getting at, we all shared in an apologetic chuckle.

I took my status for granted. Many of my classmates came from dirt-poor families who desperately struggled just to make ends meet. A kid named Hassan sat directly behind me in school, and he used to make fun of me. It was no big deal. However, every so often he'd flick his finger and give me a crack in the back of the head. One day, we exchanged some nasty words in regards to his mother; over there, that's the worst kind of insult you can give someone. After school, he was waiting at my turnoff with his hand in his jacket pocket. I knew he had a knife. Instead of hightailing it the other way, I approached him, but not before picking up a hefty rock and stopped ten feet short of him. We had a modern-day standoff, ten feet apart. We held our ground, but then started talking. Within the hour, we actually became good friends.

My first year passed very quickly, but no matter how hard I tried I wasn't successful in making it to the next grade. Given the circumstances, everyone but me accepted this as an undeniable reality. It was already predestined that instead of the three years it normally took someone to complete the trade qualifications, I'd end up doing it in five years. Looking back on it from a fresh perspective, in no way should I have been discouraged; many who weren't faced with my disadvantages never graduated to the next grade.

On the last day of school, about ten of us got some alcohol and went to a park four blocks away. It didn't take me long to get falling-down drunk. It should have been my first indication that alcohol and I just didn't see eye to eye. My only true friend, Hassan, had had the sense to get straight home. Luckily for me, he saw the disaster about to unfold and came back to check on his Canadian friend. He got me on my bike and wheeled me the mile-long journey home, which ended in a nasty confrontation between me and my aunt. Being falling-down drunk was looked upon as shameful. For the second time, my aunt had slapped me.

Off I went, weaving down the road. I intended to stay with my mom's sister in Petrinja. How I was going to get there, I didn't have a clue. My cousin Kreso caught up to me and talked me into coming back, but it was never the same again. Shortly after this, I flew back to Canada to spend the summer with my family. Until I returned, I didn't realize just how much I had missed them. The summer passed quickly. Just before I came back to Yugoslavia, a crisis of astronomical proportions took place which would affect us kids for the rest of our lives.

One day we all went to the beach, except for my mom, who said she wasn't feeling well. At the end of the day, when we returned home, she was gone. All we knew was that she had taken her personal stuff. Before leaving, she emptied the contents of the huge safe we had in the basement. It was light by about a hundred and fifty thousand dollars. This caused much grief and suffering.

While an ugly divorce played itself out in Vancouver's highest court, at my dad's urging, my brother Danny went on a rampage of terror, fueled by fear, intimidation and violence. Danny, by his own reputation, was an extremely dangerous individual, and when his wrath was imposed on anyone the consequences were severe. Unknown to me, my dad was heavily involved in organized crime and Danny was a feared mob enforcer in Vancouver's violent underworld.

Beyond a shadow of a doubt, more than fear drove my mother underground for twenty- five years. She was in fear of her life. My dad had enlisted the services of Danny and Gill, a contract killer from Chicago, to find her. Once the divorce was finalized and the chase began, I'm sure she knew on many occasions how close she came to losing her life. They were always missing her by a day. Within a year, the chase ended, as she managed to disappear completely, like a puff of smoke. For the longest time, I actually thought she was dead.

On my flight back to Yugoslavia, I had two stopovers. The first was in London, England. Heathrow was all it's claimed to be—a regular zoo. I didn't stray too far and managed to buy five cartons of cigarettes. Next, we landed in Stuttgart, Germany. I had a crush on two girls from Petrinja, Marianna and Ljubica. While roaming the airport terminal, I bought each of them a gold necklace with a matching heart pendant.

Immediately upon returning, my aunt took me to Zagreb, Croatia's capital, and enrolled me at Rade Koncar, a well-recognized trade school. My new home was a college dormitory. For whatever reason, there had been a huge argument between my dad and his sister, and as a result I wouldn't be returning to school in Sisak. In the weeks before school started, I was to stay with my aunt and uncle, but things were just never the same there anymore. Any chance I got, I was on my bike or on the bus to Petrinja.

Once situated in Zagreb, I became very impressed. The dormitory building held a total of one hundred fifty students. This time around, I didn't have the guidance, control, support, or more importantly the one-on-one attention I had received the previous year. It wasn't long before I started hanging out with the wrong crowd. To make matters worse, my dad sent me fifty dollars every month as spending money. This was the worst thing he could have done. One dollar would buy sixteen dinars, which at that time could buy eight packs of cigarettes. In terms of wages, the average worker received about thirty dinars a day, so at fifteen years of age I had more money than most families earned monthly. I'd roam the city with my new friends, and as expected my studies went down the drain.

Within six months, I returned to Canada. My dad figured, why throw away good money, especially when there were no positive results? Before I left, sometime in December, I was awakened late at night by the people running the dormitory. They told me my mom was downstairs and wanted to see me. I was very excited, as this was the first time I had heard from her since she disappeared. We visited for about an hour. Before leaving, she gave me about a hundred dollars. It would be eight months before I saw her again, and then it was only briefly.

Before leaving Yugoslavia, a meeting was arranged for me to meet the woman who would become my dad's fourth wife. Her name was Milka and she was twenty-six years old, still a kid when compared to my dad's fifty-four years. No matter how hard we try, it's tough to break away from our inbred patterns of deviancy. Looking back on it today, deception and deceit lurked in every corner of my father's actions. Let's be realistic; if he had really had our best interests in mind, why did he need a wife half his age? He just wanted someone he could manipulate and control. She picked me up on a Friday afternoon and I spent the next two days on her family's little farm in the town of Karlovac.

It didn't happen immediately, but through the passage of time all of us kids grew to hate this woman. As a result of her own manipulations, we were left with no alternative but to leave home. By 1975, none of us were living at home anymore. We were either in prison, or living and surviving by the only method we had come to know: crime.

I returned to Vancouver in January 1973. Had I known what lay ahead, I wouldn't have come back.

DESCENT INTO HELL 5

At sixteen years of age, my global travels were at an end. Within five months, the next phase of my life began. For the following twenty-five years, my life was a continuous rollercoaster ride into hell itself; the worst thing about it was I didn't even have a seatbelt. Instead of world travel and discovering exotic places, I embarked on a life filled with petty crime, violence, and drug addiction. I would also find myself incarcerated in many prisons throughout Canada.

As a homecoming gift, Danny gave me my first car, a black 1964 Pontiac Parisienne. I quickly took the necessary tests and received my driver's license. From the beginning, I had a hard time handling this car, so my dad bought me a 1970 Vauxhall Viva, a small compact car which I had no problems with.

With my family, there never seemed to be a dull moment. Danny had a very explosive temper, and in 1973 that temper made him the subject of a Canada-wide manhunt. He and my dad were working in Victoria, in the final stages of wrapping up another bank remodeling job. Danny was living with a woman named Charlotte, and together they had a son: Danny Junior. As the project was ahead of schedule, Danny got to return a week earlier than expected, and he did so unannounced, as he wanted to surprise his girlfriend. In his living room, he found a half-naked, tattooed biker. Instead of flipping out, he calmly told the guy to grab his clothes and get out. The biker, who was taller than Danny and outweighed him by about sixty pounds, decided instead to come at him with a knife. This was the wrong move, as it resulted in his death. Somehow during the fight, the guy ended up with the knife embedded in his head, killing him instantly.

Danny called the police and quickly explained the circumstances of what had just happened. Given his reputation, and since he was well-known by the police, Danny didn't hang wait around for them to arrive. He jumped into his beautiful 1956 Crown Victoria and went into hiding. A few months later, when the dust had settled, he turned himself in and was placed in Oakalla Prison to await the outcome. His lawyer, David Gibbons, was one of the best, and at the time he was widely known across Canada for taking high-profile cases. I'm not sure of all the circumstances surrounding the defense, but eventually Danny walked out of prison a free man. While incarcerated at Oakalla, he had quickly earned a reputation as someone you just didn't mess with. To him, Oakalla was nothing compared to Sydney's infamous Long Bay Penitentiary.

Most of the self-proclaimed tough guys found in Oakalla wouldn't have survived in Long Bay; they would have easily fell victim to its brutality.

If I had to blame any one thing for the devastating hardships of my life, my greatest downfall by far would be the crippling addiction of alcoholism. It was about to embrace me in its inescapable grip.

Every couple of days, I'd drive my brother Mike to False Creek Park. At fourteen years old, Mike was always welcome to join in and practice with the Vancouver White Caps soccer team. His skill with a soccer ball went beyond exceptional; if he'd been given a little more guidance and direction from my dad, he would have been a very successful professional soccer player. Almost every week, there'd be an article about him in the local newspaper.

In 1973, the Yugoslavian soccer team Dinamo came to Vancouver to play the White Caps. There were talks between the general manager and my dad of the possibility of Mike going to Europe to further his training and eventually play for their team. Unfortunately, this once-in-a-lifetime opportunity never took place.

The division of our family had long since taken hold. All the signs were there, if only someone cared enough to look. On one hand, my dad was extremely busy attending to his huge divorce case, but that wasn't the only thing he was attending to. He placed an ad in the Yugoslavian newspapers about looking for a wife, and he quickly received a dozen letters in reply. The divorce papers weren't even drawn up, but in April 1973, my dad and two younger brothers boarded a plane to Yugoslavia so he could meet his future wife.

While away in Europe, my dad's friend Zagorac and his wife Ankica came to stay at our house. Instead of making fun of Zagorac, I could have learned my most valuable life lesson. He was my first glimpse into the life of an alcoholic. It could be that he was too busy fighting his own demons to notice mine taking shape. At sixteen years old, by all appearances I was already deeply enslaved by the early stages of chronic alcoholism. Hanging out with my so-called friends, we'd drink ourselves silly and then drive around town. One day, I sped around a corner while drunk, at about sixty miles an hour, and I wiped out five parked cars, totaling mine in the process. Luckily, no one was seriously hurt. I spent the night in the Oakridge police detachment, charged with impaired driving. I was released in the morning after being given a court date by the judge.

I was now in serious trouble and needed a way out. This trouble had nothing to do with the courts, but rather my dad's viciousness. He would be back in less than three weeks. Left without a car to drive, I started driving my dad's brand-new van, and it didn't take long before I smashed its windshield. I wasn't scared; I was desperate. Out of the blue, I found myself pulling burglaries with a friend of mine named Rick. We were two idiots looking for a pit to fall into! In the spur of the moment, we decided to steal a car and go to Toronto, but we only got as far as Chilliwack, almost a two-hour drive from Vancouver. We needed gas and Rick told me to pull up to a semi-truck and fill up the tank with that famous Mexican credit card—a siphoning hose. We drove about three blocks away from the station when the car suddenly died. Turns out the trucker had been filling up with diesel fuel. It didn't take long before the police were questioning us about what we were doing prowling the street in the middle of the night. They held us in a cell until Danny came and picked us up.

With one week left before my dad returned, and not wanting to face the consequences, Rick and I pulled a string of burglaries. Armed with stolen credit cards, we stole a 1963 Pontiac which belonged to a priest. We made it a little further this time, to Brandon, Manitoba, about a thousand miles away. Things appeared to be going all right. While driving down the highway in the middle of the night, instead of just pulling over to the side of the road to relieve myself, I pulled in behind some buildings just off the highway. Out of nowhere, a police car pulled in behind us. I gave him a pretty good story, which I'm sure he was buying, as he was prepared to let me go—that is, until Rick screwed everything up.

Rick had a number of warrants out for his arrest, so the cop was going to take him to jail. While the cop was handcuffing him, I got back in the car, wanting to leave. Rick started crying and spilled the beans. We were both remanded into custody while arrangements were made to transport us back to Vancouver. It goes without saying that the goof got a beating. I never saw him again after that.

Now facing a number of charges, my first stop was the Vancouver city jail, a grim and dingy place. The judge, not taking anything I had to say into consideration, denied bail, pending trial, and sent me to the Haney Correctional Center in Maple Ridge.

That was May 1973, a month whose significance didn't mean anything to me at the time, but in the distant future it would be as powerful and impactful as a crack of thunder.

The road leading to Haney, a fairly new facility, was a half-mile long, and from this vantage I quickly realized it would be a dangerous place. My immediate thoughts were those of survival. In shackles, the guards led us to an area known as receiving and discharge. Once the shackles were removed, we were placed in a holding cell to await the next process of admittance. A short time later, a guard came for us. One by one, we were taken away to be fingerprinted, have our picture taken, and told to strip. After a full body search, confirming that I wasn't concealing any contraband, I was sprayed down with a disinfectant and told to take a shower. Afterwards, I was issued prison greens, blankets, sheets, and a pillow, along with a small bag containing a comb, toothbrush, toothpaste, and soap. If you smoked, you were given a package of daily mail tobacco and rolling papers. Depending on how many new arrivals came in, this process could take anywhere from a couple of hours to most of the day.

After everyone was processed, we were escorted single-file through the prison to the second floor, which housed up to a hundred prisoners. Once designated to either the A or B Unit, I was told to report to a guard whose desk was situated halfway down the tier. I guess it gave him the best observational advantage over the prisoners. I was then assigned a cell—or house, which was how most prisoners referred to their cell. Mine was number ten, and I've seen bigger bathrooms. But what would you expect? My cell measured seven feet by four feet was bare except for the metal bed bolted to the floor. On the back wall was a small porcelain sink, with a mirror above it, and next to it was the toilet.

Before even attempting to make my bed, I placed my belongings on the thin mattress and went down to the end of the tier, where all the cleaning supplies were kept. I grabbed what I was looking for, along with a mop and bucket. I returned and thoroughly cleaned the cell from top to bottom. I had just turned seventeen and didn't know a single person in this strange and hostile environment. It made me extremely apprehensive.

What does one do in remand? Actually, your day is very repetitious. The only time we ever left the tier was to go to court, or to see visitors. On rare occasions, we were permitted to go outside in the fenced yard, which for remand prisoners wasn't that often. All meals were brought to us on a food cart, so basically there wasn't much to do besides sleep—which, by the way, is a valued commodity in any prison, as it's the easiest way to escape pressures or frustrations.

It was highly advisable at all times that you remain aware of what was going on around you. We definitely didn't want to inadvertently awaken someone from a deep sleep. A lot of beatings and stabbings occurred over this. To fill our days, we either read or played cards. Lockup at night was usually the time most prisoners did their letter-writing home; that was when we had the most undisturbed privacy.

By talking and listening to the countless stories told by my fellow prisoners, I got the impression that most of the repeat offenders could be classified as losers. One thing they all had in common was that they'd gotten themselves caught up in a vicious revolving door of crime, with absolutely no means of escape. Little did I know that I would follow the same beaten path for the next twenty years.

A lot of "fish," as all newcomers to the system were called, were picked on and tested. I was fortunate to be not only left alone, but treated with respect. The reason for this was that in the early 1970s, Danny was well-respected by the notorious East End gang known as Clark Park. In the group there was Jimmy Gee, who's now dead; Morgan; and Chief, a small but extremely dangerous Native man. They were there as the result of being charged with a violent murder. From this assortment of characters, I got my first schooling in prison life.

Jimmy was the type of guy who you'd run the other way from if you saw him coming. He was a walking crime spree just waiting to happen. He exhibited a cruel sadistic nature and had a vicious streak which made him unpredictable. From him, I learned that regardless of the situation or its outcome, a man was to meet his challenges head-on. Chief, on the other hand, was the opposite. He was a dangerous individual, made obvious not only in the way he carried himself, but in his mannerisms. From him, I learned that I didn't have to beat everyone's head in to prove I was tough. The way a man carried himself told its own story.

Within a very short period of time, I developed a hatred for everyone who worked at the prison. This is not to say some of the guards weren't decent people, as I have encountered a few. One thing I discovered through my many years of incarceration, though, is that the majority of guards were lazy. Whenever they were bothered from their dull routine of sitting down and reading books, they tended to exhibit a cruel nature. The less contact I had with them, the better. Most people who haven't been in a prison before often turn to the guards when finding themselves in some kind of trouble with other prisoners. They think the guards can help solve their problems. This is the worst thing anyone could ever do.

Most of the guards really don't care about your problems. Their outlook is that during their shift, they'd like things to run smoothly. Turning to the prison administration for help of any kind automatically labels you as a rat, and words alone cannot begin to describe the hatred prisoners feel toward such a lowlife. It doesn't matter the reason someone rats out another prisoner, there's absolutely no forgiveness. No matter the beef, you're expected to take care of the situation yourself. If you show violent resistance to your fellow prisoners, even though you might get punched, you'll be given respect and left alone.

I learned early on that my main associations in prison consisted of bank robbers, lifers, or your hardcore rounders. It was evident that these types of offenders had the most to offer in knowledge and seemed to keep a very low profile while serving out their sentence. I also learnt early on that in prison, regardless of who you are, the most valued form of respect comes from your word. Without this necessary quality, you are nothing.

In the two months I was in remand, I was involved in only one violent incident. We had learned that a guy was on trial for raping a ten-year-old girl. Quite often, the guards leak this kind of information to inmates, as no one likes a molester. We confronted this guy about it, as we still needed to be certain. When all suspicions were confirmed, we beat him black and blue, then smashed all the bones in his arms by slamming the cell door on them a couple of times. There was absolutely no pity, remorse, or mercy for such a lowlife.

It's strange, but true, how easily you can grow accustomed to acts of brutal violence. The two main ingredients are the environment in which you find yourself and the associations you make, the people you surround yourself with. I was never much of a fighter, although when the right buttons were pushed I could handle myself pretty good. Looking back on the violence I've committed throughout my life, I'd have to say I was completely unpredictable, which made me dangerous. I would do everything necessary to inflict the most damage as quickly as possible, regardless of the consequences.

On her only visit, my mother assured me that her lawyer, who was representing her in the divorce proceedings, would defend me in regards to my own legal problems. She said he was a very good lawyer, and he probably was in cases related to marital law. He briefly saw me before my court appearance and assured me I would be out in a couple of hours. However, when we appeared in front of the judge, the first words out of his mouth were, "Your Honor, I'd like to recommend nine months prison and nine months probation." Bang goes the judge's gavel in agreement, and instead of getting out of jail, I quickly found myself on the next bus back to Haney.

I wasn't fully aware of the extent of charges against me, or what the crown prosecutor had expected in terms of a sentence, but that lawyer probably did save me from going to the penitentiary.

Back at Haney, I saw the classification officer, who decided where to place a prisoner depending on the risk he might pose. Being a first offender, I was a likely candidate for rehabilitation. Within the week, I was scheduled to go to the New Haven Correctional Center on Marine Drive in Burnaby.

Long before I left Haney, I already had it in my mind to escape.

New Haven, by all appearances, seemed like an okay place for doing time; it just wasn't for me. I stayed for a few days in order to familiarize myself with the institution and figure out when would be the best time to leave. Leaving was really a walk in the park, made easier by the fact that we were allowed to wear our street clothes, as opposed to prison greens. Not that it mattered in the end. If you're going, you're going no matter what.

I left on a Friday evening, just after the supper headcount, as there wouldn't be another one for three hours. It was very foggy that day, and I had trouble seeing ten feet in front of me. I slipped behind the industrial trailers, broke into a run, and almost ran directly into a tree. Three blocks down the road, I hopped on a local bus. This was the first of my many escapes.

In prison, the conversation is endless when it comes to convicts talking about their crimes. If they were actually any good at break-and-enters, they certainly wouldn't be in jail telling me about their great scores.

However, it was definitely a learning experience. They would go on in detail how about this burglary or that one went. After listening long enough, I had a crash course in the fine art of burglary. Each person had their own way of doing burglaries, ways of casing a place, entering a place, and disabling alarm systems. I filtered all this information and put it together. I took something from all the stories and actually came out with a good method, minimizing the risk of getting caught.

Within hours, I committed my first successful break-and-enter, netting about six hundred dollars. I then rented a motel room by the week and took a few days to formulate my plan. During the day, with a map of the city, I traveled by bus and cased places out. If I felt a place as accessible, I'd mark it on my map for future reference. Once I had about twenty marked, I'd steal a car, sometimes hitting two places in one night. I did this twice a week, always stealing a different car.

The places I chose were restaurants, hardware stores, or paint stores. A lot of my dad's friends had their own construction or painting companies. No matter how much stuff I brought, they would always buy it. A lot of the houses my dad's friends built were painted with stolen paint. I'd get meat from restaurant freezers and lots of liqueur, which also sold easily. I was making about a thousand dollars a week.

It was at this time that I met my first girlfriend. Although it was a rocky relationship due to my lifestyle, it lasted a year and a half. Marlene was a beautiful, blue-eyed blonde I met in the Vic Way Inn, a restaurant located in the East End of Vancouver. I'd often hang around there with my friends Ross and Paul, and one day they introduced me. I couldn't take my eyes off her, and it wasn't long before we were going out.

Things appeared to be going okay for me, as I had lots of money, freedom, and a beautiful girlfriend. However, as I was an escaped convict, it was to be very short-lived . In fact, it only lasted three weeks.

One evening, I was having supper with a couple of Danny's friends in their home. I didn't know it, but Art had major warrants out for him. Suddenly, we heard a pounding on the door, followed by the words, "Police, open up." Art had already been through this drill a few times and had prepared himself for their arrival. He headed for the kitchen, where all six feet of him fit in the kitchen cupboard where the dishes normally went. He had taken out the middle divider shelf, and you know what, it worked. They didn't find him; instead they found me under the bed.

Luckily, I was only charged with escaping custody, as the burglaries I had committed, along with the cars I'd stole, had gone undetected. The police took me to the Burnaby police station.

In the morning, the judge asked me how I wanted to plead to the charge. I thought to myself, *What's this supposed to be, multiple choice or something?* If I hadn't been guilty, I'd still be in New Haven mopping floors. What did the judge think? Did he imagine I'd been abducted from prison? I pled guilty and received an extra four months added to my sentence, which I now had to serve at Haney. Once back, I was quickly classified to unit eight, which was basically a unit for first offenders and those not considered violent.

The tier was two hundred feet by sixty feet. Instead of cells, as the other units had, we had twenty cubicles on either wall. Up front by the gate was a little office where the guards were stationed.

Life in the main population, as opposed to the dreaded remand units, improved a hundred and fifty percent. I definitely had more freedom, as well a choice of activities to keep me occupied. My time went by very quickly. I went to school for a while, then transferred over to Mr. Pope's cleaning crew. I also kept busy by being active in sports, lifting weights, and writing to Marlene. She came to visit once, and you could tell she'd never been in a place like that before. It must have been very intimidating for her, as she didn't come to visit again after that.

In May 1974, I was granted a twelve-hour day pass, and three weeks later full parole. My dad came to pick me up in his brand-new Lincoln. Marlene came as well. It was nice to be out and just walk around and spend some long overdue quality time with my girl.

Not much had changed in the eight months I'd been away. My dad had opened a business, which Mike and Danny ran—a small pool hall called Mike's Funland. It had three pool tables and thirty pinball machines. It was the only one around for a fifteen-block radius, and as a result was very profitable.

My dad lent me the Lincoln and I went with Marlene to meet her parents, who really liked me. I didn't lie to them in regards to where I'd been all this time. On the drive back to Haney, Marlene cried most of the way. As I wiped away her tears, I reminded her that in just three short weeks, I would be home to stay. This almost didn't happen, as for weeks the tension in the prison built to such a climax that I thought it might escalate into a full-scale riot. Two months after my release, a riot did actually take place, and shortly thereafter they closed the center down.

Back in Society 6

On May 23, 1974, I was granted full parole. The prison gave me a little Mickey Mouse suitcase for the few belongings I had, along with a bus ticket and ten dollars. After signing my release documentation, I was handcuffed and driven to a bus station in the prison van. I could clearly see that it made no difference to the guards who was around. They made a big production of taking my cuffs off. I didn't really care, as it was nice to be rid of them.

The first thing I did when they drove off was walk over to the nearest garbage can, open the suitcase, and take out my letters from Marlene and the things I wanted to keep. The rest went into the bin, as I didn't need or want the suitcase. It felt as though everyone was staring at me, and I just stared back in open defiance.

The bus ride to Vancouver took almost two hours. I sat in the back by myself and thought about where I had just been and where I might go in the future.

I didn't head straight home. Marlene knew I was getting out, but she didn't know which day. I went to her school and politely from the office found out what class she was in. I waited in the hall until she came out and surprised her with a big hug. It was easy to see she was filled with happiness; she skipped the rest of her classes that day to be with me. From the school, we went to Mike's Funland, about four blocks away. Mike was glad to see me. After we talked for a little while, he gave me the keys to the house and a hundred dollars from the cash register. He suggested I take Marlene out for a nice lunch. I took his advice, and afterwards we went to my place and spent the rest of the afternoon in each other's arms.

I knew Marlene loved me with all her heart, but prison had somehow changed me, and many times I had put a heavy strain on our relationship. However, she stuck by me… until she could no longer compete with the negative influences around me. If it wasn't for this, we would have one day gotten married. Even now, some forty years later, I often find myself thinking of her.

Within a week, the thrill of being back on the street subsided, and it was time for me to get on with my life. I worked for my dad during the day, and in the evenings I hung out at the pool hall. It wasn't long before I slowly drifted back into drinking. I knew Marlene always had my best interests at heart, but it seemed as though she was constantly nagging at me for one thing or another. After a night of drinking, I told her to get out of my life. We separated for about a month. After talking things through, we eventually reached an understanding: we'd get back together as long as I quit drinking. However, before our reunion took place, I was off on an adventure in Toronto.

Milka, the woman my dad was to marry, arrived from Yugoslavia and almost immediately tried to dictate how things were going to be from now on. She left me alone, but continually picked on Mike and Tomo. Mike has always been very outspoken. Whenever she'd ask him something, he'd tell her to leave him alone. As soon as my dad would leave for work, Mike would open the pool hall, not closing up until really late, knowing or hoping she'd be asleep afterward so he wouldn't have to look at her face. She constantly pestered him, being a royal pain, but Mike always stood up for himself. To him, this was our house, not hers. More importantly, she would never be able to replace our mother. The quicker she realized this, the better off she would be.

After eight months of operation, the pool hall shut down. A petition was signed throughout the neighborhood, alleging that since Mike's Funland had opened the neighborhood had been plagued by a rash of crime. This was probably true, as there was quite an assortment of characters in and out of the place, selling all kinds of merchandise which no doubt had been stolen. With the closure of the pool hall, Mike and Milka were steady at each other.

One day, Mike lost his temper and physically threw her out of the house, locking the doors behind her. She sat on the porch all day crying, waiting for my dad to come home. She gave her version of events, and then Mike explained his side of the story. Seeing as there was no compromise between the two, Mike had to leave.

I was troubled over this decision. What in the world was my dad thinking? She was the guest in our house, not Mike. If anyone had to make allowances and learn to adjust, it should have been her. Mike and I made a plan of our own. We decided to take my dad's van and head for Toronto.

After about a week, when everyone was asleep, Mike and I, along with our friend Gary, stole the van, rolling it down the block so as not to wake anyone up when we turned it on.

Off we went, without a dime in our pockets. As it turned out, the van had been full of my dad's power tools. Each time we needed gas, we'd tell a story like this: "I must have dropped my wallet at the last stop. Will you take a skill saw as collateral, until I return?" Which would never happened. Now and then, Gary would do a smash-and-grab, or steal a purse, so we had money to eat. Just outside Toronto, the last thing to go was the van's stereo system. By the time we reached Toronto, the van was completely empty. Even the spare tire was gone.

When we arrived at my mom's sister's place, naturally she phoned my dad, who wired money with instructions to put us all on the next train back to Vancouver. On the trip back, I did a lot of thinking about what had just taken place. I figured that if my dad wasn't fuming by now, just wait until he got his empty van back. Also, he had to fly someone out to drive it back. I definitely wanted no part of that action, as I knew he wouldn't be waiting there for us with open arms.

Just as the train pulled into the Vancouver station, we decided to jump off. I went to stay with my mom for a couple of months. During this period, Marlene and I started seeing each other again on a regular basis.

Around this time, I started my infatuation with tattoos, which by 1987 would end up covering most of my body. I went to the oldest tattoo parlor in town, operated by Curly Allen. On one arm I got a perching eagle, and on the other arm a couple of hearts with ribbons, and had mine and Marlene's names inscribed in them. I also gave myself a homemade tattoo. I wound some thread around an ordinary sewing needle, then dipped the needle in a bottle of black pelican ink and put the letters F.T.W. on my fingers.

Mike had moved in with Danny, and it was only a matter of time before my dad caught wind of it. Eventually he persuaded Mike to come back home. He often tried reassuring me that all was forgiven and that he had explained the facts of life to Milka. I did go back to work for him, but as far as I was concerned the house I had come to know as home didn't exist anymore.

It took almost three years before my parents' divorce was finalized. The divorce actually began with my dad doing a favor for a friend; he brought the man's brother, Goljub, over from Yugoslavia and helped him get established with a place to live, gain employment, and find a car. In time, Goljub became friends with the whole family. Apparently, he was getting more than just friendly. Whether he and my mom were having an affair goes beyond speculation; it was very evident. However, in any relationship where there's abuse, sooner or later the abused person will turn somewhere else for emotional support. Throughout my parents' marriage, my mother had been on the receiving end of constant abuse, both physical and mental.

Regardless of why their marriage of almost twenty years failed, my dad should have never closed his eyes to the true facts of their life together. She followed him in times of great hardship and struggled alongside him. She bore him three sons as well, trying to raise Danny as her own. Many times, she was left on her own for months at a time. She did all this while moving from city to city all over the world. Whatever she may have been guilty of, my dad was twenty times worse. Unquestionably she wasn't afforded the credit, nor proper respect, she wholeheartedly deserved. She did take a large sum of money with her, but why wouldn't she have taken something that in all fairness had been her just entitlement?

Shortly after I moved out of her place, she disappeared into seclusion, surfacing only for scheduled court appearances. Whatever friends she had, Danny and his gangster friends drove away. They would smash windows, make ongoing threatening phone calls, and even physically beat up anyone they felt might have been involved with her leaving.

One day, while she was visiting some friends, Goljub showed up. As he got out of his car, Danny jumped him and proceeded to beat him to a bloody pulp. The only reason he survived the attack was that my mother's friend Ivo had bought a rifle for personal protection. From his second floor balcony, he aimed the rifle directly at Danny and stated that he was prepared to fire if he didn't leave Goljub alone. Once the divorce was finalized, after escaping a contract killer's guaranteed bullet many times, my mom and Goljub went into deep seclusion.

After twenty-five years of looking over their shoulders, they're still living together, in hiding. The only difference is they now try to run from their own conscience, from which there is no escape.

7
Oakalla Prison Farm and Beyond

In 1975, my dad had bought an old four-story house located at 1835 Francis Street. After a thorough remodeling, it was turned into a rooming house, and in the beginning I was the caretaker. My tenants were the thieves and undesirables of society. Marlene and I had separated for the final time, and I slowly drifted back into the familiar pattern of criminal activity while things looked good. If only my dad had known how many safes I cracked open in the basement. After we emptied the contents, all traces of the safes would be thrown into the Frazer River, under the cover of darkness, from the Second Narrows Bridge. In April, I was arrested on numerous charges and my trial was set for November. As I was denied bail, I was now sent to one of Canada's most well-known prisons, Oakalla Prison Farm.

As I remember it, there were three five-tiered wings with barred cells and catwalks, holding a thousand prisoners in the main part of the prison. The west wing was for those awaiting trial, the east wing for the sentenced, and the south wing for the unmanageable. Each wing had its own separate exercise yard. There was also a single level unit known as Westgate B, which was fitted with prefabricated metal cells. This unit could house up to a hundred and fifty prisoners.

My first stop was the west wing. Like at Haney, as soon as my name came over the loudspeaker, I was approached by hardcore cons who wanted to know if I had a brother named Danny. These were his friends. Being a first-timer here, they sort of took me under their wing. I hung out with this group, by whom I was not only accepted but placed under their blanket of protection. This sent a clear and menacing message through the prison: "You mess with Mino, you mess with us."

From this group of colorful characters, I received an advanced course in prison life and survival. I lost all fear of what prison was supposed to represent. Simply put, as the years passed me by, I became more comfortable in prison than society.

My time went by fairly quickly and without incident. Most days when we were given yard time, I'd either play hand ball in the court or just pace back and forth with the guys, mostly listening. Every day was a learning experience for me. The worst thing about Oakalla was the chirping birds. Due to the extreme heat, the windows were left open and there would literally be hundreds of birds chirping all day long.

After seven months, I thought I was smart—but not smart enough to outsmart old Judge Hyme, my trial judge. I took the stand in my own defense, and when I was done all five feet of him stood up. While glaring at me, he directed his comments to my lawyer, "Mr. Lacovin, from the moment your client stepped on the stand to the time he got off, as was very evident to me, every word that came out of my mouth was a direct lie." After going through the normal song and dance of how I hadn't learned from my previous incarcerations, he sentenced me to two years less a day.

Being a sentenced prisoner, I was quickly transferred to the east wing. Shortly thereafter, I was classified to go to Boulder Bay Camp, a four- to six-month wilderness survival program. In most cases, if you completed the program successfully, you received a parole. I became friends with Danny Plumber. We were scheduled to leave within the next few weeks, but we had our own ideas.

We were transported by prison van to a dock at Stave Lake; the drive alone took about an hour and a half. We then got on a boat. I believe its name was *The Sea Otter*. The boat trip took about an hour. The camp itself was literally situated on top of a small mountain. A path led half a mile straight up at a seventy-degree incline. From the walk up the hill, Danny and I knew we didn't want any part of this place. We even told the guards this. Their response was, "The only way you're leaving is by escaping."

Which is exactly what ended up happening.

We hung around for a few days, turning their advice into a plan of attack.

From the start, Danny and I tried to disrupt everything. The guards knew what we were up to, that we were trying to be troublemakers. As a way of keeping us out of the way, they'd give us the crap detail, meaning all day long we'd pack supplies up and down the path from the boat. Thank God the camp itself, situated at the top of the hill, was flat.

The camp had six or seven cabins, and a small lake with a little alcove where there were two docks, one at either end. Every morning, being as it was the middle of December, the ice had to first be broken. Then everyone was required to swim from one end to the other.

It was a no-nonsense kind of place. Every day after work, you had to run around the two-mile perimeter of the lake. Swearing cost you anywhere from twenty-five push-ups to a couple of laps up and down the hill while dragging a heavy boom chain. It wouldn't have been such a bad place had it been summer; I think I would have actually enjoyed it.

We found out there a homemade brew—made by a group of inmates scheduled for graduation—which was just about ready for drinking. Once we got our mitts on it, we drank that night and nearly ended up burning our cabin to the ground. A guy who was asleep in the corner bunk had a glass eye that he took out at night. Being mischievous, we set the corner of his blanket on fire and then woke him up. He freaked out trying to put it out. We handed him a tobacco can full of gas, telling him it was water. He managed to get most of it on the bunk, but about a third sprinkled the cabin wall, which started to burn immediately. While everybody tried to put the fire out, Danny and I roared with laughter. That night, after things settled down, the guards locked us up in the vegetable storage shed until morning.

When the warden showed up, he said, "Fine, you got your wish. You're going back to Oakalla, but not to stay. You'll get thirty days in segregation, and then you'll be coming back."

Upon arrival at Oakalla, the guards escorted us to the upper wing of Westgate B, which was now officially the segregation unit. The cells were bare except for a steel bed, a lavatory bucket, and a burning light bulb that stayed on twenty-four hours a day. We endured twenty-three and half hours of lockup per day. I was only allowed out once for thirty minutes, just long enough to shower and clean out my bucket and cell. To tell you the truth, I kind of enjoyed the solitude. Of the fourteen years I spent in prison, I probably served two and half years in segregation. It never seemed to bother me.

Thirty-five years have gone by since I was there. Looking back, I'd have to say it was then that I had my first experience with a person I now would describe as an apostolic Christian. I don't remember the guard's name, other than to say we nicknamed him "The Preacher." Whenever he was on shift, he would make his rounds and stop at each cell, striking up a brief conversation with its occupant. Eventually, the conversation would somehow find its way to God. More often than not, within an atmosphere of hostility and cold indifference, the prisoners would send him on his way.

Now, I fully appreciate the guard's true nature. He didn't take offence at the repeated insults and rejections thrown his way. This earmarked the strength and credibility of his Christian heritage. All those times when he sat in the office, carefully reading each prisoner's file, when he closed his eyes and it appeared as though he was asleep, he was actually praying for each individual's salvation.

Once the thirty days were up, we were on our way back to Boulder Bay. Danny and I had already decided that once back we would get out of there. As soon as the lights went out for the night, Danny, another inmate, and I proceeded out the door, grabbed a canoe off the rack outside, and headed down the path for the last time. We got as far as the Narrows—about a twenty-minute ride, before the sirens went off, signaling that an escape was in progress. Nice of them to let us know they were on to us! We quickly paddled to shore, where we filled the canoe with rocks and sank it; it was no good to us anymore. The guards were already on the water, in their boats with the heavy searchlights on.

We went the rest of the way on foot, through thick shoreline brush, seven miles to the road. Then it was yet another fifteen miles to the nearest town, Maple Ridge. We were already frozen, as we hadn't been dressed for winter. Getting wet while sinking the canoe hadn't helped. Every time the searchlights came our way, we dropped to the ground and waited until they went by. Once we managed to get to the main road, it wasn't much use to us, either. That night, it was snowing heavily and the police had vehicles patrolling up and down the road. Walking there was out of the question, as they would certainly see our footprints. Why alert them as to how far we had traveled?

After twelve hours of treacherous travel, we finally reached Maple Ridge, and within a matter of hours we were caught. It didn't matter, because we were frozen. We were paraded that same day in front of the judge, and given a four-month sentence for the escape.

Once back in the east wing of Oakalla, the warden from Boulder Bay came to see me. He tried to soft-pedal me, saying how sorry he was for the way things had turned out, when in actuality all he really wanted was to get his canoe back. All I said was, "We sank it in the lake." I never did tell him where.

In May 1976, the authorities wanted to send me back to Stave Lake. I made it very clear that I was fine just where I was, but as is the case in most prisons the administration doesn't listen. They insist. There was only one thing to do. Once at the camp, I went to the first trailer and opened the first door. After closing the door behind me, I immediately started punching and kicking the room's occupant. As I hit him, he screamed that he hadn't meant to do it; he hadn't known she was only twelve years old. While beating this goof, I thought to myself, *Where in the world did they send me?* I went back to the office with blood on my hands, saying that some dummy had spit on me and we had a fight. They took me away for reclassification. This time, they sent me to Cedar Lake Camp, and I fit in perfectly.

To get there, we took the same dirt road that led to Stave Lake camp, but we passed right by it and continued for twenty miles. As we came around a small mountain, Cedar Lake awaited in its valley. As the camp was still in the early stages of being built, it only consisted of six buildings. There was the guards hut, or office, and a double-wide trailer which had been converted into a kitchen. Our recreation hut doubled as a TV room and weight pit. Our living units were two trailers, the kind used in logging camps. Until the camp was fully operational, I had my own room, which was twice the size of a normal cell.

Directly across the way from us was a brand-new trailer that had been converted into a bathroom with showers. Finally, we had the pump house where we'd find tools and the generator which supplied power to the camp. The cons had cleared a path about a hundred yards through the thick tree line, providing access to our own private lake and four canoes. For obvious reasons, this was my favorite place in the summer. I enjoyed my fourteen-month stay here. In the beginning, we worked around the camp, setting everything up. It took about five months.

Ninety-five percent of the population was made up of misfits and hardened repeat offenders. In this type of environment, there were no misunderstandings. I knew the rules of the game. If you didn't, believe me, you weren't going to stay too long.

There was a great amount of respect amongst us in the beginning. The unauthorized version of the prisoner's code of ethics was strictly enforced. This meant that as long as you minded your own business and did your time, you'd fit in. If you didn't, retaliation was often swift and brutal. Even the guards, who themselves were old-timers waiting for their pensions to kick in, were under the same understanding. If we caused them no problems and gave them no reason to fill out paperwork, they'd basically leave us alone.

Once the camp was set up, we got a new work project that I really enjoyed. There was ten miles of driftwood on the landing between the lake and the road, and it was our job to pick a spot and light a fire, slowly cleaning up and burning the driftwood. I'd go off by myself and pick a spot to burn. I've always been somewhat of a loner.

In the fourteen months before my next escape, there were a few incidents. We swore that Pope, one of the guards, was part bloodhound. No matter where or how well we hid our home brews, he always managed to sniff them out. We later found out he was getting his information from one of the cons. When our suspicions were confirmed, we got rid of the mole in short order.

Prison justice is swift and often brutal. As in any prison, the administration always tries to slip in a few undesirables, but eventually we'd weed them out; either they'd be transferred right away or they'd be carried out on a stretcher. In the prisons I've been in, the guards' main concerns always have to do with pills and alcohol, because someone would usually end up getting hurt; it could very easily be one of them. They seemed to tolerate smoking pot, as they knew it mellowed us out and there'd be no trouble. Usually the cons shared their dope, especially since there was plenty of it coming in. I still remember the guards doing their evening count. They'd come down the trailer boardwalk, opening each door to do a head count. Sometimes they'd open a door and a cloud of marijuana smoke would engulf them. They would just count you and go on their way. Cedar Lake Camp was pretty laid back.

One day on the landing, I got my fire going and was doing my own thing. A new guy kept hanging around, and I'd tell him nicely to beat it. He just wasn't listening, so I pushed him into the fire. Luckily, he didn't get seriously hurt, but he never came around me after that. Some people just have to learn the hard way.

Many times as I sat in the quiet solitude of my fire, my thoughts would briefly linger on the realities of prison existence. I've often asked myself the same question, what's it all about? I don't care who you are, or how tough you think you are, never disillusion yourself; prison will emotionally, physically, and mentally cripple you in unimaginable ways. I've seen and participated in countless acts of barbaric violence, without regret or even a hint of remorse. Just as you would cover an innocent baby in its crib with a blanket, so too did the environment of prison embrace me. However, there was absolutely no warmth in this blanket. Instead of comfort, it offered a chilling air of deception and manipulation, and everyone ensnared in its grip was left a victim!

For whatever reason, we had to clear out an area behind the camp. I ran the chainsaw, bucking up trees and old logs which were to be burned. As I was cutting, I made two piles and stacked them four feet high and ten feet apart. I didn't have a clue that while I was in the bush cutting wood, someone had dumped ten gallons of gas on the two piles; they never lit it. While I was on my way up the hill to sharpen my saw and take a break, I had my saw in one hand and a can of gas in the other. I was walking between the two piles when I spit a cigarette butt out of my mouth. All I remember was this huge explosion. It rocked the surrounding trees and I flew ten feet into the air, blowing back fifteen feet. If it wasn't for my buddy, who was taking a break on the hill, I probably would have been seriously disfigured. In the year he had been there, I had never seen him move so quickly. I didn't think he had it in him. He was on top of me almost immediately, patting my head because my hair was on fire, as were my clothes. I was taken right away to the hospital at another correctional center, where I remained under observation for a couple of days.

A couple of months before this, I put in paperwork requesting parole, and I had a really good shot of getting it. However, a parole wasn't in the cards. When I got back to Cedar Lake, my friend Tom knocked on my hut door and told me he was leaving. Instead of trying to talk him out of it, I left with him like a dummy. We went deep into the bush. For almost two days, we followed the power lines out. As it turned out, we were going in circles. Eventually we were caught, not by the police, but by the guards. It was back to Oakalla for me.

Jimmy Jose, the warden of Cedar Lake, came to see me. For the life of him, he just couldn't understand why I escaped. Especially when I would have been granted a parole in two weeks. To a certain degree, he went to bat for me, as I ended up getting only thirty days tacked on to my sentence for the escape. I was then placed in Westgate B, and remained there until November.

During this time, I assisted in a mass escape, but for whatever reason I didn't choose to run myself. Westgate had a fenced exercise yard overlooking Deer Lake. On the north side of the fence were two manned guard towers, one at either end. The grounds crew specifically left the grass there to grow. It was about three feet high. A group of us sat against the fence, somewhere in the middle, then cut a two-foot opening in the fence—with a butter knife. While crawling on their bellies, twelve guys made it through. They made it about a hundred yards down the hill before the guards spotted them. A few warning shots were fired. They started running in all directions in the open field.

The guards immediately corralled us in the yard and did a name count, as they needed to know exactly who was missing. When they called my friend's name, I yelled out, "Here." As a result of my actions, I almost got charged for aiding and abetting in the escape. My policy had always been that if you're not going along personally, then at least do all you can to assist someone willing to take the risk. There was one guard, a real gung-ho type, whom everybody referred to as German George. As soon as the alarm was sounded, he was the first one with a shotgun in hand, running down the hill chasing escaped prisoners.

In November, I was sent to the Marpole Correctional Center, a halfway house in South Vancouver. I don't really know why, but within days I escaped. I managed to get to Nanaimo on Vancouver Island, where my dad and brothers had moved. My dad had been very successful in Nanaimo, as he built many beautiful houses and commercial buildings. Keeping a low profile, I stuck around until Christmas. My dad threw a huge Christmas party with about sixty people in attendance in his workshop. Some of the people he did business with on a regular basis were alleged to have strong ties to organized crime.

My brother Mike had gone from bad to worse. It wouldn't be long before he found himself going to the B.C. Penitentiary, which at the time was like a bubbling volcano, ready to explode. Tomo still had his head above water and seemed to be doing great. However, this was about to drastically change. Milka had finally reached her one true objective. In view of her manipulations, she forced even Tomo to leave the house. He, too, was to follow suit and begin a life of crime.

After the new year, I went back to Vancouver. Two weeks later, I was arrested. After receiving a four-month sentence, again I was placed in Westgate B. I had befriended an American kid who was a very good artist. I told him that if he came across any good patterns, I'd consider getting a tattoo. He showed me a devil's head, which I thought was cool; I immediately had him tattoo it on my back. About a month went by before he showed me an article from *Time* where he had gotten the pattern. The magazine had done an expose on Satan's Choice, an outlaw motorcycle club from Toronto. What I had on my back was their crest. Understandably, I was very concerned about this, so I had him doctor it up a little to give it a new look.

I now only had six months until the completion of my sentence, and I intended to move to Nanaimo. In September 1978, I was shipped to the Redondo Bay work camp on Vancouver Island. There was only one way in, which was by seaplane from Campbell River. They had a chainsaw, and I was actively involved in tree spacing.

In the five and a half years since my return from Yugoslavia, I had spent four of those years locked up in various institutions. This alone was enough to send a tremor through the depths of my soul, but it wasn't enough to put my feet on solid ground. Not only had prison hardened me, I was what they called institutionalized.

December 24, 1978, was the day of my scheduled release, and it's surprising I made it through the first six hours. The day began in disaster. A couple of other prisoners were going out on Christmas passes, and one of them, as a result of gambling debts, owed me money. We were given our personal belongings, so we could change and be ready to go when the seaplane showed up. I took the kid's black leather jacket and a real nice ring. This made us even. Besides, he was in no position to argue.

When we got to Campbell River, we had about an hour to kill before our bus was scheduled to leave. As always, being the instigator, I talked everyone into going for a few drinks in the bar. Before heading back to the bus station, we stopped at the liqueur store, where I bought a small bottle of whisky. One of the other guys bought himself six beers.

Even before I got on the bus, I had drunk most of my bottle. Everything seemed peaceful as the bus made its way down the beautiful scenic highway. The guy sitting beside me, drinking his beer, was throwing his cans out the window. The bus driver noticed it through his side-view mirror. He pulled the bus over and came back to where we were sitting. He saw me with the tattoos and right away picked me out as the culprit. Somehow, the issue got straightened out and he went back to driving the bus. As a result, I was mad at the kid and gave him a punch in the head. The bus driver caught this action in his rear-view mirror and immediately radioed the police.

Unbelievably, from the time we had gotten on the bus, no more than a half-hour had gone by before the RCMP pulled the bus over, just outside Parksville. They wrestled me out of the bus and decided to take me to the city jail to sober up. After five hours of yelling at them and wanting to fight, I fell asleep. Around one in the morning, the police politely escorted me fifteen miles outside the city limits and dropped me off in front of the Arbutus Motel. It was snowing heavily, and there was no traffic at that time of night on Christmas Eve. I thought to myself, *Merry Christmas, Mino.*

I finally did manage to catch a ride into Nanaimo, at five in the morning. I called my dad and met him for breakfast. Afterwards, he took me to the local barbershop for a haircut, where I sold the ring to the owner for a hundred and fifty dollars. It was three days before I started working for my dad, so he gave me five hundred dollars as an advance.

It didn't take me long to get settled in. Within a very short period of time, one of my dad's business associates, George Holland, who owned a masonry company, gave me a full-time job. Just like that, he signed me into the laborer's union, which at that time paid fifteen dollars an hour.

Nanaimo Masonry was a very successful company. We were always busy. The company had seven bricklayers, and me and one other guy were laborers. Not many workers could keep up with the pace of keeping them supplied with materials, but this seemed to be right up my alley. There was no pressure and I liked hard work. I managed to keep up by developing a system: I came in an hour early every day and stayed half an hour longer at end of the day. I would come in one day on the weekend and load the scaffolds with blocks. That way, I always managed to stay ahead of the bricklayers. I held on to this job for eleven months.

With steady employment, my next move was to get away from the motel scene. An excellent opportunity came my way, as I hooked up with a girl named Jessica, a friend of my brother Mike. We quickly became friends. Within a couple of months, I moved in and split the rent with Jessica and her sister in a beautiful three-bedroom apartment that overlooked Nanaimo's harbor. Throughout this period, I kept my nose to the grindstone and gained a considerable amount of stability within my life. I went once with Jessica to visit Mike, in the B.C. Penitentiary, and a couple of other times before his release from William Head Penitentiary, near Victoria.

Within a few months. he would be given early release. As Nanaimo was about to find out, he had an explosive temper. If Mike was a fair size before entering prison, now he was a monster, weighing in at over two hundred pounds and over six feet in height. In one word, Mike was uncontrollable and unpredictable. His parole officer, a sweet woman from the John Howard Society, couldn't get through to him. She pleaded with me that a condition of his parole was that he be gainfully employed. He was supposed to be working for my dad, but he wouldn't have any part of that nonsense. It seems prison had schooled him well. In the four months before his parole was terminated, he spent over forty thousand dollars and never worked one day. Mike quickly established himself as the new tough guy in town, and took on everybody, not just one on one, but in pairs, threes, or however they wanted it. Before long, no one wanted to fight him.

Tough Guy at Wilkinson Road Prison 8

It took me ten months to get established in this small community. As soon as Nanaimo Masonry shut down for the winter, within fifteen days I was given another sentence of two years less a day. I started hanging out with Mike on a daily basis, and old habits resurfaced. I continuously drank in nightclubs and fought. Mike had a new girlfriend named Jane, and the nightclub we frequented was owned by her father. One night, I came out of the club somewhat intoxicated and saw there was some pushing and shoving going on. I got myself involved in it and ended up fighting three guys. I got the worst of it, but I always remember faces; nine months later, it wouldn't do one of the attackers any good, as he received a vicious beating.

I became friends with one of Mike's buddies, Darin, and together we started taking down some good scores. During the day, we cased a leather goods store from the inside, and found which racks held the most expensive leather coats. Understandably, it was heavily alarmed. The only way in was through the thick round Plexiglas windows on the side of the building. That night, timing it just right with the traffic lights, we made our move. After Darin smashed in the window with a sledgehammer, I jumped in with bolt cutters in hand, snapping the chains securing the racks. We took both racks of coats and were gone in less than three minutes. While all this was going on, the alarm was blaring. We fenced the coat through Nick, a Greek mobster who was a good friend of my father's.

My freedom abruptly ended a short time later, just before Christmas. Leaving the nightclub somewhat drunk, I decided to break into a car lot by going in through the side window and grabbing the petty cash. I located the safe, which I intended to come back for later that night. However, while coming out the window, I was greeted by the police, who had guns pointed at my head. The next day in court, I said to myself, "The hell with it," and pled guilty. This being so close to Christmas, I thought maybe the judge would take it easy on me. He sentenced me to two years less a day. I was off to Wilkinson Road Jail this time.

At one time, this was a prison for the criminally insane. On the back wall of each cell, I could see where chains used to come out of the wall. I guess they had shackled prisoners to their bunks.

Within days, I was classified to the Jordan River work camp. Upon arriving, I was approached by a guy who was a good friend of my brother Mike. J.P., as he was widely known, was a career criminal from

Toronto, and as sharp as a whistle. In the next eight months, I was to learn a great deal from him. As a result of a vicious attack, the bond between us became irreplaceable. In addition, my reputation as a solid tough guy was to precede me to every prison I found myself in.

I had only been there a couple of days before J.P. and I were smoking a joint in the washroom. A kid named Ranger, who was scheduled for release that very morning, came in without asking and decided he was entitled to join us. J.P. had absolutely no tolerance or patience for punks, so he gave him a slap to the face, telling him to hit the road. Ten minutes later, while we were sitting in the truck, waiting to go to work, somebody came and told us that Ranger had written "J.P. is a goof" on the bathroom wall. That's all it took. We both got out of the truck and made our way to the trailer where the kid was housed. On the way there, passing by a pile of construction garbage, I picked up a three-foot length of two-by-four, which had a couple of nails sticking out the end of it. Upon entering Ranger's hut, as J.P. punched and kicked him, I repeatedly whacked him with the two-by-four. It was all over in a couple of minutes, with Ranger twitching in a pool of blood on the floor.

On the way out, a guy who was keeping six[1] said he'd burn the two-by-four in the fire out back. Not thinking, I handed it to him. J.P. and I went to the washroom and quickly washed the blood off, then to our hut to change clothes. Before returning to the truck, we made sure to put our blood-soaked clothes in the garbage. We got back in the truck and went to our worksite.

Not even half an hour went by before two RCMP cars pulled up. They arrested us both in connection to an assortment of charges. We were questioned, and naturally we denied everything. Then they came out with a blood-stained pillowcase containing the two-by-four, the one my buddy was supposed to have burned. We clammed up and headed back to Wilkinson Road to await formal charges.

The warden of Wilkinson Road was Harry Bacon, and from the beginning I could tell that he didn't like us at all. The guards were very inexperienced in dealing with hardcore cons, which was understandable given that their typical prisoners were first offenders. Nothing had prepared them for the likes of us, or for how we were about to turn their institution upside-down. I was completely unaware of it at the time, but the rollercoaster ride was yet to begin. This time it was a journey of high times, violence, extortion, loan sharking, and drug dealing. In the coming eight months, I earned my reputation as a hardcore con and a tough guy.

As a result of his injuries, Ranger was in the intensive care unit of the local hospital. In view of J.P.'s violent criminal record, I wrote a letter to the attorney general, absolving him of any involvement in the attack. Someone from the AG's office came to visit me and tried to intimidate me with an attempted murder charge. I questioned him on his ability to understand the English language; I remained firm in my conviction that J.P. hadn't been involved.

Next, J.P. and I were concerned that the authorities would try separating us by sending one of us to the mainland, which meant Oakalla. Our only alternative was to admit to a charge to be dealt with in court. J.P. waived in some Mickey Mouse charge, and I admitted to the leather store burglary. I adamantly stressed that I had done it by myself, even though the police knew differently.

---

[1] "Keeping six," in prison parlance, means "keeping lookout."

A trial date was set for August. The police tried to trick me by saying I should waive my right to weekly remands and just come back to court in August. Had I done this, they again could have easily shipped me off to Oakalla. I didn't agree to this, so once a week they had to take me before a judge in Nanaimo. Now firmly situated without any possibility of a transfer to worry about, J.P. set up a network through his wife. Through her, we received an ounce of marijuana every day. We also put together a five-man crew, and for the next seven months—through extortion, intimidation, and drug trafficking—we were the unofficial ruling body of the prison population. Within a short period, we had cornered the entire prison drug trafficking market.

J.P. was a master of manipulation, cold and calculated in his every move. He fully understood the rules of prison survival. From a population of two hundred, there were thirty prisoners at any given time we considered to be prison smart. By supplying them drugs on a regular basis at a low cost, this group became our silent partners. They unknowingly became the eyes in the back of our heads. Our main interest was in first offenders, of which we had an endless supply.

Within a short period of time, we were making around a thousand dollars a week. Our only real concern was from those who refused to buckle under our rule, and more often than not they ended up getting punched out. As a result of fear, many would check themselves into protective custody. As in any prison where one conducts some form of illegal activity, one's measure of success depends not only on the security precautions one has undertaken to avoid detection, but also on the silence of one's fellow prisoners.

Some of the prisoners housed in the protective custody unit were tough, but because of their crimes they couldn't be in the main population. They just wouldn't last. In order for us to have control over this unit, J.P. had to enlist the cooperation of some of those prisoners. He did this by striking an agreement with them, where he would supply them with pot at a low cost. However, there was an understanding in place. From time to time, some people might need a little further intimidation or persuasion, not only in keeping their mouths shut, but also in recanting their testimonies, if any had been given. It was all strictly business. Everyone paid.

Having secured all these avenues, we were just about fully set up.

In any prison, if you're willing to take the time, you can always find a corrupt guard. It didn't take J.P. long to find him, and this made smuggling drugs in all the easier. Most of the other staff were clowns; either they were too stupid to notice what was going on, or they just didn't want to know. Once everything was in place, we set up a loan-sharking operation in the prison, which was very profitable. In prison, you needed money either to buy drugs or get out of debt. When it came to gambling, we controlled the crooked card game. I would lend out ten dollars, and in a week the person had to pay back fifteen. The beauty of it was that they were all excellent customers, as they weren't going anywhere. Sure, there was always protective custody, but no one with any self-respect wanted to wear that jacket. And if we really wanted to, we could get someone there as well. They all had family on the outside; if they happened to get in debt too deeply, the family always paid. At any given time, we had about twenty guys on the hook.

In February 1980, we had some celebrities come to stay with us for a while. There were two Americans and five Colombians, and they became known as the Tofino Mob. They were being held pending a hearing in regards to thirty-three tons of marijuana that had been found on their ship. Since J.P. had an excellent working knowledge of Spanish, he unofficially became the translator between them and the prison administration. Needless to say, we used this to our advantage. We singled out the most gullible guard, and through him we arranged for the Colombians to get whatever they wanted from their personal effects. This is a prime example of just how inexperienced the guards were; in their luggage, the Colombians not only had lots of pot in hidden compartments, but bottles of whisky as well. Within a four-month period, it was all brought into the institution. Another method is that J.P.'s wife would drop off two huge plastic shampoo containers during our court appearances, and concealed inside each bottle was two ounces of pot.

The prison van that transported us back and forth was fitted with a small wire cage, used for transporting protective custody prisoners. One week while returning from court, a big guy was in the cage. I started swearing at him, but he never said a word; he just stared straight ahead. I let go with a big one and spit right in his face. He didn't even wipe it. He stared at me with a cold, menacing glare and said, "You don't know what you're doing." He then went silent. I knew at this point that there was more to this guy than met the eye, so I left him alone for the rest of the ride back to prison. I asked a guard what the tag on this guy was. What they told me sent shivers down my spine.

"That's Shilling," the guard said. "He was charged with stabbing his mother twenty-three times."

They were going to have him on forty-eight-hour observation, to see if he was suicidal. Then he was to be shipped over to our side.

To me, it was obvious that this guy was very unbalanced. I only had two options available to me. I could wait until they shipped him over and jump him, or I could try to get in contact with him and use some form of diplomacy. Right away, I headed between the catwalks and called to him. Finally, he showed himself at the little window at the back of his cell. I apologized and admitted that I was wrong. I wanted to know if we were going to have a problem. He assured me that we wouldn't. I think the only reason was that his defense had rested on an insanity plea. Any violence on his part would have thrown out that defense.

While I was at Wilkinson Road, I got my first glimpse of what life was like as a hardcore intravenous drug addict. Brian, a friend who was heavily addicted to narcotics, one day asked me if I'd keep six for him—in other words, be his lookout. He had some dope smuggled in and wanted a fix. I'd never witnessed the rituals of a dope fiend until now, and watching Brian do his thing made me sick. Most long-term addicts' veins would slowly start collapsing, and before they knew it, they wouldn't have any left, which made fixing all the harder. Since Brian fit into this category, finding a vein was a crap shoot. This experience further re-enforced my conviction to never use heavy narcotics. Little did I know that it would be just short five years before I started my twelve-year affair with narcotic drugs.

I had no doubt that the warden was on to us. During his weekly inspections, he would stop by our cells, which were next to each other. With his hands behind his back, he would glare at J.P and I and say, "I know you guys are responsible not only for the drug activity going on, but the continued violence as well." He let us know that eventually he would catch us. I'd give him a deadpan look and state that he had a better chance of catching a cold than he did of catching us.

Eventually, the Tofino Mob won their freedom on a technicality. Their defense had been that it had never been their intention to import drugs to Canada, but rather Alaska. However, as their ship had been in need of serious repair, they'd had no other alternative but to come to shore. We were thrilled when they had gained their freedom, but it was also a sad time for us, as we had formed a solid friendship with them. As they were leaving soon, they got to go through their personal effects. The last of the pot and alcohol was brought in and we had quite the farewell celebration.

True to his word, the warden did catch me. The day after the Columbians left, I screwed up by letting my guard down. I was hung over and mad at someone on the range (the cellblock). Instead of dealing with it in a cell, out of sight, I gave him a punch to the head in plain view of everyone. I received thirty days in the hole, which to me was really no big deal.

In handcuffs, I was led to the basement of the prison. The heavy metal door was unlocked, and I was led into a room containing six cells, three on either side. It gave you the impression that you were entering a medieval dungeon. My handcuffs were removed and I entered my new home. I could tell that these cells were barely ever used. Up until the time J.P. and I arrived, I don't think the guards had too much trouble running the prison. The cell smelled like a toilet bowl, probably from the last tenant, and the smell was overpowering. As the cells were located in the belly of the prison, it was a regular sweatbox.

Each cell had a solid metal door, with a three-by-five-inch square peephole. The cell was completely bare except for a thin mattress on the floor, a lavatory bucket, and a Bible. As luck would have it, during the evening shift an old-timer guard who was a pretty decent guy came down to check on me and give me a blanket. It would be taken away each morning at 6:00 a.m. We exchanged words for a few minutes, and then I asked if I could have a mop bucket to clean this pigsty out. After briefly observing the condition of my cell, he did go and get me some cleaning supplies. After examining the other cells, he quickly realized that cleaning just my cell wouldn't get rid of the smell, so he asked me if I wouldn't mind cleaning out the other cells as well. This made my living conditions more bearable. After he left, I heard the distant slamming of the outer door and I realized the place was soundproof.

While looking around at my surroundings, I let my thoughts wander. I thought about what it must have been like when the prison was full of lunatics and these six cells were all occupied at the same time. Imagine six lunatics all at once, screaming gibberish, singing, or carrying on conversations with themselves. With all that in mind, it wasn't hard to envision a good many prisoners going around the bend down here. The heat was incredible, to the point of being suffocating. I felt like I was in Australia all over again. I solved this problem by stripping to my underwear, and this is how I remained for the next thirty days. There was no set time, but once a day I was given a shower and allowed to clean out my lavatory bucket.

As J.P. wasn't one to turn his back on a friend, within days some associates came to occupy the surrounding cells, bearing gifts. One person had a suitcase of pot, while another had one containing tobacco.[2] The problem I faced was how to get the goods from them to me, as we were never allowed out of the cells more than one at a time. I gave this some thought, and within a couple of hours came up with the answer. First, I unraveled the corner of the blanket they had given me, until I had about fifteen feet of string. The distance between the cells was about ten feet. Next, I took out the cardboard roll from the middle of the toilet paper. To give it some weight, I stuffed the roll with toilet paper. Now all I had to do was securely tie the string to the roll. I had the kids do the same thing. I dropped about ten feet of the string

---

[2] A "suitcase," in this context, refers to a balloon in the rectum, containing contraband.

out the peephole, then placed the roll in the slot and gave it a whack, sending it flying across the room, to land in front of the intended cell. The other person would do the exact same thing, but in the middle of his roll he'd secure the contraband. The strings would overlap, and then I'd carefully and slowly reel them in. It didn't work right away, so we did many trial runs before finding success. Within a few hours, I was getting high and having a cigarette. My following twenty-seven days in the hole were definitely a little more bearable.

Little did I know that the warden had another surprise waiting for me. When my thirty days were up, instead of going back to the main population, as I expected, I was transferred to the segregation unit, located on the tier directly above the protective custody unit. I immediately put in a formal request to the warden, wanting to go back to main population. After all, I had done my time in the hole. His response? Since I had established myself as a hard rock, he found me to be a danger to the operation of his institution. Until every staff member spoke to him in my behalf, I could consider this cell my new home. A good percentage of the prisoners in protective custody were there, as a direct result of J.P.'s and my actions. The first couple of days were a nightmare, as I found myself ducking knives being thrown at me. It quickly got straightened out, although until it did I had my mattress propped up against the cell bars for protection.

I wasn't going anywhere, so J.P. sent me a care package. It took the guard three trips to bring me everything. There were a couple cases of pop, six huge bags of assorted chocolate bars and chips, a bag of toiletries, and a couple of cartons of cigarettes. There was even a radio. Each cell had a square wire window in its rear wall, and through this enclosure J.P. managed to send me about a hundred marijuana joints. The first joints he sent me were my first experience with cocaine, as each joint was laced with some. I had no knowledge of this.

He told me to just take one puff, then put it out, as it was very potent. Since I never could take or follow advice, I smoked a whole one. I had never been as high as I was then. I had thoughts running through my head that J.P., my partner-in-crime, was trying to poison me. I even entertained thoughts of calling the guard, to take me to the hospital. Instead, I remained silent. If I was going to die, it would be like a man. A short time later, I heard a voice in the distance. It took me a minute to realize it was J.P. Looking through the little wire-meshed window, I explained what I had done, and how I felt. He burst out laughing, then said I should just lie down and relax, as it would pass.

It's surprising how when you're restricted from doing something, regardless of the situation you find yourself in, you'll somehow figure out how to do it. J.P. had taken five pages from the newspaper and spread them out flat. He then placed a line of joints across each page, tightly rolling up each page and tapping it as he went along. He secured one length into another. When he was finished, he had an eight-foot paper pole. He passed this through the window on his side into my cell. I unraveled the paper, taking out the joints. He also told me to hide them really well. The only safe place was a suitcase.

He told me that he was about to make a move, which just might get me released back into population. I didn't know it, but he was about to rock the prison. The next day before lunch, ten people got beat up badly. When the warden went on the tier to find out what was going on, J.P. said to him, "If Mino is put back in population, there probably won't be any more violence." The warden himself, being from the old school, wasn't one for intimidation or threats of any kind. He immediately locked down the whole prison, then set the ground rules over the loudspeaker. The prison would resume normal procedure the following day, but if there were any more acts of violence, the whole prison would go on indefinite lockup. The next day, I thanked J.P. for what he had tried to do, but I told him to drop the issue. I knew the only thing the warden wanted more than having me locked up was to get J.P. as well. Besides, we couldn't make any money with the prison locked down.

I remained in this cell for the next two months. As was the pattern with me, there was never a dull moment.

One day, Darin showed up. As a result of certain information he gave me, I knew I could take care of the charges J.P. and I faced over Ranger's vicious beating. In the end, it definitely was a small world. Not only was Ranger from Nanaimo, but he was going out with the sister of a good friend of mine. Ranger had never mentioned my name, just said that somebody had attacked him. Immediately, I got on the phone with my friend and explained how this kid was planning to testify against me in court. Within a matter of two days, the cops came to see me. They stated that Ranger was back in intensive care, as a result of another beating he got. He also retracted his whole statement and wouldn't be testifying against us in court. As they no longer had a material witness, there was no other alternative but to drop the charges. My final words to the cops were, "You could have saved yourself the trip and just sent me a letter."

I had served a total of eight months now, with eight more to go. It was time for me to appear in court on the leather store burglary charge. I got in front of the judge and he gave me a speech about how I was compiling quite a list of serious offences. With this in mind, he gave me a brand-new two years less a day sentence. Since it was a consecutive sentence, which now overrode the old one, I was back at square one, with sixteen months remaining to serve.

They put me in a holding cell along with a group of other prisoners who were awaiting transport back to Wilkinson Road. Upon entering the cell, I scanned its occupants and began smiling. There, sitting in front of me, was one of the guys from the fight outside the nightclub. I could tell as his face registered recognition. He had been hoping I wouldn't recognize him. Since our last encounter, I'd put on some weight, and with my shaved head I looked very intimidating. I immediately attacked, giving him a couple of boots to the head, along with seven punches. It was over in twenty seconds. He lay on the ground bleeding.

Hearing the commotion, the sheriff came around the corner and wanted to know what had happened. Before I could say anything, the guy on the floor said that he had slipped and hit his head on the bench. He was quickly taken to the hospital for stitches, and they had him back in time for transport. I went over and shook hands with him, letting him know that he was okay by me. As far as I was concerned, he'd have no further problems from me.

Back at the prison, I went back to the main population, as now I was a sentenced prisoner, no longer awaiting trial. However, the warden didn't waste any time having me transferred out. Within four days, I would be on my way back to Oakalla.

Another solid friendship I had was with a likable old-timer by the name of Norman. He had begun his career in crime back in the early 1950s, specializing in the fine art of burglary. He had extensive knowledge in the area of alarm systems and safecracking. Fascinated, I used to sit down with him whenever the opportunity presented itself and listen to his amazing tales. He'd tell me about the different types of acid that would eat through a safe, or about the high-tech equipment on the market used by locksmiths, which could open any door. One day I asked him to teach me about different ways of disabling alarm systems and better ways of cracking a safe. I was never one for taking advice, but what he told me obviously came straight from the heart.

"In view of rapidly changing technology," he said, "you'd be better off going to school for three or four years to become an electrician. By then, you'd know everything you need to know about alarms."

Then he pointed out a simple truth: once I'd spent all those years in school, why would I want to be a thief, when I could legally make a hundred thousand dollars a year?

In the days prior to leaving Wilkinson Road, J.P. and I had no room for sad goodbyes. Our friendship was built on solid principles, and was therefore forever cemented. Maybe somewhere down the road we'd bump into each another again. I had a couple ounces of pot hidden in bottles of shampoo, but more importantly I had a thousand dollars in cash, suitcased. With this, no matter where I went or what happened, I'd be okay.

At only twenty-four years of age, I had thus far spent close to five and a half years of my life behind prison bars, and I wasn't bothered by this frightening reality. Prison survival is an art in itself. It took years of experience to master the essential skills to survive an environment which in a blink of an eye could turn totally brutal, leaving even the most hardcore convict a victim.

Long before returning to Oakalla, everyone there had heard of my Wilkinson Road exploits through the prison grapevine, which I swear was quicker than the postal service. I was once again placed in Westgate B, where I remained for the next six months. After setting myself up, I kept a low profile. However, one night a full-scale riot broke out in the main prison. In any such situation, the administration likes to lock down the rest of the prison as quickly as possible, which in effect gives them more manpower to concentrate on the riot. Instead of locking up our cells, we refused to cooperate, giving the rioting prisoners an advantage. Only after they turned the fire hoses on us were we locked up; however, by then the rioting wing had already caused extensive damage.

In January 1981, I was sent to Alouette River, a substance abuse treatment center. The warden was the same guy who had run Cedar Lake. All the units except one were dormitories. Here, I made friends with Peter, a Polish mobster, and Gordie, a solid biker from White Rock. I settled in quietly and landed a job in the auto mechanic shop, changing tires and servicing the prison vehicles. It's a wonder any of them ran, considering the things I did to them.

The three of us occupied one far corner of the unit. For us, life inside this prison camp was a piece of cake. Peter, at a prearranged spot in the nearby woods, picked up a drop of contraband every week.

After three months, I submitted my parole application. In view of my performance and attitude, I was assured by my case management team that it would be granted. As had become our routine, Peter and I sat in the corner, playing chess. Like always, we were having a few drinks and a couple of tokes while minding our own business. Suddenly, this idiot who slept in the bunk next to mine, Ernie, sat down and waited for the joint to be passed his way. Many times we gave tokes or joints to fellow prisoners, without wanting anything in return. However, this had always been on our terms. Prison etiquette dictated that if we offered, then fine, but otherwise mind your own business.

Ernie was a strange character to begin with, one whom I believe wasn't playing with a full deck. I didn't physically hurt him. All I said was, "If you don't leave, you'll get buried in the frigging woods." He left without incident; sometimes a bold word did the trick. As soon as I had threatened this clown, I knew it was a mistake. Something just didn't seem right.

I used to incorporate an old trick I'd learned that had saved my neck on more than one occasion. While relaxing on my bed, I'd put my headphones on with no music playing. In that open dormitory setting, I wanted to be aware of what was going on around me.

Well, a few days later while at work, I got an unexpected surprise. When the guard came for me, I was almost positive my parole had come through and I was going to be released. When we got to the warden's office, I stepped out of the van and shook the warden's hand, figuring I was leaving.

"Mino, you won't want to be thanking me," he said. He then slapped handcuffs on me. "You'll be going to Mini Max in Chilliwack."

This was a maximum-security segregation unit. Apparently, Ernie had written a statement to the effect that I had threatened to kill him. I found myself being herded into the transport van like a sheep, without the benefit of a hearing, or even the opportunity to defend myself against these allegations.

Mini Max was a small fenced-in compound just outside Thurston Correctional Center, another work camp. It had four units that housed about fifteen prisoners each. They had quite a group of characters here. In the thirty days I spent at Mini Max, there were a couple of wild altercations involving two crazy Frenchmen. It all began because they didn't want to be there, or at any camp for that matter. All they wanted was to go back to Oakalla peacefully and do their time. It seemed simple to me, but as always the administration felt they knew what was best.

One day we were out in this little fenced yard, making pallets with hammers, when one of the Frenchmen called the guard over. The Frenchman reversed his grip on the hammer and let the guard have it, with the claw end, right in the head. There was blood all over the place. The Frenchman dropped the hammer and sat down on the ground. All of a sudden, six guards jumped him and took him away. He not only got charged for assault with a deadly weapon, but also got to go back to Oakalla, where he had wanted to go in the first place.

You'd think the prison administration would have figured it out by now. We were more dangerous than they were. They had already treated us like dogs and taken everything away from us, except our pride and determination. We didn't care about anything that stood in our way. The Frenchman only had six months left to serve. He received a two-year sentence for the assault, but it didn't bother him because he got what he wanted, even though it was at the expense of the prison guard getting hurt.

The Frenchman's partner also wanted to go to Oakalla, and truthfully they should have shipped them both out as a package. Sometimes lessons are only learned the hard way. Several days later, while he was mopping the tier, the other Frenchman dismantled the metal squeegee handle from the mop wringer and knocked on the door, telling the guard to open it. No sooner did the guard open the door than the Frenchman cracked him twice in the head with the pipe. It only cost him a year for assault, but he, too, got to go back to Oakalla

After I finished my time at Mini Max, I was sent to Ford Mountain Correctional Center, another work camp about ten miles up the road from Thurston. Since ninety percent of its population consisted of first offenders, I mainly kept to myself and worked out with the weights. Near the end of my sentence, every day on the work gang during breaks, I'd school the kids on the finer points of burglary. The guards were pissed off at me, which was no big deal, as we clearly understood each other. They didn't like me, and I didn't like them.

A couple of weeks before I got out, I gave serious thought not only to my past, but also to what lay ahead for me. I was twenty-five years old and had now spent a total of six years incarcerated. I decided I would somehow try to get my life back on track.

A Taste of Freedom 9

Within the inescapable noose of alcoholism, I once again almost didn't make it past the first six hours of release. There was one other guy getting out that day. Once the guard dropped us off at the Chilliwack bus depot, we headed to the nearest pub and had a couple of cold beers. This was followed by a quick stop at the liquor store, where we each bought a pint of whiskey for the two-hour bus ride into Vancouver. During the bus ride, I asked the guy for a drink from his bottle. When he said no, all hell broke loose. The last thing I remember was punching him in the head a couple of times. The next thing I knew, I was waking up in a cell in the Vancouver city jail. Luckily, it was just for being intoxicated in a public place, as I'm sure the guy could have easily had me charged with assault.

During my first month of freedom, I moved in with Mike and his girlfriend Vicky. From the first moment I laid eyes on Wendy, Vicky's younger sister, I fell in love with her. Through the International Laborers' Union, I managed to get a really good job. The Supreme Court building was being remodeled, as it was now going to be the new Vancouver Art Gallery. Mike was still involved in semi-criminal activities, but I wanted to distance myself from that lifestyle. I decided to get a place of my own. I found a beautiful fourth-floor apartment overlooking a park in North Vancouver. For a while, Wendy and I were seeing each other on a regular basis.

My dad had recently liquidated all his assets in Nanaimo and moved to West Vancouver, where he was building half-million-dollar homes. He and Milka had two daughters, and there would be another to follow. Four months out of prison, and to me life was good. However, as was my experience, anything good was short-lived.

In December 1981, Tomo was released from the penitentiary to the Robson Center, a halfway house in downtown Vancouver. Since I hadn't seen him in two and a half years, I wanted to do whatever I could to help him out. I told him to use my address as a means of securing passes from the halfway house, and also as a reference on his parole application. The problem was that Tomo was an exceptional thief, and he had no desire to change his lifestyle.

One time he asked me to do him a favor. A friend of his from the halfway house was getting out and needed a place to stay. I said sure, I'd help him out for a couple of weeks, until he got settled on his feet.

Within two days, I threw him and his stuff out the door. I was working every day, only to come home to find the guy with his head stuck in a plastic bag, sniffing glue. I also noticed he had a stereo hooked up which he had obviously stolen. If I had wanted to get into trouble, I could very easily have done so on my own. I didn't need any help from this idiot.

Not one for wasting time, Mike had took the stereo. Seeing as the guy was a glue head, though, he took offence to his stolen stereo being taken. I certainly didn't want it around. That same night, he was hiding behind a bush near the halfway house. As Tomo was heading back for the night, he called out his name. Tomo turned around and the guy cracked him in the face with a two-by-four, shattering his nose. Mike, Danny, and I went looking for him, but the next day he scammed a bus ticket from the welfare office and left for Calgary.

Within a matter of weeks, Tomo moved in with me. I offered to try and get him a job in the union, but work was the last thing on his mind. As they say, old habits are hard to break. It always began with a slow progression, and once I was ensnared in that all too familiar net, there was no escape. I was working like a dog, getting home late and exhausted, and there was Tomo, counting out thousands of dollars he had made the night before from burglaries, which only took him a couple of hours to commit.

First, I slowly got back into the routine of drinking, and within weeks I started missing days from work. It wasn't long before I found myself out of a job and stealing full-time. Wendy didn't have a clue what was going on. As far as she knew, things were okay.

One night, Tomo and I hit a high-profile fashion store in West Vancouver, along with a drug store. My storage locker downstairs was full of brand-new clothes, which I slowly sold to strippers from local hotels. Under my bed, I had half a drug store; we were taking more pills than we sold. We tried to hit a jewelry store that was just down the street from the police station. In a final attempt, we even tried to go through the wall with a skill-saw, only to find out that the fifty-foot wall was made up of solid two-by-eights.

One night, Tomo asked if I want in on a couple of scores he had lined up. As I planned on spending the evening with Wendy, I passed on the offer. However I did arrange for him to have a driver.

Around three in the morning, for some reason I just couldn't sleep. I was worried about Tomo. He hadn't called, nor had the driver gotten back to me. I'm sure if there had been any kind of problem, he would have called. Something just wasn't right.

Just as I was getting ready to take everything out of the apartment, the door got kicked in. I knew immediately that the cops had Tomo in custody. I told Wendy to keep quiet and let me do the talking. Seven cops burst in, and they had a field day. They found all kinds of stolen goods, to which I played the clown, denying all knowledge.

At the police station, they got me in a small interrogation room, and the questions kept coming in rapid succession from all sides, as if fired from a machine gun. I figured out who was in charge and told him to get rid of the other cops. I would only talk to him. After he did this, I told him the facts, as I knew them. In the first place, the only reason they had kicked in my door was because they had caught Tomo in the middle of a break-and-enter. At that very moment, they had him sitting in a cell downstairs. Knowing Tomo, I went on to say that whatever they had found in the apartment, Tomo had already taken responsibility. Of that I was certain.

This left them with only two alternatives. They could either release me or charge me, in which case Tomo would take the Canada Evidence Act, absolving me of any knowledge or guilt, and within thirty days I'd be back on the street. I said to him, "Whatever you're thinking of doing, let's get on with it. I'm tired. One way or another, I want to get some sleep."

I wasn't afraid or intimidated by them, or the possible beating I might get. I'd been down that road many times. I'd had some beatings where after they'd finished with me, you'd think my hat belonged to a midget.

The cop left and returned within ten minutes. He said that Wendy and I were free to go. They even gave us a ride back to the apartment. After a couple of days, Tomo called me from Oakalla and suggested that I leave the province. A girl had been involved on one burglary, and somehow the police had gotten a hold of her. He was concerned she might say something to implicate me; I wanted to go and pay her a social visit, since intimidating witnesses was nothing new to me. Tomo strongly argued against this. I thought it was because he was sweet on the girl. After the nightmare Wendy had just gone through, she left me like a bullet. I couldn't blame her.

A guy I knew from the bar was looking for a place, so I told him that my apartment along was his, along with everything in it. I just wanted one favor in return. My mother had put together twenty-six extensive photo albums of our travels; as you can imagine, they were quite heavy. All I was taking was a suitcase with some clothes. Once I got to Calgary and was settled, I'd send for them. He said it wouldn't be a problem; he'd look after them for me.

This was the last time I ever saw my father. After I left, it wasn't long before he packed everything up and disappeared, not bothering to stay in touch with anyone. Twelve years later, I managed to have one brief telephone conversation with him. I'll never forget that conversation. I could tell by the tone of his voice that his health was rapidly in decline. We only spoke for a few minutes before he passed the phone to Milka. Her only words to me, before she slammed the phone down, were "Hi and bye." Her opinions of us should have never been allowed to enter the picture. He was our father, and we were flesh and blood. The only thing that could have escalated the bad blood between us and Milka would have been if my father passed away, and she didn't even try to contact us when it happened. In my mind, that was sacrilegious. Inexcusable. If she prevented me from seeing my father while he was still alive, that's fine. I could live with that. But I would at least have liked to know where he was buried.

Drumheller Penitentiary 10

Within six hours of my conversation with Tomo, I was on a bus for Calgary and once again in violation of my parole, a fugitive from the law. Danny and Mike had already been living there. Danny's racket had always been the used car business. As it turned out, the auto body shop next to theirs had a clientele of wrestlers who would eventually become known as the world-famous Hart Foundation. Danny had somehow gotten his foot in the door, and was also the manager of a huge apartment building.

Once I settled in Calgary, I put together an elaborate scheme for burglarizing homes. What I did was grab the local free ad newspaper, such as the Buy and Sell. Then, armed with a large city map, I'd go through each ad, looking for ads that specified for people to phone after four o'clock. Nine times out of ten, no one was home until that time. To confirm this, I wrote down each ad on its own page in my notebook. When I had about thirty of them, I'd go to work. The following morning, I'd call each number. If there was no answer after fifteen rings, I'd put a checkmark in the first column. On each page would be ten columns, and every hour I'd call each number, leaving a checkmark if unanswered. I'd do this for four days. By then, I'd be sure no one was home during the day. If anyone answered, I'd rip out the page and throw it in the garbage.

Usually on a Friday or the weekend, I'd phone in the evening, pretending to be interested in whatever they were selling. If it was still available, I'd ask for their address, which went into the notebook. Within a couple of hours, I'd phone them back to let them know I wouldn't be coming by, as I had purchased something somewhere else. I thanked them for their time. I would then mark all the addresses on my city map with a number. During the day, I'd take a bus and check out each house. I was mainly looking for places that had enclosed entrances, either in the front or back. All this was important information, and it always went on the page with the corresponding phone number and matching address. The only things I needed now were a light parka with a hood, gloves, and my favorite tool—a carpet layer's pry bar—which opened most residential doors. It was two inches wide and eighteen inches long, and ideally S-shaped.

Mondays and Tuesdays were the best days of attack, as most people were just getting back into their routine from the weekend. I'd be in the neighborhood around nine in the morning, and call the house from the nearest pay phone. I'd let the phone ring as I went to the house, where most times I'd still hear the phone ringing. If I went in the front door, I'd leave by the back door, just in case a nosy neighbor happened to spot me going in. That way, I would leave the impression that I was still inside. I never stayed in any place for more than five minutes, as that's all it would take. Once inside, I went straight for the master bedroom, where most of the valuables were hidden. They'd all go into a small briefcase or suitcase I would find in the house. During these daytime burglaries, I never had to steal a car. My best transportation was provided by the city—the bus. Through Mike, I met a guy named Bobby Nickels, through whom I fenced most of the jewelry and other valuables.

Inadvertently, I managed to get on the bad side of the wrestlers. One of the apartments I burglarized happened to belong to Tony Miller, their insurance broker. I had his wallet, which was full of personal identification, usually the kind of stuff I threw away. I was talking to a friend of Danny's about it, and the following day he said to me that the wrestlers wanted the guy's identification back. By this time, I had already thrown it away.

I usually got together with Bobby twice a week, and he'd buy whatever goods I had. One day I phoned him, saying I'd be coming over with a load of jewelry. Instead, we arranged a meeting for the next day, by my place. He was very interested in a six-hundred-dollar camera I wanted to sell. What he didn't know was that I had just moved into my new place the night before and had given someone the camera as payment for moving me. No one knew where I lived. As far as Bobby knew, I still had the camera. I told him to meet me in the restaurant around the corner. I got there early, and oddly this one table seemed to draw my attention. There were six big guys there, all talking loudly about the stock market. Bob showed up, and immediately I could see he was nervous about something. I didn't think anything of it. After a quick cup of coffee, we headed over to my place. On the way, I mentioned that I no longer had the camera, which didn't seem to bother him. I did have a small Crown Royal bag full of jewelry. As for a price, we settled on a thousand dollars. He then asked me to come by his place later; he had to swing by the bank before paying me. I found this to be a little strange, as he always had large sums of cash on him. I was a little suspicious, but he had never done me any wrong, so I let it slide. No sooner had he left and my door was getting kicked in. Sure enough, it was those six goons from the restaurant. They were cops, and on their search warrant they were specifically looking for a camera. It was clear that Bob had just set me up.

The stolen property they found only connected me to a couple of burglaries. They also found my little book with all the addresses. Luckily for me, after each house was burglarized I had ripped out the incriminating page. Instead of sitting in the remand center doing dead time, I pleaded guilty. The judge said that in his opinion, I had put together a highly sophisticated housebreaking scheme, and luckily for me no one was ever home. He sentenced me to three years. The prosecutor immediately appealed the sentence, as he felt it wasn't enough. At twenty-five years of age, I had thus far accumulated about fifty adult convictions. Thirty days later, I received an additional year, making my sentence four years. Classification came to see me in the remand center, and it was decided I would be sent to Drumheller Penitentiary.

Drumheller was an overwhelming place. It contained four separate wings, each housing two hundred prisoners. I was placed in the indoctrination unit for the first week, then classified to unit eight. For the first week, I got used to the place before deciding what I wanted to do. I knew about twenty guys there.

Some were from Wilkinson Road, while others from Oakalla. Even my old escape partner Tom, from Cedar Lake, was there.

I started working out with the weights and decided to get a job in the kitchen, which only took up a couple of hours each day. I began eating like there was no tomorrow. Not only did I maintain my rigorous weight training, I faithfully did eight or nine hundred pushups daily. Within a year, I went from a hundred and fifty pounds to a solid two hundred and fifteen. I was in the best shape of my life. Understandably, given my lifestyle, I was full of hostility, frustration, and pent-up anger. The weight pit was a wonderful place to let it out.

Regardless of the prison, there's always someone willing to test you, to see if you've got any heart. Stories about my past exploits got around, so there was always some clown who wanted to see if he could make a name for himself. I don't care who someone is, or how big they are; anyone can be beat. However, there's a big difference between a fight and a funeral. If a guy didn't leave me alone, regardless of the consequences, I would seriously hurt him.

My first and only beef while at Drumheller took place two months after I arrived. I wasn't bothering anyone, just trying to do my own time, but this guy on the range was steadily pushing my buttons. Each cell had its own buzzer, so you could close your door whenever you wanted to. By pressing the buzzer, the guard in central control would reopen your cell. One day I'd had enough of this clown and caught him just after he entered his cell. I went in right after him, closing the cell door behind me. When he saw me, he went white as a ghost.

While repeatedly punching him in the head, I told him that we definitely didn't want to have any more problems in the future, as next time only one of us would walk out of the cell. I hit the buzzer and let myself out.

In the remaining two and a half years I spent at Drumheller, I never had a problem. I survived two riots and one racial war.

I managed to get a hold of an electric shaver, and converted it into a tattoo gun. This was considered illegal activity in prison, and I made good money at it. As a result, I added seven tattoos to my increasing collection. One in particular, on my right leg, is three skulls surrounded by ribbons with the letters L.I.T.F.L. (Life in the fast lane). Up to this point in my life, I'd seriously hurt three people who had been placed in intensive care. Had I known then the damage I was yet to inflict, I could have added more skulls.

After a year and a half, my thoughts drifted to early release. In talking it over with my counselor, he stated that in view of my lengthy criminal career, along with my high-profile prison file, I would first have to participate in one-on-one counseling with the prison shrink. I agreed, and an interview was arranged. The next step in the process involved completing psychological tests, which took about a week. I then began my weekly, one-hour sessions with Dr. Holden, which continued for the next ten months. I found the first few sessions to be very intense, but quite stimulating, as I was gaining a better understanding of myself.

Once the psychologist determined that we could go no further in this fashion, he wanted me to participate in his biweekly group sessions. He thought I'd be an excellent contributor. Of course I went along; doing otherwise would have jeopardized my release plans. His positive recommendation would greatly influence any decision regarding early release. In the beginning, it was all a con to get out quicker, but after a while I came to enjoy these sessions.

To get anything out of them, you had to be totally honest. This being a prison group therapy situation, it just wasn't happening; everybody was lying. The only factor to be taken into consideration was trust, and absolutely none existed in this environment. I was in a room with six total strangers, and we were expected to reveal what was going on inside our heads. Not too likely! I played this game for another six months, all the while sharpening my manipulation skills. What nobody realized was that I didn't care. I had never been interested in what the prison thought of me, and this invalidated all their tests—and more importantly, their opinions.

I started lifting weights with my neighbor Stuart. He was just a kid, but he knew his way around the weight pit.

Shortly, everything I had worked for throughout the last year and a half came crashing down around me in a twelve-hour period. In May 1984, I was granted a forty-eight-hour pass to Calgary. I had a letter from the local union hall informing me that I would be reinstated as a member upon my release. Stuart went on this pass with me. We were to stay in the local halfway house. After we had dropped off our stuff, the first item on my agenda was to locate Bobby.

I did this by going to his uncle's place. I didn't even knock; I walked right in. The sight of me was very intimidating, as no longer was I that skinny kid he had once known. I was built like a brick wall now and had the attitude to go with it. I didn't do anything to him, as it wasn't his fault that his nephew was a piece of garbage. I simply explained that I had taken the four-year sentence and now I wanted money. He reached into his pocket and gave me what he had, which was about a hundred dollars. I told him to get hold of Bobby and make sure he came to see me at the local bar. If he made me come looking for him, I was going to get mad.

With this done, Stuart and I headed to the nearest mall, where we found some kids selling pot. This was the whole purpose of the pass. We went into the washroom, where one of the kids handed me an ounce of pot to look at. I simply stuck it in my pocket. There was no altercation as we left without paying.

Our next stop was the bar. In the washroom, using two condoms, I evenly divided the pot and immediately suitcased my half. I now knew that no matter what happened, the goods were in the vault, safe and secure.

A couple of hours later, instead of Bobby showing up, the weasel had sent his uncle, who gave me a few hundred bucks. I was far from happy, but I was in no position to do anything about it at the moment.

Since we'd already had more than enough to drink, before returning to the halfway house, we thought it a good idea to first have supper. Suddenly, the live band began to play "Been a Long Time Since I Rock-and-Rolled," a classic Led Zeppelin tune. That's all it took. I started ordering doubles. We ended up fighting with four or five guys out back. The police showed up, and once the dust settled, Stuart and I were in handcuffs, on our way back to the penitentiary.

Right off the bat, I was informed by my case management team that any chance I had of getting paroled had gone out the window. To me it was no big deal, as I only had eight more months to serve until my mandatory supervision date kicked in. Mandatory supervision refers to a prisoner's right to release after completing two-thirds of his sentence. Stuart, on the other hand, being a first offender, was just nineteen years of age. They figured I must have influenced him. They were prepared to overlook what had happened and grant him a parole. I still don't understand it, but he told them that he didn't need their sermon. If Mino wasn't going, then neither was he. Because of his remarks, he served an additional five months. I told him that he should have just taken the parole, but he remained insistent. It was the principle involved.

That kept Stuart in my mind forever. He was a friend who could be counted on, which in prison was a rarity.

Stuart and I continued our weightlifting activities. I sold some of the pot, but most of it I shared with my friends, all of whom I could count on one hand. Ross Chamberlain, another buddy of mine, was one of the few people I've come across to actually do what he said he would upon release. Most promises made in prison are as dry as a peanut butter sandwich in the desert. Ross surprised me, especially in that he was a first offender. Once he got released, I received a postcard from him. It was picture of a menacing shark, and the only words he had written were, "A shark for a shark." To this day, Ross and I are friends.

My time at Drumheller was coming to an end, as within thirty days I was to be shipped to Bowden Penitentiary.

Bowden Penitentiary 11

Bowden was a medium-security institution built in 1974, and it housed close to six hundred prisoners. It was located in the town of Innisfail Alberta, halfway between Calgary and Edmonton. At the time of my arrival, Bowden was in the process of getting a fifty-million-dollar facelift, which would take fourteen more months before completion. In the meantime, I was housed in a brand-new three-wing trailer unit, along with a hundred and fifty other prisoners. Gone were the bars, as each wing had twenty-five small rooms on either side. We had our own doors with glass windows in them.

I immediately landed a job as a cleaner, taking care of my wing. Once Cecil and I became friends, we started working out together every day in the weight pit. One day, my friend Tony was housed on my wing. He was a medium-build Sicilian kid, about twenty years old. He wore a complete body suit from head to toe, which is why we all called him Spiderman. He and his so-called partner had planned to set a building on fire. They soaked the place with a hundred gallons of gas, but as Tony dumped the last of the gas and turned to head towards the door, the last thing he saw was his partner throwing a torch through the door—and closing the door on him. According to Tony, there was fifty feet between him and the door. As he made a run for it, his body was engulfed in flames. Losing his sense of direction, he went straight for the nearest picture window, having made up his mind to throw himself through it. On the first attempt, he bounced right off, but was successful on his second try. He crawled to safety away from the burning building. When the police arrived, they rushed him to the closest hospital.

Ninety percent of his body received serious third-degree burns. The police tried to find out from him who else was involved, by saying that whoever it was had obviously set him up. They had intentionally left him to die, so why would Tony protect them? He was very principled and took pride that in view of possible death, he remained silent. The police even had a priest come to see him, as they didn't think he was going to make it. They didn't know Tony too well. He told the priest to save his sermon for someone who cared.

Being strong-willed and determined, Tony survived the initial shock. Before coming to Bowden, he spent six months in recovery. I took an immediate liking to Tony and we became good friends. After a tremendous amount of encouragement, he finally joined Cecil and me in the weight pit. I started him out slowly, lifting five-pound weights, as he was only about a hundred pounds. Within three months of disciplined working out, he put on fifty pounds.

After my first month, I added another job description to my cleaning duties. It wasn't a job paid by the administration, but rather by the prisoners themselves. I decided to be the coffee man, making sure that at any given time there was always a pot brewing. It was understood by the prisoners that when they received their pay tokens on payday, they would either throw a dollar or fifty cents in my coffee can. There were a hundred and fifty prisoners in the trailer, so it amounted to a fair chunk of change.

As always, I had another lucrative side line. I'd get vials of hash oil at a low cost and make a hundred and fifty tokens from each vial, which when converted to hard currency was about a hundred dollars cash. I let it be known that the other prisoners could get credit or a loan from me until payday. It wouldn't be out of the ordinary to collect four or five hundred tokens in a two-week period.

From my days in Drumheller, I kept a journal of personal thoughts. I even wrote down my housebreaking exploits, which looked like a textbook for crime. As I'd been waiting for a scheduled parole hearing, when that day finally arrived I was in for a shock. Instead of questioning me, they threw fifteen pages of my journal on the table, found while searching my cell. By the look on their faces, I knew they had already made up their minds not to grant me release.

In the weeks that followed, I resigned my coffee job, as the administration was about to make it a regular job. Before that took place, I badly burned two fellow prisoners with boiling hot water. It had come to our attention that these two weasels were writing kites[3] at night and reporting any kind of illegal activity. They used to hang out in the common area of my wing, watching TV. One morning, I was bringing over a two-hundred-cup pot of hot coffee that had been freshly made in another wing. I pretended that I slipped, and in the process I overturned the coffee pot on these two clowns. Because it appeared to be an accident, nothing ever came of it. Those stoolpigeons never returned, as I'm sure the guards knew we were on to them.

With less than four months left to serve until my mandatory supervision kicked in, I was transferred to the Grierson Center halfway house. Before leaving, I said my goodbyes and wished Tony all the best.

Grierson Center had at one time been either an army barracks or an RCMP training center. It was located minutes from downtown Edmonton. A halfway house was an ideal stepping stone in preparing a long-term offender for re-entry into society. Prisoners were gradually granted passes, which allowed them to leave the institution on a daily basis. All passes were progressive in nature, which meant you started with a four-hour pass, followed by six- and twelve-hour passes, which eventually progressed to weekend passes just before full release. All prisoners except me got these passes. My first two months were spent restricted within the institutional grounds. Finally, after appealing this runaround of institutional policy, I was allowed twelve six-hour passes in a one-month period.

It had been almost four years, and without realizing it I was about to be reunited with my old friend J.P. There was a program offered prisoners called Life Skills, which taught offenders from every category the skills necessary to function or readjust into society. A wonderful lady named Linda ran it, and I was

---

[3] A "kite" was a note to the guards.

lucky to even get in, as the program had already been running for a week. The group had agreed amongst themselves that they'd take no one else in. Understandably, this revolved around the issue of trust.

After Linda explained my circumstances, being that the program was a hoop I needed to jump through to secure my passes, everyone except one hardcore drug addict named Doll was in agreement. She had served many years in prison as a result of her involvement in heroin trafficking. She protested my joining the group right up to the time she first laid eyes on me. At twenty-nine years of age, weighing in at a solid two hundred pounds, I was impressive looking. She latched on to me like a bee to honey. Doll was a prostitute right off the strip; she had no other alternative when it came to supporting her addiction. None of this appealed to me, but for some reason I never made an issue of it. Loneliness was probably the biggest factor in the equation. Having the added experience of group therapy behind me, I fit in like icing on a cake. As I was well-liked and influenced the group's direction in many ways, at one point Linda arranged for Doll and I to have some privacy in an office across the hall.

After about a month into the program, I apprehensively talked about my Wilkinson Road exploits. J.P.'s name came up. It just so happened that a kid in the group, Rob, was good friends with him. No sooner had he mentioned my name then J.P. showed up. It was great to see my old friend again. In visiting, he brought along his wife Cindy and their beautiful daughter Elizabeth—Beth, for short.

That's what I liked about J.P.; he was like the proverbial leopard, never changing his spots. He had put a crew together that was heavily involved in nighttime business burglaries. Once my passes were approved, it didn't take me long before I started getting involved in a low-key way. One night, we hit a Hudson's Bay fur store, where I was the six-man (the lookout). Most of the money I received from the scores went into Doll's arm.

I completed Life Skills and was voted by my fellow group members most likely to succeed. A month later, I wanted to take the course again, as it made my days in the institution go by faster. This time, not only did no one like me, but after only a week they politely asked me to leave.

I would drink while out on passes, which greatly contributed to my unpredictable, Jekyll-and-Hyde personality. A couple of weeks before my release, my relationship with Doll progressed to the next level. I was now using drugs intravenously, and for the next twelve years, narcotic drug addiction would be an inescapable monkey on my back.

While at the halfway house, I became good friends with Allen. He was a small guy with coke bottle glasses, and was on the tail-end of a six-year sentence for a five-million-dollar fraud. At one time, he had been an accountant for one of the local bike clubs. Another guy I liked was Gordie, who by nature was notoriously violent. His motto was, "In life, there's only two things people really understand: money and violence, and I'm usually broke."

Through J.P., I was about to meet a guy named Dale. For the next three years, my life would be turned upside-down.

Puzzles of Treachery 12

December, 22, 1984, was my release date from the halfway house. Doll and I got a small apartment in the Stony Plain area. With the rising pressures of my newfound addiction, I found myself heavily involved in crime once again. I spent a lot of time with J.P. casing places which would get burglarized at night.

One day while sitting at home, I got a call from Dale, a guy J.P. knew. He asked me to meet him at a certain location, as he had some stuff he wanted to sell, and maybe I could help him out. Always looking to make an easy dollar, I agreed to meet him. When I arrived at the address he had given me, he was standing near the alley with a couple of suitcases and said he had just called a cab.

No sooner did I get into the cab with him when out of nowhere the place was swarming with cops. They stopped the cab and began the fine art of interrogation. They started by questioning Dale, who was sitting up front with the cab driver; I could tell by his responses that he had already tried to give them two fake names. The irony behind it all was that I'd only been out three weeks! Finally, they got around to me and wanted to know what I was doing there. I gave them my name and told them I was just giving Dale a hand moving. By this time, they'd figured out that the stuff found in the suitcases was stolen property. They didn't even bother handcuffing Dale; they put him in the back seat of the police car.

Because I had an extensive criminal record, before placing me in the police car they searched me completely and handcuffed me with my hands behind my back. At this point, I had nothing on my person; they had emptied out all my pockets. On the way to the police station, they spotted Dale twice trying to stuff something under the back seat. We went to court, and naturally I pleaded not guilty. Two weeks later, I was at a trial which seemed to come right out of the comic books. The judge left the courtroom after hearing most of the testimony, then returned in less than five minutes. In his wisdom, he stated that he found me guilty as charged. He went on to say that his findings were based on the fact that a stolen gold watch had been found under the back seat of the taxicab where I'd been seated. Certainly, since Dale had been in the front seat of the taxi, I was the only one who could have put it there. He went on to say that I had persisted in my life of crime and hadn't yet responded to lenient court sentences in the past. In his opinion, the only deterrent was to keep me locked up. He gave me three more years. As evidenced by my extensive record, I'd engaged in a number of different criminal offences, but in view of my lengthy periods of incarceration I had obviously been held accountable.

Most of my court appearances had been dealt with and finalized in one swift move. In and out, found guilty, sentenced, and shipped off to whatever institution to serve my sentence. I readily accepted this as part of the program. Do the crime, expect to do the time. There was never any whining on my part, but this time was different, as I knew I was being hoodwinked. They must have thought I would just go along with it like the rest of the sheep. I knew that based on the evidence presented, I should have never been found guilty. I spent the following three years in legal proceedings defending myself. I appeared in many different hearings and eventually wrote my own arguments, which were accepted and placed before the Supreme Court of Canada.

The gold watch the judge referred to was the only piece of evidence the judge could have possibly convicted me on. According to police testimony, it hadn't been found in the taxicab, as suggested by the judge, but in fact was found in the police car. I most definitely could not have put it there, as again seen in police testimony; I had been searched and handcuffed before being placed in the police car. The judge had clearly found me guilty of a crime I hadn't committed. I still had all the legal documentation, which clearly substantiated these facts.

While I was in the Edmonton Remand Center, I met a guy who was to point me in the right direction. Damon was a self-taught jailhouse lawyer, and given time I would become one as well. He was serving fifteen years for bank robberies he hadn't committed. With Damon's help, I filed for an appeal, outlining the grounds. I had been the victim of a conspiracy—and I don't use this term lightly, as the documentation provided insurmountable credibility to that fact.

While in reflection of my criminal record, it should be easy to understand that the prison term itself meant nothing to me. Prison was just another place to visit. The cat-and-mouse game I was about to play with the Alberta judicial system could make anyone pull their hair out. It's unrealistic to think that our judicial system could or would operate in this fashion.

The sad part is that in my coming years of incarceration, I came across many fellow prisoners who should have never themselves been convicted. Once I had become a self-taught jailhouse lawyer, many prisoners came to me seeking legal advice. Sadly, in view of the tremendous amount of pressure and work required in preparing my own legal briefs, as well as lacking the necessary concentration, I had no choice but to turn most away.

It all began when my trial lawyer wrote a letter to the Legal Aid Society, stating that I had no legal grounds for a successful appeal. Based on that letter, I wasn't to be given a lawyer for my appeal. I received fifteen letters from the Society in this regard, as I continuously appealed their decision. I even tried another avenue: I petitioned the court to appoint counsel, which I did ten times throughout these proceedings, all without success. They refused to grant counsel, which in itself was ludicrous. Having no alternative but to try representing myself, I again asked the Legal Aid Society to at least to provide me with a copy of the trial transcripts, as I could not afford them. They refused to even grant me this accommodation. I tried many times, but all approaches were unsuccessful. After numerous letters and three appeal court hearings, the court finally, and somewhat reluctantly, provided a copy of the trial transcripts.

While all this was taking place, I was sent back to Drumheller, where I found Damon's brother Stephen, who just happened to be in my unit. Stephen and I became very good friends. In my quest for justice, not only was he always helpful and supportive, but he offered tremendous encouragement. At his urging, as the legal burden I was about to undertake was extremely extensive and time-consuming, I got a job in the prison kitchen, working with him and a few other old-timers in the bakery. This required only three hours of my time every day, allowing me the rest of the day to pursue my legal presentations. Stephen used to help me prepare for my scheduled court appearances. Without his support and guidance, I might not have seen this thing through. He had a way of making everything seem more enjoyable. Just before going to court, he'd say, "Meet me in my cell after supper, and make sure you bring your legal papers." I'd show up to find him sitting in a chair, trying to resemble a judge. He often made me laugh, although to him it wasn't a game. We went through many such rehearsals, as he wanted me to be confident and sharp in what I was going to say.

I quickly got fed up with the obvious game of "letter tag" with the Legal Aid Society. I submitted a formal application to the Court of Queen's Bench, and in April 1985 I appeared before them. This was a hearing to see if there were grounds for an appeal, and also with regards to an application I had submitted requesting that the court appoint counsel. The judge listened carefully, and once I was finished he stated that, yes, I may indeed have valid grounds for an appeal, but unfortunately he would not deal with the issue of appointing counsel. I was slowly removing the lid off a can of worms that would have the legal profession pulling their hair out. Right after this detour, I wrote a letter to Else Rempel, a reporter for the *Edmonton Sun*, which read as follows:

I am writing to you regarding my appeal court hearing, which is scheduled to be held on May 13. Briefly, my concern is that the Alberta judicial system is dealing with me very unfairly. In my opinion, they are embarking on a doctrine that could possibly open the door to a fundamental reordering of our adversary system into a system more inquisitorial in nature. I strongly argue that in the proper review of my case in any court, it would be apparent that I'm being maliciously prosecuted.

I'm appealing to you, the press, as certainly this case should be brought to the public's attention. My rights, as guaranteed by the Canadian Charter, are not only being seriously violated, but denied as well. I feel as though I'm being buried alive by the Alberta judicial system. I will give my strongest argument that my case constitutes a farce, a mockery of our judicial system. Not only am I forced to defend myself in a hearing of this magnitude, I am left without the benefit of my trial transcripts, which prove my allegations.

In this case, the puzzles of treachery are everywhere. You must ask yourself why, if what I'm alleging is so outrageous, the court won't order for re-examination the production of the transcripts, as clearly allowed by law under Section 610[1] of the Criminal Code, to get at the truth. It would be far less expensive than these numerous court hearings. In that sense, one way or another, we could be done with this case instead of creating more puzzles.

I cordially invite you to attend my hearing, where I will once again show that my rights are being violated, as they won't produce the transcripts. Simply put, why would the court want to produce evidence which undoubtedly shows that the administration of justice has been brought into serious disrepute? Ms. Rempel, it is time not only to question but fully investigate the operation of our judicial system and its conduct here in Alberta. One thing I can assure you is that you will not be disappointed.

She did appear and wrote an article which should make anyone wonder what was going on.

All my legal notes were handwritten. Due to the volume of paperwork I was compiling, Stephen enlisted the assistance of Gerry, who also worked in the kitchen. Gerry became known as the secretary, as he typed everything out for me. On May 13, 1985, I appeared in the Court of Appeal to determine whether or not my appeal had any grounds of merit.

As had by now become a ritual, in my opening statements I strongly voiced my need for counsel. Being inexperienced as to the rules of the court, I bluntly stated to the tribunal, "Just produce the trial transcripts and I will prove that a miscarriage of justice occurred." They took sharp notice of my outburst and remanded me the next day. Reappearing the following day before the same tribunal, also present was counsel for the Legal Aid Society. As directed by the court, apparently I was to present legal argument against this fully experienced counsel, as to my right to have counsel assigned by the court. His arguments rested mainly on the comments of my trial lawyer, stating that there were no grounds for an appeal.

Doesn't it strike you as odd that my own trial counsel, whose professional ethics should have dictated that he champion my best interests, sought to deliberately discredit me and my case? In my argument, I had only one question for this experienced liar: "Has my co-accused, Dale, in view of us going through the same trial, been given legal representation by the Legal Aid Society for his own appeal?"

This not only stunned him, but rocked the three judges, for I had done my homework well. The lawyer looked to the judges for help, and they told me that he'd answer that question at his own discretion. I had "material evidence" that Dale had, in fact, been given counsel for his appeal. I would not be dismissed. I went on to say, "Since I've made numerous attempts to obtain counsel, it has to leave doubt in your mind as to whether or not justice has been properly administered in this case." I put forth an extremely relevant question that, if answered, could have cleared everything up without wasting any more of the court's valuable time and money. Either Dale had, in fact, been given counsel, in which case I should have been afforded the same consideration, or he hadn't. All I received in return were more evasive answers! I let this slide for the moment.

"The actions of my trial lawyer are in themselves among my grounds for an appeal," I said. "Therefore, his comments should carry no weight in this courtroom. Based on what I've said here today, if even a small part of it is true, we have issues which need to be fully examined and addressed by the appropriate body. However, the only way to get to the truth is to view the trial transcripts, which I cannot afford on my own."

I baffled them with many of my points, which filled thirty-six pages of transcripts. They left to make a decision, returning in a half-hour. I was shocked by their decisions. They decided not to grant counsel, but since "my case had merit to be heard," I would be brought back to be heard in the September sittings. Without any material evidence on my part, the court granted that my appeal wasn't frivolous. However, they still wouldn't appoint counsel.

One could only assume that such a finding should have placed an altogether new obligation not only on the Legal Aid Society, but the court as well. Also puzzling was the decision, in which the court said they couldn't give me a copy of the transcripts. I found this to be totally unreasonable. Now I had to try to defend myself, but they didn't even want to give me the trial transcripts, which undeniably proved my case. I bitter and frustrated.

I'll now quote directly from an article written by Else Rempel of the *Edmonton Journal*, dated May 15, 1985.

> The Charter of Rights and Freedoms does not guarantee the right to be represented by a lawyer in an appeal, says the Alberta Court of Appeal.
>
> In a unanimous decision Tuesday, the three-member appeal tribunal rejected a prisoner's bid to have court appoint a lawyer to handle his appeal against a break-and-enter conviction.
>
> The Charter does not give everyone the right to counsel "regardless of the offence, the circumstances or the merits of the appeal," Justice J.W. Clung told [Mino] Miodrag Pavlic.
>
> Pavlic, 29, serving a three-year prison sentence, had argued he had a constitutional right to a lawyer during his appeal…
>
> "Under Section 15 (of the Charter) I should receive assistance free of charge because I am poor and indigent and can't get counsel on my own," he said.[4]

This provided more bullets for my shotgun. In doing my homework, I found that when an accused person asks a judge or the court to appoint counsel to represent his interests, the request must be thoroughly considered. As per the governing guidelines of the Supreme Court of Canada, some factors to be taken under strict consideration were as follows:

1. Is the accused not in a position financially to retain counsel himself? (Yes.)
2. Is the case one in which the Legal Aid Society may, or should, grant a certificate for assistance? (Yes.)
3. Are there grounds for appeal? (Definitely.)
4. Does the case seem to be a difficult one? (Yes.)
5. Would it be difficult for the accused to marshal relevant evidence? (Certainly.)

They must have issued us different law books in prison. I just found it unexplainable. Why did the judicial system not just admit that there were errors of law made in regards to the case and that proper procedures hadn't been followed? Then they could either acquit me or order a new trial.

Back on the homefront in Drumheller, trouble was brewing. A friend of mine had gone out on a pass to Edmonton and I had him deliver a message to J.P., who in turn sent me back eight vials of hash oil. All I wanted to do was make a quick buck. Stephen and I made inquiries about dumping five of the vials, as we

---

[4] Else Rempel, "Right to a lawyer doesn't cover appeal," *Edmonton Journal* (Edmonton, AB), May 15, 1985.

were keeping three. We made a connection, and the buyer was supposed to pay us as he sold the product. After a couple of days, I went to see him and he tried laying track on me, saying that the oil was no good. Words were exchanged, and later that evening I got a call from my unit. Apparently some guys wanted to talk to me, out back in the ball field. I told them I'd be right out. I was no stranger to this game; I told my buddies what was going on, and to give me a minute before they came out. They brought golf clubs with them. What I didn't know was that the guy we had made a deal with was dealing with some bikers. I guess they figured they'd get me out back and give me a beating.

While walking around the field with the original buyer, I saw three other guys closing in on us fast. When they were almost on me, my friends with the clubs were on them, wondering if there was a problem. In order to avoid bloodshed, I immediately approached three well-respected cons who were on the inmate committee. In explaining the situation, I gave them a vial of hash oil to smoke, to verify its quality, and asked them to intercede on my behalf; a battle would have brought a lot of unnecessary heat, and nobody liked a lockdown. Within a day, it was all straightened out. I was given six grams of hash. From that moment on, my friend Stephen gave me a nickname: Don Vito. It would stick with me well beyond my incarceration. I still laugh about it.

It was obvious by the way they treated me in Edmonton that I wasn't getting a fair shake. I had put together an argument and filed it in the Provincial Court of Calgary, on July 31. It explained my attempts to get a lawyer, and briefly detailed my court appearances. I had a ton of case law, which clearly stated that any judge, even a provincial court judge, has the power to appoint counsel. I understood all too well that an accused doesn't have the absolute right to have counsel appointed by the court. However, where an accused makes application to the court for the appointment of counsel, the judge *must* take into account all relevant considerations. The decision of a judge who failed to consider everything would be quashed, based on his erroneous view that he had no power to appoint counsel. I was starting to really enjoy myself, fighting toe to toe with the system and being able to hold my head above water.

Another principle I put forward was this: Every person charged or convicted of an offence is entitled to have counsel, unless he chooses to represent himself. An accused pending an appeal should most definitely have the benefit of counsel assigned by the court to represent him, if not for the reasons of being poor and indigent, or in the interests of justice. Without question, counsel should be appointed on those grounds, if the appeal has meritorial value. In addition, I submit that this case constitutes a statement of law from our highest court, in that where the offence is serious enough to result in a term of imprisonment, counsel should be appointed. Our criminal system is an adversary system—that is to say a system where when a conflict arises between a citizen and the province, the two are to be regarded as adversaries and the conflict is to be resolved by fighting it out, according to fixed and sometimes arbitrary rules. The tribunal settles the dispute, based only on such evidence as the contestants choose to present. However, there are rules of procedure and rules of evidence which can only be properly understood and applied after years of training and experience. For the court to project me into such an arena totally unequipped by experience or education, to defend myself against Legal Aid's counsel, is shocking. It's unrealistic to believe that in such a contest, against an experienced and learned counsel, I could be afforded a fair hearing."

I was once again transferred to Bowden, and Steven followed shortly thereafter. Again I found myself in the luxury trailers. However, it would only be for a short period, as the new facilities were almost completed. The place was gigantic. It had five units surrounding a park-like setting. Once we moved over, I was placed in unit five, which housed about a hundred prisoners. It was all very impressive and state of the art. My cell looked better than some of the rooming houses I had lived in, and came with its own key to the door.

Once I was settled in, I befriended an old-timer named Dean Rose, who in his own right was skilled in the fine art of advocacy, as he had filed hundreds of actions in the Federal Courts. He gave me a tremendous amount of assistance, anytime I asked. Almost immediately, I got a job in the kitchen, which gave me lots of free time to work out with the weights and deal with my upcoming legal issues.

On September 8, 1986, I was again brought before the tribunal, consisting of three judges, to be heard in full. I was more than prepared for them. They weren't really mad at me, but my cleverness bothered them. As a direct result, they entered the treacherous web of conspiracy. I was already in their bad books, as I had gone outside their jurisdiction to another court. No one likes to have their dirty laundry on display, especially in terms of an institution in the public spotlight. As soon as I was allowed to speak, I firmly stated that I couldn't possibly receive a full and fair hearing without at least the benefit of the trial transcripts. In light of the press in attendance, an appearance of fairness had to be shown. The court now invoked Section 610 of the Criminal Code and supplied me with a copy. They could have easily done this months earlier, which would have given me time to properly prepare.

Also present at this hearing was my co-accused, Dale. I immediately requested that he be allowed to give testimony, as what he had to say would certainly absolve me of any guilt in the whole affair. One judge was very much interested in what I to say, but for some reason the head judge had cut him off, saying no. Ten minutes into the hearing, they remanded me once again to October 28. I found out later that Dale had appeared in court the next day and his sentence was reduced from three to two years.

This time, with the transcripts finally in hand, I went to town. I appeared in October before the same tribunal, and this is a matter of public record; the hearing was held in camera, meaning it was closed to the public. My big question was, why? It wasn't a murder trial, just an idiotic break-and-enter offense. Could it possibly be because they didn't want the press there?

My verbal argument took up thirty pages of transcripts, as for two hours I presented substantial arguments on all issues in question. As the Supreme Court had clear guidelines for the Appeals Court to follow, I put for the following argument.

As the appellate courts will usually be assisted by the reasons of the trial judge, as a general rule the appeals court has neither the right nor duty to access the evidence, for the purpose of determining the guilt or innocence of the accused. Its duty is to review the record, to see if the trial court has properly directed itself to all the evidence bearing on the relevant issues. If the record (trial transcripts), including the reasons for judgment, disclose a lack of appreciation of the relevant evidence, or a disregard of it, then depending on the nature of the errors, it will fall to the reviewing court to step in and either order a new trial or set the verdict aside.

I assumed this was a cut-and-dried direction from the highest court in the land, yet in view of my outstanding argument, the tribunal dismissed my appeal on the grounds that while they had read the transcripts and agreed that the trial judge had, indeed, misdirected himself—both regarding the facts and the law, they still found no fault and thus dismissed the appeal unanimously. They were adamant that this case had finally reached its conclusion and that there was no further recourse available to me.

We'd see about that.

Going to the Supreme Court of Canada 13

I was beginning to understand the treachery. They had a closed hearing, as they didn't want to advertise the treachery, and secondly, they thought I'd be easier to intimidate in such a hearing. No such luck. I still believe now, after twenty-five years, that the Court of Appeal was wrong in their judgment.

The very foundation of our judicial system is based on the following principle: if a trial error is of such a forceful nature that it leaves a tainted mark on the judgment, then the trial itself has been contaminated. Anyone whose rights are violated in this fashion should then be accorded a retrial. Retrial would be a small price to pay in order to ensure fairness in the courts. If the Appeal Courts were more prone to reversing the verdict in cases of clear doubt, this would instill a closer safeguard against errors at trial.

Another legal issue which I extensively researched was the invalidity of my sentence computation. I had indisputable evidence, from the highest reputable source, that the issue could very possibly be resolved in my favor. Once again not able to secure counsel, I was cheated out of eighteen months.

There's a specific section of the parole act which deals with federal prisoners being released on mandatory supervision. It states that if there is a new sentence, they will be merged to form one aggregate sentence, but the judges refused to apply it in my case. Another Supreme Court ruling states that where a plaintiff (me) brings an action before the court and there's clearly an uncertainty in the law, the action shall be decided in favor of the plaintiff. This should have also been cut-and-dried. After a year of fiddling around with the sentence administrator, as well the correctional investigator, who it seemed didn't do much investigating, I filed legal argument.

I received a letter from the Director of the Correctional Law Project at the Faculty of Law at Queen's University. It read, in part:

> I inspected the student's work and felt she may have overlooked the impact of the Burn's ruling as it existed prior to July 26, 1986. To this end on May 10, 1987, I sent a telegram to the Sentence Administrator at Bowden and to the Chief Sentence Administrator in Ottawa, drawing this matter to their attention.

> On May 14, I received a telephone call from [the Sentence Administrator in Ottawa], who indicated that National Headquarters has received your sentence and is of the opinion that Section 15[4] of the Parole Act applies to interrupt the sentence you were serving until the sentence for the consecutive term was served. As such, it is an exception to the Burn's ruling.
>
> [The Sentence Administrator] admitted that the case law on how such an interruption would impact upon the automatic consequence of loss of remission was inconclusive. If the Burn's ruling applied, you would [according to my calculations] be entitled to immediate release…

He suggested that I apply to Legal Aid, to launch a habeas corpus application, to test this point of law. They had refused six times to provide a lawyer.

I submitted an extensive argument to the Federal Court, and in conclusion stated that to suggest I defend myself in such a complicated area of the law as sentence commutation, which cries out for reform, would deprive me of my entitlement to a full and fair hearing. I also requested damages for negligence, as to unlawful confinement. However, due to my inexperience, this case had been swept under the rug, leaving no one accountable. I'm sure, if I had been given a lawyer to properly argue this complicated area, it most certainly would have been decided in my favor. I had my sights on the Supreme Court. To me, this case was more than just a court case; it honestly seemed as though they thought I was stupid. From that moment on, my every waking moment was spent researching and drafting an argument to the Supreme Court of Canada.

I was looking to find a prison job which paid top dollar, as it was costly to send all my documents by registered mail. One day while at work in the kitchen, I spotted a kid by a new machine that had just come in. I went over and found out it was a potato peeler. I immediately saw the potential and gave the kid a couple of grams of hash to trade jobs with me. The kitchen guards/staff explained how the machine worked. First, you put so many potatoes in the machine and turned it on for two minutes. Then, by hand, you had to cut the eyes out. My idea was a lot better. I'd fill the machine with potatoes the size of baseballs, then turn the machine on for twelve minutes. The potatoes would come out the size of golf balls, all nice and clean. No wonder the kid had been there all day. Once the potatoes were peeled, I placed them in plastic garbage pails to soak in water. In a matter of four hours, I had all the pails full and in the fridge. This would be a three-day supply. I really liked this job. Who wouldn't? I worked two days a week and was paid for seven. It took them quite a while before they caught on. I'd hear the guards now and then mumbling amongst themselves, trying to figure out why all of a sudden the potato bill was so high.

Another thing that kept me going about these legal proceedings, besides knowing I was right, was the tremendous assistance I received from one guard in particular; I owe Ray many thanks. He was a third-year law student and took a deep interest in what I was doing. One day, I gave him my trial transcripts to read. A couple of days later, he gave them back, all the while sadly shaking his head, with just one question: "What are you doing in prison?" He brought me lots of relevant case law, which I used in most of my arguments to the Supreme Court. Even though he was a guard and I was a prisoner, he knew I was being hoodwinked. I'll always remember him in a respectful way. He went out of his way to help me.

For the next two months, I spent up to ten hours a day preparing my argument for the Supreme Court, writing and then rewriting to get the argument just right. This was a tedious and frustrating procedure. I found someone to type out my documents for a fee, and by mid-December my argument was completed and ready for filing with the registrar in Ottawa. From what I understood, the Supreme Court received thousands of cases each year wishing to be heard. Only a few hundred cases, based on issues of significant general and national importance, were accepted.

Based on the merits I had presented in my argument, my case was placed on the docket to be heard in June 1987. Since my argument is too long to list, I'll just put forward the issues of national importance, along with a brief summary, as it's important in understanding the further injustices and treachery committed against me. These further injustices were not committed by the Supreme Court, but again by the Legal Aid Society and a questionable lawyer.

Anyone would appreciate my elation at having come this far, not only in view of the insurmountable obstacles I faced, but also my inexperience in the art of advocacy. Each step of the way, I was becoming more skilled in this complicated drama. Regardless of the countless spears of discouragement thrown my way, I always managed to remain one step ahead. However, nothing prepared me for what was to come.

My issues, which sparked the Supreme Court's interest, were as follows:

1. My trial counsel was not only ineffective in the preparation of the case, but incompetent as well.
2. The misdirection of the trial judge in this case wasn't only an error of mixed law and fact, but also a critical error of law, in which my constitutional rights were invaded.
3. The Alberta Court of Appeal severely denied me my constitutional rights.
4. Fairness in any court is regarded as the core requirement of natural justice, and throughout my whole argument, the four Court of Appeal hearings I attended were all dealt with in a very unfair manner.

As you can see, not only were all my issues valid, but when viewed in their entirety, the Supreme Court wanted to take a closer peek. To date, everything I have alleged remains undisputed. It is my understanding that the Crown must prove all elements of the offence charged to the satisfaction of the court, beyond any reasonable doubt. If he cannot do this, then he has failed in his burden of proof, and accordingly, as prescribed by law, an acquittal is required. Suspicion, no matter how extensive, is not grounds for conviction in any court. As I understand, suppositions must be substantiated by rigid premises, which give suspicion its sustenance.

It was my argument that within the nature of the trial judge's misdirection, the only impartial remedy was to quash the conviction and enter a verdict of acquittal. My argument was that the trial judge, as noted in his reasons for judgment, found me guilty without having any reasonable doubts. He referred to a watch, which he stated was found under the back seat of the taxicab where I was seated. This is where the trial judge had seriously misdirected himself, not only in respect to the facts, but also in law. The facts I put forward, were as follows:

1. At no time was there a watch found in the taxi where I was seated, but as indicated by police testimony, the watch was found underneath the back seat of the police car, upon arrival at the police station.
2. As indicated by police testimony, the other person charged with this offence was the first to be placed in the police car, and he was not searched before being placed there.
3. As indicated by police testimony, I was searched and handcuffed before being placed in the police car, which logically would exclude me as the source of this watch.

I went through four Court of Appeal hearings without any other alternative but to defend myself, as I was continually denied assistance from the Legal Aid Society, nor would the courts appoint the much-needed assistance of effective counsel. I found it impossible to conclude that no miscarriage of justice had occurred, for it was my understanding that a person charged with the commission of a crime was entitled to a fair trial according to the law, and any errors which occurred at trial which deprives the accused of this entitlement were in and of themselves a miscarriage of justice. Certainly, not every error results in a miscarriage of justice, which is recognized by the very existence of the provision to relieve the court against errors of law which do not cause a miscarriage of justice.

I received the follow letter from the Legal Aid Society, dated August 28, 1985:

You have already applied and numerous times been refused the appointment of counsel at the highest level of appeal with legal aid. Evidently there is no other recourse available for you with Legal Aid.

This meant I was not able to reapply, or appeal this matter any further. The decision was final. It would seem that I had exhausted all avenues with the Legal Aid Society. Imagine this: four months later, as I was headed before the Supreme Court of Canada, on my own submitted argument, I received a puzzling letter from Legal Aid. This letter, dated January 9, 1986, states that they "are now willing to approve a lawyer for me." If you think this puzzling, buckle your seatbelts. What happened in the following eighteen months was just incredible. Had it not been for indisputable certified documents, no one in their right mind would ever believe such a conspiracy actually occurred.

Naturally, I was highly suspicious of their generosity at this time, as according to them I had absolutely no grounds for anything. Why then would they not just let me continue on my own, as in all probability, according to them, the Supreme Court would dismiss my appeal as frivolous.

I was assigned a lawyer, however, and I wanted to see what this puppet of theirs had to say. This was his first of many letters to me, dated February 20, 1986:

I understand that legal aid has approved the appointment of a lawyer and I have agreed to take the case. However I can tell you in brief, that various arguments about incompetence of counsel, lack of a fair trial, or your right to a lawyer are all hopeless and have no prospect of success in the court of appeal, the Supreme Court, or any level, as this simply is not the law in Canada.

They must have found this guy in the funny pages, as all my issues had been drafted in reference to valid legal principles which defined supreme law in Canada. I found it comical that a lawyer would tell me that my arguments about the incompetence of counsel, lack of a fair hearing, or my right to a lawyer were hopeless and had no prospect of success at any level. I don't know where they got this clown, but it would seem from these comments that his knowledge of the law was seriously flawed.

In his continuing letters to me, he would further contradict himself many times. Firstly, he tried to cover up for my trial lawyer by stating that when he had written his letter to Legal Aid, saying that I had no valid point for an appeal, the Fanjoy case hadn't yet been written.[5]

As I was being tried under the Doctrine of Recent Possession[property recently stolen]. By law, in order for the judge to convict me, he needed to show that I had direct knowledge and control of the stolen property in question, his misdirection of the facts put me in direct control and knowledge, as such it was an irreparable error of law and the only remedy available to any court, was to step in and set the verdict aside.

Regardless of what had and hadn't been written, the misdirection itself was a solid, arguable point of law. He also tried to pull a fast one by suggesting that my case should be reheard by the Alberta Court of Appeal. I immediately wrote the following letter to the Supreme Court registrar, on February 21, 1986:

> I am writing to you at this time in regards to the recent decision, dated February 14 by the Legal Aid Society of Alberta, to grant coverage and provide counsel in this case. Also with respects to the fact that they would like to have the case reheard once again by the Alberta Court of Appeal. Sir, under no circumstances do I agree to this condition, and I inform you that my decision is to pursue this case in the Supreme Court, even if it means being left with no other alternative but to defend myself.

I then wrote the lawyer a reply, dated February 24, stating,

> In your letter, you have stated that certain issues are simply not the law in Canada and have no hope of success at any level. I hope you can understand and appreciate this simple fact: I am very concerned with all the merits of this case and can only hope that you will give them full consideration.

I explained certain issues in detail, always reminding him that he was supposed to be working for me, not the Legal Aid Society.

> In conclusion, accept this letter as one of many concerns. You may think I'm questioning your ability, which is simply not the case. I don't mean to sound bitter or harsh, it's just that like you,

---

[5] Regina vs. Fanjoy was a decision of paramount importance. Prior to it, reviewing appeals relied heavily on Section 613 of the Criminal Code, under which appeals could be dismissed where errors at the trial were clearly noted. The Fanjoy case outlined that Section 613 couldn't under any circumstance be applied when those errors were in regards to the facts in evidence, or on a point of law.

my trial lawyer assured me of certain things, and now, as a result of those assurances, I'm doing three years for something that could never be proven, and one day someone will have to be held accountable.

In spite of the atmosphere of uncertainty on my part, he proceeded to the Supreme Court on my behalf and, you guessed it, I was royally deceived again. On June 23, my appeal was dismissed. He sent the following letter to me in that regard, dated June 30, 1986:

This is to confirm that an application for leave to appeal to the Supreme Court of Canada was made on Monday, June 23, on your behalf, and was argued but dismissed. I do not feel there is any court or body to which you can now appeal this matter any further and I think you will have to consider the case at an end. The fact that you did not give evidence, to deny knowledge or participation in the break-and-enter, that the co-accused obviously committed, did not help in the case.

This guy was nothing more than a puppet on a string. It's my understanding that in a court of law, you don't have to say one word in your defense, as the Crown must prove every element of the crime charged. Why would I have wanted to take the stand?

His letter continued:

As I have discussed with you, the comment the co-accused made to the taxi driver, or the police, that the goods were his and not yours, were inadmissible, as it was hearsay for the police or taxi driver to say it. You could have applied for separate trials, in which case it would have then been admissible.

This statement of his allows for my argument of incompetence and unfairness by the Crown. If a separate trial was the only way in which the judge would know all the pertinent facts, this was certainly the right way to proceed.

He goes on to say,

Also, your trial counsel indicated to me that had that been done, the co-accused would have denied making that statement. Also, why call a witness and then discredit him?

Again, this was totally idiotic. Firstly, who had said anything about calling Dale as a witness? The purpose of separate trials would have been to have the police and taxi drivers testimony entered.

In closing, this baloney sandwich said,

I therefore feel that you had a fair trial and were competently represented. I was unable to persuade the Supreme Court that your case presented any issues of general or national importance. So I suppose that one could say, in retrospect, that Legal Aid's decision not to appoint counsel had been justified by the way things finally turned out. I would recommend that in your own best interests, you now accept the fact that you have been convicted and work towards reforming yourself within the prison system, so that you could qualify as a candidate for early release, who is unlikely to reoffend in the future and has learned his lesson.

Compared to my submitted argument, his was twisted. All the facts were not brought to the court's attention. He mentioned the watch found in the taxi and said that as a result of it, the judge had found us both guilty. This was wrong, for if the watch was in the taxi, the judge could only convict me, for at no time was the co-accused ever in the back seat of the taxi. It's hard to explain even now, after so many years have passed, how I felt at learning that my appeal had been dismissed. I know I felt betrayed, and very angry and bitter.

In his letter, my lawyer said that I should consider the case ended, and then he casually reminded me that there was no further recourse available to me. I do remember thinking, again, that we'd see about that.

14 — THE TREACHERY PLAYS ITSELF OUT

I've been in several prisons and courts, and between the two there always remained a distinct commonality. Courtrooms and prisons are government institutions that possess an awesome aura of power. Both are institutions with stages, where real-life drama is acted out for the benefit of society. Human passions live and die there, yet no one seems to care or realize that the common currency in these institutions of misery are cunning, madness, greed, poverty, fear, hatred, deceit, and suffering. Prisoners bring their desperation, brutality, and ignorance to the scene, and too often it all goes unchecked.

It was beginning to become clear to me that I couldn't win, even by playing by the rules in a court of law. Beware the gullible who believe in our justice system, as you surely could find yourself the next victim. Just because a crime has occurred and the elements of one are present, a person shouldn't be held accountable or responsible for that crime until the crown prosecutor has done everything he or she can to prove otherwise, beyond a reasonable doubt. In my case, clearly the judge's conviction was based on an inference clearly unsupported by the evidence. It would certainly seem to me that this was a misapplication of the law. The law was made to protect people from the barbarism of society, but who is to protect us from the barbarism of the law?

I'm sure you can feel my anger, frustration, and bitterness through my words. The only evidence I stood convicted on was my past.

Not too long after this, the parole board came to see me. They asked me to forget about the legal proceedings and consider a parole. No way. I wasn't going to admit defeat.

While at Bowden, I continued my drug activities, but everything was very low profile; I didn't want to jeopardize my next legal sucker punch. A few people I knew were going out on a pass, so I'd get them to see J.P., and on their return they'd have a package for me. I'd give them their end of the dope and then sell the rest. One time, instead of pot or hash oil, J.P. sent me a couple hundred prescription pills, known as seconals, a heavy sedative. They were nothing but bad news. I gave fifty of them away and sold the rest. All of a sudden, there were twenty guys walking around high on pills, looking for a fight.

One night while I was visiting Stuart, two guards entered the cell and asked me to follow them. I knew something was up. In my hand, I had three crunched up twenty-dollar bills and a vial of oil. I put everything in my mouth, trying to make it into a ball I could swallow before we entered the office. I tried to swallow, but it got stuck in my throat. I was hunched over the table gagging, and one of the guards started slapping me on the back, wondering if I was okay. In that moment, I managed to swallow what I had lodged in my throat. Now, out of immediate danger, I asked what they wanted. They must have had their suspicions, as they were concerned about pills. I told them that maybe now and then, like anybody else, I'd smoke some pot, but no way would I have anything to do with pills. All the while, I was trying to think of how to get rid of the four pills in my pocket.

They were concerned that I didn't look well. My explanation was that with all my legal headaches, I'd been rather stressed out lately and not eating right. I told them I'd been feeling a little sick, so I took five aspirins I had in my cell. They asked me to go over to the hospital with them to see the nurse. On the way, I managed to pop the pills in my mouth. The nurse gave me the old flashlight test to see if I was high. She asked me to close my eyes, and after a moment she had me open them. While pointing the flashlight directly into my eyes, she gave them a casual inspection. To my surprise, she told the guards I was fine. Before leaving the hospital, I asked her to give me some Maalox for my upset stomach. On the way back, they asked me to stay in my cell for the rest of the night. I didn't mind, as I had my own color TV. Besides, I knew the pills would start hitting me shortly.

For all my time at Bowden, my living unit officer was a guy named Wayne. He wasn't a bad guy, but I always seemed to give him a hard time. I just didn't want any part of whatever the guards had to offer. I wanted to be left alone, as I had enough of my own problems. I think the warden, Mr. Hanna, respected me; he seemed to always extend me courtesy in regards to my legal concerns, but then again this may have been because the Supreme Court called him a few times regarding my case. I had sent a letter to the Supreme Court, which in short read,

> Sir, as you are aware, even before this application I voiced my concerns to you many times in our numerous telephone conversations, regarding this lawyer's effectiveness to fully deal with all the issues in question. I referred to his letter, simply stating that these issues were not the law in Canada and it is this letter that gives considerable weight to his incompetence. The issues in question are, in fact, considered to constitute the three most basic requirements in obtaining a fair hearing in any court. I would like this honorable court to extend me the benefit on the merits enclosed and review my application in its full capacity without my appearance and render its learned judgment, which I will honorably accept. Then and only then will I be satisfied that I have been assured a full and fair hearing.

He sent me a letter back, informing me that there could not be a rehearing at this level. I made several attempts to regain entry to this court, all of which were unsuccessful. I now planned on taking my argument to the Federal Court of Canada. The court at first tried to discourage me by sending a copy of the court's rules and regulations, and stated that I either was to follow these rules or not to bother them anymore. I guess they thought I'd be intimidated. Being very determined, I introduced myself by fully complying with all the rules and procedures. Again, it began as a game. Whatever I sent, they'd counter with a motion to strike the claim, as having no bearing in the court.

In between all this, I also found time to write extensive letters to Ray Hnatyshyn, the Minister of Justice; Clayton Ruby, a prominent lawyer specializing in criminal and constitutional law; and also the NDP party. The one thing I respected about the Federal Court was that, regardless of their continuous opposition, if there was something I didn't quite understand, they would explain it to me in detail. They were always procedurally fair to me. My hearing date was September 17, 1987, and I arranged for the prison administration to be responsible for insuring my appearance on that date.

About a month before the hearing, members of my case management team grabbed me and put me in segregation based on nothing more than suspicion of drug trafficking. I remained locked up there for fourteen days. Appearing in front of the prison's kangaroo court, I was told I would be shipped back to Drumheller the next day. All I asked for was some paper and a pen, as I had a letter to write. Within the hour, I wrote the warden a three-page letter. As the guard read it, his eyes blinked like a flashing light bulb. I told him to just deliver it to the warden.

Within half an hour, I was released back into population, where I found the guards had turned my cell upside-down. However, they didn't do too good a job. They had gone through everything, but whatever they were looking for, they missed it. When I saw all their cigarette butts in the black astray, I couldn't help but smile to myself. If they had cared to empty it, I would have been pinched, as stuck to the bottom was a two-gram piece of black hash. In view of the prison's attempt to have me transferred, I had to ensure that under no circumstances would this take place. I still had a lot of preparation ahead of me for my most important court hearing.

It had taken me two days to write my argument against Bowden Penitentiary, which I immediately filed in the Federal Court. This meant that no action could be taken against me until the courts dealt with the matter. I needed a smokescreen. My argument went as follows:

1. While serving a prison sentence at Bowden Penitentiary, I was deprived of my rights to prepare a defense against the penitentiary staff's function of acting on suspicion.
2. On September 1, 1987, I was suspected of being under the influence of a controlled substance. I was placed in solitary confinement and held for fourteen days.
3. Being held in solitary confinement incommunicado is a direct infringement and denial of my charter rights.
4. The facilities of the regular cell blocks were adequate to confine and deter me, pending an investigation and hearing.
5. The solitary confinement unit is a means whereby a prisoner is deprived of his rights to defend himself, and further a means whereby a prisoner is subjected to intimidation, duress, compulsion, and threat exercised by the penitentiary staff.
6. My case management team interviewed me after the security investigation was completed, and as a result no charges were laid. In the alternative, my case management team recommended a transfer to another penitentiary, based on nothing more than suspicion.

It was time now for me to appear in Federal Court, where I gave my best performance yet. The final scene in this incredible legal adventure, filled with betrayals and deceit and played out to the highest court, was about to reach its conclusion. No one really knew what I had prepared as an argument for the Honorable Justice Hugessen of the Federal Court of Canada. Certainly, they had the documents I had filed, and in that regard they weren't going to underestimate me. However, the oral argument I intended to present was more secretive and guarded than Colonel Sanders's chicken recipe.

I knew that the prosecutor wanted to throw my whole case out, as he thought I was trying to appeal the Supreme Court's decision to this lower court, but I had a twist of my own that caught him off-guard. Arriving in court that morning, even my prison escort was excited, given my many previous courtroom dramas. I was something of a celebrity in Bowden.

"The floor is yours, Mr. Pavlic," Justice Hugessen said to me. "What do you have to say?"

The courtroom was in total silence. When I spoke, my voice echoed off the walls.

"Your Honor, my clear intention has always been, while trying to defend myself, to place before this court substantial legal proof that indeed shows a grave injustice has occurred. If that injustice is to be left unchanged, it would on its own merits undoubtedly place the administration of justice in disrepute."

I argued that I had undeniably shown that my counsel at the Supreme Court appeal had not only been incompetent, but negligent in his duties. As a result, I had been deprived of my entitlement to a full and fair hearing.

"I have made two attempts to try to have this case reheard by the Supreme Court, based on those arguments," I continued. "However, I have remained unsuccessful, as there can be no rehearing on an application for leave to appeal."

In view of these very unusual circumstances, as well the merits of the case, I had no other alternative but to now seek, in the interests of justice, a recommendation for a rehearing before the appropriate body, from this honorable court.

After I was done, the judge sat back in his chair, looking at me while collecting his thoughts. The courtroom was silent, waiting for the judge to speak. I felt like a diplomat. It was as though what I had said had been a powerful statement. When the judge finally directed his comments to me, what he said elevated me to such a level of self-esteem that if I never saw another courtroom in my life, I would forever view my accomplishments in this intricate case my highest level of personal achievement.

I remember the judge's exact words, as though it were yesterday: "Mr. Pavlic, it's not often that a man in your position comes before this bench so well prepared and advanced in the art of advocacy."

He went on to say that he had read my argument, which was quite extensive, and that it contained many issues that should be addressed by the appropriate court, but unfortunately it was not the Federal Court. He added that I should try addressing my concerns under Article 53 or 55.

His statements hit me like a runaway train and had me feeling dizzy with emotional gratitude. Here was a highly respected and intelligent, professional man, who sat on the bench of the Federal Court of Canada, telling me that indeed my argument had many significant issues to be addressed. Up to this point, I had been starting to wonder if I hadn't just fabricated the whole thing. Up to now, not only did people not listen, they turned a blind eye, as though I was stupid. I extended my deepest thanks to the court and its members.

"Your Honor," I said, "my faith in our judicial system, which had all but disappeared, has been reinstated here today. I came empty in spirit, expecting nothing, and now leave with everything, as my dignity has been rightfully restored."

On the ride back to the institution, the guard kept telling me how sensational she thought my argument was. I told her that I always performed better in front of an audience.

Within days, the whole prison knew of my outstanding performance. Regardless of the outcome, I never lost faith, as far as having my concerns heard in court. In view of the Justice's remarks to me, which could not be disputed by any lawyer, the door was left wide open for me in regards to civil proceedings. In view of how far I had come and the knowledge I had acquired, had I remained in prison instead of being released within weeks that would certainly have been my next move.

After thirty-three months of incarceration, I was scheduled to leave the next day for the Seven-Step Halfway House, located in Edmonton. Just before lockup that night, my caseworker tried to give me the farewell sermon. He started by wishing me well, which seemed like a nice gesture on his part. Then he said, "Mino, it's over now. You've paid your dues to society."

I looked at him as though he was from another planet. "You still think, after all this legal aggravation and frustration I've been through with the courts, that I was guilty?"

"It doesn't matter. You did your time."

What a balloon head, I thought to myself. I had just been robbed of three stinking years of my life, and to this guy it didn't matter. To add further insult, he wanted to shake my hand. I gave him a classic Clint Eastwood stare as I walked past him to my cell, letting the door quietly shut behind me.

Surprisingly, I spent a good part of the night reflecting on the times Stephen and I had talked as we walked the prison yard. In the years I knew him, not once had he ever talked to me in regards to crime. If anything, he continuously tried to influence me into straightening out my life. His words, even now, echo in my head from time to time: "Mino, when you get out, no matter whom you meet, ask yourself what that person can do for you. If it isn't to your benefit in a positive way, distance yourself from them." It was only common sense. If you surrounded yourself with successful people, eventually you'll become successful. Hang out with losers, and sooner or later you'll become one as well. His most famous line to me was this: "Once you're back in society, take a break from the destructive lifestyle for six months. Who knows? You might just get to like it out there."

Stephen was a true friend and was always there for me. He was principled and strongly believed that when it came to justice, there was none; there's just us.

EIGHT MONTHS OF FREEDOM 15

The first thing I did when allowed to go out on a pass was visit the Edmonton courthouse. After explaining myself to the clerk, I was informed that the only remedy available to me was a civil action, a very complicated process. I wasn't in the least disappointed, as I still had an ace or two up my sleeve.

As I headed towards the exit, the last person I expected to bump into was the idiot who had sabotaged my case in the Supreme Court. Understandably, I had a few choice words for him. He must have felt protected, as he got very brave. Waving his hand in the air, he said, "It doesn't matter what you do now. You won't get anywhere." The full meaning of his bold statement wouldn't fully hit me until a few weeks later. If it wasn't for the fact of being surrounded by police, the dummy would have definitely gotten a shot in the head.

My ace in the hole was that I would try to obtain legal representation, on a percentage basis, where if the action were successful, they'd get a percentage of the damages awarded. I visited two law firms, explaining the whole mess and leaving a copy of the trial transcripts, along with my argument, for their consideration. When I returned a week later, both firms paid me a high compliment, saying that I should have been a lawyer. Unfortunately, there was nothing they could do. In that moment, I understood why. Not any lawyer, quite possibly anywhere in Canada, would get involved due to my implications and allegations. Careers would be lost. The treatment by the Alberta Court of an accused unrepresented by counsel would open the door to many issues of procedural misconduct. The courts would be swamped with a succession of similar claims, for I was nowhere near the only individual to whom justice had been denied.

I knew that the only alternative left for me was to submit my own representations in a civil suit. However, the chances of this happening were slim. I knew the excitement of having my freedom wouldn't allow me to stay focused. Stephen had been right in describing me as an angry young man. Over twenty-five years had now passed by, and still all my legal documentation sits idle in a box, collecting dust. If I couldn't get the public's attention through the courts, hopefully I've now done so by what I've written.

One day before returning to the halfway house, I decided to stop at the Cromdale Hotel for a couple of drinks. I wasn't supposed to drink, but with only a couple of months left before my mandatory supervision kicked in, I really didn't care. If they wanted to send me back to the penitentiary, my stuff was already packed. For some reason, I really liked the atmosphere at Cromdale, so I asked for a job as a bouncer. Because of my size, I was given the job on the spot, and there was no opposition from the halfway house. I worked there without incident up to my release.

While working there, I became close friends with a girl named Wanda, and slowly a relationship began.

The Cromdale brought its own joyful surprises for me. One night while working, the last person I expected to see came through the door: Stephen. He had just been recently released and his mother happened to live around the corner. About a week later, Doll showed up, which turned out to be quite the reunion. She told me I was now a father, and that our son, Jessie Rafe, was two and a half years old. Don't get me wrong, it was great visiting with my son, and I really was a proud father. However, it was the same old story with Doll. It wasn't long before I got back into using drugs intravenously. Somehow I managed to make it to my automatic release without getting revoked. When I was released, I got my own place, and Wanda moved in with me. Stephen, who hated me working at the Cromdale, got me a job in the bakery where he worked. Momentarily, I did manage to break away from Doll and the drug use.

Trouble always had a way of finding me, though. When the job came to an end, I bumped into J.P. again, and this time I met his younger brother, Mark, and a guy named Mac. They were working a burglary crew which consisted of six kids ranging in age from fifteen to eighteen. It didn't take me long to get involved. Soon the burglary task force was on to us, and we found ourselves under heavy police surveillance. I kept thinking, what if one of these kids got pinched and under pressure decided to write a statement against us? I was worried about landing before a judge and hearing him say, "You're guilty of counseling minors in the commission of an indictable offence." This would justify a fourteen-year prison sentence.

Even with the police breathing down our necks, it seemed as though we were on a roll. But eventually crime has a way of catching up to you. One day, after returning home from a burglary, the cops pounced on us with guns drawn. I still remember Mac trying to walk away with a case of beer under his arm. He deadpanned the cop, "I don't know what's going on." He said he could had come by to watch a hockey game and drink some beer." I have to admit it was quick thinking on his part, but as they had us under surveillance, it did him no good.

Since she was in my house, the police also arrested Wanda. She was released within a matter of days, as I stated to the court that she had absolutely no knowledge of what was going on. Before she was released, I told her, "Wanda, forget about me and go live with your mother." I encouraged her to finish her education, as those had been her original plans. Instead she persistently remained by my side for the next year, coming to visit me weekly.

In March 1988, my mandatory supervision was revoked. Instead of doing dead time, I intended to plead guilty and go back to the penitentiary. Mac and Mark asked me if I would hold off on pleading guilty for thirty days, as they were positive that any sentence I received would have a negative influence on their own sentences. I did as they asked, and it did help them out tremendously; one received nine months while the other received a year.

I went for sentencing, and the judge, without so much as looking at me, added three years to my existing sentence. While in the remand center, awaiting transfer back to the pen, an interesting offer was placed before me which I immediately accepted. I was one of the first federal prisoners to accept a federal/provincial transfer, meaning that the remainder of my sentence would be served in Fort Saskatchewan, a provincial institution.

Fort Saskatchewan Provincial Prison 16

The Fort, as it was widely known, was located an hour's drive from Edmonton. The original prison was about to be shut down, as the new seventy-million-dollar facility would be completed in a matter of months. Prior to entering the new facility, I didn't do much of anything except a lot of reflecting on the mess I had made of my life. It was now May 1988, and up to this point I had served eleven and a half years of my life in prison. Imagine a hundred and thirty-two months, or almost four thousand days, locked up in a cage. The thought sent an electrifying chill through me. I couldn't even try to justify this wasted life. It's a wonder I was never suicidal, or maybe I was all along and just didn't know it.

When we finally entered the new institution, I was impressed. It was state of the art. There were five units, with one reserved for female offenders, as this was a co-ed prison. I took the job of being the unit cleaner. The circle of prisoners I surrounded myself with were those who would directly influence my achievements, which in great measure became their own. The two which stood out most in my mind were Ann and Grant, who worked in the prison canteen. They were very intelligent, and through the duration of our incarceration, we developed a solid friendship. However, as always, I had to have an angle. In view of the programs I involved myself in, I achieved my goals tenfold.

The three of us decided that by combining our extensive experience, we could put together a document outlining the basic principles of best surviving the prison experience, and the steps necessary for obtaining the earliest possible release. Such a document would invaluably assist all first offenders in helping them best complete their sentences. If we were successful, we could write our own ticket within the institution.

With the prison administration's approval, we were given access to a room we could use. For the next month, we met almost every night and brainstormed, putting our every thought or idea on paper. Once completed, this impressive fifteen-page directory was viewed by the administration as an exceptional document. We now held open meetings once a week; we had ten youngsters at any given time. We were all proud of what we had accomplished.

Eventually, we were approached by the administration about participating in a new program they wanted to initiate. It went along the same principles as the legendary Scared Straight program. Every week, a group of troubled kids from the outside were brought in. I enjoyed those weekly sessions very much. They gave me a great sense of fulfillment. No matter my motive, if what I had to say helped even one kid turn his life around, no words could describe how great I felt. Through a program sponsored by Edmonton's John Howard Society, I could have involved myself in similar sessions, talking to kids at high schools. I made all kinds of promises, but it never became a reality.

In view of my achievements, the prison administration respected me in their own way, but they never for a moment trusted me. My thick prison file told a different story from the one I was trying to project.

I also befriended two guys who at a later date were to play a major role in my drug activities. There was Danny, a fellow Yugoslav, who would eventually supply me with "pink champagne," a highly desirable quality of cocaine, almost ninety percent in purity. Then there was Rick, a hardcore speed freak.

In view of what I had done for his brother, J.P. made sure I was well looked after and always had a constant supply of either marijuana or hashish. Getting high was tough in the Fort, they did random urine testing. I knew the administration was just waiting for me to step out of line. To get around this annoyance, I read somewhere in a book that if you took a small amount of bleach and drank it, no drug in your body would be detected. It actually cleaned the urine of all illegal substances.

The bleach we had was powdered, and it tasted terrible. I used to put a small amount in a little ball of bread, then swallow it in one shot. Once the bleach was digested, it remained in one's system until flushed out, which could take up to a week. I knew this trick, but the kids who bought drugs from me didn't. I used to laugh uncontrollably—still do, when I think about it—as they'd take a big spoon of this stuff and mix it in a cup of water before drinking it. They used to do it almost daily.

I was touched by the way Wanda adamantly stuck by me. Most times, her only way of getting to the prison was by hitchhiking. Eventually her visits got further apart, until one day they stopped altogether. I understood this all too well. Just as with Doll, when I got my three years, she sent a card wishing me luck and hoped to see me when I got out. I respected Wanda's decision, as it would be unrealistic to expect anyone to wait faithfully for who knows how many years. I knew where to find Wanda, and once released I'd look her up. If she still felt the same way about me, we'd start up again from scratch.

I took it upon myself to help a guy named Ray, who was doing time on an impaired driving charge. I prepared and obtained all the necessary documentation for him to establish a fiber optics company in Edmonton. He went on to make it a very successful business. He told me about a program he and his wife had seen on TV regarding a fiber optics company in New York. I found it fascinating, so I wrote to the network and they sent all sorts of information. I then formulated a lengthy plan which Ray could use to start a similar business in the Edmonton area. I firmly believed that if he applied the same principles, it would be successful, regardless of where he applied them. Based on what I put together, Ray's father-in-law invested in the venture, and within a year it was on its way to being a very profitable company.

Ray had an unusual way of showing gratitude. Instead of helping me, he eventually tried to ruin my credibility with the institution. Before he got out, he suggested that I apply for a day pass and use his house. In the course of events, it was granted. Regardless of whatever my motives were, he should have had the understanding that I worked hard at his interests. Left on his own, he never would have been able to put together the business plan. My first clue should have been that he was a chronic alcoholic. Sobered up, he was a great guy. In most cases, alcoholics are highly intelligent with easy going personalities.

I got out for the pass and saw that Ray was still battling with alcoholism. His wife Susan continuously voiced her appreciation of the assistance I had given them, and she went out of her way to make me feel at ease. In his clouded judgment, Ray took this the wrong way and proceeded to drink himself silly. Since there were a few things I needed to take care of, I said that I'd be back within a few hours. I left, and when I returned, it was obvious that he had gotten physical with Susan, at which point I gave him a couple of shots to the head. Being that he was intoxicated, Susan had to drive me back to the Fort.

After we left, Ray telephoned the institution and told them that he believed I was smuggling heroin back to the prison. What a goof. As I had been playing this dangerous game a long time, in the event of the unexpected, I always remained one step ahead. Certainly, I had picked up some packages, but there was no way I'd be the one bringing them in. I dropped them off at a prearranged address, where there was a kid scheduled to go out on a pass the following day. He'd be bringing the drugs back with him.

On my return, I was immediately escorted to the segregation unit, where I exchanged my street clothes for prison coveralls and then placed in a dry cell. It was completely bare except for a plastic bucket, which was one's toilet. It took three days before the guards were convinced I was clean. As a result of always thinking one step ahead, whether in prison or out in society, I have never been charged with anything that could implicate me in the drug trade.

After almost two years at Fort Saskatchewan, it was time to move on to yet another adventure. Regardless of how clean I appeared on paper, since I still had over two years remaining on my sentence, the administration refused to grant me anything resembling parole. Instead, they decided to send me to the Belmont Correctional Center, a provincial co-ed halfway house in Edmonton.

While at Belmont, I was never underestimated by the administration. By the way they treated me, it became obvious that under no circumstances were they about to trust me. Within days of my arrival, they made it clear that while I was in their institution, I wouldn't be allowed off the property. Their logic bordered on the idiotic, as Belmont wasn't a fenced complex; leaving would have been as simple as walking away. It would have proved more beneficial had they dangled a weekly six-hour pass and allowed for me to earn those passes based on my performance.

If this was how the game was to be played, then at least my stay was going to be a comfortable one. The first offenders that didn't have a clue what doing time was all about, so I always had an endless supply of puppets doing my bidding. My first order of business was to create a job which was tailor made for me. Just like the chirping of the birds in Oakalla drove me crazy, if I didn't get away from it fast, the chirping of a hundred clueless kids would quickly drive me off the deep end. I found my peace as the cleaner of the gym and its built-in weight room. In the morning, after a hearty breakfast, I'd go work out for three hours with the weights. There wasn't a soul around to bother me. After lunch, I'd sweep and mop the gym. This arrangement lasted for my whole stay at Belmont. I made friends with two dope fiend prostitutes who worked in the kitchen. One was Fran, who was serving an eighteen-month sentence. She liked to rob guys who picked her up, by putting knockout pills in their drinks. However, one guy overdosed. The other was Sherri, with whom I immediately entered into a relationship. She used to come and see me every afternoon in the gym.

Once all the puppets were in place, I had J.P. come to visit me. I explained the rules of the game and that I didn't want to risk overexposure. He came twice a week and left prearranged packages of marijuana hidden on the grounds for me.

I slowly began to turn their Mickey Mouse institution upside-down. It was Wilkinson Road all over again, only better. Every day, there were fifty people getting high from the marijuana I supplied. It brought in a profit of three hundred dollars daily. Someone working on the grounds crew brought the drugs in, another rolled the joints, while others sold it for me. Only I knew all the pieces, and nothing could point back to me. My butt was covered.

Every Friday was movie night. On one particular night, the feature was called *The Drugstore Cowboy*, which dealt with one man's journey into the nightmarish world of pharmaceutical drugs. I had smoked some pot and was pretty high. When the movie got to the part where the main character was preparing his injection and finally injecting himself, I almost fell off my seat. The filming of this scene gave me the sensation that I was injecting myself, and I swear I could taste the metallic taste of the drug as it entered my system. I'm sure the guards must have known something was going on, but since everyone in the joint was drinking bleach, they couldn't figure it out.

In not being able to catch me, they decided to transfer me out of their hair. I was once again transferred back to the Seven Steps Halfway House. They told me that a structured pass program would only be granted if I completed the thirty-day program at the Henwood drug and alcohol treatment center. More and more, I was beginning to feel like a seal jumping through hoops. What choice did I have?

Henwood was another state of the art facility, and for those truly wishing to address their addictions, even I had to admit the program was commendable. However, each and every day the staff and I butted heads. Understandably, in order to even be there, you needed to admit to some form of addiction. When asked what mine was, I said I didn't have one. I had spent the last three years in prison, so what addiction did they expect me to have? In the first week, they often threatened to send me back to the halfway house. I'd defiantly answer, "My bags are packed; don't let the bus leave without me." It's still not clear to me, but somehow I managed to survive the thirty days.

With six months left before my mandatory supervision came into effect, I started going out on passes. Many things happened which could have landed me back in prison. I really didn't care about anything, a predictable attitude for an institutionalized drug addict. I started using drugs with Sherri on a regular basis. Seeing how her life mainly revolved around the city's skid row, it wasn't long before I broke free of the relationship.

At the halfway house, I became friends with a guy called Fred, and the scam he introduced me to could be considered an art form. He was an expert in credit card fraud. He could create his own keys to open mailboxes, such as mailmen carry.

First, we'd find a rundown apartment building where security wasn't an issue. With a Phillips screwdriver and wire cutters, we'd go to work. On the outside of the entrance, there's a little box where a mailman inserts his key to open the front door. We'd quickly dismantle it, cutting the wires which held it in place. Then we'd take the whole unit back to the halfway house. From a hardware store, we bought an assortment of the smallest files they had. Once Fred had the locking mechanism open, which was itself quite a task, he'd take an ordinary butter knife, which he had filed square, and heat it until it was red hot. This way, it could be bent at the right angle to fit in the slot. Inserting it a little at a time, the pins in the lock would scratch their markings, which he'd file again precisely. Once finished, we'd have a perfect homemade key.

We would usually, roam the richer neighborhoods in the morning, hitting apartments. This wasn't as easy as it sounds. Trouble could erupt at any time. Once inside the building, he would let himself into the mailman's room and scan all the boxes in search of gray envelopes; these were the ones in which we'd find credit cards. We always remembered which building the cards had come from, as it allowed us to carry out the scam to its fullest potential. In the days following, we'd have to do this all over again, as the credit card companies would send another gray envelope, known as an interception, which informed the customer that they'd mailed a card.

Once you had this information, you were set for thirty days, as that would be when the card owner would receive his first credit card statement. By that time, the total owing would have amounted to tens of thousands of dollars, and right about then we would be in the process of maxing out the next card. The money to be made in this game was astronomical, and things were going great for two months. Due to my lifestyle, Fred abandoned me; being a drug addict made me unpredictable and unreliable. The continuing success of this high-stakes game depended on us being in control and having our wits about us at all times.

I ran into my friend Rick and tried to teach him the credit card game. He learned very quickly, but he didn't have the patience or skill required. He would get a card, run it for a day, then go on the prowl the next day for another. Rick and I worked together for about a month.

By this time, I could have been considered a speed freak. Speed was a combined mixture of cocaine and heroin. Any money we made went straight into our arms. One night while drinking at the Cromdale Hotel, I ran into Doll. She took me to her place to once again introduce me to my son, who was almost six years old. It's amazing how time can quickly pass you by.

Doll had always craved heroin, but now she mostly used cocaine. I was getting weekend passes, and it wasn't long before Rick, Doll, and I were getting together and going on binges, shooting up drugs at her kitchen table.

By chance, I happened to bump into my friend Yugoslavian Danny, which was to my advantage, as he was a major player in the Edmonton drug trade. I would buy ounces of ninety percent cocaine, known as "pink champagne," for as little as fifty dollars a gram, about fifteen hundred an ounce. I more than doubled my money after slightly cutting the dope with baking soda. One day, I was told that all further passes would be suspended for thirty days. This was probably the best thing to happen to me, as I was just waiting to be caught. During this time, Rick managed to make his way back to prison.

Once I regained my passes, I stumbled upon Wanda and we started seeing one another again. While I was in prison, she had hooked up with a guy who turned out to be a real idiot. She had been trying to avoid him but wasn't having much luck. One day, we ran into him at the bar. I went over and told him it was over between them; to avoid any complications, he should just stay away from her. Seeing as he was strung out on pills, he seemed to have a problem understanding plain English. Maybe I should have drawn him a map, which in view of what happened the next morning, is kind of what I did. Only, he would remember this map for the rest of his life, each time he looked in the mirror.

He knew I was in a halfway house and had to be back by a specific time. He got himself high on pills, and after midnight he showed up at Wanda's place with a friend of his. He beat her up—badly. His biggest mistake was in passing out. When I showed up in the morning and saw Wanda covered from head to foot in dried blood, I completely lost it. I asked what had happened and she pointed to this goof passed out on the floor. I grabbed a butcher knife from the kitchen and got ready to carve him up like a Christmas turkey. His buddy, who was a big guy, stepped in my way. I threw the knife down and picked up a bloodied crib board that he'd probably used to beat her. I deadpanned the guy, saying, "Are you going to interfere?" He shook his head and stepped out of my way.

With my first swing, I cracked the goof full-force on the nose, breaking it. Well, let me tell you, he came out of his pill-intoxicated state in quite a hurry. I cracked him again and he went down. With my knee placed heavily on his head, I grabbed hold of his hair with my free hand and began methodically cracking him in the face. As each blow struck, blood flew all over the place. He received ten solid whacks, but then it suddenly hit me in a fit of rage: I had to get out, not only because the guy was bleeding profusely, but his screaming would have certainly caused someone to phone the police. This vicious beating took about three or four minutes. By this time, Wanda had gotten dressed. Before heading out the door, I put the crib board in a bag. I planned to personally get rid of it. The police and ambulance showed up a few minutes after we had left. He died on the way to the hospital, but luckily they managed to revive him. Since he had minor warrants out for his arrest, when he recovered, the police took him into custody.

A couple of days later, while I was at Wanda's, the phone rang. I answered only to hear him on the other end. He told me that the police were pressuring him to lay charges against me, as they knew I was involved. He assured me that he wasn't going to say anything, but he reminded me that the issue was far from over between us. I coldly told him that if we ever met again, I would get really mad.

Sure enough, about a month went by and he showed up with his brother. He looked like a remake of Frankenstein, as he had required over thirty stitches in his face. We got into it, and both he and his brother took a beating. Since then, I haven't seen either of them again.

It didn't take too long before Wanda and I started drifting apart. I was just a little too wild for her. One day after a heated argument, on my way out the door, I smashed a window. The police were called and I ended up going back to Bowden for six months. I was, to all appearances, trapped in a never-ending cycle.

My Brother Mike, the Gentleman Conman 17

After serving six months, I once again found myself in the Seven Steps Halfway House. I went to see Doll, and to my surprise she had straightened herself out considerably and was living with an ironworker named Rob.

It had been nine years since I'd seen or heard from any of my brothers. One day, after returning from a pass, I was both elated and stunned to find the message waiting for me. Tomo had somehow tracked me down and left his telephone number. It took a few days before I returned his call. What do you say after nine years of absence? I eventually talked to all my brothers, at length, and they wanted to know only one thing: when I was returning to Vancouver. I immediately put in my parole application, which was granted three months later. In the meantime, I stopped almost all forms of illegal activities that might jeopardize my parole.

I spent a lot of time visiting with my son at Doll's, and the sad part was that once I was gone, who knew when I would get to see him again, if ever? During this time, the only illegal activity I committed was using stolen calling cards, as I was constantly on the phone to Vancouver. This probably amounted to thousands of dollars. In talking with Mike, he put me in touch with my old girlfriend Wendy. In the three months I waited for my parole, Wendy and I spent three to four hours daily on the phone. It was evident that upon my return we would find ourselves in a relationship.

About a month before I was to leave for Vancouver, Mike showed up and introduced me to a beautiful con game, as well sharing a few others. In the following ten years, I got to see him at work many times in the extraordinarily fascinating game of the confidence artist. Mike, regardless of the company he found himself in, always presented himself with an outstanding image of friendliness and self-assuredness, accompanied by a smooth sophistication that gave him an almost mystical charisma. I never viewed what he did as criminal, as he didn't steal; he survived by his wits. His unsuspecting victim, be it a large department store or the ordinary citizen on the street, had to be a willing participant in order for the con to work. Usually, after he baffled a person with his story, he was walking away with their money, which they willingly gave him in the first place. So where was the crime? In almost all his street cons, people were looking to get something for nothing. With Mike, he gave you nothing for your money.

He had too many award-winning performances to mention, and some may still be in use. In the years I've watched Mike in action, no matter who he crossed paths with, all of them were conned. In the original con he taught me, you'd begin to understand how even the most intelligent person, from any walk of life, could be relieved of their hard-earned money. Make no mistake about it: if you allow yourself to be charmed by his extraordinary personality, he'll take everything you own and laugh about it at the end of his workday. His motto is simple: if you're too stupid to keep what's yours, it will eventually become his. All his cons are borderline criminal. The fact that people willingly participate in them destroys their hopes of criminal prosecution.

I went to see Mike in the motel where he was staying, and he mentioned something about putting Irene to work for a few days. I looked around, but I didn't see any woman. Mike's Irene was a code name for a fourteen-carat jeweler's stamp. He had located the specialty stores in town and bought cheap costume jewelry. He'd buy sixteen necklaces for about twenty dollars, then carefully punch the fourteen-carat emblem on the clasp and artfully sell them throughout the bars at thirty bucks a pop. Only after three or four days would the mark know he'd been fleeced, as the cheap chain would begin to leave a green ring around his or her neck. Everybody thought they were getting a hundred and fifty dollar chain for next to nothing. Depending on how you made your presentation, nine times out of ten you were guaranteed a sale. Mike would have no problem selling thirty of these chains a day, which he needed to do since he had a very expensive drug addiction: narcotics. His dependency cost at least five to six hundred dollars every day.

Mike stayed about two weeks, then continued on his way across Canada, doing a circuit with Irene. He had already done this four or five times in the past. I firmly believe that if Mike were to apply himself fully in any legal venture, he would be very successful. At the same time, I understand what it's like to have a serious dependency on drugs. Some people can never rid themselves of an addiction, no matter how hard or how many times they try.

I've been there.

Reunion in Vancouver 18

My parole was granted in July 1991. Before I left Edmonton, I had one final visit with my son. Leaving him was a very sad experience, as even at that age he wanted to leave with me. My life was still pretty disorganized, and I didn't have a clue what to expect in terms of my future. In the best interests of my son, he was better off being with his mother.

Finally leaving Alberta filled my thoughts with the promise of a new beginnings. I hoped I'd be able to break free of the tormented existence I'd subjected myself to for the past eighteen years. All I had to do was surround myself with positive people and positive thoughts. It sounded simple, but unfortunately it wasn't the way things were meant to be. At least, not yet.

Arriving in Vancouver, Tomo met me at the bus station. It was great seeing him. I was glad to hear that in the past eight years he had managed to turn his life around. For the last six years, he'd been working full-time in the laborers' union for the same company. He was rising quickly up the ladder, as an industrial first aid attendant. Eventually, he'd also become the safety officer. He and his girlfriend, Gabriel, lived in a modest apartment; they were also the caretakers of the small complex, located in an exclusive south-end neighborhood. He had just bought himself an almost brand-new Mustang convertible.

Reflecting on all this, I'd shake my head in disgust. If I hadn't had so many negative influences in my life in 1978, when I belonged to the union myself, who knows what accomplishments I might have achieved? Tomo and I discussed my re-entering the union with his help, but again this just wasn't meant to be. No sooner had I arrived at Tomo's than I was on the move again, this time to White Rock, where Wendy lived. It was wonderful to be reunited with her after almost ten years. Tomo understandably kept me at arm's length. In view of my immediate actions, it was evident that straightening out my life wasn't my main priority, as it should have been.

Tomo understood that I could have easily jeopardized everything he had worked so hard for. He wasn't about to let anything impede his success, even me. He had rid himself of all the negativity in his life and surrounded himself with positive people and friends. Why couldn't I get the simple yet valuable message that Stephen had been steadily trying put in my head?

The John Howard Society was responsible for my parole, in that I reported to them. They would always have my respect. Throughout my dealings with them, they always showed a great deal of consideration. My caseworker, as I liked to refer to her, was a fantastic lady named Kim. She went out of her way to assist me in any way possible.

My relationship with Wendy was short-lived, and I moved back to Vancouver. Danny was living in Gibson's, located on one of the many islands off the beautiful coast of British Columbia, with his then-girlfriend Diane. I met my nieces Tanya and Natasha for the first time. At two and three years old, I couldn't help but fall in love with them. I stayed with them and their mother Ann for a little while, but due to my reckless behavior, I knew I had to find my own place. I was frequently drinking.

One night I was in New Westminster, in a bar known as Hotel California, a biker hangout. It seemed to me that I was being tested; after all, I was a new face with a lot of tattoos. I was somewhat under the influence when I flicked my cigarette butt in someone's face. A fight broke out. All I remember is finding myself outside, covered from head to toe in my own blood. I don't know what was used. My guess is that my attackers used a pool ball, as they caved the side of my head in. A few days later, while at Tomo's, he looked at my face and asked if it hurt. One side of my head appeared to be indented. I said that there was a throbbing ache. He advised me to go to Vancouver General Hospital, which I did. Once the x-rays were completed, the doctors scheduled me for immediate plastic surgery, as my cheekbone was badly damaged. Since it was a recent injury, they could still repair it.

Mike had returned from his recent "tour," as he liked to call it, and I spent the next month with him. We made lots of money, but again, the bulk of it was spent on drugs. He had an uncontrollable appetite for drugs.

A month later, Danny decided to move to Toronto, where he'd previously lived for a number of years. Mike was going with him. Now I was left on my own with a heavy drug addiction. I tried putting Irene to work, and I did make money, but I lacked the confidence required. I could never match Mike at this game of wits.

The people who hung around me were all involved in criminal activity, although they found Irene to be the ultimate for making easy money. It only stood to reason that they would all become accomplices in the game. Looking back, what we did was very stupid. Every day we'd make a few hundred dollars. There was absolutely no reason for shoplifting to enter the picture, but our mentality was that the less cash we'd have to spend, the more we had to spend on dope. In any department store's jewelry section, they would have cheap imitation gold-plated chains that sold for ten to thirty dollars. We started using these, as they were thicker, heavier, and more impressive looking. Once stamped, they would sell for a couple hundred dollars—not a bad return, even if you spent the thirty dollars. We had one guy who insisted on shoplifting these chains.

One day, we all got pinched and I ended up in the Vancouver city jail. I phoned Kim, my caseworker, and gave her a story that she bought. Instead of revoking my parole, she had me released. I resumed my activities, but with no more shoplifting, for the moment. I could have found myself back in prison very easily, as one of my parole stipulations had been to abstain from alcohol.

One night, four of us decided to go to the Coachhouse Club in North Vancouver for drinks. One guy decided he wanted to have sex with a girl who had tagged along with us. She was his friend's girlfriend.

Unaware of his treachery, he was spiking her drinks with a drug called helicon. Typically known as a sleeper, it quickly knocked you out.

When the effects started to hit her, she said that she wanted to lie down and have a sleep in the car. About an hour went by, and the guy who had spiked her drink was missing. Another guy went out, and on his return he told me that the girl in the car had her pants down around her ankles. I was livid! It was obvious what had taken place. The goof had probably raped her as she lay there passed out. Naturally, I lost it. I went out to the car and readjusted the girl's pants. She was out-of-touch with reality. On re-entering the bar, I went to talk to the waitress, whom I knew, and explained what had happened.

I was seriously going to hurt this idiot. I went back to the table, where I finished my glass of beer, then said it was time to go. I hung onto my glass and hid it inside my jacket. I got ready to leave with the guy, then positioned him behind me as we got out the door. That's when I turned around and smashed the glass in his face, seriously cutting him up. I tried to grab him, as I wasn't done with him just yet, but he managed to slip away. Luckily for him, and possibly for me; who knows what I would have done? Just as we were ready to get into our car, the police showed up. Naturally, we had nothing to say.

They talked to the waitress, who I imagine explained what took place. Although the police had to act accordingly, even they frowned heavily on date rape. After all, everybody has daughters or nieces. They overlooked my drinking and called an ambulance for me, as I was bleeding profusely from a cut I had received from the glass. They took me to the North Vancouver Hospital, where they not only stitched my finger up but allowed me to sleep it off.

One day in the bar, I was trying to sell a chain when some idiot came over, trying to hit me up for a beer. He tried to take a sip from my glass. I told him to get lost. He started screaming that I was selling phony chains. Out back, I gave him three shots, and down he went. I didn't really want to hurt him, because he was harmless to everyone but himself. As I tried to help him up off the ground, he said, "Wait until I get up, I'll show you." That was the wrong thing to say to me. I laid the boots to him and left him there.

I watched him come back into the bar bleeding, and he immediately went over to the payphone. Not once did it enter my mind, in my drunken state, that he wasn't trying to call the police, but instead an ambulance, as he was hurt pretty bad. I went over and told him to stop being a jerk. So he headed to the bar across the street and I followed. Just as I entered the lobby, again I saw him on the phone. The only words he was able to get out, before I cracked him five times in the head with my cane, were, "Hello, 911?" I left him in a pool of blood. Luckily, he didn't know my real name. When dealing with this downtown crowd, it was always best to use an alias.

ON THE RUN AGAIN 19

I had met a girl named Brenda and, knowing better, involved her in my criminal activities. According to her, she was a skilled shoplifter, but apparently not skilled enough, as we both got pinched trying to steal some chains. Incredibly, once again my parole officer believed my story and allowed me to be released pending trial, refusing to revoke my parole. With the prospect of an upcoming trial on two counts of shoplifting, the only thing I could see in my future was a return to prison. After a month and a half of freedom, as was my pattern of unpredictability, I decided to break my parole and go on the run. However, before I could do this, I needed two things: money and false identification papers. Given my network of friends, both were easy to obtain. Within a few days, I had six hundred dollars and a false picture ID.

Getting on a bus, this time I decided to join Danny and Mike in Toronto, some three thousand miles away. Danny was in the beginning stages of remodeling an old four-story rooming house, and for the time being that's where I settled. Once all renovations were completed, with its three-story glass enclosed solarium, you would have never guessed this same house had been ready to be torn down, as in condemned. Pero and Vera, a beautiful couple who had just recently arrived from Yugoslavia, were also living there and we quickly became friends.

When Mike and Danny had lived in Toronto years earlier, they'd worked at the Parkdale Hotel as bouncers. They acquired quite a reputation as tough guys. Danny worked there once again, in the evenings. Mike, on the other hand, was involved with drugs and continued his con games. With my fake ID, in what was a very bold move, I made application for assistance from social services, which was granted. Each month, I was now guaranteed some form of income.

In the bar where Danny worked, it wasn't unusual to see members of the Satan's Choice bike club, which had colorful roots going back to 1965. Danny had become friendly with many of them, and they respected his toughness. That was as far as the association went.

To see Danny in action was to believe the only way you would ever beat him, regardless of the odds, was to kill him. One Friday night, the place was packed with four bouncers working. At one table sat six huge black guys who were causing problems. None of the other bouncers wanted anything to do with them, so Danny handled it. This was an amazing thing to see, as Danny, at five-foot-five and weighing two hundred pounds, was a loaded stick of dynamite. Not only did he possess tremendous courage, but the viciousness of his temper was frightening.

Sitting a few tables away, I watch as Danny approached their table and addressed the biggest guy, telling him that if they didn't keep it down, they'd have to leave. The guy, who had to be over six feet tall, looked up at Danny and told him to beat it. Danny briefly studied them all, and then, with a determined glare, said, "Only because I'm in a good mood, I'll let you stay and finish your drinks. But then it's time to say goodnight." The guy made a move to get up, and Danny peppered him with ten solid punches. Before it started, it was over. The guy was knocked out and bleeding on the floor, and Danny wasn't even out of breath. He asked everyone else at the table, "Who else would like to stay?" Needless to say, they all left without further incident.

Regardless of the circumstances, I loved being around Mike, as there was never a dull moment. This time he led me on an adventure as we went through an assortment of crack houses. Mainly we'd go to his friend Ronnie's house, where we'd remain in the basement for days shooting dope. Looking back on it, I'm positive it was during one of these sessions that I contracted HIV.

Mike, Ronnie, and I each took turns fixing. When it was coming to the end of the dope and they had each done their fix, Ronnie took his time preparing the last one, which just happened to be mine. All the while, you could tell his brain was working overtime trying to figure out how he might scam me out of my fix. Finally, he said to me that he had screwed up by using his needle instead of mine. This is an old dope fiend trick in order to get that extra hit. Clouded by weeks of continuous drug use, I said, "Just fix me."

Four months later, these words would come back to haunt me.

On welfare day, my check arrived, so I bought a couple of grams of coke, which Mike, Ronnie, and I fixed through most of the day. It was my intention to go drinking afterward. Mike convinced me that I should leave the bulk of my money with Ronnie's wife, which gullibly, I did. Returning the next day, I found that there wasn't one dime of my money left, as they had spent it on drugs. What could I do? It was my fault for leaving it. I told Mike not to worry about it, as it had been free money. However, I did manage to break away and went back to stay with Danny. I got a legitimate job working for an asbestos company, and for the next two months I did quite well.

One day, Mike showed up and I was shocked. In his schemes, he had easily made four hundred dollars a day. Where he had always prided himself in his appearance, he now looked no better than a bum off the street. I told him, as we all did, that the drugs were crippling him. This must have left its impact, as within a week he came back to stay, somewhat clean in appearance, and gave me a few hundred dollars, explaining how he was sorry for what had happened. I'm sure he had begun to realize that living on Queen Street was a dead end. He did partially straighten out, breaking free at least from the intravenous drug use. However, he reverted instead to smoking crack cocaine.

While working for the asbestos company, I used my own name, as I was still receiving welfare checks under my alias. The company had lots of work, but my time there was coming to an end. The foreman liked me. One day he approached me, saying that the company had been awarded the contract to do a two-week job at one of the local police precincts, but he had to submit all the employee names for a security clearance. He was smart enough to realize that, in view of my tattoos, he'd better first ask me if it was okay. I thanked him and told him that my employment with the company had just come to an end.

One day, I was sitting on the porch with Danny's dog Digger, a wolf/malamute cross. I watched two clowns across the street who appeared to be just hanging around; they gave me no reason to be suspicious in the least. They continued walking up the street. Suddenly, they were on the porch with guns drawn and pointed at my head. They told me to hold the dog, otherwise they would shoot it. It turned out they were undercover cops. They took me to the 42nd Division, where they tried to convince me that I had been continually involved in criminal activities since being in Toronto. All I told them was that I was a parole violator and nothing else. I was taken from there to the old Don Jail, which was Toronto's remand center. Three weeks later, my parole was officially revoked.

The suspension didn't anger me; it was their reasoning that ruffled my feathers. I ended up writing a brilliant letter to the parole board. They had received a special report from the arresting officers, stating that I had been spotted frequenting numerous crack houses and that I seemed to sleep late in the day and stay out all night. That report, for many reasons, should have left anyone scratching their head. This was my reply:

> In reply to your letter dated November 1991. This is to inform you that my intentions are to make a formal complaint, not in regards to my parole being suspended or the loss of remission, but in strict reference to the information contained in the post release decision sheet, which I strongly proclaim is not only a lie, but a complete fabrication made against me by the Toronto police. In my case, there is not one iota of legal justification to warrant the fairy tale. It is therefore my contention that part of the board's decision is based on wrongful information which does not represent the facts. Had your representative, who interviewed me after my arrest, cared to properly and fully investigate the information I put at her disposal, there would have been no question as to what I was doing in my three-month absence. All of which has been fully confirmed by many reputable sources.
>
> I have spent-one third of my life incarcerated. To even consider that my problems end upon expiry of sentence would be an error not only on my part, but also on the part of the parole board. I feel that instead of trying to punish me with the few remaining months I have left until the completion of sentence, as it serves no purpose, I would ask that I serve the remainder of my sentence under strict supervision in the community. Remaining in prison is of no benefit to me or the community.

You have to admit, it was a nice try, but they told me to forget about it. I was shipped to the Millhaven Maximum Federal Penitentiary, located a couple of miles west of Kingston, which rightfully was one of the most hated and feared prisons in Canada. It was a common ground for brutality, murder, suicide, assaults, and gang warfare. Millhaven was home to a few hundred of Canada's most dangerous offenders, with additional prisoners housed in its special handling unit, a special prison within a prison, one of only two such facilities in the Canadian federal prison system.

I was there for close to a month before being transferred to Joyceville Penitentiary, a medium-security institution. The building itself was old, and anyone who's been there will remember the thousands of cockroaches, many as big as one's thumb. Once you're there for a while, you don't even notice them.

Upon arrival, I had Danny send me a regulation fourteen-inch color TV, which I was allowed to have in my cell.

Within two months, I became so sick that I was transferred to the local hospital for a week. My vital signs were steadily weakening, and from what I understand my blood was racing at a life-threatening level. As a result, I was placed in a bathtub full of ice cubes three times daily. The doctors monitored me numerous times daily, but there was mention of the possibility of transferring me to the Toronto General Hospital. I did recover, but even when I returned to the penitentiary, I was placed in the infirmary under observation. I remained there for about a month before returning to the population.

Looking back, I believe it was at this time that I contracted Ronnie's Hepatitis C. What else could it have been? Even the doctors, after extensive tests, had no logical explanation for my condition.

RETURN TO EDMONTON 20

Upon my release, with only three months until the expiration of my sentence, I took up residence again at Danny's place. For the longest time, I seemed to be haunted by one continuous thought. I had served nearly fourteen years of my life in prison. As a result, I was mad at everyone but myself. I fully understood this undeniable reality: if I didn't want to spend another fourteen years in prison, I desperately needed to change, if that were even possible. I would try, although I knew this was easier said than done.

I started to view my whole incarceration as an addiction, but I still lacked answers. I remained in Toronto for a month and a half before transferring my parole back to Edmonton. I started hanging around the bar again and got to know a few of the local hookers.

I briefly got involved with Diane. She was an attractive blue-eyed blonde, sophisticated in her own way. Although she sold her body, she wasn't what I would call a hardcore drug addict. It's too bad it didn't work out, but in view of my principled manner I just had a hard time trying to make love to her wholeheartedly, knowing she had been with five or six tricks throughout the day.

Before taking off to Edmonton, I spent a few days with Mike, but it was the same old story of money and drugs. I was glad to be leaving, as I wanted to distance myself from his lifestyle, although I couldn't have picked a worse destination.

With what little money I had, I checked in to a local hotel and immediately applied for and received assistance from social services. In order to continue receiving benefits, I needed a suitable address. It didn't take me long to start drinking, and even less time to hook up once again with Sherri. This arrangement worked to my advantage, as she lived in a huge rooming house with thirty suites. For a small percentage, the manager would gladly fill out my intent to rent form for social services. He must have had at least thirty checks coming in for people who didn't even live there. At fifty bucks a pop, he had a good sideline.

Living with Sherri was hard due to her chosen occupation. I found myself spending most of my time in the skid row hotels, drinking while she sold her body outside. As she was a hardcore dope fiend, it didn't take me long to fall back into the drug scene. With my money gone, I was living off what Sherri made, with the stipulation that I'd reimburse her when the welfare checks came.

My sentence finally expired on June 23, 1992. A memorable day, as this was the first time I had been unconditionally free since May 1973—nineteen long years in which I had never been completely free of halfway houses, parole, or prison. Certainly, it was a tremendous feeling to be cut loose from the noose which had been around my neck for the past twenty years. Yet, in a twisted, almost morbid way I felt abandoned by the correctional system, which throughout my adult life had represented the only family I'd adopted as my own.

Prison and violence have been written about in many books. Whether accurate or not, we all have our own perceptions. What I do know is that I've served over five thousand days in various prisons across Canada. This could make me an expert on the topic of what life is truly like behind prison walls in Canada. Understandably, the very words "prison" or "jail" generate fear when the average person tries to imagine themselves locked up in them for any length of time. They have thoughts of an awesome-looking complex surrounded by fences with razor sharp Constantine wire, with gun towers manned around the clock. That's before even stepping inside one of these human meat grinders.

This leaves one to believe everyone contained in these facilities should be regarded as extremely dangerous. This is an illusion or fallacy that has been fed to society. If you treat me like a dog, day in and day out, eventually I'll become that very callous and cold animal; like an abused dog that one day breaks free of his chain, I too will become a threat, a direct product of my abusive environment. I've spent one-third of my adult life locked up in prison, and I'll be the first to agree that society as a whole couldn't function properly without them. Some form of order must be maintained. Without punishment, our very foundation of a just society would deteriorate, leaving total chaos, if not anarchy.

From my perspective, prisons are a small community. Therefore, why should they be any different from the outside world? Society has general rules and standards which people as a whole live and abide by. The same holds true of any prison, as they too have rules, but not the ones set by the prison administration, which to most prisoners mean nothing. The administration is nothing more than a keeper. The rules of importance are the convict's unwritten code of conduct, and unfortunately these rules won't be found in any book or manual. You pick these up very quickly by remaining silent and observing and learning. In some cases, if you're lucky enough, you may get the help of a rounder to teach you these skills. Respect and privacy are very important. Since I always found myself doing time, the less contact I had with the outside world, the better off I was. The more I associated myself with thoughts of the outside, the harder it was to do my time. Dwelling on things I had no control over was pointless. Depression would set in, followed by frustration, irritation, and then anger.

Sometimes that pent-up anger would erupt, and I'd issue a verbal warning; this allowed everyone to see that my patience had reached its limits. I might just say, "To hell with it," and attack someone, allowing for a situation that would condemn me to segregation in the hole. Most times this was a welcome result, as it allowed me to escape the frustrations of general population and give me the opportunity to collect my thoughts. This isn't to say that segregation doesn't have its long-term disadvantages; when completely isolated, you become bitter and extremely antisocial.

In my last years in prison, I saw more and more that the ethics of the old school were slowly disappearing. Not because there were more first-time offenders entering the system—or, as everyone would have us believe, because of drugs. Drugs have always been and will always remain part of prison subculture. I believe there are too many carrots. Prison has become a comfortable place, where all the luxurious privileges can be taken away at any time, for whatever reason. Therefore, the more you have to lose, in my opinion, the less important the prisoner's code becomes.

It goes without saying that the majority of prison violence is connected to drugs and gambling. Many people get heavily in debt because of this. A cardinal rule of surviving in prison is to not get involved in drugs or gambling, unless you can afford it. It's the same principle of any downtown area, where more brutal acts of violence are committed than in general society. How many prison murders do you read about? How many rapes?

There is a certain amount of prison violence, but you have to view it in its proper context. Most often, brutal violence in prison is committed against undesirables—sex offenders, followed by stoolpigeons (snitches). Throughout my years of incarceration, I have participated in countless beatings of such offenders. There is a huge distinction between these two categories of offenders; they're both considered lowlifes, but there *is* a difference! Stoolpigeons go to the administration in hopes of gaining some form of consideration, in fear or as a result of intimidation. Unfortunately, some follow this path and it hangs over the rest of their life like a cloud.

Sex offenders, on the other hand, are a different breed. Through the course of our lives as children, we experiment with sex, although in most cases it's not until some time in our early teens that we start to develop relationships of serious consequence. All sexual abuse is degenerate behavior. Especially in cases of sexual abuse involving children, such behavior is intolerable, inexcusable. The depth of the invisible scars and devastation caused by such a predator escapes our immediate comprehension, but rest assured that they will haunt the victim for most of their lives. Such an offender acts in a malicious, if not premeditated manner, preying on the vulnerability and gullibility of children, who more often than not remain the victims.

Since there are more predators than space available in protective custody, where they rightfully belong, the prison administration often tries to quietly slide them into the general population, but it doesn't take us long to weed out such an offender. In these instances, the harsh realities of prison justice are fully exploited by the media. Regardless of society's perception of who we may be, each time we're so fortunate as to expose one of these lowlifes and beat his brains in, in our minds we're giving society justice which the court cannot condone, but at the same time we're giving ourselves satisfaction. We also have girlfriends, wives, and kids. Don't think for a moment that the guards care about some child molester getting a beating, for if they did, they wouldn't place him in general population, where his safety is at maximum risk twenty-four hours a day.

Any prison is a closed community, and tension is a constant companion. If you involve yourself in illegal activity, such as drugs or gambling, it's understood that you've allowed for the very real possibility of violence.

There's no road map for successfully completing your sentence without trouble, but there are some guidelines that should be considered. It starts with the sentence received at court, but also the attitude you portray at that time. Once you're sentenced, that's the time to seriously consider what direction you want your life to go in. As you take a good, hard look at your surroundings and the people around you, don't be wondering what prison is about; it's not the kind of place where you want to be. Prisons are full of men and women of all ages wondering what the heck is going on. For those who've spent a great deal of their life behind bars, they just don't care about choices anymore. If you don't want to be a carbon copy of my life, make the correct choice while there's still time.

A Change in Direction, Tree-Planting 21

The social assistance checks would arrive soon, and I realized that most of mine would go to Sherri. Many thoughts ran through my head regarding the direction of my life. Did I really want to continue in this destructive lifestyle, which was headed nowhere except straight back to prison?

Knowing that I had to break free, I made a plan. Since I had to pick up my check at the social services office, I told Sherri I'd meet her in the bar. She agreed. After cashing my check at the bank, I took a cab to Sherri's place, grabbed my stuff, and never looked back. I checked into a hotel on the other side of town, and two weeks later I was broke. Some plan!

I decided to call Tomo and explain the reality of my present situation. I stressed my need to disassociate myself from this dead-end crowd and drowning lifestyle. He had an alternative for me which I readily jumped at. What other option did I have available to me, short of the revolving door leading back to prison? He told me that if I could meet him in Prince George in a week, he would introduce me to the tree-planting industry. I had never heard of it before, but at this point I was willing to try almost anything. He had all the gear I would require. I told him I would be there.

I kept thinking, how hard could it be to plant trees? I was about to find out. At thirty-six years old, all the possessions I had thus far accumulated fit into three cardboard boxes and one suitcase. Since I had no way of taking this stuff with me, I told Tomo that I was going to send it to him by bus. I'd square up with him afterwards. Now I only had a small suitcase containing some clothes.

On my last day at the hotel, I awoke early and got ready for my journey, which I hoped wouldn't take too long, as I was hitchhiking. I didn't have a dime to my name. This tree-planting seemed totally alien to me, but maybe this was what I needed.

After twenty years in the system, I knew I was highly articulate and had a certain degree of intelligence, but then again, after fourteen years in prison even a chimp would be well-read. Rehabilitation doesn't come from the prison system, as society may think. It was something I had to continuously decide to do. Many wouldn't believe that someone with my past could become a productive member of the community. Trying to put all the pieces back together wouldn't be an overnight thing. After twenty years in the system, you don't just forget about the abuse. Straightening myself out would take many years, if not the rest of my natural life.

One thing had become evident: I was now guarding my freedom as something sacred. Just one wrong turn and it would all be taken away from me. I had decided to do everything I could to remain free. I had no job skills, but regardless of what I found myself doing to earn a living, I would try and survive it by sheer determination.

From the moment I walked out of that hotel room, suitcase in hand, I never had a single regret, nor did I look back. I have never returned to Alberta. I wasn't too sure what lay ahead, but in my mind it had to be better than what I was leaving behind. This was going to be a major turning point in my life, a promise of a new beginning.

It was Tuesday, and I was to meet Tomo in three days. My only hope was that this would be enough time to complete the thousand-mile journey between us. I made the trip in three rides and arrived in Prince George the following afternoon. Someone was looking out for me.

I was dropped off two blocks from the hostel, which I immediately checked into. My final act before falling into a soundless twelve-hour sleep was to call Tomo and let him know I had arrived and was staying at the hostel. Then I made an appointment to see social services the following day.

Being hungry after a day and a half of traveling, I sat down to my first meal since leaving Edmonton. I had spent my last ten dollars on a pouch of tobacco, the only addiction I could never seem to turn away from. I awoke early the next morning to the smell of fresh coffee brewing from the kitchen down below. After a shave and shower, and putting on my cleanest clothes, I went in search of the smell. I had three cups of coffee with my breakfast and felt good about everything. I didn't know a soul, which was the way I wanted to keep it. When my laundry was done, I folded it in my suitcase and left it on the bed they had assigned me.

I went out and familiarized myself with this small but beautiful town that would be my home for the next year. First, I located the social services office. Since my appointment wasn't for a couple of hours, I went in search of the Nechako Inn. This is where Tomo was staying, and within a short while I was to find out it was widely known as the tree planter's meeting spot.

My appointment with social services could do no more than produce a check for a hundred dollars, but it was more than I'd had before. Walking through town, I wondered where I was, as there were hundreds of hippies. I was later to learn that most tree planters were either hippies, students on their semester break, or immigrants. People from all walks of life have tried tree planting, but only one out of every three is successful.

When Tomo showed up the next day, I was off for my first experience as a tree planter. We headed up to Chetwynd, located within the northern regions of British Columbia. In a tree-planting camp, your first priority is to find a suitable site and pitch your tent. This proved to be quite a chore. Next, I had to make sure all my gear was ready to go in the morning. I needed a planting shovel, the bags in which the seedlings were carried, and most importantly my work boots.

I learned quickly to make sure all the corks were in place, as they were one of the more important tools in this occupation, especially if you planned to make any money. The ground we traveled every day wouldn't only be covered with mangled trees left on the block, but slash (logs, branches, and stumps). Slash piles, as I was to learn, could be over ten feet high, but they were mostly left covering the ground.

Stumbling and falling down has been known to result in fatal injuries, as you could easily impale yourself. I found it essential every day after work to replace all missing corks on the bottom of my boots.

One of the first things you learn is screefing, where you remove any organic layer above the soil where the tree is to be planted. This usually consists of one or two swipes with your boot, but it doesn't necessarily work so easily all the time. You also need to take care of the extras—such as sunscreen, sunglasses, and a water bottle—so you don't become dehydrated. Lastly, you need a whistle, in case you spot a bear. All of this was new to me, but I was learning as I went. Remembering that I was the visitor in the bear's environment, the safest precaution was to tie a few loud bells to my bags. This way, I was sure to alert the bear to my presence, and also any other wildlife that might be lurking nearby.

The wakeup call sounded at five in the morning. From then on, I had about an hour to wash up, eat breakfast, and make my lunch from a variety of luncheon food spread out on the table. We all piled into different vehicles and drove for a half-hour up a dirt road into the wilderness, where we finally reached the clear-cut block or landing to be planted. This would consist of a vast tract of logged forest ribboned off in sections. Everyone, either in teams or on their own, was given a section which could extend two to three hundred yards long, by fifty to a hundred yards wide.

Between every three sections, there'd be a covered cache of seedlings. Everyone would fill their bags with two to three hundred seedlings per load. The more you could carry, the better; the pay scale was usually between fifteen and twenty-five cents per tree. Tomo was an excellent teacher, as well as a good planter. On any given day, he'd plant his normal fourteen hundred trees. If I got five hundred planted in a day, I considered myself lucky. At least for now, it seemed as though I had freed myself from institutions and the drug lifestyle.

With my shovel in one hand and seedlings in the other, we'd start up planting our line, with me following Tomo. I'd have to open a ten-inch hole in the ground with my shovel, stick the seedling in, then with my boot securely close the hole. Every five feet, a tree would go in the ground.

I'd follow in a different line five feet away, between Tomo's planted trees, putting in one of my own. This sounds easier than it is. Tree-planting is an art, and either you develop a rhythm or remain a mediocre planter, in which case you don't really make any serious money at it. After my first day, I realized just how monotonous and physically demanding tree-planting really is. Not only do you work in all kinds of weather, which can be very challenging, but also the terrain is best suited to a mountain goat. Had it not been for Tomo, my first day could have very easily been my last.

I must have stumbled and fallen down at least a hundred times. I received what seemed like a thousand mosquito bites, not to mention the blisters on both my feet. I had scrapes and cuts on both hands, along with rips in my new clothes. For all this agony and torture, I made about forty dollars, half of which went towards camp costs. Even if I really wanted to leave, where and how would I go? I had no money? After my first day, I truly felt as though I had substituted one prison for another. With each passing day, I was improving in technique and the number of trees planted. The frustrating part was watching someone like Tomo, known in tree-planting terminology as a "high-baller." He made it look like child's play, and made between two and three hundred dollars a day. A good many high-ballers were women, making it even more humiliating for me.

I have been in many scary situations, but nothing was to prepare me for the bush. In all the years I worked in the bush, my worst nightmare was the thought of running into a bear. Like many other planters, I was soon to be known as a "llama." They have their heads in the air, looking from side to side. Instead of planting trees, this seemed to be my favorite pastime. I was always on the lookout for bears.

Down around the landing, the section was bare and therefore easy going, but up on top, about a hundred yards from the tree line, it was all thick grass five feet tall and very dense. I never had a problem as long as Tomo was there.

No matter how horrendous the job was, tree-planting did have an upside to it. The food was excellent and you could eat as much as you wanted. On your days off, you could go swimming in the lake, and at the end of a planting contract, there were a series of great parties.

Tomo, having somehow decided I had enough training, wished me luck and headed back to Vancouver. I was doing all right, until one day a checker came over. A checker is someone who checks to see that your trees are planted correctly. He's probably even scarier than the thought of running into a bear. A checker has been known to break many planters so they never come back, with just one simple word: "Replant." Imagine the helplessness and frustration you would feel after five days of planting, in which you put a couple thousand trees in the ground, only to be told to replant them all at your own expense, as a result of screefing or unevenly spaced trees.

One day in talking with the checker, he wanted to know if I'd seen any bears. I asked him what he meant. He pointed to the tall grass up by my tree line and calmly said that grizzly bears liked to sleep in it. Now I was all freaked out. It took me a long time to feel safe again. I finally came up with a plan for how I would plant from then on. It seemed that being near the tree line was the most dangerous place to be. On my first run, I'd load up with trees and follow the lineup, then work from side to side, coming down from the top. This seemed to work out pretty well.

I stayed planting for the rest of the season, which was another three months.

You may be wondering how I managed to stay tree-planting, as I'd been a thief, drug addict, and con for nearly twenty years. There was always quick money to be made in the many things I'd tried before. By selling fake chains, I could make more in an hour than I would ever plant trees all day. So what would possess me to even consider tree-planting? Maybe it was the new beginning, or the way it gave me my pride back. Or perhaps it was knowing I could function in society by their rules, instead of those of the jungle. I noticed that everyone took an interest in me; they found me quite pleasant to be around. If you can endure the harshness of this sort of work, it will instill in you a rigid work ethic that will remain part of you forever.

My Last Prison Sentence 22

When the planting season ended, I returned to Prince George and rented myself a nice apartment. I tried tree-spacing with a chainsaw for a while, but my limited experience made it difficult to make any serious money at it. However, it was something I wouldn't close the door on; maybe in the future, down the road, I would give it another try. Being that it was firefighting season, I managed to secure steady employment with one of the many companies working in the area.

One day while having a few drinks in a local bar, I spotted an old family friend sitting a few tables away. I hadn't seen Johnny in more than twenty years. He was well-known as Jumping Jack, on account of how he was always moving from one spot to the next. He had worked for my dad back in the early 1970s.

I joined him and his friend Bruno, another Yugoslavian. We talked most of the afternoon. In terms of employment, Johnny proposed something to me which was far better and certainly less dangerous than my current line of work. How could I refuse? It paid more. Johnny was working for a guy who owned his own construction company. I was hired full-time, and over the next six months we built a new Mazda dealership.

Life really was looking up. I was seeing a beautiful lady named Cindy. However, due to my excessive drinking, the relationship was short-lived. I fell into a pattern of heavy drinking with Bruno and Johnny, who were themselves chronic alcoholics. And whenever I had periods of uncontrollable drinking in my life, you just knew what was coming over the next horizon…

In the bar one night, I met a woman named Donna, who was single and had a young daughter, Crystal. Donna's stepmom had known my brother Danny very well when she'd lived in Vancouver a long time ago. Danny had gone out with her daughter Margo, and her memories weren't good. Donna and I were immediately attracted to one another and had a crazy relationship, which lasted about a year. Had I known what lay ahead, I would have run away instead of moving in with her. Donna was a beautiful woman in her late twenties, and our drinking is what brought us together.

The first couple of months were great, but as in even the best of relationships, where there's substance abuse, there's bound to be problems. I was working in the forestry industry when we met, but I just couldn't keep up with the constant pace of drinking. My lack of proper sleep and not eating right wore me down considerably. All Donna wanted to do was party continuously, and when I tried to initiate a chance, to slow the pace down, it was met by fierce resistance, which often resulted in confrontations during which we'd scream at each other.

At one point, having had enough, I stayed at Bruno's for a few days. His being an alcoholic didn't help the situation. If anything, it just added fuel to the fire. After a long conversation on the phone, I decided to go and see Donna and try to patch things up. Naturally, we started drinking and an argument started up. While I was in the washroom, she phoned the police. This episode in court was to cost me either one week in prison or a five-hundred dollar fine, which I had a year to pay. I chose to pay the fine, as a year was a long way's off, and I could always not pay and just do the week. I now also had a restraining order, in that I was to keep away from her.

This time I got a room in the same building where Bruno lived. Donna started to come by to visit, but I was serious about putting my life in some kind of order. One day I called her and said that I was coming over to get all my stuff. She replied, "Don't bother, as you're not getting it."

Fuelled by alcohol, I thought to myself, *Enough of the Mickey Mouse games.*

I headed over to her house. Arriving there, I found that she had a two-by-four propped up against the door to give it added security. I started banging on the door, but she wouldn't open it. Instead, she phoned the police.

No sooner had I kicked in the door than four cops showed up. They jumped me as if I was a loose football in a game. Eventually they got the handcuffs on me and wrestled me into the back seat of the police car. Only when I was locked in a cell downtown did I start to realize the seriousness of my predicament. I was charged with breach of the restraining order, and with forcible entry as well.

I saw the duty counsel in the morning, before going into court, and I figured it was just a minor domestic dispute. I instructed the duty counsel to go and talk to the crown prosecutor, to see what I was looking at in terms of pleading guilty. I was thinking I would get probation, at most.

The lawyer came back, shaking his head. "You really must have a bad record, as their offer is a sentence of three to five."

"Months?" I asked.

"No, years."

At that point in time, there were many write-ups in the local papers about spousal abuse. It was and still is a big issue, and in me they found the perfect patsy. I sat in the city cells for almost a week before the duty counsel came to see me again. He told me that the Crown's final offer was that if I pleaded guilty, they wouldn't ask for more than eighteen months. Naturally, in view of my record, which certainly was not impressive, I took the deal. However, I didn't let the lawyer know what I had up my sleeve. I let him think he was going to represent me, as I needed him to do the legwork.

I wasn't allowed to talk to Donna, so I had him interview her. In a statement, she retracted everything she had said to the police. With this in my favor, I sat down and wrote a one-page presentation that I would read to the judge in my own defense. The crown prosecutor, true to his word, asked for a sentence of eighteen months. The judge asked me if I wanted to say something before he pronounced sentence. The lawyer had told me earlier that when we got to this point, I should say no and bow my head. Instead, I said that I did.

I didn't deny that the situation had occurred, as that's what would had been expected. I didn't try to put the blame on Donna, either. I went on to explain how we had both abused alcohol, and that even in the best of relationships, where there's abusive activity involving alcohol and drugs, there's bound to be a number of problems. I agreed that some form of punishment was required, in view of my breach of the restraining order, but I felt that eighteen months of incarceration was excessive; there was no rehabilitative purpose to such a sentence. The judge gave me six months of incarceration, followed by twelve months of probation. If I had taken the advice from that idiotic lawyer, I'd have done eighteen months in jail.

I was sent to the Prince George Regional Correctional Center, where I was required to take the spousal abuse program. This took a month, and then I was shipped to Huddle Lake Work Camp. The camp was okay. I liked the people I met, and my time went by quickly.

I guess I like adversity in my life, or I was just plain stupid, as I found myself writing to Donna daily. After two months, I requested to go back to the main jail with a month remaining on my sentence for what amounted to the stupidest of reasons. Donna couldn't come to visit, as it was too far. When I transferred back to the main jail, she only came to visit once. On the day of my release, she was there to pick me up and we spent five wonderful days together, and there was no drinking involved.

What could have been a promising relationship ended when eventually alcohol reentered the picture. I informed my probation officer that I was going to move back to Vancouver, and he made the necessary arrangements. When I was allowed to travel, I just left, as I knew Donna would have tried to talk me out of going. Little did I know, but Donna and I were to have one last encounter later in life, compliments of the attorney general.

When I was in Prince George, living at the rooming house, I made friends with Terry, a colorful character who said he was from New York. Often when he got in a drunken state, he would ramble on that at one time he had belonged to the Genovese mafia crime family. Whether fact or fiction, he did know a lot of details.

One day, we ran into a kid I had planted trees with, who just happened to had gotten in town from a camp. He had a pocketful of money. Due to lack of funds, as well the fact that it was dirt-cheap, we started drinking Yugoslavian stomach bitters—Travarica, which is forty percent alcohol. The kid came drinking with us, and my mobster friend figures he'd relieve the kid of his paycheck. I told him that I wanted no part of it, and I didn't want it happening in my room. The kid sensed that something wasn't right and decided to leave, with Terry right behind him. I don't know what happened, nor do I want to know, but apparently Terry gave the kid a couple of karate chops, a technique in which he was highly skilled.

Sometime later, while in Vancouver, I received a summons to appear in court in Prince George, as a witness for the Crown. I wondered what was going on and called them. Obviously, the kid had fingered Terry. Since we had been drinking in my room, my name had come up. I told them that nothing I could possibly say could be of any help, but it seems they wanted Terry badly. I told them that I had no funds, so I wouldn't be able to make the trip. They said that they were going to take care of all my expenses. So, including the four days I spent in a four-star hotel, where all I did was sign for everything, it ended up costing them a thousand dollars. I saw Terry a couple of days before the trial, and he was stunned to see me. I told him that the Crown was calling me as a witness, and he started shaking.

On the morning of the trial, he pulled me aside and told me not to put him in a jam, to which I replied that I was only going to tell the truth. On the stand, I said that we had all been friendly and drinking in my room for a couple of hours. The alcohol had started to seriously take effect, so the kid decided to go home. Within twenty minutes, Terry also left. Because they didn't leave together, this testimony got the case thrown out. Terry was a free man.

Outside the courthouse, I said to him, "I told you I was going to tell the truth, and now you owe me bigtime." He bought drinks all night, celebrating his victory. Donna stayed with me for the four days in the hotel, but I knew there would be no reconciliation between us.

My Friend Brad 23

When I originally left Prince George, I was living at my nephew's place. Now, on the bus ride back, I decided to get my own place. Upon arriving in Vancouver, I immediately rented a room in the downtown area, just a few blocks from all the drug activity. As I was on a collision course with disaster, what happened next couldn't have come at a better time.

I still had a fine to pay. Well, I didn't pay it, and one night I was picked up for being intoxicated in a public place. Now I had to serve a week in prison. You'd think, in view of what I'd already been through, this would have been a piece of cake. Let me tell you, that week seemed like six months. The only explanation is that for the first time, I was having serious withdrawal symptoms from the drugs.

Tomo once again came to the rescue. He definitely didn't like my downtown address, nor the direction in which I was headed, so he made a call to a guy he knew who had his own tree-planting company. Tomo had worked a couple of seasons for him; he explained my situation and asked him to give me a job, which he did. Within days of being released, I was on my way to the British Columbia interior, to the beautiful city of Vernon. The camp was situated on one of many surrounding lakes. There were only a few people around, as everyone else was at work. I found a suitable spot and pitched my tent.

Once everyone returned, I met the main characters who would play a role in my life in the years to come. I liked Brad the owner right from the moment I met him, and we remain friends to this day. Then there was his girlfriend, Lori. The camp's checkers were John and another Lori. John, I was to learn, had an incredible talent. He was an accomplished flutist, and at one time he played in a symphony orchestra. I have a few of his cassettes, as he now has his own band. I was fascinated by his extraordinary ability. In the evenings, we'd get a fire going. Providing he was in the mood, he'd bring out his flute and captivate everyone. There was no end to the variety of people one could meet while tree-planting. Finally, the story wouldn't be complete without mentioning Black Label Garth. He was an old-timer, from the old school. On a slow day, he'd drink at least twenty cans of beer. He didn't make any money planting, but it kept him supplied with beer.

The job almost didn't last, as I'd brought a couple of bottles of Travarica with me, a potent alcohol. One night while sitting around the campfire with seven planters, we drank the bottles. It took the kids three days to shake their hangovers. Never again would they drink something I brought into camp, unless it was something whose label they could read in English.

Looking back now, I'd have to say the company wasn't an important source of income for Brad. He came from a very wealthy family; his father could easily be considered one of the early pioneers of B.C.'s logging industry. Because of the many characters Brad employed, from all walks of life, it was more like entertainment to him. In a sense, this company and all its people became my new adopted family.

The part of planting I liked most was that you didn't just stay in one area. When a block was finished, you'd literally pack up camp and move to a different town, perhaps a hundred miles away or more. Each block brought its own new adventure.

After four months went by, the season ended. It was time for everyone to leave and go back to their families. For most, it was time to prepare for going back to school, with the promise of returning the following season.

Back in Vancouver, I rented myself a bachelor suite at the Sharp Villa Apartments, located on the south side. I lived there for eighteen months. I made a few close friends, like Terry, in his early fifties, who was a hardcore alcoholic. Due to financial hardships, he was comfortable drinking Chinese cooking wine. Let me tell you, it had quite a bite to it. I'd usually bring a good bottle when I went over to his place, but as our friendship progressed and my financial situation went from good to worse, I often found myself sharing in the cooking wine. Your environment and associations will eventually come to govern your lifestyle, as slowly you become part of it or it becomes you.

The best friendships I developed there were with Randy, his wife Linda, and their little son Michael (The Dude). They liked to drink, and not just occasionally. Randy was in the construction field and a very good worker. During this time, I had few relationships, all of which were short-lived; the women were often prostitute drug addicts.

I went tree-planting again the following year, and this time we moved camp twice. We went from Clearwater to Revelstoke. Tree-planting gave me a peace such as I hadn't yet experienced. It was like a vacation, and given the breathtaking natural beauty and spectacular scenery, I viewed it as my own private treatment center. During the season, the drug use was gone, to be replaced by positive people who not only never used hardcore drugs, but couldn't even begin to imagine such an existence. My health always improved tenfold, as I ate like a king three times a day, as opposed to once a day.

We had at least ten women planters in camp. I never tried to establish a relationship with any of them, and my reasoning was as follows. After so many years of being in prison, I couldn't imagine any woman without an addiction would want to share a life with me. From my standpoint, they would have a hard time empathizing with me, trying to understand some of the things I had done, even though I was trying to forget the past and get on with my life. The thing no one really understood was that I was constantly tortured. All I wanted was to be like everyone else, not the hardcore con drug addict, or whatever it was they perceived me to be.

In view of my extraordinary life, even upon meeting people today, or just observing them, I have no problem spotting the signs of addictions. Such was the case with one new fellow we had in camp. Within an hour of his arrival, I knew he had a drug problem; his mannerisms gave him away. He was an excellent planter, and had he stayed in this type of environment he may well have overcome his need for cocaine. We did, however, form a friendship, and after the season ended we took a bus back to Vancouver together. He checked into the Cobalt Hotel, where for a week we got heavily involved in drug use.

Eventually, I managed to break away from him.

HIV Confirmed 24

Recuperating for about a month in my apartment, this time I decided to try tree-spacing. One day I was over at Tomo's, where I met his friend John Doe. He had just finished a twenty-year sentence and was going to work in the bush. I asked if I could tag along, as I knew I had to get out of town. We went to the small town of Port Alice, located on the northern tip of Vancouver Island. I really enjoyed this work, as it made for strenuous physical activity. You have to wonder what was going through my mind, though, as the weather conditions were horrendous. It was December and we were twenty miles deep in the bush, surrounded by mountains. The snow was two feet deep on the ground and each time you cut a tree, snow from the branches fell on your head. It was very frustrating, but at the same time rewarding. Looking at this vast forest covered with snow from different vantage points was captivating. Regardless of the situation, the job wouldn't get the best of me. I would see it through to the end.

For months, I had been telling Tomo that I wasn't feeling well, and finally he set it up for me to go see his doctor. I liked and appreciated his professional service, as well as those of his receptionists, Anna and Helen. We developed a fond liking for one another, and were it not for this unique relationship, which has always been full of support and encouragement, I don't know if I could have survived the turbulent years to come. The doctor had me take blood tests, and when the results were ready I sat in his office in quiet thought, wondering what I would be told. After ten minutes, which seemed like hours, I was ushered into a small office and shortly thereafter joined by the doctor. We spoke a little, and then he told me that things weren't good.

"As of this moment, you are formally diagnosed as having the HIV virus," he said.

He sat there for a minute trying to read my face, perhaps thinking my expressions would give away my thoughts. I've poker-faced with the best of them throughout the years, and my present situation was no different from the others. Though this should have been crippling news, it really had no effect on me; I'd come to accept the reality that I'd always been playing Russian roulette, not only in the use of drugs, but also in my continuing involvement with prostitutes. This was just another obstacle I'd have to deal with. I understood my doctor's lack of direct knowledge regarding the issues surrounding this incurable virus, as he was a family practitioner.

I was totally in the dark about this illness, so I asked him what he could tell me. He said that a movie called *Philadelphia* had a good insight to it.

I went downtown to St. Paul's Hospital, where I had an appointment with Dr. Julio Montaner, the HIV/AIDS specialist. He was incredible, both professionally and personally. I could sense that his receptionist Patricia had a deep understanding of human nature, as she actually made me feel like a human being.

If I had immediately taken a plane back to the Island, as had been my initial intention, I wouldn't have seen Tomo for at least a couple of months. I decided to visit him at work and tell him face-to-face what was going on with me. Although he tried to repress his emotions, I could plainly see that the news devastated him. Before leaving, I assured him we'd get together when I returned from the Island.

About a month went by and *Philadelphia* aired on TV. I completely lost it watching this tragic tale. If this is what I had to look forward to, I definitely didn't want to reach the final stage of the illness. The movie heightened my sense of compassion and empathy. Two things became clear in my mind. Because of the seriousness of my illness, the last thing I need or wanted in my life was a woman. The thought of willingly or unintentionally infecting someone was horrifying in itself. For fourteen years in prison, I had used my imagination and a hand slippery with Vaseline. I would do the same now.

Secondly, I was concerned about winding up in a jam and returning to prison. I had no desire to die there. I wanted to control the decision of where, when, and how I was to die.

Once again, I started using drugs and drinking heavily. Really, I had no desire to continue working. What was the point? After partying with John for a week and seeing that this was going nowhere but down a dead-end street, I bolted like the roadrunner. I took a plane from Port Hardy to Vancouver.

I again saw Dr. Montaner, and he informed me of many things. He stressed that if I wished to remain healthy, drug use would be detrimental to my health. If I wished to persist in this activity, then regretfully my life would be short-lived. Another factor to consider was my alcohol abuse. I understood it was important to keep my liver functioning at a healthy level. He stated that I had to take charge of my life to ensure its continuance.

A great many things happened in 1995. Tomo showed considerable concern and bought me a book about AIDS. He located the local organization that dealt with the illness, called the PARC (People with AIDS Resource Center). The center was full of every imaginable piece of information one would need, but I don't think I read even one book on the subject of HIV. I thought I didn't need to mess up my head any more than it already was. I would just play it by ear.

One day while walking downtown I passed a bum sitting on the street in front of the Hong Kong Bank on Georgia Street. He had a sign asking for food or shelter. I couldn't believe my eyes. It was my old friend and crime partner Mac from Alberta. I grabbed some beer and we went down by the waterfront and talked for hours. while getting out of a burglary in a hurry, he had jumped from a second-story window, shattering both ankles in the fall. He told me he was living underneath some building now. I invited him to come stay at my place, which he did for a couple of months. He had a very simple life, when you think about it. He'd sit there for his eight-hour shift. A woman used to bring him a lunch from home every day and he'd make about seventy dollars a day, which paid for his dope, booze, and cigarettes. Every night when his day finished, he'd come home and we'd fix dope together. Tomo and I discussed that in view of my medical condition, he should phone my mom's sister and explain this to her, in the hope that she would relay the message to our mother.

For the 1995 season of tree-planting, I arrived in Lynton. B.C. Almost everyone noticed the change in my attitude and sensed something was terribly wrong. After a few days, I explained everything, as these were people I considered friends. I have been fortunate, as everyone I've crossed paths with has shown me respect in view of my illness, giving me tremendous encouragement and support. I've never had to deal with the rejection factor, which I'm sure often accompanies this disability which almost sixty million people share.

The stupidity and ignorance of rejection is inexcusable. Regardless of how a person contracts this incurable disease, whether from their own high-risk activity or due to circumstances beyond their control, they still deserve our respect. They're already at their lowest. Why strip them further of their dignity? Instead of treating them like outcasts, we should open our hearts with a little compassion, and hopefully some empathy. From my experience, this helps in a medical sense, as the stress of rejection can lend to the progression of the illness. A healthy mind aids a healthy body.

Three months of planting once again found me in great health, except I still drank excessively.

The end of the season was tough for me, as I had to say goodbye to most of these people for the last time. Returning to Vancouver, I went for my scheduled three-month blood test and it seemed that my liver count was at an alarming level. The counts were not to be above forty, but mine were at 341. This was puzzling to everyone, as I appeared to be in good health.

One day, while walking downtown, I ran into Ross, my good friend from Drumheller. He was very heavily into smoking crack cocaine, and it wasn't long before I was drawn into this activity. Crack cocaine—or rock, as it is widely known—is consumed by smoking it. You seem to get a better high this way rather than snorting or injecting the drug.

The most effective and inexpensive crack pipe available is an empty can of soda pop. They are very thin, which makes them easy to work with. The opposite end from the one you drink out of needs to be flattened, then six or seven holes are made. You then put a layer of cigarette ash over the holes, which prevents the melting crack from falling through. I learnt the hard way that a lighter isn't a good method for lighting the pipe, as it just gets too hot to keep holding upside-down. As a result, it wasn't unusual to see me with huge blisters on my fingers. Matches are by far the best way, as your rock melts by the time the matches burns. You inhale the vapor as the rock melts, holding it in as long as possible. The high lasts between ten and fifteen minutes. Knowing this, it's easy to understand how a couple hundred dollars a day just doesn't cut it, especially when there are three of you smoking. Crack cocaine addicts you after a very short period of smoking.

Not only did I have to deal with smoking crack, but I also contended with intravenous drug use. When Ross and Mac weren't around, my other friends were all heavy drinkers. You'd think eventually this destructive behavior would land me in the hospital, giving me a brutal awakening to the dangers involved. In view of my chronic substance abuse, and the amazement of my doctors, I've never been hospitalized and remain in great health.

Twenty-Five-Year Reunion 25

October 1995 was ending, but it wouldn't end without me seeing my mother for the first time in twenty-five years. I had a month to straighten out my act before she arrived. I got rid of Mac and Ross—without any ill feelings, as they realized the significance of the reunion which was about to take place.

Tomo and I waited at the airport for my mom's plane to land. I stood quietly, deep in thought. What could I tell her about the son she hadn't seen in over twenty years? No sooner did the thought enter my mind when instantly I knew the answer was nothing but the truth. To do otherwise would discredit her as my mother and me as her son.

Realizing this as the gates opened, I stood not in apprehension but exhilarated anticipation. How could one possibly begin to entertain the thought of not recognizing the woman who gave you life? As she came down the escalator, and from the very moment our eyes met, once again she was the mother I knew and I was the lost son. She held my trembling body as only a mother could.

This was a very emotional time for me, and for her as well.

"I love you and missed you, Mom," I said. She desperately needed to hear these words.

Her visit was a short one. It lasted only three days, as she didn't feel comfortable during her stay. She was very restless, which was understandable. She often found it necessary to try and justify why she had been in hiding all this time, trying in her way to explain all the facts regarding her marriage to my father, things we hadn't known as children. None of this mattered, as nothing anyone said could take away the deep love I had for her.

After twenty years of complete seclusion, such a reunion had a stressful impact. Even though we had a great visit, it wasn't long enough to explore all the submerged emotions that had been buried by the passage of time. As I silently watched her plane climb and then quickly disappear into the distant horizon, I was left in a state of surprised sadness, with an overwhelming longing for her quick return.

We spoke several times a year on the phone after this—until her next visit, six years later.

RUNNING WILD 26

I tried hard to stay away from using drugs, but I just didn't have the strength, courage, or (more importantly) the inner desire.

In December 1995, Mike and Danny came back from Toronto. Until he could get himself situated, Danny and his family lived with his son, Danny Junior. One night, Mike, Ross, and I were smoking crack cocaine when Danny and his common law wife Joanne came over for a visit. Danny despised all forms of drugs, as he had witnessed over and over again how they controlled people's lives. In the early 1970s, he had been involved in trafficking but he had never used drugs. His only indulgence was good alcohol, and even in this activity you would never see him intoxicated to the point where he didn't have control of himself.

It had been four years since we'd last seen each other, and even though Danny despised the drug activity going on, for the moment he tolerated it. Then he noticed Joanne hanging around the kitchen, where the drugs were being smoked

"Jo Jo, let's go," he said. "We're going home."

By his tone, you could tell it wasn't a request; it was a demand.

"You go," she replied.

Before anyone knew what was going on, Danny was on top of her. Even though there were five of us there, no one made a move to intervene. The attack had been severe, and quick. For her defiance, Jo Jo received a couple of kicks and five slaps. When Danny lost his temper, it didn't matter to him who was on the receiving end of his rage. Without a goodbye, holding Jo Jo by the scruff of the neck, they were gone out the door.

About a month later, my nephew's eight-year-old son Kyle was run over by a truck when he tried to cross the street. After an investigation was conducted, it was ruled that Kyle's death was an accident. The funeral spoke to just how well-liked this young boy was, as there were over three hundred people in attendance. Kyle hadn't even begun to reach his prime, but he already had an impressive list of accomplishments to his credit. I wasn't only enraged, but saddened beyond belief. I would have gladly sacrificed my life for his, as I'm sure he would have had a very successful and fulfilling life. I've often asked myself, why an innocent like him and not me? I had done nothing with my life. What was my purpose in this game we call existence? I really wasn't much of a religious person, but even I could see that I had a guardian angel or two watching over me.

In the summer of 1996, I went for one season of tree-planting for a company called Brinkman's. They were well-known all over the world. This time I went with Chris, a friend of Tomo's, who had never planted a tree in his life. He was a good kid and I liked him a lot. Our first stop was in Hinton, Alberta, where we stayed for about a month. Chris made me laugh a lot, as he thought there was nothing to planting. Once we got to the block, I showed him what was required and told him to just take his time, following my line. I got about a hundred trees in and turned around to see how he was doing. To my surprise, he was right behind me.

"What are you doing with the trees?" I asked, seeing that he was out of seedlings. "You couldn't possibly have planted them all."

He swore that each tree had been put in the ground. I noticed that he didn't have a shovel with him. As you need it to make the hole deep enough for the seedling, I asked him, "Where's your shovel?"

He said he didn't need it, so he left it by the road.

Curious, I went to have a look at what he was doing. All he'd done was jam part of the root into the soft ground, leaving about five inches of the root exposed.

I shook my head. "Let's go get your shovel, and I'll help you plant them properly."

Our next stop was Dease Lake, B.C., just a couple of hours from the Alaskan border, right near the town of Hyder. Everything seemed to be going well, except for the fact that it was a vegetarian camp and Chris couldn't stomach the menu. He lived on peanut butter sandwiches. What finally made us quit was that our final planting block was about a forty-minute drive from camp, and then you had to hike straight up the side of a mountain, which took the better part of an hour. One day, about halfway up, we both looked at one another with the same thought: *What the hell are we doing here?* We hiked back down and took one of the vehicles to camp, where we hit the boss up for an advance in pay, which was against policy. He gladly gave us one, just to be rid of us. This was definitely the end of tree-planting for me.

Randy, Linda, and I had spoken many times about renting a house together. Finally, in November 1996, we found a nice four-bedroom house that we could afford on 50th Avenue. The basement suite was available, and I got Ross to rent it. For the next six months, my life was one constant drug party. It got so bad that I started doing burglaries again with Ross, which I hadn't done since 1988.

Because of the volume of drugs we were consuming, and because there was no rational, organized thinking between us, one day I almost got caught. Everything we did was spur of the moment. One day, just blocks from where we lived, we came across an empty house. I guess we spent too much time circling the place, as one of the neighbors phoned the police. Before they arrived, I had boosted Ross through an open window. While waiting for him to unlock the front door, a cop identified himself directly behind me. He lightly grazed the back of my jacket as he reached for me. I bolted like a jackrabbit.

I never realized I could run that fast. The cop chased me for three blocks before I managed to give him the slip. Running the two extra blocks to get home, I was formulating my intended course of action. As soon as I got in the house, off came every stitch of clothing I had on. It went into the washing machine, along with the running shoes I was wearing. Turning it on, I ran past a startled Linda up the stairs, telling her to just say I had been home all afternoon. No sooner did I get in the shower than the police were in the house with the dogs.

They pulled me out of the shower and started questioning me. Unless Ross directly implicated me, they didn't have anything, as I knew the cops' dogs could easily have been following Ross's scent. As we were playing cat and mouse, the clothes I'd been wearing were being washed. Finally, they asked if I knew Ross. Sure I did; he lived in the basement. Knowing they had been beat, they left.

A week later, Ross was back. He had fabricated some story and was given a five-hundred-dollar fine. This incident made me realize how close I had come to returning to prison, for what could have been a very long time. From that moment on, I wanted nothing to do with any crime, or to have it associated with me in any way.

I didn't realize it but within a matter of weeks, without the benefit of any treatment center or counselling, I was about to quit drugs forever.

Another thing that made me think about what kind of animal I was becoming had to do with a woman named Karen. She used to come to the house and party with us. She was a hardcore alcoholic. Very often when she got loaded, she would talk about ending her life. One day, clouded by drugs and alcohol, I said to her, "Let's grab a case of beer and go to the park." It was about ten in the evening and we had drunk half the case when she started up again about ending her life. Just as she was taking a drink, I grabbed her by the throat and started slowly squeezing. I felt her go limp. Suddenly, thirty yards behind us, I spotted a person walking by. As I let her go, she started gasping, trying to get air into her lungs. Once she regained her composure, she told me that I shouldn't have stopped.

On the one hand, I understood the complexities of her inner demons. I truly felt her pain in my heart, as I too had indirectly wanted to end my life on many occasions. I found myself wondering what dreadful incident had happened to her. All she was doing was crying out for help, in what must have obviously been a very traumatic personal experience. After this, I spoke to her at length and we remained on friendly terms, but for understandable reasons I backed out of her life.

Danny was always interested in sharing a house together, so when the opportunity arose I jumped at the chance to rent his basement. Danny only had one rule: no drugs in the house.

The Process of Change 27

It is my observation, especially in regard to addictions and carrying out positive changes in our lives, that almost everything we do can in some way be considered an addiction, whether positive or negative in nature. In most cases, until these character traits become overwhelming, we're neither aware of their existence nor just how much they actually govern our lives. Most of my life has been played out in an arena of cold deception and calculated manipulation. My addictions and criminal lifestyle were so deeply ingrained that the only way I could truly rid myself of them was to find a stronger addiction. This seemed like an impossibility, although in a matter of days it would be as though I stepped into a different dimension, like something right out of the twilight zone.

It seemed inconceivable to me that I could ever completely detach myself from my tormented past of addiction, which for so long had created in me its own inescapable prison. I would face many obstacles and hardships along the way, possibly even more overwhelming than the reality I'd been living these past thirty years!

When I talk of change, I'm just scratching the surface. It's more complex than simply putting on a new pair of socks. In view of the rocky road that had been my life, thoughts of change generated paralyzing fear. Around every corner was the very real fear of failure. The unknown lingered in the shadows of my thoughts. Even when you know everything around you is negative, at least it's an arena of familiarity.

In reading my further adventures, you'll come to the same conclusion. Regardless of our circumstances, positive and constructive change is always possible. However, don't for a moment misunderstand me: it doesn't come easy. As in everything you want from life, there's a price to pay. Are you prepared to do whatever is necessary to succeed? Are you willing to go the whole nine yards? Change isn't only a lengthy process; to begin with, it takes a tremendous amount of courage and strength, coupled with great determination and persistence. It all begins with a desire. Where does this desire come from? It's the missing link. It could be a need for stability, acceptance, or unconditional love. The list is endless, but rest assured that we all desire something. Most people are fortunate enough to realize their desire, while others wander, lost in their own self-imposed hell, just trying to survive another day.

It has been said that the person who doesn't know where they're going in life, has no hope of ever getting there. Only through deep reflection will you be able to make a positive connection for a brighter future. Whatever it is you want in life, unless you have a continued desire to achieve it, your chances of achieving and fulfilling your goals and dreams are greatly diminished. The road to recovery is difficult.

Throughout this transitional process, you'll slowly begin to notice people who are willing to help. You must without reservations accept and welcome the support of these positive people, as they'll be instrumental in your recovery. If you believe you can do it on your own, you're not even out of the starting gate, and already destined for definite failure. Then there's the issue of disclosure; everything about you must become an open book, even if only to one person. This is imperative in your progression towards a positive transformation. Any hesitancy in this regard is a good indication that you're not ready to cross the street just yet. Also, you better learn to laugh at yourself a lot. Trying to straighten out and fly right is similar to learning to walk all over again.

You'll make many mistakes along the way. People will laugh at you, and some will look at you as if you're stupid. The easy way to handle ridicule is through anger. For me, it's all too easy to do the wrong thing. It comes naturally. I definitely had to harness this untamed anger, for it would lead me towards failure.

Why is change so difficult? I'll share with you an invaluable secret. The process of change revolves around many intricate factors, but in looking back now, I've come to understand the simplicity of this process. There's nothing difficult about effecting positive change; the difficulty comes from underestimating our own ability to change.

I don't have any theological degrees; my degrees come from the school of insufferable hardships. Only when unraveling the unimaginable in our lives can we truly begin to understand the unlimited certainties in the unexplored world of the extraordinary, which is all about the Sovereignty of God. I've often heard it said that Satan roams about looking for those he can kill and destroy. I'd like to briefly put this phrase in its proper perspective.

The words of Jesus are self-explanatory: *"The world cannot hate you; but me it hateth, because I testify of it, that the works thereof are evil"* (John 7:7).

We are all born into this world with a sinful nature. Satan leaves us alone, as he's already got us. However, from the moment we consciously decide to come to God, to the point of complete surrender through baptism in Jesus name, Satan wants to kill you; he knows the greatness you are destined to obtain. Once you are a new creature in Christ, as is clearly stated in 2 Corinthians 5:17, *"old things are passed away; behold, all things are become new."* This verse unquestionably speaks of transformation. When there's a progressive, positive transformation in your character, conduct, and conversation, your life becomes a thunderous roar of undeniable testimony.

Once you've been baptized as a new creature in Christ, the last thing Satan wants to do is kill you—and this is a fact. If I were to drop dead right now, just as the story of Job goes on living forever, my powerful testimony would continue to leave its influence and impact. Above all else, if Satan can get me to walk away from Jesus and go back into the unimaginable, then and only then will he succeed in extinguishing my testimony.

Hitting Rock Bottom 28

In looking at the shipwreck of my life, it seemed a safe bet to assume that when it came to the things of God, I was definitely what you would consider an unbeliever. Probably the only thing I believed in with any certainty was bad luck, as I've definitely had my share of it. You could have never convinced me in a million years that God existed. The Bible clearly states,

> *There hath no temptation taken you but such as is common to man: but God is faithful, who will not suffer you to be tempted above that ye are able; but will with the temptation also make a way to escape, that ye may be able to bear it.* (1 Corinthians 10:13)

In my blind ignorance, my argument was always the same: "Where was God during my early childhood abuses, which left its filthy stain upon my life? How can you believe in a God when you have no faith in your own parents?" I still felt the sting of my parents' callous abandonment. Surely a Sovereign God would have intervened at some point, during twenty-five years of criminality or my fourteen brutal years in prison. The cold indifference in my heart kept me void of all emotion. I just couldn't understand a loving God who would allow the continued torment of thirty years of chronic alcoholism and drug addiction.

To put the icing on the cake, as if I didn't already have enough on my plate, I also had to deal with HIV, which threatened to extinguish my life. I saw nothing but a dark, empty void ahead of me. There's a huge distinction between me and those who one day decide to become followers of Christ after seeing the light. It's quite something else to be chosen by God, to be plucked from the unimaginable depths of darkness, to become the miraculous! This may seem like a bold statement, but as I unravel the mysteries of my shattered life, you can draw your own conclusions.

There are many instances in the Bible where God took an absolute nobody and made them into a blessing to others. I was clearly a nobody. Even if I had been able to have somehow grasped Christian faith, would it really have been enough to bear the spears of discouragement and failure which daily hammered away at me as if fired from a machine gun? When you're standing in a pit surrounded by complete helplessness, how could it be possible to cling to an unseen and unknown faith?

I would now leave my past behind and venture towards a greater destination, one I had never before imagined or thought possible. What had appeared to be a hope beyond hope would soon be reality, a journey to the glory of God.

I received a call from the doctor's office on April 23, 1997, urgently requesting my appearance. I really wasn't in the mood, as I had been up most of the night partying. Looking in the mirror, I was a mess. My constant drug and alcohol abuse had rapidly progressed in the last couple of months. I was out of control. I knew that I had boarded that speeding train which was headed towards a final destination. In many ways, I welcomed the brick wall at the end of the line. I had nothing to look forward to, and this urgent appointment didn't look good.

As a result, I openly entertained suicide as my easiest and quickest escape. If there were a God, only He could now roll the dice in my favor. No matter how you looked at it, from all appearances I was beyond human repair.

I wasn't left waiting long in Dr. Webb's examination room. As the doctor came in, I noticed his uneasiness. It really didn't matter what he might have to say. I was happy to see him; to me, his expression seemed to confirm that I'd be leaving shortly. I could see out the window over his shoulder and the liquor store across the street.

The doctor himself looked everywhere but at me, then suddenly said, "Unfortunately, Mino, your HIV has progressed into its final stages. You're now in the process of slowly dying."

If he thought his directness would startle me, he guessed wrong. I was momentarily embraced in a feeling of complete emptiness, void of any external emotion. My whole life seemed to flash before me. On the inside, I felt as though the lid was coming off the pressure cooker. I wasn't mad, just lost in a state of helplessness. I could find no justification for all the suffering I had been through. My life seemed to lose all its meaning.

While in thoughts of self-destruction, for the very first time in my life I found the courage to ask God for a miracle. It's very strange that I would even make such a request, as I had never before embraced faith, or belief of any kind. I wasn't even sure if I was capable of doing this, as I don't ever recall having a hope that could have been extinguished. Almost from birth, my mind had been a continual habitation of one demon or another. The powers and principalities of darkness had manipulated my life like a puppet on a string.

Believe me, it wasn't a fluke that on this day, in exactly my fortieth year, I asked God to step in. I remember my feeble plea as if it were yesterday: "Big fella, if you're up there, I could sure use a hand right about now." My plea didn't represent any expression of remorse or helplessness. It didn't have a spark of sincerity to it, nor was there anything in its simplistic ignorance to suggest God would even want to listen. Even as I softly mumbled the words, I knew the plea would go unanswered.

Without realizing it, I had just invoked the greatest promise given to mankind! However, it would be another fourteen years before I fully came to realize it. All I knew with definite certainty was that my life was quickly reaching its tragic conclusion. No matter what anybody thought, there would be no reprieve for me.

One of my favorite verses in the Bible is found in the book of Jeremiah 33:3. There can be no greater promise from God Himself: *"Call unto me, and I will answer thee, and shew thee great and mighty things, which thou knowest not."* It's a three-part promise of direct interaction between God and His creation. We first need to call upon him, and He will answer. As a child playing, you could be off somewhere out of sight, but when your father cries out your name, you don't ignore him; instead you recognize his familiar voice and quickly respond. Since our God is one of complete order, anytime He talks to anyone, rest assured it will be in that recognizable, familiar voice. As long as we remain obedient to His call, God will show us—through signs, wonders, and miracles—great and mighty things which exceed our wildest expectations. Don't ever forget this. Jesus came to *restore* all the things that Satan destroyed.

Regardless of how or where I called out to God, the essential requirements of a just prayer were met. It didn't matter to God whether my plea was one in faith or complete unbelief, as they are closely related. The necessity of brokenness was clearly evident. In my helplessness, I had lost all confidence in myself and the world around me. In that moment of despair, I had momentarily stepped into another dimension, gone beyond the walls of this world and asked for God's help. Imagine for a moment a God whose very breath and Word created the universe, speaking to us just as He spoke to Abram: *"And I will make of thee a great nation, and I will bless thee, and make thy name great; and thou shalt be a blessing…"* (Genesis 12:2–3). These same promises have always been available to us.

As you've read my story, you might agree that my name wasn't great, that I wouldn't be a blessing to anyone. However, the following words go beyond human expression. They'll eternally be a tender endearment inscribed upon my heart. Each time I meditate upon them, the indestructible nature and resilient power of God's spoken words embrace my soul in a merciful reminder of His amazing Sovereignty: "No one but God, the very pulse of the universe, could make such promises. No one but God Almighty could deliver such promises. More importantly, no one but God Himself could enforce such promises."

While exploring the complicated and entwined paradoxes of my life, the evidence clearly and unmistakably manifested itself. God had all along patiently carried me, and it didn't matter whether it was in faith or unbelief. He was waiting for my cry of help, which ignited a spark of hope with fierce and persistent determination. Anyone who God brings forth as a messenger has already been authenticated by Him. Don't ever fool yourself: miracles aren't a result of God having something He wants to say or do. Before anyone is ever willing to listen, one first has to *believe* in the existence of God. Through signs, wonders, and miracles, God performed the supernatural through all His chosen ambassadors, so people would know that these men were of God, and spoke the truth.

I finally realized that Dr. Webb had been talking to me. Lost deep in my own thoughts, I never heard a word. He had his receptionist book me another appointment, two weeks from then. The receptionist also gave me the telephone number of an HIV specialist who urgently wanted to see me. I crumpled the piece of paper in my jacket pocket and assured them I would call, all the while knowing I wouldn't. The best thing anyone could do for me was show mercy and give me a loaded gun. I shook the doctors' hand before leaving, and I don't think he suspected this would be our last meeting. I wouldn't be back. My fate had been pre-determined.

I phoned my friend Ross, telling him that I'd come over to see him in a few hours. Together, we would have a wild weekend. I was in a partying mood. Hanging up the phone, I headed in the direction of the liquor store.

I grabbed a couple bottles of Jack Daniels and headed for the nearest park, just a few short blocks away. I desperately needed to collect my thoughts. After several drinks, I was angry at everyone. I looked everywhere except within myself for reasons to justify what was happening. The worst of my problems was my inability to find a glimmer of hope to somehow lessen the harshness of what remaining existence I had left. These thoughts of self-destruction further weakened my resistance. The odds were insurmountable. If I was in fact dying, I would choose my own destiny in ending my life. It definitely wasn't going to be as a result of an HIV infection or the horrific illness known as AIDS.

An overdose from drugs looked like a welcome alternative.

Finally, I got on the bus and headed towards Ross's place, not caring if that's where it was all going to end.

Daniel, while in prison, prayed nonstop for three weeks before an angel of the Lord visited him, saying that his prayer had been heard on the first day he spoke it. Here was a man who walked with God most of his life. He believed and prayed constantly for three weeks for God's intervention. Have you ever asked yourself why people in the Bible prayed as they did? It's because they had an expectation that God would answer their prayer. I, on the other hand, never wanted to know God.

It's often said that you must first hit rock bottom before you can put the pieces back together. I was beyond rock bottom. What was about to take place in the following three days could only be described as having one foot in the grave. All I needed was a little push and for someone to close the lid on the coffin to contain the smell.

However, from the moment I uttered my feeble plea, God was already at work in my life. The events which were about to take place would change its destructive course forever. But first, I needed to be stripped of everything.

Separation and Faith 29

Our greatest stumbling blocks in life will always be found in the principles of establishing and maintaining a persuaded faith. Even though it now seemed like I continually stepped into the miraculous, it took many years before my hardened heart was unshackled to the unmistakable truths I so passionately write about. The process of actually stepping into an unwavering faith, which will not be moved or shaken, really isn't a great mystery. I'm here to tell you that the beginning of all wisdom starts with the fear of the Lord. As strange as this may sound, regardless of what Satan has thrown your way or how weak you may think you are in mind or body, if you sincerely desire to break free and separate yourself from worldly spirits of suffocating oppression and depression, whose only desire is your destruction, there is a way out—and it's all about Jesus.

In the moment when you surrender your life to Jesus, He'll place His hand upon you. When He does, nothing in this universe can come against you without His consent. It saddens my heart that with such blessed assurance, many today would rather turn their backs on the promises of God and drown themselves in the storms of their lives, unwilling to make an attempt at survival. The heart of God is full of sorrow over this; why would you allow the enemy of all mankind to have victory over your soul?

However, before anyone will be willing to consider entering into a journey of deliverance from invisible principalities, they first need to be persuaded as to whether such things even exist. As history confirms, the greatest impacts on individuals, communities, and nations come as a result of personal experience. In this, the uniqueness of my testimony is immeasurable. If you're truly looking for a way out, perhaps my story will help persuade you.

Three characteristics clearly present themselves in all those who have been used mightily by God. They have an abundance of situations in their lives which they couldn't have fixed on their own. Also, the things that come against them are beyond their control, because they are preordained by God. Understandably, many have a hard time trying to wrap their minds around this concept, but in the coming chapters I will persuade you of even that. Lastly, their lives will have been miraculously transformed from crippling impossibilities to living realities.

Many will strongly oppose these claims, regardless of whether or not they are biblical. Let's then look at a miracle from the world's perspective. It's said that a miracle is an event which has no human explanation, therefore by scientific admission it can only come from beyond the walls of our present realty.

In order for someone to have such a testimony, firstly their life's journey will have left a trail of tests to pass. For such a person to be considered triumphant, they'll have suffered and endured through many trials. To be truly considered victorious in these battles of unseen principalities, a kaleidoscope of insurmountable obstacles must exist to be miraculously overcome.

During the first fifty years of my life, I didn't so much deny the existence of God as I could never bring myself to entertain such a concept. Now, after four years as a born-again Christian, baptized in the wonderful name of Jesus, I'm here to tell you that I don't need anyone to try and convince me. As sure as I'm breathing, I know that He stepped into my life and supernaturally turned it around. I haven't only survived crippling impossibilities, but had them wiped out as though they never existed. These are miracles of astronomical proportion.

However, my journey has been nothing short of a mathematical improbability. Countless people can't seem to break free of the suffocating nooses in their lives. The number one reason is that they've admitted defeat without going that extra mile.

I find it very strange that so many today oppose any form of religion, yet everyone on the face of the planet at some point, whether directly or indirectly, desires God's intervention in it. You'd be a complete fool not to have. No one wants a progression of hardships, poverty, and illness in their life. Even those who have never opened a Bible have hoped for the miracle they never expected or believed in, and no one understands this better than I do. There really is an invisible presence of darkness all around us. Throughout most of my life, a dark cloud of oppression embraced me like an ill-fitting coat. The more I struggled to remove it, the tighter it wrapped itself around me.

We've all entertained thoughts of changes, but without recognizing them as such, those changes always bring with them a degree of fear. If we could only, for a moment, grasp what's really going on. That fear was never ours to begin with; it belongs to that oppressive force known as Satan. Think about it for a minute! When the tide is about to turn in your life, that's when all hell seems to break loose and come against you. Satan's worst nightmare is that you might discover the potential of your true glory.

Our lives are very much like a jigsaw puzzle. For some of us, trying to put the pieces together becomes its own obstacle course. However, from the moment we allow Jesus into our lives, we enter an extraordinary journey of self-discovery in which the once broken and shattered pieces are put back together again. Imagine! Where there never existed a glimmer of hope, suddenly you find yourself at that elusive crossroads, where the physical world meets the spiritual one.

Regarding faith and belief in the unknown, many of us lose sight of a simple yet powerful principle. Every time I experience moments of weakness or doubt, and we all have, I pull back the curtains of those faded memories of so long ago, exposing a nightmarish past. Ever so briefly, I travel down the roads of my greatest and fiercest trials. Whether saint or sinner, we need to constantly remind ourselves of where we would be had He not intervened in our lives. Only now, looking back upon my life, can I see it with clarity.

Each and every time I step into the unknown dimension of God's presence, His Holy Spirit takes control of my life, its supernatural power guiding my every step. As long as I am willing to follow its direction, I cannot fail.

Hopefully I'll be able to help you better understand your own Red Sea experiences, and we've all had them. When it comes to acknowledging the existence of an unseen God, many are stopped dead in their tracks. Always keep it in mind that the God we worship, the creator of the universe, is not made of flesh and bones. He is a spirit, and unless He chooses to reveal Himself to us, He will remain invisible to the human eye.

As with anything in life, whatever you desire, there's a process in obtaining it. Unfortunately, this is also true when it comes to stepping into the presence of God. It never used to be like that. From the moment we were created in God's image, He continually desired to be in our presence. However, with the entrance of sin through man's disobedience, God's holiness demanded that He separate Himself from us. God continued to speak to us, but it could only happen through His chosen messengers—His spokesmen—through signs, wonders, and miracles. The reason God has chosen to speak through individuals rather than speaking directly to the people is that we always question and rebel against authority, even God's. More importantly, it doesn't take Him quite as long to get an individual's undivided attention.

So why did God choose me? He could have chosen many that were more worthy than I was, and certainly more obedient. After considerable thought, I've come to this conclusion: my most important characteristic is that my life has literally been drenched in human suffering. It escapes rational comprehension. Certainly my resilient and determined nature is an admirable quality. However, it wasn't the climbing out of the pit, but rather the *miraculous transformation* that sculptured my character, testifying to God's amazing love, mercy, and grace.

It is said that when you ask God for anything, as long as you're willing to walk in His way, He will enter your life, and from His grace shall flow an abundance of goodness. My life still had many trials and tribulations; it would take another ten years for me to register the significance of the divine intervention. The events about to unfold could certainly be considered a supernatural phenomenon. Some would dismiss them as blind luck, but the reality is that God was about to step in, and nothing could change what He had planned.

Again, you be the judge.

Miracles of Restoration 30

After three days of constant partying, I looked as though I had just crawled out of a grave. My clothes were dirty and smelly, and I looked horrible. Just about broke, I headed in the direction of the nearest bar, just a few blocks away. Catching my reflection in the glass doors of the beer parlor, I decided I looked like somebody's worst nightmare. As I entered, all eyes were on me. Truthfully, I couldn't understand how they even let me in, never mind served me a drink.

I needed both hands to lift the glass of beer to my lips, as my hands were shaking with an intensifying frequency. I knew all too well that the withdrawal symptoms would soon be so severe that I'd get unpredictable. Each time I took a drink, I could see the surrounding people staring openly. Regardless of why these people were staring at me, what they didn't understand was that when I stared back it was through the eyes of a predator sizing up its next prey. What was about to take place, I'm now convinced, wasn't of this world. No human explanation can justify it.

Out of nowhere, a woman appeared and sat down across from me, trying to strike up a conversation.

"Listen," I gruffly said, "you don't want anything to do with me. I'm no good to myself, never mind to anyone else. Just leave me alone."

Seeing that I was extremely rude, the woman got up and went out the front door. It couldn't have been more than thirty seconds later before she was standing right beside me again. Without a word being spoken, she gently took my trembling hand in hers. It was as though an electric current passed through me. Fifteen years have now passed and I still clearly remember everything as if it happened yesterday. The only explanation I have is that it was spiritual in nature.

God, in answer to my plea, had sent an angel my way—and it only took three days. I believe that when she left the first time, God turned her around. When she grabbed my hand, time stood still; God parted the curtain which separates the physical world from the spiritual. If God has ever spoken to me, it was in that moment: "Mino, my precious son, I know you've had a life full of insurmountable hardships and sorrows, but it had to be that way. You see, I have a special purpose for you, and it's now time for you to fulfill that role. If you really desire a change in your life, you must take the first step. I've sent this angel to help you in the journey."

Without questioning anything, I got up and walked out of the bar with this woman, whose name I didn't even know. I know it sounds ludicrous, but here's the first miracle. From then until now, I've gone fifteen years without ever going through drug rehabilitation or counseling. I never touched drugs again. The addiction was miraculously gone, as though it never existed.

I couldn't understand what was going on. From the moment this woman took my trembling hand in hers, I was embraced in a cloud of warmth and tenderness like nothing I had ever experienced. Given my appearance, the attraction was *not* sexual in nature. Six weeks would pass before we decided to enter into a relationship, which continued up until her death a short five years later.

I learned later that evening that her name was Debby, and she was a forty-one-year-old single mother with an eight-year-old son named Jayson. She took me home and put me in a hot bath. Once she had my filthy clothes in the washing machine, she returned with razor in hand and proceeded to give me a shave. I seriously thought she was a nurse or caregiver of some sort. As she handed me a housecoat, I didn't ask whose it was. It seemed to fit. She sat me down at the dining room table, where I enjoyed my first meal in three days. After I finished eating, she took me upstairs and put me in her son's bed, where for the next twelve hours I fell into a soundless sleep. I was to learn much later that while I slept, she sat in a chair watching over me.

In the following three days, Debby, with the extraordinary depths of her compassion, understanding, and affection, raised me from a pit. She became my nurse, my mother, and more importantly, my guardian angel. What made her so unique was that for the last seven years she had suffered from multiple sclerosis, a crippling disease in its own right which immobilized her coordination. Even though she was only five feet tall and weighed in at a hundred pounds, she was always very energetic, steady on the go. Jayson, as we were to eventually learn, was also at a disadvantage, being diagnosed with attention deficit syndrome.

I woke up in a terrible sweat, my body shaking violently. This could only be rationalized as some form of withdrawal. Again, Debby bathed me and literally hand-fed me. I still remember her holding me in her arms, ever so gently rocking me back and forth, assuring me that everything would be all right, until I once again fell asleep.

With Debby's help, I'm convinced those three days were a major breakthrough in regaining control of my life. Imagine the beauty of this extraordinary woman's character, which went beyond commendable, completely ignoring the filth and stench of my appearance. She opened her heart and brought a total stranger into her home. Maybe she somehow knew I was on the verge of becoming nothing more than a faded memory.

Or perhaps it was destiny.

On the third day, I phoned my brother Danny to let him know where I was. Strangely enough, my friend Brad was with him and wanted to see me. I said I'd be there within the hour.

Even somewhat cleaned up, I looked rough. I didn't know where to begin to thank Debby. She set the atmosphere in letting me know that she wanted to see more of me. Before leaving, I assured her she would.

True friendship comes from the heart, with no limitations attached; this was proved in Brad's response to seeing me. He could only shake his head. I realized it wasn't in disgust, but rather empathy and deep concern. In that instant, he probably decided how he was going to try and help me. He told me to pack a small bag, as I was going with him to Armstrong, B.C. He had a beautiful forty-acre spread on the side of the mountain. In order not to strip me of what little dignity or pride I still had, he said he had some work for me to do.

I did lots of yard work, but this was basically just to keep me busy. Whether it was destiny or unknown forces at work, Brad nursed me in his own way for two weeks, bringing my health back to an acceptable level. As he didn't drink, there was no option for me to do so either. Most of my thoughts centered on Debby. I knew she was the missing link in my life. Once we entered into a relationship, a unique bond was formed, and we became inseparable, two great oak trees standing side by side deep in an untouched forest.

Brad mentioned that he had a new venture about to start up in Squamish, a small logging town about an hour's drive from Vancouver. He wanted me to become involved in creek-cleaning. I thanked him very much for all he had done for me and reassured him that when he was ready to start work, I would definitely join him.

When I arrived back in Vancouver, everyone was greatly impressed with the status of my health. I had some blood work done, and a week later I went to see Dr. Webb to get the results. I was in great spirits when I found out that my CD-counts had gone from 270 back up to 900.[6] I was spending a lot of time with Debby, and we started the slow process of a courtship.

I sincerely believed this relationship was to be forever, as our love for one another was never in doubt. In the years we were together, I tried to be all I could and then some. Debby was a wonderful partner and loving mother to Jayson. However, she had her own demons that just wouldn't let go. She had an ongoing alcohol addiction, and in view of her medical condition, which directly affected the central nervous system, she was continuously reminded of the dangers of drinking. After two or three drinks, her motor skills became very impaired.

I soon met two of Debby's ex-boyfriends. The first was Wayne, Jayson's dad, although the parentage is questionable, sometimes even by him. He has never done me wrong, but I've always had a hard time accepting him as a friend; he was selfish and extremely obnoxious. For the most part, he was tolerated. The second ex was Donny, and to this day I have a solid friendship with him. Donny had a protective nature about him, and it took six months before we actually felt comfortable with one another. I also met Debby's best friend, Jessie, and realized that she was dealing with her own demon—bipolar disorder. These were just a few of the many people who each in their own way helped to shape my life into what it is today.

Since I was spending most of my time at Debby's, I gave Brad her number. Debby lived in a beautiful three-story, two-bedroom townhouse. In June 1997, I moved in with her and Jayson.

One of the first things Debby did, as she was an extremely organized person in all areas of her life, was to help me restore all my personal identification, which I had lost in 1973 and never bothered to replace. She just couldn't understand how a person could live for twenty-three years without identification. I was surprised at how quick the process was. I soon held a valid driver's license. Within weeks, I went from riding a stolen bicycle to an appearance of respectability; I now drove her car.

---

[6] The CD-count measures the level of CD4 helper T-cells in one's body. These are cells that vital to immune function, but are the target of HIV. As HIV gradually depletes these cells, the body becomes less able to defend itself from a wide range of opportunistic infections.

Near the end of June, Brad called and said we would be starting work in a matter of days. Monday to Friday, we'd be staying in Squamish, having our weekends free. Debby, as was her nature, packed me a duffel bag with everything imaginable in it. However, the most important considerations were found in her many handwritten notes. In my four months of working in the bush, I always looked forward to unpacking and finding her little hidden treasures; I was to learn so much more of this extraordinary woman.

Creek-cleaning, which became an artistic expression, took place in what could only be described as God's country. Each morning, we would drive for an hour into the wilderness, on what appeared to be long abandoned logging roads. Then we hiked on foot to the intended restoration site. I should thank the environmentalists, as without their love for the preservation of nature's beauty I'd be out of a job. When the block of land had originally been logged, the creeks that ran through the forest had been destroyed. Our job was to restore them. This was a time-consuming process. Brad's son Brook and I, armed with chainsaws, would start at the bottom, by the existing tree line where the creek was supposed to tie in. We would slowly work our way up, cutting a six-foot berth which wound its way up hundreds of yards through dense rotted logs. The creek once again began to take on a new life of its own. Hopefully it would remain undisturbed for decades to follow, as the newly planted seedlings grew.

It was physically demanding work, although I can't begin to describe the satisfying reward. When each restoration was complete, we would just sit in silent awe at the newborn creek in its majestic beauty. I have hundreds of pictures. Sometimes there would be three restorations in the same block. After four months, the project was terminated due to the cost involved. I thought any price was small compared to the damage caused by logging companies. Seeing the creeks restored was priceless. Even now, in reflection, someone should and must be held accountable.

Often while taking a break on the block, my mind would slip into the nightmare of what had once been my life. I still never reflected on issues of spirituality, as I never professed or proclaimed myself to be a man of faith. After thirty years of surviving through deception and manipulation, I was an expert in the complicated art of treachery. I had seen it all.

Frightening HIV Decisions 31

From the moment Debby entered my life, almost twenty-five years of narcotic drug addiction was wiped out. I still drank, however, as did Debby. It only took a few drinks for her unpredictability to rise to the surface; she would become as deadly as a loaded powder keg, looking for a match.

Even though she and Donny had been separated for a number of years, it wasn't uncommon to find them in a heated argument. When I returned home for the weekend once, I walked through the door and knew something was terribly wrong; I could literally feel the tension in the air.

A couple of nights before, a neighbor had phoned the police, who didn't just break up the argument between the two, as there seemed to be a pattern of progression. Being that a child was caught in the middle, the police involved the social services department, who basically gave Debby an ultimatum: either she would straighten her life out and quit drinking or she would lose Jayson the next time. To make matters worse, several complaints had been made to the apartment caretakers, and she received a three-month eviction notice.

She had run out of options. It was either quit drinking or lose her son.

"Debby, if you're serious, let's quit drinking together," I said in all seriousness. Tears of respect welled up in her eyes. "As to the eviction notice, we'll start looking for a house."

She readily agreed, and it wasn't long before we found a cozy two-bedroom house. My health was rapidly improving, probably as a result of the demanding work, fresh air, and proper diet. Everything seemed to fall into place... well, almost everything. Dr. Webb's words constantly thundered in my ears: "Mino, your HIV has progressed into its final stages. You're now in the process of slowly dying." How could I get around that? Debby was almost to the point of nagging, twenty times a day, for me to go see the specialist. Finally, she broke through my stubbornness and I made the appointment.

Dr. Montaner put before me a proposal regarding an HIV drug trial involving one hundred participants worldwide. Ten of those people would be from Vancouver. With my viral load rapidly escalating, amongst other factors, he felt I'd be a responsive candidate to these treatments. I liked him a lot, as he didn't sugarcoat things. And why should he, with people's lives held in the balance?

He gave me all the necessary forms and information regarding each drug, outlining the side effects, which were both horrific and numerous. I told him I would take everything into consideration and let him know within a few days.

Unclouded by drugs or alcohol, I was able to make a rational judgment. I discussed the matter over with Debby and Tomo, carefully weighing all the facts. I didn't totally understand why I had been asked to participate, but I assumed the infection was taking control of my body. I must have read the information Dr. Montaner gave me at least fifty times.

In reaching my decision, for the first time in my life I experienced genuine fear. Firstly, there was no guarantee that the medications would work, and there also remained the very real possibility that the drugs could speed up the progression of AIDS. Secondly, the only studies researchers had conducted so far had been with monkeys, many of which had shown abnormalities. It wasn't known whether these same abnormalities could happen in humans! At one time, this would have been enough for me to say the hell with this, but I promised the specialist I would take every piece of information into consideration.

Lastly, there was the issue of side effects. The most frequent side effects could include rashes, diarrhea, headaches, fatigue, abdominal pain, dizziness, herpes simplex, insomnia, vomiting, back pain, along with a host of other things. The major side effects included inflammation of the pancreas (which in some cases had been known to be fatal), pain in the arms and legs, and leukopenia (a decrease in white blood cells), which could result in organ failure, anemia (a decrease in red blood cells), hair loss, hallucinations, and convulsions along. There were many more.

No one knew what my decision would be, as this decision needed to be made by me alone. I knew I would participate, though, because up to this point my life had been one adventure after another. Regardless of the outcome, by participating I was placing myself on the front line of a long struggle to maintain this devastating illness. I couldn't just think of myself; my participation would make a difference for other people. This decision was met by approval, along with encouragement and support from everyone associated with me.

As it turned out, it was one of the most important and promising decisions of my life.

Positive Transformations 32

In September, we were finally able to move into the house we had rented. I couldn't remember when I had been happier. The only thing missing was getting to marry this wonderful woman who had given me a new lease on life. As creek cleaning came to an end, I secured a job with a company that made pre-fab trusses for roofs. I couldn't have envisioned a better home life, although Jayson proved to be quite the challenge.

Since I've known Jayson, he's displayed a high level of intelligence. He was always one of the smartest kids in his class. He seemed to act more like an adult than a little boy. I now understand why: any child growing up in an atmosphere of alcohol abuse either falls into a similar pattern of dysfunctional behavior or grows up in an awful hurry.

Dealing with his anger was a different matter. We weren't aware of his hidden disability at the time. Some days, he would blink uncontrollably; or, instead of blowing his nose, he'd loudly draw this back into himself. After any period of time, it became very annoying. We could see it really bothered him. I felt helpless, as I had no way of helping him.

I knew one thing for certain: his anger, if not harnessed now, would rival my own temper as he got older. Being so young, he had no fear. When this Tasmanian devil got mad, he would black out and fly into a rage. Ten minutes later, he'd be having a wonderful conversation with me as though nothing had ever happened. I'd step in when he violently argued with his mother, and he'd storm off, telling me where to go, slamming his door. Ten minutes later, he wouldn't remember the incident.

As I learned more about attention deficit syndrome, I began to empathize with him. It seemed that stress was the main trigger; however, like anything else in life, you learn to adapt. I thought a dog might help relieve some of his tension, so one day I brought home a four-week-old Labrador. He had a black coat with a white chest and Jayson named him Toro. As Toro got older, we learned he wasn't pure lab, but a pit-bull cross. We still loved him.

My employment opportunities constantly improved. The laborers union finally called, after years of waiting, and placed me in a company that performed repairs at grain elevators. Our job was to chip, sandblast, and patch the outside of the silos while suspended in a little spider cage as high as three hundred feet. Every morning, Debby would pack me a lunch. It was more like a regular cafeteria, as there would be enough there to feed the entire crew. Again, I'd find hidden notes in my lunches, in which she expressed her love for me. I was very content and happy.

I was taking my medications regularly. Debby took it upon herself, after reading a book on HIV, to go out and buy certain vitamins she felt would benefit me. Every morning, she'd make sure I took all my pills along with the vitamins. Unbelievably, after just four months on these new trial medications my viral load disappeared, leaving all traces of HIV undetectable. Occasionally, when I was drinking, my liver count would climb to alarming level. Also, my weight went from 150 pounds to 185. My other tests showed an overall improvement.

Amazingly, to this point I'd had no side effects whatsoever, and I could tell that everyone at the trial center was very impressed with my progress. I also began to consider the full implications of my illness, not only medically but socially. I understood the various ways the virus spread. I had no more involvement in drug use and didn't miss it at all. My concerns, however, had to do with social interaction. Violent physical confrontations had to be avoided at any cost. It's easy to say, "HIV… it'll never happen to me." That's a famous last line for many who become ensnared in its web. Here's something everybody should consider when deciding to get involved in a fight: the person you find yourself challenging may be HIV-positive. A person's reluctance to fight shouldn't be looked on as a sign of weakness or lack of courage. As everyone infected with this illness knows, a punch in the mouth could result in the aggressor contracting HIV, through no fault of their own.

My drinking went from excessive to moderate, to ensure no unnecessary altercations arose. I quit going to regular pubs and only drank in Canadian legions. Debby and I went without drinking for about five months. On our first Christmas together, however, we did the unthinkable. On Christmas Eve, Debby and I decided to get a bottle and have a few drinks at home. An argument erupted, spoiling the whole spirit of Christmas.

Another issue I had a hard time dealing with was the ever-increasing influence of her so-called friends. I hold them partially responsible for our relationship falling apart. The only one who fully acknowledged how well we were doing and how far we had come, and meant it from the bottom of his heart, was Donny. No one else really gave me the credit due. Everyone knew of Debby's health problems and the fact that we were trying not to drink. Most of her friends were phonier than a three-dollar bill, and were easy to spot. On the one hand, they would tell me how we all had to watch out for Debby, yet they'd go to the pub with her. Most of Debby's friends had their own problems, and if they weren't strong enough to deal with them, they should have distanced themselves from our lives. The people you hang around with on a daily basis—be they successful people, drug addicts, or criminals— will eventually draw you into their lives; you'll become as they are. This is an undeniable fact of life.

Shortly after we got settled in, Debby befriended a family that lived down the street. There was Dave, a mechanic, who like me had taken a wrong turn in his younger years. However, he found the strength and wisdom to better himself in prison by learning a trade. In getting to know him, it was easy to see that he was honest, a hard worker with a great disposition. His wife Kelly was a very thoughtful person. They had two beautiful daughters, a young teenager named Lynn, and Kailey, who turned out to be the same age as Jayson. Both were kind, friendly, and respectful, which reflected their parents.

However, from our introduction, we were to always have our differences. They both drank often and liked to smoke marijuana. They kept trying to convince me that there was no harm in Debby having a few drinks or smoking pot. Well, they didn't live with her; I did. I don't think they understood the seriousness of her multiple sclerosis. Then again, in my mind, it was a wonder they understood anything. Don't misunderstand me; their intentions were anything but malicious. They felt she just didn't need any medication. Their backward thinking rightfully earned them my nickname, "The Hillbillies."

If there ever was a poster child for the healing effects of prescribed medications, it would have to be me. Taking my meds for almost ten months, my health improved a hundred and fifty percent. My viral loads remained undetectable, without any major side effects, which was a rarity considering the toxicity of my medications. However, these issues really had nothing to do with Dave and Kelly, for if Debby didn't have the strength, desire, or willpower to say no, there was nothing I, or anyone else, could have done.

In September 1998, my life was about to enter an extraordinary period which would demonstrate how much I had changed as a person. Jayson wanted to play soccer, so we signed him up at Kensington Community Center, where I had played soccer as a kid thirty-five years earlier. About a week went by before Debby received a call from the hall, saying there might not be a soccer team, as they didn't have a coach. Without missing a beat, she said, "Well, my boyfriend Mino will volunteer." I didn't want to discourage her in any way, so I agreed. All the while, I knew it wasn't going to happen in a million years. Firstly, it was going to be a team of mixed nine-year-olds. Since there were children involved, they would require a criminal record check. That's where the problem would surely begin. When they went to punch my name in the computer, the lights would start blinking like a neon sign. I went and filled out in the forms and had no problem with a criminal search. I had sixty-five adult convictions, all related to theft and violence, and twelve escapes. My immediate thoughts were that I was as likely to get this appointment as penguins moving to Australia.

A week went by and the center called to tell me I could come up and pick up the uniforms and all the additional information. I was now the new coach. My brother Tomo was laughing, but not for long; I drafted him as the assistant coach. This was truly a rewarding experience. For the first time in twenty years, I felt like an active and productive member of the community. Instead of taking, I was giving back. My feelings were inexpressible, especially in view of the fact that just eighteen months ago I had been ready to pack in my existence on the planet.

It was set up for all the kids and their parents to meet us at the center; we received the schedule and exchanged addresses and phone numbers. Within the first few practices, we established who was going to play which positions, but more importantly we had to agree as a team on what we were going to call ourselves. This was easy; we came up with three suggestions, then took a show of hands on each. We finally agreed on the Red and Black Express. It matched the color of our uniforms. Through it all, Debby was a driving force behind our success; she always brought snacks for the team during intermission. During the Christmas break, she invited the team and their parents to our house for a get-together. She was truly a very dynamic person.

Occasionally, my mind reflected on my many walks around the penitentiary yard with my friend Stephen. Something he'd often said now struck me like a lightning bolt: "When kingdoms unite, you lessen the fight." In applying those words of wisdom to my present circumstances, those kingdoms were the people around me offering positive encouragement and support, which gave my life new meaning and direction.

Donny turned out to be our number one fan, and he always got a laugh out of me and Jayson, as we often butted heads. Jayson prided himself on doing everything well. It didn't matter what position he played, and he was a very good player. I was supposed to be the coach, but at times he'd act as though he was.

Debby started drinking again, frequenting the legion. One day she said they were going to make her a committee member, but I saw right through that nonsense. She was trying to create a reason to spend more time there. I was mad at Dave and Kelly, as this had all started with them and had now progressed. This decision of hers was heading towards a cement wall and I wasn't having any part of it. Instead of allowing bitterness to fester in me, I made plans to leave her. I simply saw no alternative. It wasn't because our love was fading—with all my heart, I would love her forever—I just couldn't take all the other nonsense.

In January 1999, the union sent me to work for a company called Narco Construction. We would be working at the huge Lafarge cement plant in Richmond, which was undergoing a two hundred million dollar reconstruction. I really enjoyed this job and the money was fantastic, especially as I was working the night shift. In a fourteen-hour shift, I'd take home five hundred and forty dollars. Our job was to go inside each kiln (huge ovens) and insulate them with new fireproof brick. This particular job lasted three months.

Our soccer team's goalie was a kid named Rory, and it was through his father that I was offered a deal too good to pass up. He heard I was in the market to buy a truck. Well, he had a 1983 Ford truck with a canopy, which I could drive away for seven hundred and fifty dollars. I was amazed at the shape it was in, as I had pictured a rust bucket. Basically all he wanted was what he'd paid for the canopy. We struck a deal for me to buy the truck in two weeks' time, when I got paid; it was also the day I would leave Debby.

She never saw it coming. She had wanted to visit her mother, so I dropped her off, went to pick up the truck, stopped at home long enough to pack a bag, and headed to Tomo's. Donny was very understanding, as he had been through it himself for five years. Debby and I talked extensively afterward, where I outlined my concerns. I moved back about a week later and it seemed for the moment as if everything was back to normal.

Our soccer team was chosen to participate in the annual Safeway soccer tournament, which always took place at the B.C. Place stadium. Thirty teams were chosen from all over British Columbia. The teams would play each other not in competition, but in sportsmanship. Everyone involved, from the players to the spectators, had a terrific time. At the end of the event there was a big ceremony, where we got to personally meet the players of Vancouver's professional soccer team, the Whitecaps. I felt honored and privileged to be given the opportunity to participate as a coach.

Our Farm in Langley 33

In May 1999, once the soccer season ended, Tomo planned on moving to Saskatchewan. Without admitting it, I know that he had enjoyed his coaching role as much as I did.

After eighteen months of peacefully adjusting to our quiet neighborhood, regrettably our cozy little home was sold. Whenever I look back, I can't help but shake my head in amazement. From the moment God steps in, when one door closes, a more beautiful one opens. Our landlord liked us a lot and went out of his way in helping us secure another place. He had a house available in Langley, about a half-hour's drive from Vancouver, which in actuality turned out to be a small farm.

The house was a small two-bedroom dwelling with a couple of barns and sheds, situated on five acres. We loved it. What made it more incredible was that our rent would remain the same. There was a lot of work involved initially, as the house had been vacant for some time. However, I knew that once I had cut the grass (which was well over two feet high), painted the fence, and cleaned all the junk out of the barns, the place would take on its own attractive appearance. Coupled with Debby's creative decorating skills and love of gardening, we turned this once rundown farm into a welcome addition to a fast-growing community.

Many factors influenced our decision to move away from the city. The two most important were that the school Jayson would attend was a block away, and Debby's sister Darlene lived ten minutes away.

It was August when we moved in, and it took about a month of hard work until the place looked great. I started working for a company called Primary Liner's, and the job lasted four months.

Regarding the impossibility of my declining HIV counts, until about three years ago I had honestly never given it much thought, other than luck being on my side. I saw it from a different perspective now. For two years, I had been taking the toxic antiviral medications religiously—sixteen pills daily, along with whatever other vitamins Debby shoved down my throat. My weight was a steady 175 pounds. I looked and felt great. The specialists always referred to me as the "star." Keep in mind that I remained consistently undetectable, with no major side effects. Meanwhile, most people on the regime would cry at the prospect of taking them; the reactions were sometimes very severe. Could it be that my heavy drug addiction had somehow built up my body's tolerance?

For the moment, Danny had settled down in the small town of Mission, an hour's drive away. Now and then, Debby and I would drive out for a visit. Although he was skilled in all aspects of the construction trade, and even though it brought him a nice living, his passion had always centered on automobiles. He was what you would call a car broker; whatever you were in the market for, he would find it, at a profit. This had always been his most lucrative form of livelihood.

It was always a pleasure to see my nieces, Tanya and Natasha. I couldn't believe how quickly they were growing into beautiful young women. It seemed like only yesterday when I'd been bouncing them on my knee.

On one particular visit, Danny had a mobile trailer for sale, and Debby wanted to buy it. That really made no sense, but there was no point arguing with her. This trailer caused many a headache, as it took almost two months to get it, even though it was paid for.

Around the end of November, Tomo called to say he was on his way back to B.C., but he wasn't coming alone. He had met and fallen in love with a woman he'd known for twenty years, Kim. She was the sister of one of his childhood friends. When they arrived, Tomo, Kim, and her twelve-year-old daughter Sunsherra settled in the trailer until he got himself situated. It was a hectic three weeks, but it all worked out. Kim was a very attractive woman in her thirties, with an energetic personality. It was plain to see they were very happy together. Sunny took after her mother, and once I got to know her I realized she was very considerate.

Tomo returned to work with the union full-time, and just before Christmas they rented a huge five-bedroom house just down the street.

Again I was harboring thoughts of leaving Debby. We were drinking in moderation, if that were even possible; however, when Debby went overboard, out came that Jekyll-and-Hyde personality which I hated so much. I really had a terrible time coming to terms with it. She had a heart of gold when sober and couldn't do enough for you, but after a few drinks she went on the warpath. The alcohol completely disagreed with her multiple sclerosis medications; it irritated me tremendously. Only my deep love and devotion for her kept me hanging in, hoping things would somehow work themselves out.

Throughout my life, there's always been one very manipulative, scheming, yet inescapable addiction: alcohol. It had been three years now, and still I remained completely drug-free. I'd distanced myself from my lifestyle of criminality, too, but alcohol continued to strangle me in its suffocating grasp. Possibly I was caught in state of continual denial, or was it my rationalization that alcohol offered me an avenue of brief escape from the pressures in my life? We can rationalize just about anything with a firm conviction.

Alcohol remained a serious threat to all my accomplishments, on many different fronts. When I drank enough, I would start thinking with that penitentiary mentality. I turned into that tough guy all over again. In that frame of mind, if pushed, I was likely to push back. If words escalated to an altercation, instinctively I would go on the defensive. This was an extremely dangerous threat to my freedom. Because of my HIV status, regardless of whether I was in the right or not, I would always remain a loser in the court's eye. If such a case went before the courts, not only would my criminal record convict me, but my medical condition would be a critical factor. Certainly everyone has the right to protect themselves, but my own self-defense would only apply if all other avenues of disconnecting myself from the situation had been tried.

Another dangerous game was my willingness to drink and drive. Up to this point, I'd been treading a very thin line. You'd think I would clue in! It would take another five years, and a life-altering experience, to trigger my abstinence from drinking. Just as with everything else in life, eventually it all catches up to you.

In January 2000, the union placed me in an excellent job. Vancouver had a transit system known as the sky train, an elevated train that went from the heart of downtown Vancouver and ended up deep in the suburb of Surrey. Its path was close to thirty miles in length. Finally, after long negotiations, a thirteen-mile expansion was approved. The job was in Port Moody, where we made each individual segment; the plant alone cost twenty million dollars to construct. This project employed up to a thousand workers. The work was demanding, but once I became accustomed to the construction process I was responsible for, it became a matter of repetition.

Debby and I had now been together almost three years, but changes just over the horizon would dramatically alter our lives. I've always prided myself on being a hard worker, sometimes to the point of overextending myself. My medical team would repeatedly remind me not to overexert myself, as it could have an effect on my illness. Throughout life, regardless what I was doing, I always applied myself a hundred and fifty percent. That wasn't about to change just because I had a few health issues.

I fit right in at work and made a few friends. No one knew of my medical status, as it wasn't their business. I often wondered what they would think if they knew; I was considered a hard worker by all, yet many fellow workers, some of whom were half my age, just couldn't keep up. As a result of my disability, I had to show that regardless of the work or the weather, I was as capable as anybody else, if not better.

Around this time, Donny received unfortunate news that a loved one was terminally ill and wasn't expected to survive much longer. Donny suffered greatly from anxiety attacks, which I believe were mostly due to the amount of stress he allowed to influence his life. Donny and I were very similar in nature. Donny had his way of dealing with it, and I had my way; I usually ended up in prison! I'd seen him under enormous pressure, almost to the point of snapping, and it often seemed as though my way was the easiest.

Donny returned to his hometown to attend the funeral, and while there he was reunited with a beautiful woman named Sandy. In their younger days, Donny and Sandy had shared a brief relationship. Now, after many years, they fell in love again. Perhaps they just reignited what had always been between them. Shortly thereafter, Sandy and her two sons, Josh and Sean, who displayed many of their mother's wonderful characteristics, joined Donny.

As a result of one of his unbelievable fights, Danny spent a few of days with us. Over the years, he and Joanne had many altercations because of drinking. One particular evening started out as a backyard get-together, with twelve friends in attendance, some of whom were hardcore bikers. Seeing that the party was starting to get out of hand and trouble was in the air, the bikers left. It was well into the morning hours when Danny decided it was time to shut things down, as everybody had had a lot to drink. Jo Jo wasn't ready to pack it in just yet, and this caused the fight. When Danny told you it was time to go, it was best to take his advice. Instead of people leaving the party, though, people told him to relax, which to him meant "Take a hike." Danny's theory of life was when you're in his home and he politely asks you to leave, after he's given you all the hospitality he can, you've given him the right to torture you.

Like something out of the movies, without saying a word, he got up, went over, and locked the front door. He rolled up his sleeves. "Now even if you'd like to leave, you're out of luck."

Total chaos broke out as he started punching and kicking anyone in his reach. Someone whacked him in the back of the head from behind with a two-by-four, and without losing stride Danny turned around, saying, "Now you got me mad."

The fight lasted ten or fifteen minutes, and the house was a mess, with blood from one end to the other. Once outside, Danny, with the two-by-four in his hand, chased anybody and everybody. One guy even managed to drive straight at Danny in a truck, just missing him. Danny gave the truck a few dents on the way by.

Danny managed to make it to his friend's place a few blocks away, where he phoned Tomo to come and pick him up. The police, no strangers to this address, cordoned off the block. You'd think it was Christmas Eve, from the way their patrol cars lit up the dark street. Five people were treated at the local hospital for cuts, broken noses, broken ribs, and broken arms.

Tomo described Danny's appearance as scary. He was soaked in blood from head to toe. They took him to the hospital, where he was stitched up.

I asked him how he felt the next day, and his reply was, "Good. I haven't had exercise like that in a while." Danny had just turned fifty. I knew the only way you could ever beat him was by killing him. He was like a Timex watch; he takes a beating and keeps on ticking.

Disaster on the Horizon — 34

It was April, and again I seriously considered leaving Debby. We had been together three years, which for the most part were terrific. It seemed I had done everything humanly possibly in pleading with her to let go of alcohol, and it really saddens me to say that Debby just didn't have the courage. I constantly voiced my concerns to Dr. Webb, in the hopes of possibly gaining a better understanding of how to deal with the situation. His advice to me was to consider myself; there was nothing I could do until she chose to help herself. I understood that remaining in such an abusive situation put my own health and progress at considerable risk. Regardless of this sound advice, I continued not only because I loved her, but because when I most needed support and encouragement, Debby gave it unquestionably and unconditionally. My brother Mike often reminded me that she had in many ways literally given her life to me when no one else was able or willing to make such a commitment. I would forever cherish the beauty and kindness of her giving heart.

Another source of friendly understanding was Donny. He better than anyone could empathize with my dilemma. He had been through it all for five years prior to me. I explained to him that it wasn't so much the drinking itself, because I knew I could adapt to this aspect of our relationship. What went beyond stressful was her verbal abuse after a few drinks; not only was my family no good, but suddenly I was an idiot. Plain stupid. These words from someone I adored. It really hurt. She never had a recollection of the abuse in the morning, but it had a devastating impact on me. Donny was placed in a no-win situation. On the one hand, there was Debby and Jayson to consider. But since we had developed a good friendship over the years, he had to consider the situation through my eyes as well. He didn't want to offend either side, so he tried to remain neutral. She was so far into her pattern of destructive behavior that she was beyond changing, let alone listening to the few people who really loved and cared about her.

I finally found the courage to leave.

The date I chose was May 24, the day before Jayson's eleventh birthday. After work, I drove to Danny's and traded my Grand Marquis for a Toyota minivan. When I arrived home, instead of having supper waiting, Debby was with a couple of friends getting very intoxicated. I sat silently, watching the circus unfolding before my eyes. About an hour later, I let her know that it was over. I went out the door, taking my dog with me. At that moment, it appeared Toro was the only friend I had. Heartbroken, I grabbed a six pack of coolers and went down to the river. I sat for an hour in darkness, sobbing like a baby, trying to understand why things had to be this way. Toro, sensing something was terribly wrong, sat quietly by my side, letting me know he still loved me. After getting it out of my system, I tracked Tomo down and told him there was no going back this time. He had heard this song and dance in the past, so he didn't comment one way or the other.

I showed up the following day around noon and started packing my most important personal possessions in the van. Debby, true to form, didn't remember much and expected me to just make like it never happened. Part of me wanted to do just that. Her sister was there, along with Jessie and Donny. Donny gave me tremendous support that afternoon. Even with her tears piercing my soul like bullets, I remained in control, firm in my decision. I was proud of how I handled the situation.

Instead ending it on a negative note, I hoped we might still be able to salvage a friendship. I knew she was desperately trying to understand why I was leaving. At that particular time, especially in front of a mostly hostile crowd, I didn't know how to explain that the love we had cherished so long ago was all but gone. I knew this in my heart.

The next year proved to be very difficult for me. Not only did I feel completely lost, but I was detached from everything around me. Within six months of my departure, I had two serious automobile accidents in which I should have lost my life.

Close Calls and the Sasquatch 35

It didn't take me long to realize just how dependent I was on Debby. Gone were the daily doses of vitamins and the healthy meals I'd grown accustomed to, replaced now by a constant supply of alcohol. Instead of carrying on with my life in a responsible manner, I fell into a vicious pattern of drinking. Within a matter of two months, my weight dropped from an impressive 175 pounds to 140. At the start, the drinking didn't affect my employment. I continued to work on the sky train project for another nine months.

I had no logical answers for my destructive behavior. Nothing really made sense, nor did it seem to matter. I had left due to Debby's drinking, yet I now fell into the same routine. My only conclusion was that I drank excessively in order to remain strong and keep my mind a blank. Tomo and Kim realized I was having a difficult time; however, they frequently reminded me that if I persisted in drinking and driving, I was going to have serious problems one day. Their sound argument was based on this one simple fact: my vehicle was my main source of livelihood, and if I lost my license I would become unemployed.

On July 20, I went to the bar in Port Moody after work. It was my birthday. My friend bought me four or five exotic drinks, which was all it took to get in the party mode. I had made prior arrangements at work to take the following day off. I spent five hours in the bar drinking before I decided to head back to Langley, a half-hour's drive. I didn't go home right away; instead I went to the local bar, where I continued drinking myself silly for the next couple of hours. Just after midnight, the waiter finally cut me off. I remember getting into my van… why I didn't just go to sleep in the thing is still beyond me. Taking to the back streets, I turned on Logan Avenue, where during the day a crew had been doing road construction. Going about fifty kilometers an hour, I smashed through a couple of barricades and luckily ran into a four-foot pile of sand, which stopped the van instantly. Not wearing a seatbelt, my head literally went through the windshield. I got out of the van, somewhat sobered up from the impact, and tried to push the van free of the sand. It was firmly embedded.

Almost immediately, a police car and an ambulance showed up. They looked at the punched-out windshield and couldn't believe I didn't so much as have a bump on my head, let alone any cuts. It was apparent to everyone but me that I had a guardian angel watching over me that night. The seriousness of the scene escaped me; had it not been for the pile of sand, I would have been killed instantly! Directly behind the sand was a big front-end loader, with its bucket raised. Not only was I walking away from this, but the police only gave me a twenty-four-hour suspension and had my van towed. They called Tomo and Kim, who came and picked me up right away, before the police changed their minds. Tomo and Kim just shook their heads at how fortunate I'd been. I stopped drinking for three months after that.

In view of the three years Debby and I had spent together, from time to time I dropped in to see how Debby was doing. No matter what, I would never turn my back on her. I came by after the accident; she was horrified by my appearance and the tremendous amount of weight I had lost in such a short period of time. We came to a suitable arrangement: I would give her some money to help her out with groceries, and I'd come for dinner every day after work. She would also make me a lunch for the following day. Truly an angel. This worked out fine for two months.

My brother Mike was in prison in Toronto, doing six months. Cathy, his girlfriend of three years, was returning to Vancouver. She and Debby had reached an agreement where she could move in, which certainly helped Debby with the bills. However, in the long run, it was a big mistake, as Cathy was a chronic alcoholic. In a short period of time, Cathy was introduced to an old friend of Debby's named Murphy, with whom she started a relationship. At first I didn't like him at all, but as I got to know him we actually developed a friendship.

Murphy's attitude seemed to be a product of the old school. Having never met anyone in my family, and hearing so much about us, he was always on guard not to offend in any way. There really was no need of this, as Mike made it clear Cathy was on her own. His intention was to finally try and get his life reorganized, especially in regards to his fifteen-year drug addiction. He signed himself into a treatment center. I think even old Murphy, who was a drinker himself, wasn't prepared for Cathy and the headache this relationship would bring.

As the sky train project neared its completion, I was informed that the following Monday I would work on Roy's crew. Everybody who worked for Roy had the same thing to say about him: he was an idiot and yelled at everyone. Well, I felt that if I just did my job as I had been for the past nine months, I shouldn't have any problems. On the first Monday, Roy let me know what was expected, which I had no problem with.

But it didn't take me long to see what everyone was talking about. Not only did he yell at people, he did it to belittle you. I just continued going about my job, but I was warned that it was just a matter of time before Roy turned on me. My turn was coming. The following day, not even an hour into the shift, he started in on me. Everybody watched to see how I would handle the situation. I told him if he kept yelling at me, we were both going to be out of a job, with me facing assault charges and him eating hospital food through a straw. I went on to say that if he had something to say to me, he had better talk to me man to man and not treat me like some punk kid.

Instead of letting the matter slide, I immediately voiced my concerns to Mark, the supervisor, at which time I also explained my medical condition. The next day, I was transferred to a different job.

That same week, I had problems with Toro. First he had viciously attacked a woman, chewing up her arms. I then gave him back to Debby, explaining the circumstances and that he had to either be kept tied up or put to sleep. This lasted all of two days before he attacked someone again. Without hesitation, I took him in to be put to sleep. We all cried, as we really loved him. Jayson wrote a letter outlining how things just weren't fair. He wrote about how when a human hurts someone, they put him in prison, releasing him sometime later, so why couldn't they do the same with Toro? For an eleven-year-old, it was an amazingly emotional letter.

In January 2001, I stepped into a bar for a couple of drinks and ran into Murphy. I joined him at his table, and sitting with him was a guy named John. After a while, Murphy had the good sense to leave, but I stayed and drank doubles till closing time. I offered to give John a ride home, and he invited me in for a couple of beers. As I sat on the couch, I got caught off-guard. John got out of his chair and, without warning, punched me in the head between the eyes; I was on him in a flash and peppered him with an assortment of punches and kicks. Not wanting trouble, I said to him, "I didn't come here to fight." He quickly agreed.

Again, I should have seen it coming. When I tilted my head back to take a drink, the idiot punched me in the side of the head. Once more, I laid into him. Why I just didn't leave is beyond me. About ten minutes went by and suddenly he was standing right in front of me, catching me square in the chest with his boot. This resulted in several fractured ribs. I flipped out and jumped on top of him. As we went down, I must have whacked my head on the corner of the coffee table, as suddenly I was bleeding a lot.

He kept trying to poke my eye out. Finally realizing there was no way this idiot was going to admit defeat, I started thinking about how I could get away. He had me by the throat, and on the coffee table beside us I noticed a big lamp. I let go of him and grabbed the lamp and smashed it down on his head. This seemed to stun him just long enough for me to get out of the house. It was around three o'clock in the morning, and with all the noise we had made the neighbors were awakened and must have phoned the police. The clown was most likely well-known to the police, because when they showed up he was taken away. Due to my intoxicated state, my vehicle was again towed and the police decided to give me a ride home.

It was the middle of January 2001, and the winter was extremely cold. Being prone to bouts of bronchitis, I should have guarded myself at all times. Because of the high level of concentrated dust in the air at work, I was accustomed to wearing my respirator. For some reason, I didn't have it one morning. The cold air immediately gripped my lungs. In a matter of days, I was running a high fever. I went on sick leave for the following three months. By the time I was well enough to return, the project was winding itsel down.

January 27 was a memorable day, as Tomo and Kim became proud parents of a beautiful baby girl they named Saffron. She wasn't even born yet and already had her own fan club. About six people spent the night in the delivery room with Kim. Someone was always watching, and at 7:20 a.m. Sunny's friend Tanya noticed the baby coming out—with the umbilical cord wrapped around her little neck. The room went into a panic, as the nurse called for the doctors. The delivery was successful, although Saffron was kept in hospital for an additional four days, as a matter of procedure rather than caution.

When they first brought Saffron home, she was fairly quiet. At least for the first month. Once she got active, she made herself heard. Actually, the joy and happiness of the sounds of a newborn baby filling the house brought its own atmosphere of tranquility.

Many of my concerns still revolved around Debby. Despite keeping my distance, I was courting her all over again. We had discussed the possibility of reconciliation and looked at a number of houses for rent. Since my leaving, Al, a friend of ours from Vancouver, moved in as a boarder. It worked out great for Debby, as she couldn't afford to keep the place on her own. He was transferred to his company's Langley branch, which was a five-minute cab ride from Debby's place. However, Al was yet another chronic alcoholic. It wasn't long before Debby was drawn into that old vicious cycle.

Next thing I knew, she had some guy named Bob hanging around the house. Where or how she found this idiot, I'll never know, but from the moment I met him I didn't like him. I just didn't trust him.

"You'll be seeing a lot of Bob," Debby said to me one day. "He'll be doing the yard work from now on."

Who was she trying to kid? I had always done that for her; it would have been a chore for this clown to remember his own name, let alone do yard work. I knew one thing for sure: we were both lucky I quit drugs a while back, as I'd be in prison and Bob would be eating through a straw. At first, it could have easily gone either way; in my own way, I terrorized him every time we crossed paths. I asked him to step out back several times so I could show him what I really thought of him, but he knew better. He wanted no part of a fight; he had no chance of winning.

One day Debby, phoned me and said, "If you persist in your terror tactics, Bob will have you killed." At no time in my life was I ever worried about dying. My disability was its own death sentence. Threatening my life had no impact apart from adding fuel to an already raging fire.

The next time I saw Bob, I laid into him. "Listen up, very carefully. The next time you want to run off at the mouth, remember not to push me past the point of no return. I'll plant you myself and never give it a second thought."

Obviously I was speaking from anger and resentment, not thinking in a rational manner. It never failed. Anytime alcohol entered the picture, I would go back to my familiar prison mentality. Although buried deep within me, it was still a very real part of who I was. I knew I had to watch myself extra carefully. Jealousy always plays an important role in crimes of passion; it's sent many good men and women to prison for life.

Eventually, for my own selfish reasons, I came to terms with things. Simply put, if I had persisted, I wouldn't have been welcome there anymore. I did, however, slowly cut the emotional ties. It couldn't be done overnight.

One day while visiting, we were all drinking heavily. I got pretty drunk and was going to leave. Bob suggested I take a nap before heading out. I didn't have a clue what was going on, so Jayson had to explain everything to me the next day. After I passed out, Bob went to the bar, Debby having drunk too much herself. She then lay down next to me on the bed. When the dummy finally made it home, all hell broke loose. You can't really blame him for flipping out; if the circumstances had been reversed, I'd hate to even speculate on what I would have done. We started fighting. Judging from the marks on my throat, he was trying to choke me; by the marks on his forehead, I must have head-butted him a few times. That was the extent of our fight.

That night, I slept in my car. In the morning, we both laughed about the whole thing, but it could have easily been very costly.

From that incident, I realized a crucial truth: I was fully to blame for my erratic behavior. I had allowed myself to become involved and enraged over a situation I had no control over. With this realization, I finally managed to walk away.

Because of my dislike and mistrust of Bob, I periodically went by to see how Debby and Jayson were doing. She has never left my heart. To this day, my love for her is very much alive. Debby will always be my diamond in the rough.

THE COQUIHALLA CLIFF 36

Being impulsive, one day I decided to take the five-hour drive and visit my friend Brad. Sounds simple enough, but there are a few things you should keep in mind. Absolutely no one knew I was making this trip, and it was one o'clock in the morning, in the middle of winter. The pub had just closed, and instead of going home I figured to pay my friend a surprise visit. Traveling the Coquihalla Highway during the winter, especially when ill-equipped, can be treacherous. I reached the tollbooth, located on the mountain peak, almost five thousand feet in elevation.

I had only gone a couple of miles past the booth when suddenly the unimaginable happened. It was three in the morning and pitch-black outside. I was going about fifty kilometers an hour, and while maneuvering a slow turn I hit a patch of ice and lost control of my vehicle. First, my car slid into the guardrail. It bounced off, gaining even more speed. The car then completed two one hundred and eighty degree turns and slammed into the embankment, sending me and the car over the edge of the cliff. The car was airborne, flying into the emptiness of a black void.

The car came to a sudden stop some thirty feet down, luckily wedging itself in the snow behind a huge boulder. Momentarily disoriented, I sat in stunned silence. There was no hiding my fear. As I stared into the darkness below, the only thing I was certain of was the direction I needed to go: straight back up. I tried opening my door, but it was sealed shut. Almost as if in slow motion, I carefully climbed out of the passenger side and crawled back up the side of the cliff. Once I reached the highway, I made my way to the other side and managed to flag down a passing trucker, who gave me a ride back to the tollbooth.

I called a tow truck, and it took him almost an hour before he arrived from Merritt, the nearest small city. With his powerful searchlight, we slowly traveled along the highway. It was easy to spot where my car had left the road. The seventy-five-degree angle of my car, plus where I had gone over the cliff, left the tow truck driver in amazement that I had survived. He said something about having angels watching over me, but at the moment his words had no impact.

Not only was it three hundred feet straight down, but the cliff dropped into a frozen lake. According to tow truck driver, if I had continued down the cliff, the car would have smashed through the ice, plunging me into cold water. Even if I would have somehow managed to get free of the car, I would never have made it back to the top. Having had very little sleep in the past twenty-four hours, the implications of what he was telling me didn't fully register. Pulling the car up over the embankment was an eerie sight. Looking straight out, the car slowly appeared out of nowhere.

Instead of going back to Langley, I continued on my journey, even though my car now wobbled down the highway. I arrived at Brad's place at about six in the morning. After waking him and his girlfriend Kristi up, we had coffee together. Being very tired, they put me in the guest bedroom, where I slept for five hours.

When I awoke, the realization of my ordeal took effect. Brad looked at my car and said I had bent the frame. I was totally shaken, both mentally and physically, so within a few hours I decided to return home. This time, the trip took almost eight hours. When I started to climb into the mountains, I reduced my speed to a very slow ten kilometers an hour. I wasn't taking any chances.

It wasn't until I had safely returned that the full impact of going over the cliff and surviving actually hit me. It stopped me dead in my tracks, like a sledgehammer between the eyes. When I explained the nightmare of the last twenty-four hours to Tomo, he didn't believe me. He went out to look at my once-beautiful Chrysler Fifth Avenue. It had once been a powerful and heavy automobile, but now it was crumpled like an accordion; one could see its new half-moon shape.

For the next few weeks, I drifted into a deep state of depression, although it was more than that; it was almost as if I were detaching myself from the world around me. I was in deep thought of how quickly and easily my life could have ended. It wasn't dying that concerned me, but rather the thought that if my life were to end, what legacy would I leave behind? At this point, there was nothing to substantiate that I had ever existed.

The tow truck driver's words thundered in my head: "If your car hadn't stopped, you would have plummeted straight down three hundred feet, coming to rest at the bottom of the lake, after breaking the ice." I reflected on the unimaginable chapters of my life. Had it not been for the three years of peacefulness I had shared with Debby and Jayson, this incident would have been enough to drive me once again into an inescapable pit.

Whatever I got from life was a direct result of my performance; therefore logic dictated that if I changed my pattern of thinking and applied myself, as I had with everything else in life, my performance would eventually change my life. It was crucial that I focus on solutions, instead of making one excuse after another, which was always an easy pattern for me. I knew I desperately needed a goal, a sense of direction, or I'd find myself in serious trouble. As the saying goes, if you don't have a clue where you want to go in life, you'll never have any hope of getting there! I needed something powerful, but I didn't have a clue what it would be.

For the second time in twenty-five years, I was about to see my mother once again, possibly for the last time. This time, she stayed for a full week. I noticed a difference in her compared with her visit six years earlier. She was more at ease and relaxed. Not that it mattered, but she was quite the drinker herself. A few issues surfaced, over which I could have let her have it with both barrels. Firstly, after a few drinks she would continuously repeat herself, saying, "I can't believe what you kids have done with your lives." On and on, like a broken record, yet she failed to acknowledge her role in it. When it came to issues of parental neglect and abandonment, I had greatly struggled. My words may appear resentful, even harsh, but if she had been a mother, instead of a tramp, having one affair after another, things might have been different.

She never did like the burden and responsibility of children. The lowlife she had an affair and eventually went into hiding with, was supposed to have been a friend of my father's. Instead they cleaned my dad out when they disappeared back in the seventies, taking off with almost two hundred thousand dollars in cash. No wonder he had hit men looking for the both of them. Yeah, he was no angel either, with strong ties to organized crime.

Regardless of the volcano boiling inside, I kept my mouth shut. All speaking up would accomplish was forcing her underground again, never to resurface. I let her enjoy being a grandmother.

On the morning of her departure, I wrote a beautiful one-page letter which seemed to bring tears to everyone's eyes. In my heart, I believed it was the last time I would see her. Since her last visit, we hadn't known where she lived, her phone number, or for that matter what name she was using. Once again, she was leaving without offering any information. For the first little while, she'd call once a month, but with the passage of time the calls got further and further apart, until finally they stopped.

Tomo, having read the letter, said, "Mino, I didn't know you could write like this. You should be writing about your life." For the longest time, I firmly believed nothing I could say would be of benefit to anyone.

Trials and Tribulations 37

Although I still received seventy-five percent of my salary, being on medical leave had many disadvantages, as I was about to find out. I had plenty of time on my hands, which truthfully left me bored. I started hanging around Debby's, but it didn't take me long to wear out my welcome.

I'd had HIV for close to ten years, and in that time I hadn't said much about it to anyone. I saw Dr. Montaner on a regular basis, though. He was brilliant. On a recent visit, he informed me that my condition remained undetectable, which in layman's terms meant there was no sign of the virus in my bloodstream. I never questioned him on anything, and why would I? Three years earlier, I had basically been pronounced dead on my feet. My progress had been phenomenal.

Over the years, many have asked what it's like living with this illness. At first, such a question seemed to be without foundation, possibly even a cruel reminder of my carelessness in life. However, the more I thought about it, the answer revolved around my psychological well-being, my emotional stability, and my physical health, the three key elements governing one's survival. Even in my limited understanding, I knew that fully capturing the complexities of this bewildering disease would take years of study.

Living with HIV? Well, it's not a pretty picture. Everyone at the center seemed to like my attitude, even if my humor was a bit off-color. Since the drugs I took were very toxic, I used to say to the doctors, "At least now I get to save on batteries. If I go out at night, I don't need a flashlight; I'm the only one in the neighborhood who glows in the dark." Having a sense of humor was essential to my frame of mind. If I concentrated on the doom and gloom, I would find myself in a deep state of depression, the number one killer.

There has been one inescapable side effect. In the first week of taking the medications, I began to notice a chilling ache in my bones and in the joints around my hips, knees, feet, and hands. Imagine your bones to be very brittle, placed in a carpenter's vice, and constantly tightened. I was told that eventually, as my body grew accustomed to the meds, this side effect would diminish. It was a good line, but I never believed it.

Through it all, I've definitely been a survivor by my instincts and wits. I have often been given sound advice as to prolonging my life while managing HIV. Many times I was unpredictable in my behavior, flagrantly disregarding the advice and doing the complete opposite. As a result, during one scheduled appointment, I expected to see a rapid decline in my health. Instead, I was given congratulations, as all my medical reports were overwhelmingly positive. As to the reasons, I've never personally searched for any answers. I knew better than to question that which could only be attributed to fate or destiny. Or was it something even greater?

Debby and I had been separated for about a year and I still periodically stopped in to see how she was doing. It went beyond human comprehension. Regardless of the wedge between us, I refused to believe that our experience together had reached its final conclusion. I wouldn't close that door. We had crossed paths and left a huge impact on one another for a specific purpose, though it escaped both of us. As to the existence of God, I never gave such foolishness a second thought. Had I entertained such a belief, I would have viewed our separation as a cruel joke, placing a wedge between me and God.

In the last three years, regardless of minor setbacks, I had gone from crippling impossibilities to living realities. In my way of thinking, if there were a God, He had pulled the rug out from under me. Little did I know that God was slowly grooming me for things that would exceed my wildest expectations. One of the hardest lessons I needed to master was dying to my own self-will. As long as I thought I could do this or that, God was tenderly polishing away the rough edges of the diamond; I never had a clue. Like the dummy I was, God had left a trail of footprints through my life that a blind man could have followed, yet I stubbornly refused to recognize or acknowledge their existence.

I would have liked to meet someone, to fill the gap of loneliness. At first this proposition presented many challenges. Where was I to find someone who would be comfortable with my illness, and at the same time be free of addictions?

One day, while waiting to see the specialist, I looked through a local HIV magazine and learned there were many wonderful support organizations throughout the lower mainland. I visited a few to see what they were about, and immediately noticed the helpful nature of the staff. Above all else, I felt their compassionate understanding. Not that they looked for recognition, but all the people I met demonstrated encouragement and support.

However, I didn't hang around too much. I was no longer confused about the realities of HIV. I was fully aware of its consequences. I had survived this long as a result of who I was, along with all the obstacles. I knew I would fight this paralyzing illness up until my last breath. It was hard for me hang around these centers, as I would often see people in various stages of the illness. I understood their trials and tribulations. I would often fall into a deep depression, which took me days to come out of. Since I was neither emotionally nor psychologically strong enough to cope with this, I tended to stay away. As the saying goes, out of sight, out of mind.

Since my slow process of change began in 1997, I met many people from all walks of life, and they all complained about how life had been so unfair to them. Most of them were in relatively good health and half my age. I'd tell them straight up that I'd trade lives with them anytime.

I decided to take Tomo's advice and do the craziest thing I ever attempted. I was going to write a book about my extraordinary life. I didn't know how to type, other than using one finger, as I still do today, and I knew nothing about computers, or even where to start. At first I wondered whether it was a dream, a vision, or complete lunacy.

In the beginning, I stayed up half the night making notes. Then in the morning, I'd be the first one in line at the local library, waiting for its doors to open. As you were only allowed two hours on the computer each day, I would rotate between four different libraries, sometimes ending up where I first began.

It wasn't long before my writing took on a life of its own, It seemed to go far beyond mere obsession. Those in my immediate inner circle looked at me as if my mind had finally snapped. Regardless of all the opposition, I remained determined and persistent. It took a year and a half to finish. After typing one hundred thousand words, I completed my manuscript.

Whatever hopes and dreams I had, though, were about to be crushed. Tragedy beyond measure was about to strike yet another vicious blow.

Part 2

In Memory of an Angel

Shattered Dreams 38

Maybe it was preordained for Debby and me to separate. In our three years together, my life surpassed my wildest expectations. It went from the unimaginable to the extraordinary. When we reach a point in our lives where everything is beyond hope, we find ourselves in a similar situation to Ezekiel, standing in a valley of dry bones. When asked by God if he thought God could restore those bones to life, Ezekiel didn't know. In my case, without wanting to know what I thought, God just did it. In essence, He resurrected parts of my soul that had been dead, supernaturally bringing them back to life.

But I was clueless as to the majesty of it all. Maybe that was part of God's plan all along. Without knowing what the plan was, I was to write about the existence of God. As is so far clearly evidenced, only God Himself could have stepped into my shattered life and resurrected it.

From the moment I started writing about my life, I found myself wrestling with an unknown force seeking the book's failure and my very destruction. Many times, I wanted to give up. I would spend hours typing with one finger, then the librarian would tell me, "Okay, it's time to wrap it up so the next person can have their turn." Instead of saving the pages I had typed, I would inadvertently hit the delete button, losing it all. Sometimes I even tried to give the next person twenty dollars, just to give me their turn. Most times, instead of getting mad, I'd have a couple of beers and head to the next library, starting the whole process from scratch. It took me a good three months before I gained a working knowledge of computers.

Eventually, I moved with Tomo and his family to Chilliwack, which was basically the middle of nowhere. I had written fifteen chapters, and someone I knew read them. As a result, this person gave me a used computer, which helped me tremendously.

One day, while visiting Danny and Mike in Mission, I was offered a landscaping job with the same company Mike worked for. I couldn't handle the two-hour commute every day, so I moved into Danny's spare room. I loved everything about this job and worked for the company almost five years.

Realistically, in completing the first draft of my manuscript, I must have typed out half a million words. As with most of the things in my life, I discovered the hard way that an author is never happy. I seemed to be in a hurry trying to find a home for my story, although there was an important lesson I yet needed to learn: whatever is God-inspired will be promoted by Him. God wasn't about to promote something that was incomplete. No matter what I did, my book would collect dust for that very reason.

Debby and I had now been separated for eighteen months. It had been almost three months since I last saw her. I often found myself daydreaming about this extraordinary woman, as I believed she had given me a new lease on life. I was never one for superstitions or old wives tales, but there was no escaping the fact that I was guided by destiny. Out of the blue, when I had been my most vulnerable, this woman had mysteriously appeared as if from a dream.

I was about to re-enter Debby's life, in a similar fashion. It was February 20, 2002, and I remember exactly what happened as though it were yesterday.

While in Vancouver for a doctor's appointment, I decided to stop in to see Donny and Sandy before making the hour-and-a-half drive to Mission. After knocking on their door for a couple of minutes, it became obvious that no one was home. While slowly making my way to the highway, an eerie feeling seemed to embrace me. It just wouldn't let go. Suddenly, without rhyme or reason, I said the hell with it and turned the car around, driving back through the city.

My plan was to stop by the bingo hall, to see if Donny and Sandy were there; they were known to drop in there from time to time. Once I got there, to my disappointment, they were nowhere to be found.

Before leaving the hall, I thought, *I'll try telephoning them one last time.* Donny answered the phone. I could tell by the sound of his voice that he was overly frustrated and relieved to have heard from me. His first words were that Debby was at his place, and that she was in very rough shape. Usually when we referred to her in this manner, it meant she had gone on one of her drinking escapades, having had one too many, and couldn't walk. This time, however, the urgency I detected in his voice was enough for me to figure out something of a far more serious nature was wrong.

I showed up twenty minutes later to find him waiting outside for me. Before I go on, I'd like to stress the fact that no one, including myself, knew exactly what was wrong with Debby. All our thoughts were based on assumptions. Donny is a very compassion person. With tears in his eyes, he tried his best to explain that Debby was having a serious relapse of multiple sclerosis. Not until I saw her did I fully realize that her medical condition was far more complex. Donny went on to tell me that for the past month or so, all she'd been doing was asking for me. This warmed my heart tremendously, as the bond we shared still remained strong.

Debby was fast asleep on their bed, so Donny, Sandy, and I had coffee. Finally, after a while, I stepped quietly into the bedroom.

Upon seeing her, I noticed she had lost a considerable amount of weight. As I stood in the doorway, watching over her fragile frame, my thoughts wandered. I knew it couldn't have been more than a few seconds, but it seemed as though hours passed by. I felt as though I were in a dream; my whole life flashed before me.

Shaking the memories off and returning to reality, I knew I would be there to help her in any capacity that was needed. Almost as in slow motion, I walked over to the bed, bent over, and lightly kissed her on the cheek. She stirred beneath me and her eyes opened. It took a moment for her to focus properly, and when she realized it was me her eyes got as big as silver dollars. Tears filled her eyes and began running down her cheeks. As she tenderly wrapped her arms around my neck, I felt her body tremble beneath me. I somehow knew she had reached the most vulnerable point of her life. I'm sure she sensed I wasn't about to abandon her. When I turned around, I was surprised to see Donny and Sandy silently standing in the doorway, watching with tears in their eyes.

Debby tried to get up, but she had no strength to do so on her own. When she finally managed to get up, with help, she couldn't walk. Her whole body would go limp; it was like trying to hold on to a lump of jelly. Even this wasn't as frightening as the next stage. For two minutes, she went into some form of seizure. Her whole body rigidly contorted, and it felt as though she were in another world. She was just lifeless. Seeing her in this state, it was impossible for me to stem the flow of tears. Here was the woman, whom I adored more than life itself, once so full of energy; now all that remained was an empty shell. Up to this point, I hadn't given any consideration toward that idiot Bob, who had been living with her this past year, but slowly the anger deep within me burned like an uncontrolled fire, steadily growing and getting hotter.

I had told him many times to cool it with the drinking around her, for one day it would have the best of her—and then I would have the best of him. When I looked at things realistically, everyone in Debby's immediate circle had been guilty of contributing to her alcohol addiction.

After putting Debby back to bed, where we made her as comfortable as possible, we returned to the kitchen for more coffee. The moment of truth arrived. Donny had always greatly respected me, not just as a result of my achievements but for the way Debby and I were meant for one another. Looking me in the eye, in all seriousness, he says, "Mino, if you can't do it, then no one can." He wanted to know whether I'd be willing to help. Considering my reaction to seeing her, this seemed like such a silly question.

I made it clear about my intentions. My decision to assist had nothing to do with reentering a relationship with Debby. My primary concern was for her well-being. I went on to say that I would do whatever was necessary, for as long as it took, to see Debby rehabilitated. Only when she was once again in control of her faculties would we consider the possibility of reconciliation. On the same note, I said that if she returned to her destructive pattern of drinking, I would be left with no alternative but to again disappear from her life.

The next step in this tragic affair was to get rid of Bob. Only then would I return to what had once been our home. After giving this some thought, I expressed my concern about becoming directly involved in this task. Don't get me wrong; I would have gladly welcomed the opportunity to throw Bob and his stuff out the window. However, I also knew that if I made any move, it would appear as though I was the jealous boyfriend trying to move back in. Jayson's dad, Wayne, had come down to look after him until it was figured out. Wayne had said he would see to it that Bob moved out. However, before anything of this nature could take place, it was of the utmost importance for me to first see if this was what Debby truly wanted.

Donny had already made arrangements with Debby's sister Darlene to have her brought over the next day. I agreed to take her, and then was invited to spend the night.

In the next six hours, I realized just how intensely involved I would have to be to look after her. It was not a part-time obligation. I had to watch over her twenty-four hours a day, seven days a week. I literally had to carry her to the bathroom and wipe her up after she did her business. Basically, Debby needed assistance with getting dressed and undressed, and she even had difficulty feeding herself. She couldn't do any of these things on her own. For whatever reason, she had lost all motor control. I lay down with her for a while, holding her gently in my arms, reassuring her that I was here to stay and that everything would be all right. Once she was asleep, over coffee again the horror story of her ordeal was relayed to me.

She had been in this shape for the previous two months, and it was obvious to me that Bob couldn't have been bothered to help out. He was too absorbed in his own alcohol addiction. I had a hard time coming to terms with it; for the sake of his own gratification, she had been forced to suffer. With great difficulty, I tried to find some way to pity this degenerate. It would be another week before I fully comprehended just how degrading the conditions for her had been.

I didn't get much sleep that night. Most of it was spent watching over her and wiping her face with a damp cloth. She seemed to be burning up.

THE NIGHTMARE BEGINS 39

The following morning, while driving to Darlene's place in Langley, my thoughts wandered. I knew from personal experience that going to see her would be a wasted trip, as she definitely couldn't care for Debby in the manner required, due to her own alcoholism. I'm not pointing fingers; I firmly believed her intentions were sincere, but she didn't have the patience. As I pulled into the driveway, I hoped she would prove me wrong.

Once we got Debby settled in, I sat around the kitchen table with Darlene and her boyfriend, Toby. Toby commended me for stepping up to the plate. I could tell they were somewhat overwhelmed that I had taken on such a burden so easily. Once Debby was sound asleep, before leaving, I was reassured that she would be fine. I had no reason to think otherwise, yet the thought of them drinking kept nagging at me.

I was right in my first assumptions. It was a forty-minute drive back to Donny's, and no sooner had I arrived than the phone rang. It was Toby, and in his roundabout way he told me that Debby belonged in a hospital, where she could receive the attention she required. That night, we made a judgment call, deciding to have her admitted the following day.

The next morning, Darlene arranged for an ambulance to come pick Debby up, but Debby was very stubborn and would have absolutely no part of it until I arrived. From the moment I took on this role, I was constantly running around like a chicken with its head cut off. The pressure and stress was insurmountable, and this would come back to haunt me. My own medical support team had numerous times reminded me that prolonged stress was a major factor in the progression of HIV. Regardless, I remained persistent in caring for Debby.

I was disappointed to see just how uncared for Debby was in her sister's care. Right from the beginning, they had to have known what was involved. I'd carried Debby into the house, as she couldn't walk. Had they thought she would just look after herself? When it came to Debby, I didn't put any faith in others. You had to be one hundred and fifty percent committed. Her well-being was the only thing that was important to me.

I immediately went in the bedroom to check on her—and what I saw made my hair stand on end. Debby was half on the bed and half off, and in the midst of one of her seizures. She must have lit a cigarette, as it was slowly burning a hole in the blanket beside her. After I put the cigarette out and laid her down properly on the bed, I sat and caressed her face. Once again, my thoughts drifted. I tried to analyze everything I had just witnessed.

I was no medical expert, but it appeared Debby had moments when she was in total control. After all, she had lit the cigarette and tried to get out of bed. From what I could piece together, in those instances, when she tried to do something but couldn't, she became so stressed and frustrated that she went into a seizure.

Shortly thereafter, the ambulance arrived and I went to the hospital with her.

Even though I lived in Mission, an hour's drive from Langley, I came to see her for the following ten days, sometimes making the trip twice a day. While she was at Langley Memorial Hospital, I began to notice her health deteriorating rapidly. It wasn't until the ninth day that we came to understand the seriousness of her condition, which all along had been critical. My visits with her mainly consisted of catering to her every need, as she was truly helpless. It was almost like taking care of a baby, but then again she had always been my baby.

With each passing day, I became more and more proficient as her caregiver. Each day when I showed up, her first priority was to go out and have a smoke. This seemed like such a chore at first, mainly due to her arguable nature, but once I organized myself and made sure all her needs were met, I actually enjoyed getting her ready to go outside.

In the beginning, it was mass confusion, but I got organized very quickly. Before I would leave in the evening, I'd ask her what she felt like wearing the next day. This way, when I showed up the following morning, there would be no arguing. Everything would be in its place and ready to be utilized.

We basically followed the same daily routine. She'd hit the bathroom first, and while she was taking care of business I dampened the towel she would use to wash her face. This had to be done just right to avoid Debby's explosive onslaught: not too wet, not too cold or hot. With this taken care of, I'd have her sit on the side of the bed and proceed to remove her hospital pajamas. Then I would dress her in the clothes she had picked out the night before.

There were a few more items on the agenda, and then we would be ready to go outside. Debby had a big container which I always made sure to fill of her favorite juice, with lots of ice. When she first arrived, I cased out the entire floor where she was housed, and found the most comfortable wheelchair. I had her name put on the back so no one else would mistakenly take it. Then I would go to heated oven and remove a couple of warm blankets. I'd spread one on her wheelchair, which turned out to be an ideal cushion, and use the other to cover her.

In the evening, the ritual was similar, except it was reversed. Out for a smoke, then to the bathroom and change her into clean pajamas. Before I tucked her in and kissed her goodnight, I made sure the juice bottle was full.

In the following six months, I witnessed undeniable acts of greed and deception from her family members. To think that family could act in such a callous way without shame or remorse. I'm not out to attack anyone; I've faced many obstacles throughout my life, and regardless of crippling addictions, I always knew the difference between right and wrong. Whether it's facing a serious illness or a death in the family, you definitely see the best and worst in people. Their true characters come into full view for all to see.

One day, Wayne showed up at the hospital to see how Debby was doing. Through the course of the visit, he brought up the subject of Bob. Wayne wanted to know if Debby was certain that she wanted him to leave her house and life. It only took Debby a moment to confirm this, and from that moment on, as far as everyone was concerned, Bob and his suitcase were out the door. It didn't matter to us if he chose to go the easy way or the hard way; he was leaving!

Even so, I still chose to stay out of it for a few days, to see how Wayne would handle things.

ILLNESS BEYOND COMPREHENSION 40

The following day, I had some personal errands to attend to and didn't make it to the hospital until late in the afternoon. As usual, I headed up to her room, and to my shock her bed was stripped and all her belongings gone. I had to take a few moments to compose myself, as my thoughts were racing in all kinds of different directions, speculating the unimaginable. As I approached the nurse's reception area, my emotions were on full alert, expecting the worst.

I was told that the previous evening, at around ten o'clock, Debby had been flown by helicopter to the Royal Columbian Hospital. She had needed immediate emergency brain surgery. All along, Debby had had too much fluid in her brain; it wasn't draining properly, and this was the cause of her seizures. I was to later learn that if her condition had gone undetected a few more days, she would probably have died.

During the forty-minute drive to the Royal Columbian, my thoughts were hopeful, but also desperate.

She was in her own room in the intensive care unit and her head was bandaged. She was still groggy from the anesthetic and painkillers they had given her. The date was March 1, 2002, her forty-seventh birthday. I spent the evening watching over her and felt a tremendous amount of empathy for her. If it wasn't one thing, it was another. I searched my mind for some logical explanation as to why things happened as they did, but I found no justifiable answers.

I was deeply concerned. Within a matter of days, I was finally able to speak to her surgeon, as I wanted a better understanding of her condition. Most of her immediate problems were a result of a large cyst in her brain usually caused by a tumor. The technical term used was an arachnoid cyst, fluid-filled sacs that develop between the surface of the brain and the arachnoid membrane. This is one of the three membranes that cover the brain and spinal cord. These cysts are known to produce such symptoms as headaches, seizures, behavioral changes, weakness, paralysis on one side of the body, and a lack of muscle control. In other words, the exact symptoms Debby had. In her case, treatment warranted the immediate surgical implantation of a shunt to remove pressure from the cyst.

When I thought of everything that could have been done to prevent the progression of Debby's illness to this stage, I had a tear in my eye. I also felt rage, all directed towards that idiot she had been living with.

Because the cyst had gone untreated for such a long time, even the placement of the shunt could cause permanent and severe neurological damage. Debby now faced damage to the optic nerve (which could cause irreversible loss of vision), loss of intellectual abilities (dementia), problems with walking, irritability, abnormal eye movement, and a low level of consciousness. This could also leave the placement of the shunt inoperable.

The operation she'd had is known as a ventricular shunt, a surgical procedure where a tube is placed in one of the fluid-filled chambers inside the brain. A ventricular tube is placed to drain excess fluid from the ventricular system in the brain, to the cavity of the abdomen. In such a case, surgical procedures must be done both in the brain as well at the drainage site. The tubing contains valves which ensure that the fluid can only flow out of the brain, not back into it. Also, the valve can be set to a desired pressure, which allows the fluid to escape whenever the pressure level is exceeded.

After a few days, when her bandages were removed and I had a much clearer understanding of what her surgeon had been trying to explain, the shunt was implanted behind her right ear. The tube traveled down her throat to her abdomen, but in time this tube caused a whole new set of problems, not only for her but anyone who was to come in close contact with her. As a result of the placement of the tubing, she wasn't allowed to eat regular food; she could very easily have choked to death. All her food had to be prepared in a blender. In this, I could never blame her; never mind eating it, I had a hard enough time looking at it! It resembled porridge. She also wasn't allowed to consume fluids of any kind, which would be life-threatening. Any fluids not thickened like pudding would directly enter her lungs, causing her to aspirate, which meant that she could catch pneumonia.

In view of the seriousness of her condition, death was a real possibility.

I sat quietly, watching her sleep. My intentions when I left the hospital were to go to her place and beat the living daylights out of Bob. In the ten days that Debby had been in the hospital, Bob hadn't even called to see how she was doing. If I didn't like him before, with each passing day I grew to hate him. He wasn't going to be on any flipping Christmas list! I really wanted to throw caution in the wind and go pay the goof a visit.

Instead, I decided to take Donny up on his offer and spend the night at his place. Except for my personal satisfaction, beating the crap out of Bob wouldn't help matters any. I'd be no good to Debby in prison. In all likelihood, he would have called the police, and considering my lengthy record I would have ended up going to jail.

Every couple of months, I went for regular blood work regarding my HIV infection. Once again the results were fantastic, as the virus remained undetectable. However, from this point on, for whatever reason, I started to get sloppy. It would be five months before I got in for another test, and everyone was very concerned by those next results. In the morning, before going out to Debby's place, I visited with her for a couple of hours in the hospital.

In the ten days she had spent recovering from the surgery, I was starting to see improvements in all areas of her health, although she was still a long way from total recovery. When the doctor determined she was well enough to be transferred, Debby would be moved to the rehabilitation center at Eagle Ridge Hospital, in Port Moody. There was no concern in regards to irreversible brain damage, for her recovery was coming along just fine.

Little did I know, however, that disaster was waiting for me just around the next corner.

Escaping Death Once Again 41

While driving out to Langley, my thoughts reflected on all the precious memories Debby, Jayson, and I had shared together on this five-acre farm. This numbed all the pent-up frustration, anger, and tension I was feeling. At least momentarily, I felt a somewhat calmer state settle over me, but I certainly realized this could all change very quickly. All it would take was for Bob to say the wrong thing, and in his case anything he said to me would be the wrong thing. Luckily, he wasn't there when I arrived. It was great to see Jayson again. I couldn't even begin to imagine how he must be feeling, or for that matter what thoughts were going through his head. All anyone could do when it came to him was offer their full support and understanding.

Before I get ahead of myself, I should explain about the people presently occupying this small two-bedroom farmhouse. Naturally there was Jayson and his dad. There was also Al, Debby's roommate, who had moved in shortly after Debby and I separated. This was a good thing, not only because Al was a friend of ours, but for the simple fact that Debby wouldn't have been able to afford the place on her own. It worked out great for Al, as the company he worked for was in the process of relocating to Langley, a five-minute drive from Debby's place. Al was a very intelligent man in his own right, and he was somewhere in his late fifties. Right from the beginning, we all used to laugh ourselves silly over Al's comedy act. He still continues it to this day. Al was dependable, reliable, and a hard worker.

However, without realizing it, Al was held captive by his own suffocating addiction to alcohol. It has plagued him now for almost thirty years. Each day after work he went to a quiet, friendly neighborhood pub, and very rarely would he make it home by nine o'clock at night. This was his right; everyone is entitled to do as they please, as long as it's not bothering anyone else. More times than not, the cabdriver would have to help him to the door. He'd come staggering in, sometimes barely able to manage on his own feet. He would sit down at the kitchen table, then check to see if Debby had cooked supper; if she had, he would immediately eat, then fall asleep at the table for a couple of hours. On those rare occasions where nothing was made, he would just sit down, fall asleep, and within a few hours wake up and prepare something for himself before wandering off to his room. At first, it was really funny that he snored so loud, before it got to be annoying. Believe me when I say you could seriously hear him out in the front yard. In spite of everything, he was a welcome addition to the house.

Wayne must have sensed I was in no mood to play anymore games when it came to Bob. My patience was wearing very thin. Wayne telephoned him, relaying one simple message: as of that very moment, he was officially moved out. He could come by to pick up his suitcase, which would be waiting for him out in the garage. I think Bob realized he was no longer welcome on the property. He eventually picked up his bag, and he hasn't been back since. Just the way I liked it.

It would be an understatement to say I was in shock when I saw the state of the house. It was absolutely filthy. You could tell that Wayne had tried cleaning up as best he could, but I fully understood his dilemma; where could one begin?

My first day back could have very easily been my last. A while back, I had given Jayson a dog, a female Jack Russell which he named Spice. She definitely seemed to be popular with the males in the neighborhood, as she was very pregnant, and about ready to drop a litter. No sooner had I got there than Jayson asked my opinion as to the best suitable spot for Spice to have the pups undisturbed. There were already three dogs and a cat on the property, and in the very near future we would get two horses—and a llama, of all things.

I was overwhelmed to find that Jayson wanted to do things with me. It showed that there was a bond between us. Regardless of the differences we may have had in the past, after three years of living together, some form of closeness and trust had been established. What made it all more impressive was the fact that even a year and a half into the separation of his mother and me, he felt totally at ease with me.

Finally, after checking the whole place out, we decided that the ideal spot for Spice was in the little chicken coop out back. When we first moved to this house, I'd paid no special attention to the coop other than it being a place for storage. What puzzled me now was that it looked much bigger from the outside than it did inside. After a closer examination, I found out why. A partitioned wall had been built. Who knows when or why! Stupid me, with my curious nature, I immediately began tearing it down and found a small, elevated room five feet by five feet, equipped with lights and shelving. My only explanation was that at one time it had been used as a growing room for marijuana. I didn't make this assumption lightly, nor was it unsupported by facts. When we first moved here, there had been signs scattered all over the property that marijuana had been grown on the property. After taking all the factors of this little room into consideration, Jayson and I decided it would be Spice's new home. It was enclosed, small, and elevated eight inches. I grabbed a broom and stepped in to sweep it out. Even Spice came to investigate.

The floor creaked constantly. Jayson, not liking the sound of it, stayed out. I figured no one had been in this room for who knew how many years; the floor would loosen up and settle down in time. It frigging loosened up all right! Not even two minutes into sweeping, without warning the whole floor collapsed. It seemed as though it were happening in slow motion. I felt myself dropping straight down five feet, landing in a pool of freezing cold water. Had it not been for Jayson reacting as quickly by reaching down and grabbing my hand, I'm certain I wouldn't have survived, as I was somewhat tangled in the floorboards. Jayson most certainly was my hero that day. He acted very calmly, displaying a tremendous amount of courage in what could have been a life-threatening situation.

Shivering uncontrollably, before I could go and change, I had to deal with another immediate concern: the rescue of Spice. I didn't have a clue how long she might be able to withstand the freezing temperature of the water. Also, there were the unborn pups to consider. Wayne, having heard all the commotion, arrived on the scene.

I had already figured out there was only one way to save her without wasting time. As Wayne was much heavier than I was, we got a six-foot plank which we extended over the pit. I saw him brace himself while standing on the end of the plank; I lay down flat, suspended directly over the water. It took a few minutes, but we finally managed to pull Spice out, and within a couple of days she spit out the litter. Incredibly, she had eleven huge pups—and all of them survived.

After I had changed and warmed up, I went back out to survey the damage. It was now apparent that this part of the coop had originally been an underground well. It would seem I was fortunate it had been full of water—or rightfully, a thick muddy water. If the well had been empty, such a fall—onto the concrete floor below—could have proved fatal. I also considered that there was a makeshift light bulb hanging in the room, wound around a nail. What if that bulb had jarred itself loose and fallen in the water with me? I immediately partitioned this area off, and the remaining part of the coop was converted into Spice's new home. It took Spice a day to get used to this idea, not that I blamed her.

My visits with Debby over the following four days were for the most part great, as you could see the old Debby resurfacing. Her mind was as sharp as it had ever been; she even tried to con me out of a drink of water. You didn't have to be a rocket scientist to realize she was getting tired of the porridge they were feeding her, and the pudding as well. On the bulletin board above her bed was a note from her doctor, which read in bold letters: ABSOLUTELY NO CLEAR FLUIDS OF ANY KIND. Then it briefly explained the dangers involved. It should go without saying that I felt many times like jumping out of her sixth floor window; we had many frustrating, if not downright irritable arguments surrounding this issue. If you got her going by not letting her have her own way, she'd let go with an abusive barrage. I can tell you, she would have fit in very comfortably as a drill sergeant in the army! After a session with her, your head would be left spinning like a top. As an alternative to water, I'd bring her a small strawberry milkshake, her favorite menu item from Dairy Queen.

Wayne and I decided to clean the entire house from top to bottom. The best way to approach this task was to just pick one room at a time, and begin by washing the ceilings and walls with disinfectant. We started with the kitchen. Our first major obstacle was the fact that Debby was a pack rat; she had three of anything and everything. I knew she might eventually get upset, but I decided what wasn't a necessity would go in the garbage. Just from the kitchen alone, we had three full boxes.

The following day, Debby had a roomful of visitors, which always brought out her million-dollar smile. She just loved being surrounded by people. Jayson came, even though you could tell he didn't like seeing his mother sick in the hospital; it hurt too much, and I know he wished more than anything that she'd get well soon and be able to come back home, where she belonged. We all missed her tremendously.

Wayne had come along, too. Donny and Sandy showed up, and as they did many times in the future, they brought Debby's mom, Georgetta. Debby and her mother had a special closeness, a bond that words alone couldn't begin to explain. These were memorable occasions, and everyone thrilled to see Debby. You couldn't help but notice how well her recovery was progressing.

    The water issue turned into a game of wits between her and me. When I refused to give her water, she'd let it go until the next day, thinking she would outsmart me. She did manage to catch me off-guard once. While getting her ready to go back inside after having a couple of smokes, the conversation was pleasant and everything was going great. Little did I realize her mind was working overtime, trying to think of a way to manipulate me. When we passed the pop machine, she said, "Mino, you'll be here for a while, and you might get thirsty. Why don't you grab yourself a pop?" I figured, why not? What a mistake and a headache this was! All she wanted was a little sip… and on and on it went. From that moment on, I was on guard not to get caught in that vicious song and dance again.

Criminal Negligence 42

I was now in the frame mind to expect the worst. I decided that I alone would clean out the room which had been Debby's. When I first arrived I slept on the chesterfield, but now I carefully surveying the bedroom, the sight and state of which made me sick to my stomach. I began to understand for the first time the true extent of the abuse and neglect Bob had put her through. What I witnessed certainly could have been classified as criminal. I firmly believe had Debby passed away at home, and a proper investigation been conducted, he would have been held accountable.

Could these allegations be an exaggeration? You'll have to decide that for yourself. Her bed sheets hadn't been changed or washed for quite some time, and as a result the room smelled horrible. It was apparent this lowlife didn't have an ounce of compassion towards Debby. She had been given no choice but to release her body fluids where she lay in bed, helpless.

If this wasn't enough to make me want to rip Bob's head right off his shoulders, what I witnessed next pushed me over the edge. Scattered around the bedroom were pills of all descriptions, such as ones for sleeping, pain, stress, even her multiple sclerosis pills—all over the floor and on the bed. These medications were dangerous, and abusing any one of them could have resulted in an overdose. In view of her condition, you'd think the goof could have at least administered the medication as prescribed on the bottle. Instead he gave her free access and control of these deadly narcotics, to take as many as she pleased, whenever she pleased.

As all the pieces of the puzzle came together, even Al showed his true colors. He told me that he'd known Bob and his idiot friend Wesley had been feeding her morphine pills. If Al had really cared about Debby, why hadn't he said something a long time ago? As long as the party was on, it didn't really matter what the consequences were. I've never been to a school of dentistry, but in this case I don't think I would have had a problem pulling teeth.

It took me the better part of a day before her room was thoroughly clean. Overall, it was a good week before Wayne and I had the whole house looking presentable.

Around this period, I started working full-time for a landscaping company called Lawns Plus. I enjoyed the work I was doing, and it was great having Andy as a boss. It was his contract to look after the grounds of Douglas College, which had two campuses. Also under our maintenance were fifty private residences.

Finally, her doctor signed the transfer order. Debby was looking forward to her move to the Eagle Ridge rehabilitation facility in Port Moody. There, she would become a full-time participant in her recovery. She would be involved in various counseling sessions and the rigorous and necessary exercises. I was proud of her as she committed herself to whatever was required, a hundred and fifty percent. It was a real blessing for me when she was finally transferred to Eagle Ridge in March. It was only five minutes away from where I worked.

It was a wonder I didn't wind up in the bed next to her. I have no idea what kept me going. If I thought the pace of the last month had been hectic, it was about to get chaotic. My daily routine went like this. I got up at 6:00 a.m., went to work until 4:00 p.m., then headed off to see Debby for a few hours before heading home. For the most part, these visits were always pleasant. Debby fully accepted the fact that she could depend on me in every way. This instilled in me a feeling of unbelievable personal satisfaction, knowing I was making a difference, not only in the quality of her comfort, but more importantly in her life. Before I left in the evening, I would make sure all her needs were met. I would then rush home, attending to my own needs while washing her laundry. I'd prepare her food with the appropriate thickener (a substitute that had to be used in preparing all her food and drink), which I'd drop off in the morning. If this wasn't enough, keep in mind that since I was the one who saw Debby on a daily basis, I received telephone calls asking how Debby was progressing. If I got more than five hours of sleep any given night, I considered myself extremely lucky.

Around this time, the deceptions, hidden agendas, and deceit slowly began to filter into the picture. They formed a pattern, which through the passage of time reached unbelievable proportions. Her sister Darlene was starting to irritate me more and more. In the time Debby had been hospitalized, Darlene had only been out to visit four or five times. This I didn't have a problem with, as I took into account that she worked long hours and had to make a return trip involving an hour and a half of driving.

Usually by seven in the evening, when Darlene got off work, Debby was ready to go to sleep for the night, as a result of the exertion she put herself through during therapy. However, as I was to find out, even when the rehab staff did move Debby back to Langley Memorial, it didn't make the slightest bit of difference. Considering it was now only a ten-minute drive, Darlene's visits were still kept to a minimum—once or twice a week, and only for short periods of time.

Not only did I find Darlene's actions shameful, I found her lack of desire to even try committing herself to her sister's well-being despicable. She could have made the effort to go see Debby every night, even if only for fifteen minutes, just long enough to see how she was doing. Regretfully she couldn't even do this, and it wouldn't be long before her true nature surfaced for all to see. The cause of my aggravation was in the fact that I was the only one running around doing everything. I didn't see anyone else stepping up to the plate. True, I had committed myself to the role of being Debby's primary caregiver, but certainly others had to take into consideration the pressures and stress this position brought me. If Darlene couldn't, or wouldn't, ease some of my burden, then the last thing I needed was for her to frustrate me even more.

Whether intentional or not, this was exactly what she did. Her nightly calls and concern for Debby were fine, but then out of the blue, she started dictating what I should and shouldn't be doing. Everyone other than her thought I was just doing an incredible job, and from those people I was given an incredible amount of respect, support, and encouragement. This helped me immensely to keep it together through this painful time.

When Debby had gone for her brain surgery, her jewelry had to be removed, and it was placed in the hospital's safe. When she was transferred, the jewelry was left behind. My understanding of the situation was that only a family member could claim it. Darlene did this, but the jewelry was never returned to Debby; it seemed Darlene claimed it as her own—for the moment, anyway.

Debby, in her persistence and courage through everything she went through, never ceased to amaze me. After ten days of continuous retraining, she was so ecstatic and proud of the progress she was achieving that she wanted me to come and watch during her daily sessions. In order to do this, I started work at six o'clock in the morning and skipping lunch, which allowed me to leave at two in the afternoon.

Watching her do her exercises filled my eyes with tears of admiration. Here was a woman who for the past month hadn't been able to walk unless assisted. By sheer determination, she was working to overcome all obstacles in the path of her recovery—and making incredible gains. She pushed herself beyond what was expected of her. She'd start out by going through her stretching exercises, which to her must have been grueling; the sweat just poured off her. Next she'd work out with very light weights for ten minutes. After a little break, so she could catch her breath, she'd wrap up the session with fifteen minutes of walking and climbing up and down platform stairs.

Mind you, she was still a long ways from walking unassisted. She had to use a walker, but eventually she would walk up and down the length of the room using two canes. It didn't take me too long before I got involved as well. I used to stand at one end of the room, coaching her. I'd tell her how proud I was and how much I loved her. All she had to do, using the walker, was come to me, taking her time; I had a huge hug and a kiss waiting for her. She went through this routine twice a day, three times a week. The staff in all areas of the rehab facility was to be commended for their professionalism and dedication, given to each and every patient.

Like always, Debby had her moments. When I reflect back on some of the more memorable ones, I treasure them fondly. She hated being in the hospital with a fierce passion, not that anyone could really blame her.

One day while visiting, she said to me, "Let's go out and have a smoke." She had me wheel her around the whole complex, and we stopped at all different spots. At the time, little did I know, she was surveying the layout; right outside her room was an exit door, and on our way back she had me stop at this door. Giving me that classic look of hers, she said, "If I happen to phone you, you just come and park outside this door; I'll be ready and waiting with all my stuff packed."

Without me being aware of it, she had planned her own escape route. All I could really do in this instance was play along.

"You call and I'll be there baby," I said.

Every couple of weeks, her friend Jessie showed up and spent the day. As a result of these visits, I began to view Jessie in a different light. I started to appreciate her for the things she would do for Debby. I just couldn't do these things myself. She'd get right in the bathtub with Debby, giving her a long hot bath. She'd clip her nails, pluck her eyebrows, then put makeup on her. When Jessie finished with Debby, she looked like a million bucks, and I'm sure Debby appreciated these visits. Jessie was always meticulous.

Debby had now spent a total of two months in various hospitals, which in its own way is similar to being in prison. However, at Eagle Ridge, depending on the improvements a patient made, they would be encouraged to go home for weekend passes. As there was no therapy on the weekends, I thought this would be a wonderful opportunity for Debby. She was really looking forward to this possibility. It made her work all the harder. One thing I never deluded myself about was one simple reality: as demanding as my role was at the rehab facility, it would be increasingly more so on her weekends home. Before these passes could take effect, I had to pick up medical aids from the Red Cross.

The following week went by quickly. I took care of any last-minute preparations to ensure Debby's first weekend home visit would be as comfortable as possible.

Progressive Blindness 43

Finally, the big day we were all waiting in anticipation for arrived: Debby was allowed to come home for the weekend, which proved to be a chore in itself. I really believed Debby thought she was coming home permanently. Every weekend, she'd literally have all her stuff packed up and ready to go. As no one else volunteered, I was left doing everything. Sometimes it would take me several trips back and forth before I got everything in the car.

Before she was allowed to leave the hospital, two things had to take place. I had to sign her out, which basically meant I was assuming full responsibility for her well-being, at which time the staff would hand me a two-page questionnaire I'd have to fill out when bringing her back. The only other item of great significance was her medications; these were given to me along with instructions as to their administration. Once Debby was in the car, her wheelchair had to be dismantled to fit in the trunk, then put together at our destination. You can imagine how frustrating it could get if she wanted to go to a few different places all in the same day, as was often the case.

I really looked forward to having her come home, but at first I felt apprehensive about the idea. All she would talk about was the dynamite sex we'd have. To me, this never even entered my mind; the number one priority was to get her back to her original condition. Certainly I all too well understood the loneliness she was feeling, but what she craved more than anything was to be comforted. I spent long periods just lying with her, holding her warmly in my arms, a luxury we didn't have while she was in the hospital. I took full advantage of it now.

When Debby was home, you needed eyes in the back of your head. I had to continuously check up on her. She had always been a very independent person. Either she didn't realize or didn't want to believe it, but she was no longer capable of doing even the simplest of things on her own. However, as was her stubborn nature, she always tried to do things, not wishing to accept the dangers involved. As a result, she did fall down a few times.

We could work around this, but the greatest danger was in her smoking. On her first visit home, I understood why the hospital staff strongly objected to her having cigarettes and a lighter. Her eyesight was terrible. In all the extensive discussions I had with her doctors, Debby's recovery seemed to be progressing in all areas except her eyesight, which was an area of concern. Everything beyond three feet of her remained nothing more than a blur. We were sitting around the kitchen table one day and I lit a cigarette for her, placing an ashtray directly in front of her. I got up to do something, and upon returning she was putting out the smoke on the kitchen table. She thought it was the ashtray. Watching her do this seemed funny, but then I considered the seriousness of leaving her unattended while smoking. Very easily, instead of the table, it could have been the comforter on the bed, or the carpet! From that moment on, the cigarettes were never in her control. I watched her like a hawk.

When her mother was visiting, Debby threw her a few curveballs in regards to her make-believe world.

"Mom, I need you to do me a big favor," she said one day.

"Anything for you, my darling."

Debby continued, not realizing I was even there. "Mom, next time you come to visit, could you please bring me a box of light bulbs?"

Her mom looked around, puzzled; all the lights were on.

"Mino has turned out to be very cheap," Debby went on. "He won't even turn the lights on. Mom, he's got us in the dark here!"

Debby was about ninety percent blind, poor thing. She had always bought little gifts for her mother. Even though she hadn't been out of bed for a long time, it was no different now.

"Mom, did you get that card and the plate of fruit I sent you?" she asked.

Her mom didn't have a clue what she was taking about. "When did you send it, Deb?"

That's all it took. It was my fault now. I must have eaten the missing fruit! She kept us all on our toes, that's for sure.

Debby had always been animal-oriented, so she was just thrilled when Jayson spread out the comforter on the front lawn, made her comfortable with pillows, and brought Spice and all eleven pups to surround her. She loved the attention of the pups, but they were too much for her. In the future, I would only let her handle one at a time.

I knew Debby and I would have a problem when it came time for her to return to Eagle Ridge. She came up with a lot of excuses, which from her viewpoint seemed perfectly logical, but I wasn't buying any of it. I would remind her of the progress she was making, which had been outstanding. If she continued in the same manner, it wouldn't be long before they allowed her to come home permanently.

However, if the hospital felt there was a problem with her returning on time, it could result in her passes being cut back. Unbelievably, she bought all of this without any arguments. When it came to the questionnaire, we had a problem, though. Regardless of what she thought, I would answer honestly, whether favorable or not.

In the following weeks, everything seemed to be going smoothly. I was much more organized and Debby was still plugging away, working hard at rehabilitating herself.

Just about when I was coming to terms with my anger towards Bob, almost erasing any thoughts of him from my mind, another piece of information surfaced. I was outraged. If not for Debby's tragic situation, you'd almost want to laugh. I had assured Debby that when the bills came in—such as for the hydro, cable, and the telephone—I would pay them in full. Sitting at the kitchen table, I opened these one by one. Hydro: three hundred and fifty dollars. What had Bob been doing, heating all of Langley? The phone bill was two hundred and twenty dollars, which I didn't have a problem with, as I was in steady communications with Debby's brother Terry, who lived in Seattle. It wasn't until I opened the cable bill that I really lost it. The hell with the consequences, if he'd been there I would have personally pulled every tooth out of this dummy's head.

Donny had done an excellent job helping me control the anger which bubbled up within me, begging for the opportunity to be cut loose. In most of our long talks, I came away with the impression that he was trying to protect Bob. Now understanding it from a proper perspective, he was just trying to protect me; I'm sure he didn't really care what happened to Bob.

The amount of the bill was two hundred and sixty dollars, and again I didn't have a problem paying it. What enraged me was this simple fact. On February 20, he dropped Debby off at Donny's. Over the next five days, he rented seven pornographic movies from the pay-per-view service. Unbelievably, while Debby was close to dying, fighting for her life, Bob was at home watching pornos.

Incredibly, I didn't flip out. I believe we all have perseverance instilled within us, although to a larger extent this depends on the amount of support we receive from the positive people around us. I'm sure if I had negative people around me, things would have exploded a long time ago. Thinking of the consequences could have been still sends a shudder up and down my spine.

On one of Debby's passes, I made prior arrangements with Darlene to bring Debby up to her place for the day. Before I could do this, first I had to rush into Vancouver, pick up their mother and take her to Darlene's, then come back for Debby. In terms of Darlene, I was a puppet on a string. I had no other alternative but to project her into the same category as Bob, and her position was even worse than his, as she was a blood relative. The same holds true for Cheryl, Debby's other cold-hearted sister, who had a different agenda.

On the weekends, I often took Debby over to Darlene's place, as there was usually a fire burning in the pit out back. It wasn't out of the ordinary to find up to a dozen people sitting around it. Debby truly enjoyed these visits; she loved to be surrounded by people, along with the excitement it brought. What puzzled me, though, was that during the time of Debby's hospitalization, not once did Darlene ever offer to take her home for the weekend. She offered many excuses as to why she couldn't. I just don't understand why she didn't just say, "Mino, I have a hard enough time looking out for myself, never mind Debby." This would have been understandable and acceptable. Instead she remained persistent in playing a role she could never fulfill. I don't think she ever realized how foolish she made herself out to be. I believe she resented the amount of support I gave her sister, but she seemed blind to the fact that her own alcohol addiction prevented her from doing the same.

Finally, the concern over Debby's eyesight had to be addressed. It became very obvious that her eyesight was deteriorating on a daily basis. An appointment was immediately scheduled with the eye specialist. Debby either didn't understand or simply didn't wish to register the diagnosis the optometrist gave her. Based on the extensive testing she underwent, we were told her eyesight would not improve beyond what it was at present. I asked about second opinions, and even the possibility of glasses. The specialist said that her optic nerve had been irreversibly damaged. He went on to say that there remained a great possibility she might eventually even lose what little eyesight she had.

There were no words to allow me to explain that for the rest of her life she would remain almost blind. Therefore I never bothered to try. In the near future, I was to accept the conclusion that Debby, when it came to her condition, never fully understood what was happening to her. If she did, she hid it from everyone unbelievably well.

In the following weeks, the unimaginable started to happen.

Debby's World of Make-believe 44

Suddenly, as quickly as Debby had been progressing, for some unexplainable reason the whole process started to reverse itself. She was getting worse with each passing day. The first and immediate possibility the doctor ruled out was a shunt malfunction. On the scheduled day of her testing, I went back to the Royal Columbian Hospital with her in the ambulance. The results of the brain scan and all further testing showed the shunt was in fact doing just what it was supposed to, and was definitely not the cause of her regression.

It was now everyone's opinion that the only logical explanation was that her multiple sclerosis was going into a relapse. An appointment was set up with her specialist in downtown Vancouver; however, this wouldn't take place for another month. This wasn't reasonable, and I strongly voiced my opinions in this regard. In view of the nature of her illness, and the seriousness of her deterioration, she should have been given top priority. It would amount to nothing more than wasted breath. The medical system has its own process, and it wasn't about to change for me. Not just yet anyway. Her therapy was discontinued, since the stress might trigger further irreparable damage.

Day by day, she lost all desire to participate in the programs offered at Eagle Ridge, and this included eating. This turned out to be an issue of major concern, as within a period of ten days she lost an incredible amount of weight (twenty-five pounds). The necessity of surgically implanting a feeding tube in her stomach was seriously considered. This eventually wasn't a possibility, as the dangers of infection outweighed the benefits. However, as an alternative, they fed her by inserting a feeding tube down her nose. After a short period of time, this was discontinued as well. Debby would often pull the tube out, whether intentionally or not. Again, the dangers of continuously reinserting the tube outweighed the benefits. Since further treatment wasn't warranted, her stay at Eagle Ridge came to an end.

On April 22, 2002, she was transferred back to Langley Memorial, where she would remain for the duration of her short life. The hospital staff wasn't receptive to the idea of me taking her out on weekend passes. However, as was my nature, I remained persistent and determined to bring her home whenever possible. I believed any small luxury which brought her joy should have been a welcome accommodation. My efforts eventually paid off and I was allowed to take her home on weekends. However, due to the hospital's policy, she was only allowed to come home for one night instead of two. This worked out fine, as I'd pick her up Saturday morning and have her back Sunday night. Unfortunately, these passes were short-lived, due to her rapid decline.

Through this whole sad affair, I was very appreciative of the help and support I received from Wayne in looking after Jayson. This could at times be a full-time occupation, and also frustrating. More often than not, Jayson could be very irritating. In view of the present circumstances, this was understandable, and to a certain extent accepted. Debby had been in hospitals now for two months, and I could count the number of times Wayne had been to see her on one hand. In the beginning it angered me, but then again so did many things. My mind was always racing at a hundred miles an hour; I had no time for clear, rational thinking. Now that I've had time to reflect, I see some things in a different light.

The major factor to consider with Wayne is that his funds were very limited. The financial burden of visiting Debby, before she was transferred back to Langley, was a heavy one. I understood this better than anyone. Going to see her every day could cost a hundred dollars a week in fuel costs alone. However, from the time she returned to Langley until the time Wayne was recalled for work up in Chase, B.C., he religiously went to see her for at least an hour each day. He'd take her out for a couple of smokes and have a coffee with her. It wasn't unusual to see him wheeling her around the hospital complex, all the while giving her positive feedback and encouragement. In my opinion, he stepped up in a number of ways. And to think we had all thought he just cared about himself.

When she first returned to Langley Memorial, Debby shared a room with three other patients. This had its ups and downs. Being around people was important to Debby, and she now had people to talk to. However, as her patience level was relatively low, she could take any given thing for only so long before it became irritable. This was understandable. Try to imagine yourself in the following situation: let's assume each of the three patients had two visitors. All of a sudden, there would be nine people in the small room, each carrying on a different conversation. After any length of time, this would begin to frustrate even a healthy person.

As a result of the politics surrounding the issue of jurisdiction, her family doctor from Langley hadn't seen her for almost two months. To say he was shocked at her appearance would be an understatement. He was appalled. According to him, the last time he had seen her, he'd felt she was rapidly going downhill; she now resembled a scarecrow. What truly sent me into a panic were the tests and results of the on-the-spot medical examination he administered in regards to her reflexes. The procedures were extensive, but you could tell they showed unfavorable results. There was absolutely no response from her whatsoever. He cracked her fairly hard with his little hammer, right on the knee bone. I felt it; tragically, Debby didn't even register a hit.

Since no action could be taken regarding the feeding tube until she saw her MS specialist, that appointment was rescheduled to within a matter of days.

Debby was always happiest when I would personally take her to appointments. I don't know which pleased her more—us going together for a car ride, or just getting away from the hospital for a while. Either way, she looked forward to these trips, thoroughly enjoying herself. I wish I could feel the same way. I'm sure most of us have had the pleasure of having a backseat driver in the car with us at one time or another. We all know what a pain in the butt they can be. Rest assured, you've never had one like Debby. You would think she would just make conversation and relax, as she couldn't see due to her blurred vision. Every twenty seconds, it was "Watch out! You're going to hit the kid!" or "Watch out! You just missed the telephone pole!" or "Watch out! It's a red light!" If it weren't these colorful outbursts, it would be "Where are you going?" or "Do you even know what you're doing?" or "Don't you know how to drive?" All the while, she'd wave her arms like a traffic cop. If all this wasn't frustrating enough, she started giving directions. I look back on these moments as truly treasured memories, even though many times she had my hair standing on end.

This woman had unbelievable beauty in her heart. Her extraordinary courage, dignity, and compassion never wavered, right up until her last breath. If anyone had reason to complain, it was Debby. Devastating tragedy kept attacking her, one after another, like sharks at feeding time. Not once in the final stages of her life did I hear her complain or feel sorry for herself. As was her nature, she showed no fear. In her own way, she accepted whatever came her way. In view of all this misfortune, she still considered everyone else's needs before her own. She was truly a remarkable woman. At times she was a handful, but I'll always love her dearly.

Her friend Jessie came out to see her one day, deciding to spend most of the day and stay overnight. I truly thought this was a wonderful gesture of friendship—or so I thought! Just when I was starting to like Jessie, she had to go and spoil it. I was appalled at the comedy act that took place. First, she rented a television for Debby, which would have been nice except for the simple fact Debby had trouble seeing; Jessie didn't want a radio, so it didn't take me long to get the picture that the television was for Jessie's benefit. That was all right, though. If Debby should happen to fall asleep, it would give Jessie something to do. What baffled me was that here was Debby, who needed to be made comfortable to relieve the tension and stress she was experiencing, and Jessie got in the bed with her and turned the TV to her East Indian channel. It didn't stop there. She was steady on the telephone, and more often than not she'd be arguing with whoever was on the other end of the line. You can imagine how frustrating and stressful this was for poor Debby, never mind what I thought of the whole escapade. Debby was sharing a room with three other patients, though, so this walking headache was disturbing the whole room.

Again, don't take my words the wrong way. Unquestionably, Jessie and Debby did share a unique friendship. However, the Debby we had all known wasn't the same woman who now lay before us in the hospital bed.

Regretfully, Jessie wasn't quite through with her madness. With friends like these, there's no point in even having enemies. Debby wanted to go out for a smoke, and once outside Jessie lit up a marijuana cigarette. I looked at this lunatic and thought she was such a piece of work, she belonged in an art gallery. She took a big puff off the joint and blew the smoke right in poor Debby's face. I was on the verge of exploding. What normal person in their right mind, let alone a friend, would do something so stupid? Before I could say anything, Debby, barely getting the words out, managed to say, "Don't ever do that to me again."

Through this whole tragedy, if all I had to deal with was the likes of Jessie, I could consider myself fortunate.

After briefly examining Debby on May 2, the MS specialist scheduled an appointment for her to immediately see a neurologist, for a multitude of tests involving electrodes. I can only speculate that this was in order to assess the extent of nerve damage. Around this time, Debby started to exhibit signs of dementia. Due to the medications and changes to her environment, she was getting mixed up, having trouble understanding what was happening to her. This confusion made her suspicious of everyone's actions.

Whether Debby's frame of mind and personality was changing temporarily or permanently, the Debby I had always known would always remain. In my mind, this would never change.

In order to cope with the insanity continuously surrounding her, I believe she created in her mind a world of make-believe which to her was, in fact, her perception of reality. In the beginning stages, I had a hard time dealing with this, but when I began to understand the implications and significance of her make-believe world, I quickly accepted her reality as my own.

I began to notice Debby's state of mental confusion grow worse with each passing day. However, I didn't give it serious consideration. In view of her blurred vision, her actions didn't seem out of the ordinary. One day while visiting, she asked me if I could do her a favor and straighten out the picture on the wall; they were crooked.

"Sure, not a problem," I said.

I looked around, and for the life of me I couldn't see any pictures on the wall. I double-checked, just to make sure; I definitely didn't need her screaming at me. I then told her nicely that there was no picture on the wall.

She pointed to the wall five feet in front of me and let go with an abusive tirade. "What's the matter with you? Are you blind, as well as stupid?"

I looked to where she's pointing, and the only thing there was a small air vent. As far as she was concerned, it was a picture of a flower. Not to confuse her any further, I apologized for my stupidity and pretended to straighten out the vent. Looking in my direction, she said the picture was now straight and apologized for yelling at me and wanted to know if we could go shopping in the morning. Always looking for ways to see that beautiful smile of hers, I told her it was a date.

These countless small incidents captivated me. You had to admire her for the courage she displayed against insurmountable odds. Whether or not she was conscious of the being blind, she never once acknowledged or complained about it. She tried to give you the impression she could see as well as you could. Many times I sat in silent awe, trying to unravel the magic and mystery behind those sightless eyes.

My next act would become mandatory each and every time I stepped into the hallway leading to her room. In all honesty, the llama we had on the property could probably carry a tune better than I could, but I sang to her as follows: "Forever, my darling, I'll keep loving you. Just promise me, darling, your love in return, and then you'll know my love will always be true." I always sang the same tune, but she was just tickled pink over it. When she heard me coming, she would join in. I would be able to hear her all the way down the hall as she replied, "Hi, babe! I love you, too!" When I entered her room, she'd be wearing that million-dollar smile from ear to ear, and I just felt fantastic.

Cancer and Isolation 45

On May 9, I took Debby once again to Vancouver General Hospital to see the neurologist. For the past week, this appointment had weighed heavily on my mind. I searched for probable answers of what to expect. One thing I was certain of: it didn't look good. In my opinion, there were two questions that these tests could answer: they could conclusively determine whether her multiple sclerosis had come out of remission, and the extent of the damage sustained. Beyond this, I didn't even wish to speculate. These were my primary thoughts while driving into Vancouver. Debby, on the other hand, was oblivious to the serious nature of this appointment. She once again delighted in her role of giving me directions.

I sat silently in the examining room with Debby as we waited for the specialist. A nurse had changed Debby into a hospital gown and had her lying on a bed. I was more concerned about the intimidating machines which surrounded the bed. It was very obvious they would be used in whatever tests were to be conducted.

When the doctor arrived, she was very pleasant and had a professional nature as she began the thorough examination. Throughout the period of testing, I remained focused on studying the doctor's face the same way an interrogator would study a criminal's face, for those definite signs that might indicate something out of the ordinary.

The first tests involved the use of electrodes, which were placed on strategic spots on Debby's arms and legs. Again, I can only speculate as to the desired results. When the doctor turned up the juice, Debby's arms and legs twitched, in what I gathered was the accepted response. The doctor seemed satisfied in this area. Now, without the benefit of the electrodes, Debby was asked several times to move her limbs in certain ways. You could tell by the look on Debby's face that she was exerting herself in trying to comply. However, it was obvious her limbs were not responding to the messages her brain was sending. For the most part, they remained motionless.

I saw through the doctor's bewildered facial expressions that this wasn't a good sign. As I've said numerous times, professional people in the medical practice are to be commended. They seem to have such a grasp of human nature. When coupled with their compassion in dealing with patients, the results are just incredible. Even though the shock was clearly indicated on the doctor's face, she at no time made Debby aware that anything was wrong. She would continuously offered words of encouragement. This all made perfect sense to me; why would you want to confuse and stress the patient more than she already was?

The final diagnosis was that more conclusive testing needed to be done—at the cancer hospital. In all likelihood, according to the doctor, everything pointed to Debby having cancer. On the drive back to the hospital, I searched deep within myself to try and find the subtlest words to help me describe to Debby the implications of these tests. Within a matter of days, she'd be going to the Peace Arch Cancer Clinic for further testing. How can you find the gentlest words to tell your loved one that the possibility of cancer is very high? Debby was oblivious to everything that was going on; she was more interested in giving me directions. I decided to momentarily live in her make-believe world, as my mind threatened to jump into insanity mode. As a result of the tremendous pressure and stress, I fell into a deep depression. Luckily, I snapped out of it within a matter of days. In light of what was about to take place, Debby would need my support.

On the home front, Wayne had his hands full tending to Jayson. They were constantly doing things together, which I'm sure kept Jayson's mind from wandering. A huge issue with him was always his mother's drinking; he seemed to understand better than anyone that every time she took a drink, she was destroying her health. I knew he loved his mother with all his heart, and wished her a speedy recovery. However, he didn't go to visit Debby as much as I would have liked him to. He was hurt and mad that she was in the hospital to begin with. Looking at it through his eyes, her weakness for alcohol was the contributing factor. Therefore, part of his anger was directed at her for not having the strength to stop drinking. Although I'm sure he has a better understanding now, in some instances the addiction is just too overpowering.

Jayson was highly intelligent. He had ears like an elephant and heard everything, but his hearing was very selective; he only seemed to hear what interested him. He had a good understanding of what was going on concerning his mother's health. Going to visit her, if he wasn't prepared for it, would leave him in a state of great depression and stress. Jayson seemed to handle the whole situation quite well, but the last thing he needed was stress of any kind. I personally witnessed the effects it had on him.

Debby had to go for x-rays one day, and I didn't go to this appointment with her. Besides, I needed all the work hours I could get, as no one else was paying the bills. Since her return to Langley, once again my schedule changed. After work, I wouldn't even stop at home; I would drive right on by and head straight to the hospital. I would stay there until nine in the evening, as that's when visiting hours ended.

One day upon arriving, the same thing happened as before. Neither she nor her belongings were in the room. I felt immediate apprehension. What had happened? Where was she? Approaching the nurse's station, I was informed that Debby had been moved down the hall to a sterile isolation room. Until the tests came back negative, she had to remain quarantined; there remained a possibility that she may have tuberculosis.

When I first saw this room, I thought it looked like something out of the twilight zone. The first door I had to go through, which had all kinds of warnings and instructions taped to it, was a huge sliding glass door. Once I passed this, I found yourself in a self-enclosed room. It had cupboards literally stacked with surgical gloves and masks, and hospital gowns as well. You had to walk through here before getting to Debby's room. There also was a sink, for if you came into contact with her, it was hospital policy that you wash your hands. All this was understandable, for if she did turn out to have tuberculosis, you had to consider the risk of unintentionally spreading the serious illness. The whole process made you wonder if this was what it would have been like getting in to see Howard Hughes.

Entering Debby's room, you first had to pass through a heavy door which closed on its own. Debby's room was not too big or too small; it seemed comfortable enough. It had a fair-sized window and a private bathroom. However, what really seemed strange to me was that the staff still allowed me to take her out whenever she wanted to go for a smoke. The only condition was that she wore a surgical mask when out of her room. I couldn't understand this.

Around this time, I sat down with her brother Jerry, who lived in Seattle. I had spoken to him several times on the phone prior to this, always letting him know how Debby was doing. In the following months, he would be a big source of support, praise, and encouragement, as were Donny and Sandy. They were basically the only ones who expressed genuine concern about how I was holding up through it all. May the sun always shine upon them. Friends like these are to be treasured.

Being HIV-positive, my own health had suffered. Everything I did was out of my love and concern for Debby, and I'd do it again in a New York second, regardless of the consequences. As I know she would have done for me.

Every one of my visits with Debby was a learning experience as to her mystical nature. On rare occasions, she would astonish me. One day I took her out for a smoke, as it was a gorgeous day. There was a little park area with trees and flowers just outside the hospital's entrance. I decided we'd go sit in that area. I knew she couldn't see, so we talked about how sunny it was. Out of the blue, she said, while pointing in the general direction of the flowers, which were about six feet away, "Mino, they smell so nice and they're beautiful. Especially the red and yellow ones."

I was in total shock. At first, I thought she was just making conversation, but then I looked over, and sure enough, red and yellow flowers were growing there. Debby had always been garden-oriented, and she loved her flowers. They say that when you lose one of your senses—in Debby's case, her eyesight—the remaining senses are heightened. Perhaps by smell alone, Debby had known what kinds of flowers were growing, and in her mind she visualized red and yellow ones. As far as Debby was concerned, there was nothing wrong with her eyesight. You couldn't help but love her.

She completely caught me off-guard at other times as well. One day, she told me, "Mino, I was out today." I was thinking that maybe Wayne had come by and taken her out for a smoke. But no. She was insistent that she had gone out for breakfast, then went shopping all morning, looking for a gift for her mother and Jayson. I was aware that she hadn't left the room all day, but in her mind she certainly had done all these things, and as a result she was exhausted.

There was only one thing I could say to her: "No wonder you look tired, honey. You had a busy day, and by the way did you manage to buy anything?"

"No," she said, "but if you don't mind, maybe tomorrow we'll both go together and look."

"Sure, we'll go in the morning. But not too early."

"Mino, that would be perfect."

Most of the time, in her state of confusion, her thoughts were focused on her mother—and most importantly on her son.

One time she said to me, "Get me a beer, would you?"

"From where?" I asked, dumbfounded.

She pointed to a bare wall. "Are you blind? The case of beer is right there in the cupboard."

Well, now I was both curious and wondering who in the hell would bring her a beer, let alone a whole bloody case. I looked under the bed, in the bathroom, and in her bags. No beer to be found, thank God, and I told her so.

She got really mad and started in on me. "What's the matter with you? Are you stupid? Can't you see it on the counter?" With her next statement however, everything became clear. "It's got to be there. I just went out and bought it today." She went on to say, in her make-believe world, "Mino, it had to be the nurses. They drank it."

"Debby, it's a tough job looking after you," I said diplomatically. "Maybe they got thirsty. Possibly while you were sleeping, and not wishing to wake you, they had a drink with the intention of replacing it. On the way out, I'll check with the nurses to see if that's what happened. I'll find out when they plan on replacing the beer they drank."

"That's all I ask for, honey. And next time they had better ask."

As quickly as Debby brought about this confusion, it was forgotten. You just had to know how to defuse the situation, which I was getting to be pretty good at.

Deceptions and Unpardonable Sins 46

During the last three months of Debby's hospitalization, it goes without saying that I often felt her bitter sting through verbal abuse. Many people in the hospitals she was at just shook their heads when it came to me. In many ways, they openly expressed awe, fascination, and appreciation. Repeatedly I was told I was doing an incredible job when it came to caring for Debby, under extraordinary circumstances.

I never wanted her to be alone. No one could explain my commitment or dedication. In spending as much time as possible with her, I think I ignored my own feelings and needs; all my efforts were concentrated on Debby's. This allowed me to greatly contribute to her well-being in the final stages of her life.

Eventually I began to understand and accept Debby's frame of mind. I also accepted the role of taking the brunt of all her anger and frustration. She had to somehow release everything that was building up inside her. Besides, no one else wanted any part of this side of Debby; they couldn't handle it. At times, she could be downright vicious. I'm not a psychologist. Far from it. I do, however, believe that I have a good understanding of human nature. In Debby's case, as a result of her condition, she was prevented from making many decisions. Even when healthy people are put in the position of not being able to make decisions, they become anxious, irritable, and angry. With the passage of time, they start to be confused and unsure of themselves. They become suspicious of all those around them, and eventually stop trusting them.

While reflecting on Debby's suffering, and in view of her state of mind and frequent hallucinations, I began to understand her need to create her make-believe world. It was to become her constant companion. The pressures and stress she was enduring were of unconceivable proportions; I also had to take into account her pain or discomfort. She went into her own make-believe world to cope all the sorrow and grief which was tearing her apart, driving her mad.

Though I claimed her reality as my own, sometimes I needed a break from it. After playing this role each and every day, after a while I was scratching my head, trying to distinguish reality from insanity.

Speaking of insanity, Darlene gave the word a brand-new definition. She'd call me every night; how else was she going to find out about Debby? Her two visits a week just didn't cut the mustard. Procrastination came easy to her; she had it down to a fine art. Somewhere throughout our conversations, she'd say, "Mino,

I'll stop in to see Debby in the morning before going to work. If for whatever reason I can't make it, I'll definitely pop in right after work." Like clockwork she'd phone, giving me idiotic excuses as to why she couldn't make it to see Debby. Maybe the air conditioner at work broke down, and she was just exhausted from heat. Or a real original one: "I had to train a new girl today, and I'm really tired."

Her alcoholism was in control, but she remained in a state of continual denial. I should say, though, that I understood this aspect of her. Addictions can become so overpowering; they take control over our everyday lives. Until you recognize this fact and make some effort to regain control, you'll remain delinquent to all responsibilities, except for those that govern your addiction's continuance.

I finally came to the realization that it was a waste of time worrying about her. One thing was perfectly clear: she wasn't about to change her ways just because Debby was in the hospital. That said, I didn't expect what was to come in the following months. Her selfishness and greed surfaced in unimaginable ways. If I were her, I would have drunk as well. Something had to mask the shame and guilt—that is, if any existed.

Debby's brother Jerry had already been up twice from Seattle to visit for a couple of days. He was a very successful man in his own right and was deeply concerned about his sister, but his number one priority was for Jayson.

I had met Jerry before, and our opinions of one another were positive. Friendly even. And when he personally witnessed the lengths I went to in caring for his sister, we developed a warm friendship and respect for one another, which still remains to this day. Slowly I distanced myself from Darlene and concentrating on Jerry, Donny, and Sandy. This was only common sense; not only were they positive influences in my life, but our intentions were all focused in the same direction: Debby.

I had a lot of empathy for Debby's mother, as the experience had to be tremendously painful for her. As had been my nature throughout most of the ordeal, I considered the needs and feelings of others. I knew she would have loved to visit more often, but there were two major obstacles. First, she had no way of coming to Langley, except for when Donny and Sandy or Jerry came out, and in those rare instances when I picked her up, she was very sympathetic to me. Second, there was her health. She was in her eighties and had her own multitude of medical problems to deal with. To help relieve some of the stress and pressure she may have been feeling, whenever possible I would help Debby talk to her mother by phone, for as long as she could. I know for a fact that when such a call took place, Debby was in her glory. She always thought about her mother.

Debby had always been loved and surrounded by many wonderful people, as she left her heart and door open to everyone. If you needed help, you could always count on her. She had a very warm friendship with one couple in particular: Bill and Jean. To this day, their son Ian remains good friends with Jayson. One day, they came out to visit Debby. In a gesture of friendship and support, they gave Debby a check for a thousand dollars. This was to assist her and Jayson through their period of hardship. Up to this point, I had been looking after Debby's finances, paying them out of my own pocket. I always felt uncomfortable in this role, not because I was doing anything wrong, but because I didn't appreciate people questioning my integrity.

There was a tremendous amount of insincerity in the air all around me. Truthfully, no one seemed to care. Darlene often mumbled about how she felt left out, not having any responsibility as a member of

Debby's support team. I was leery about her wanting to take care of anything. In my eyes, she had already proved herself. I saw how she looked after coming to visit Debby.

Regrettably, Darlene was soon entrusted with a very specific responsibility, one of the utmost importance and urgency. Jayson's thirteenth birthday was just a week away, so Darlene committed herself to throwing a party at her house. Debby, as was her nature, old her, "I've got a check, and I want you to cash it for me." Her instructions were very clear: "You keep two hundred dollars of it, as I want to contribute to the expense of Jayson's party." Debby also wanted a hundred dollars for her own personal use. The balance was to be deposited into Debby's account.

It never was, nor would it be.

Suddenly, Darlene's visits went from rare to nonexistent. Debby was very angry over this, very frustrated. When Darlene finally did show up, and Debby wanted her money, Darlene said, "Oh, I forgot it at home. I'll bring it next time." It never happened. All Debby got was one excuse after another. Later Darlene even claimed that Debby wanted her to have all that money. This goes to show how stupid, callous, and self-centered this woman really was. What about Jayson? Where did he fit into this equation? Would not that money be his just entitlement?

I realize this is a strong accusation, but it's not without solid foundation. Darlene had temporarily been in charge of Debby's finances. If everything had been going accordingly, why did Debby suddenly demand the return of her bank card, which by the way was also never returned? Eventually Jerry, having power of attorney, requested that the bank cancel the card.

If you think this is bad, just wait for what unfolded next.

Indescribable Heartaches 47

I knew that everyone was understandably on pins and needles, especially while awaiting Debby's tests results to come back from the cancer clinic. I was both relieved and apprehensive when the nurse from the clinic called and asked if I would accompany her and Debby the following day to meet with the cancer specialist. This already sounded disastrous.

At the first mention of cancer, I prepared myself for the worst, not so much for my sake but in order to remain strong for Debby. She would certainly need levels of support and encouragement far beyond what had already been given. I also knew she would need a different approach in helping her come to terms with potentially devastating news. This, however, would only be necessary if she wasn't already past the point of understanding the diagnosis. I knew Debby wasn't delusional, but no matter how grim the future looked, she painted it as bright as possible.

Sitting in the reception area, the nurse and I filled out the required forms. The specialist's assistant took me aside, and as a result of our brief conversation I became weak in the knees. She wanted to know if I had power of attorney, or the capacity to make decisions on her behalf. I immediately gave them Jerry's telephone number in Seattle. It had always been Debby's explicit wish for Jerry to look after her affairs if something terrible ever happened.

While waiting in the examine room, I felt like passing out. My mind raced a million miles an hour, trying to absorb the harsh reality of the coming diagnosis.

An overwhelming feeling of helplessness and sadness overcame me. In my heart, I knew nothing positive would be said. Watching Debby, I tried to hold back the flow of tears welling up behind my eyes. She was in one of her playful moods, oblivious to the seriousness of the appointment.

Finally, the dreaded moment arrived. The doctor came in and stood beside Debby. In a clear and understanding way, he began to explain the unavoidable, the incomprehensible. The whole room was embraced in a hushed silence. Each of the specialist's word thundered a painful echo in the depths of my soul.

The tests had revealed that she did, in fact, have lung cancer, and it was inoperable due to its progressive state. Even with radiation treatments and aggressive chemotherapy, she could only hope to shrink the tumors. It was pointed out that she couldn't endure any of those kinds of treatments for long periods anyway, due to her recent weight loss. There was no escaping it. The cancer would claim her life.

When the doctor had attracted Debby's attention, he asked her whether she would like to try radiation as an option. I could only imagine he was required to ask this, as a result of professional ethics. It took Debby a couple of minutes before she answered, and I remember her exact words. "Well, yes. I have a son who needs me!"

Although traumatized, I composed myself. I stepped out into the hall with the doctor, as I had some questions of my own. He told me that the radiation treatments wouldn't make the slightest difference. At this point, there was no viable cure. The treatments could only serve to slow the progression.

As I asked my next question, already knowing it might be unethical for him to answer it. I wanted to know what her life expectancy might be. Seeing that I was depressed, all he offered was an estimation: it could be a matter of months, or even a year. However, this would depend on her physical and mental state. He went on to say that the only thing we could definitely control at this time was her level of pain. No one wished to see her suffer needlessly in the final stages of her life. This would be the direct responsibility of her family physician.

In closing, he said that for all purposes and intents it would be advisable to get Debby's affairs in order. He also said that her immediate family and friends should just continue offering support and love, as she would need it now more than ever.

On the return trip to Langley, my thoughts raced wildly. Debby was in her own private world. In the same fashion she had criticized my driving abilities, she now questioned the bus driver's ability.

My immediate obligation was to inform everyone of the painful reality. There was no delicate way in which to do this. Everyone had for some time suspected the worst, but this didn't make it any easier. Another matter troubling me was the issue of the radiation treatments. The specialist had already said these treatments wouldn't stop the progression of the cancer. Wouldn't these physically demanding treatments leave her in worse shape than she already was?

I stayed and visited with Debby for just over an hour, as these outings tired her out tremendously. Before I left, I gave her a big kiss and hug, reassuring her that I'd be back later that day. I had already decided how to skillfully and diplomatically inform everyone of the news.

After leaving the hospital, I went to Darlene's place first, as I knew she would be at work. I had no intention of telling her directly. I sat down with Toby and explained the situation. He thought it was a nice gesture on my part to let him be the one to break the news to her. To me, it seemed like the best way to handle it.

I then went home and called Donny's, relaying the unfortunate news to them.

I never even considered telephoning Debby's mother. Instead I called Jerry. We spoke for quite some time, and I let him know that the doctor felt it was extremely important to get Debby's affairs in order, including her will. I told him that his mother didn't know yet, as I felt she should hear it from him.

Having completed all this, I went back to be with Debby. She was well-rested and in a playful mood. We went out, had a couple of smokes, and enjoyed each other's company. No one else was saying anything in regards to Debby's medical needs. I imagine they just assumed nature would take its course. I understood all too well that there was to be no reprieve; Debby was in the process of slowly dying.

The last thing anyone wanted was for her to suffer. Since I was Debby's primary caregiver, everyone connected to Debby knew I had nothing but her best interests in mind. I took it upon myself to make my own rational, logical decisions as to what was best for her.

In speaking to her family doctor, I stressed that no treatment would alter her prognosis.

"In my opinion, radiation treatments don't seem to be a healthy way to proceed," I said. "The treatments are demanding, exhausting, and may cause her more suffering. They might even speed up her death."

His argument rested on one simple fact. "Mino, why would you want to take hope away from her, even if it's only a distant glimmer of hope? Give her something to cling to."

This only made sense to me if she had the slightest possibility of beating the cancer, which we all knew she didn't. "At this time, she doesn't appear to be suffering," I said. "I don't think we should pursue radiation treatments."

In a compromise, he suggested that we try two treatments. If they seemed to have an effect on her, we would discontinue them immediately. I didn't agree, but what could I say? He was a very good doctor.

The radiation treatments were discontinued after only two sessions. All along, I had been correct in my assumptions.

Again I'll say that Debbie wasn't delusional or losing touch with reality; she was just confused. She was very much aware that things didn't seem right, and sometimes her off-the-wall comments caught me off-guard.

One time, when I was ready to go home, she looked at me with a serious expression. "I'm thinking of breaking up with you!"

"Why?" I asked. "What's the problem?"

"You're never home anymore. You're always going somewhere, and for the longest time now you haven't been sleeping with me."

In her make-believe world, she was at home and we were a couple. To erase any hardship, I calmly replied, "Debby, I know I've been working a lot lately."

She tried to refocus. "Yeah, you're right, honey. We have to pay the bills somehow." She then added that maybe tomorrow, if I had time, she'd like to visit her mother.

I expected comments like this almost every day. Even though it had been three weeks since Jayson's birthday, she would say, "What are we going to get him for his birthday?" or "We have to organize his party." The two most important people in her life unquestionably were her son and her mother.

I've been through some extraordinary experiences in my life, but the most difficult was watching Debby rapidly deteriorate, coming to terms with her slowly dying before my eyes. Only now, many years later as I relive those painful memories, can I comprehend how God gave me the strength and courage to continue.

My greatest concern in the last couple of weeks had been Debby's unwillingness to eat. She was refusing to eat or drink anything other than her bottle, filled with orange juice, which I always prepared for her. Whenever I entered her room, the first thing I'd notice was the untouched food tray.

"Deb, did you eat anything today?" I'd ask.

She always answered in the same cheerful manner. "You bet I did, honey. Even if I wanted to, I couldn't eat another bite."

She needed to get some nutrition into her system. Giving this problem serious thought, I came up with a solution I knew she would accept. While at home, I made a dynamite protein milkshake with ice cream, eggs, bananas, and whatever else I thought would be nutritious. I then added to this an ounce or two of her favorite alcoholic drink. Unbelievably, it worked. Now you needed a crowbar to pry the shake from her. She drank it all. I did this almost every day, but even this only worked for so long. I didn't want to admit it, but her body was shutting down.

With respects to Debby's will, I spoke to Jerry. I told him that I could probably get all the paperwork in order, and he said it would be greatly appreciated.

As was my daily routine, I informed everyone of what was going on. I explained to Darlene that Jerry wanted me to get her will in order; she said she'd take care of it herself right away, as there was a lawyer's office right across the street from where she worked. I figured even she couldn't mess this up. Every couple of days, I asked about the will, and she'd tell me these things take time, that the proper wording had to be used. What did I know? I figured she was probably right and let it go at that.

Two weeks went by and I was still getting the same idiotic answers. I started to wonder what the hell was going on. How long did it take to draft up some standard papers? Were they coming from a different country, or what? I got on the phone with Jerry and explained the situation. I could smell the deceit and treachery in the air, and I wanted no part of it.

"If I had the funds, Jerry," I told him, "I'd have this document filed immediately."

In reply, he said, "Mino, go ahead and touch base with a lawyer. Whatever it cost, I'll pay for it."

The next day, I spoke to a lawyer from Langley and made the necessary arrangements. He phoned me back the following day and told me to meet him at the hospital in a couple of hours, with an impartial witness. I felt puzzled. What was taking Darlene weeks to accomplish, I got done in forty-eight hours. Darlene still had no idea the matter was being settled.

The next day, I brought Sandy to the hospital with me. The procedure didn't even take ten minutes. I had a tear in my eye as Debby signed each page of the will. Although she was in a pleasant mood, you couldn't help but notice the wear and tear the cancer was having on her body. Her signature resembled a chicken scratch, barely legible.

When it was done, I felt relieved that everything was in order. Jerry was to be the executor of her estate and would assume guardianship of Jayson.

For the longest time, the mystery of why Darlene had intentionally delayed the preparation of the will clung to me like a bad smell. Either this woman was in need of serious professional help, or she had treachery in her heart; if so, it hadn't just come out of nowhere. When I pieced everything together, it was obvious that her deceit and selfishness had grown roots the moment Debby was hospitalized. After Debby passed away, her agenda became all too clear. She had already been feeling Jayson out. "I'm his aunt," she said confidently. "I'll take care of him." But she was a drunk! She had a hard enough time looking after herself, never mind the needs of a thirteen-year-old boy.

We explained to Jayson all his options, along with what to expect. Jerry would be his legal guardian, and regardless of his financial success Jayson's future was secure. However, Jerry believed that his own domestic setting might not fully meet all of Jayson's needs. Where he was to live would be his choice.

Jayson was very intelligent for his age, and I knew he would figure it out. Another possibility was Wayne, Jayson's dad. The closeness they shared could never be taken away, but this was not a realistic option. Thirdly, we came to Darlene; Jayson didn't even want to entertain this option.

For most of Jayson's life, he had been surrounded by alcoholism. This isn't to say Debby wasn't a good mother; she was great. He had more toys and stuff than ten kids put together. For the most part, she tried his every need. However, in any relationship involving alcohol addiction, there's bound to be some form of abuse. Jayson's final decision rested in the fact that he had always been subjected to the pressures of alcoholism. Now he had the opportunity to change this. That's why Darlene's offer seemed so ludicrous to him. His response was that he'd have to be stupid to go from one frying pan into another.

His final option was to go live with Donny and Sandy. This certainly seemed to be the wisest choice. Donny had been more of a father to Jayson than Wayne had ever been. Their household was family-oriented, as Sandy had one of her sons living with them.

Without any tugging or pulling from anyone, Jayson made up his own mind. He chose to live with Donny and Sandy. Once this decision was made, he knew he had to remain firm in his commitment, as these wonderful people remained firm in their commitment to him. It was a huge responsibility, but all based on their love for Jayson and Debby.

Everyone except Darlene was satisfied with this choice. Jerry said that as soon as the will was validated, they would complete the necessary forms to transfer guardianship to Donny and Sandy. It was decided that when Jayson finished the school term, which was only a couple of weeks away, he would make the transition. The summer months would give Jayson a period of time to settle in, and also allow Donny and Sandy time to adjust their routine around Jayson.

It was almost time for Jayson to graduate. I knew Debby was extremely proud of him and his accomplishments. He often told her that he believed he would be this year's honor student again, meaning he would have all A's on his report card. And he did. Debby wanted to go to his graduation, and I would have gladly taken her and assumed full responsibility, but unfortunately it didn't happen. To begin with, she could become tired, frustrated, or irritable very easily. Secondly, there would just be too many people there. Again, the risks outweighed the benefits. Jerry came up from Seattle for the occasion and Wayne came down from Chase. Donny and Sandy were also there. The only person who didn't make it was Darlene, which didn't surprise me at all.

We had decided to visit Debby in the hospital after the graduation. It would have been really nice for her and Jayson to take a picture together, but she was against it. Was this the reaction of a delusional woman, or did she in fact have a better grip on reality than she let on? Could her refusal of pictures be a result of her realizing the state of her deteriorating appearance? The truth was, she didn't want Jayson to have a picture of her in the hospital; she didn't want to burden him with a painful memory.

We all enjoyed a very pleasant visit, except for one mishap. Debby rarely exhibited any signs of being in pain, except for the odd headache, but whenever you bumped her in the wrong way, or tried to comb her hair and mistakenly pulled it, she would start screaming and crying.

Which is exactly what happened.

After a while, we all decided to go outside. Everyone watched in amazement at how quickly and organized I was. When we were almost ready go, Jerry, in a gesture of what can only be described as genuine love and compassion for his sister, decided to brush Debby's hair.

The comb snagged.

Complete pandemonium broke out. Sandy and I tried to ease the situation by telling her that Jerry hadn't meant to hurt her; he had just been trying to be helpful. Jerry was quite shaken up over this. As quickly as it had happened, though, Debby refocused and everything was forgotten.

The sun was shining beautifully that day. All in all, it was a perfect day. Everyone was in a happy mood, and we got that million-dollar smile from Debby which she was so famous for. It was one of her better days, truly enjoyed by all.

48. Debby Moves into the Blue Room

Around the end of June, Debby was once again moved. This time it was to a much larger room down the hall, directly across from the nurses' station. This room was reserved for patients in need of palliative care, meaning that she would now get much closer supervision. The room was painted a pale blue, and huge in comparison to the one she had just occupied. It had its own chesterfield, chairs, and a twenty-inch television with a built-in VCR which hung from the ceiling. There was also a private bathroom. In one corner of the room was a makeshift kitchenette. On a large counter sat a microwave oven, small fridge, and coffee machine.

This room was used for patients in the final stages of their life. It could comfortably accommodate twelve people—visiting relatives or friends. However, Debby wasn't quite ready to say goodbye. As I previously mentioned, she could be quite stubborn.

I never deviated from my routine with Debby, but I began to wonder if the end was near. I'd already said what I needed to say to her, as we spoke many times about our feelings for one another. One such conversation remains vivid in my memory. While lying down with her in my arms, I talked and she just listened.

"Honey, where you're going, the sun will always be shining, and the flowers you'll be planting will look just incredible."

She had a puzzled look on her face. "Mino, that's all fine and dandy, but I'm not going anywhere without you."

I gave her a tender hug, while trying to stem the flow of tears. "Debby, I'll be with you forever and always."

"I know, Mino."

All my actions were always calculated to benefit Debby in some way. Other than myself, she didn't get many visitors. Darlene would show up twice a week, which was more of a headache than a visit. With everybody else, I understood their position; the distance was too great to make it more than once a week. Now and then Donny would slide in on the odd weekday. I figured to change this a little to Debby's advantage.

Regarding her eating habits, it was an ongoing battle between the nurses, me, and Debby. It was a standing order from the doctor that she had to sit upright, at a forty-five-degree angle, when eating. Even though she persistently complained of how uncomfortable it was, the nurses wouldn't ease up. If she wasn't in the upright position, the chances of choking or aspiration were too great. Debby, even though her struggles were insurmountable, did things to try and outsmart every one, and some of her escapades had the doctors and nurses smiling. She could be a conniving rascal at times.

One day I came in and found that Debby had completely turned herself around. The only thing that was in the upright position were her feet. She had this big grin on her face, as though she had a secret no one else knew.

"Honey, what's going on?" I asked.

She had a story and was sticking to it. I bent down and she whispered in my ear, "Mino, I'm sure the nurses are conspiring against me, but there are also people sneaking in, trying to take things." She went on to explain that in this position she could hear if the nurses were talking about her; she could more easily catch someone trying to enter her room.

After a few days of having to reposition her, even the nurses agreed to let her be. It was obvious this was how she wanted it.

I contacted the hospital's chapel service and explained Debby's situation. I requested that someone from the Hospice Society pop in from time to time to pay her a visit. They were delighted to grant my request. One person in particular made it a point to drop in. Kelly stands out in my mind as a really nice guy. We had the opportunity to talk at length many times. He was very impressed with Debby's display of courage. As he described it, she had a magical personality.

One day I came down the hall singing the usual song, and I heard her greet me: "Hi, babe, I love you, too." Before I could enter the room, Kelly appeared in the doorway, shaking his head in disbelief. We stood off to the side and talked for a few minutes.

"Mino," he began, "the love you have for one another is just incredible."

"What do you mean?"

"I've been with her now for just over an hour. The whole time she's just been mumbling, not making any sense at all, off in her own little world, staring at the wall. All of a sudden, she hears this singing and her face lights up like a Roman candle. It was like her whole body just came to life, as if awakened from a deep trance."

As I listened to him, tears welled up in my eyes. Words alone couldn't begin to explain my feelings. The impact of just how much I truly meant to her hit me. It's truly incredible to be able to make such a difference in someone's life, in times of their greatest hardship.

Since she was always in thought about the people closest to her, I had a fantastic idea. In reflection now, I know it was God who implanted the idea in my head. Throughout the five years that Donny had lived with Debby, he must have made at least a hundred video recordings on his camera. There were tapes of Christmas, Thanksgiving, birthdays, and even ones involving travel. Over the next few days, I put these tapes to constant use. I knew this added to the quality of her life in her final stages.

I had no idea how Debby would react when I played the videotapes, as I knew she definitely didn't like having the radio on. For some reason it bothered her. Probably it was too confusing, not to mention that some of the songs could be irritating.

The first tape I selected was from Christmas 1994. I plugged the tape in, then asked her if I could lie down with her. She was all for that idea. As we got comfortable, Debby rested her head on my chest, and we cuddled. As the tape started playing, I was fascinated by her reaction. I had a clear view of her face. Whenever Jayson was talking, her smile radiated genuine love. It was almost as if she had been transported back to the time on the tape; she would even engage herself in the conversations going on from the videotape. Witnessing the peaceful effect these tapes had on her will forever remain with me. It didn't matter how many times you replayed the same tape, Debby's mood toward them always stayed the same.

As the cancer ravaged her body, her desire for food would in itself become non-existent. After a few weeks, she started rejecting the spiked milkshakes I made for her; she just kept bringing them up. As a result, I started only bringing shakes twice a week. If she didn't want it, I'd drink it. This seemed like a fantastic idea in terms of trying to help Debby, but it didn't do me any good. Up to this point, I managed everything very well, but I lost sight of my own vulnerability and weaknesses. From that very first milkshake, I fell into a pattern of heavy alcohol abuse that lasted about three weeks. I still faithfully fulfilled my obligations to Debby, but no sooner would I leave her than I'd be into drinking hard alcohol.

During this period, I was lucky if I ate once every couple of days. My own physical deterioration was going into a critical state. Therefore, I discontinued my abusive pattern. The people around me often mentioned that I was looking a little thin. This started to have an effect on me, so one day I decided to get on the scale. When I had reentered the picture with Debby, I'd been a hundred and sixty-eight pounds. I was now a hundred and thirty-eight pounds. I had lost thirty pounds in five months. This realization crippled me emotionally. I was devastated. How could I have allowed myself to deteriorate to this level? Without blinking an eye, I immediately scheduled an appointment to have blood work done. I had been very negligent in this area, considering it had been almost six months since my last test. I started to worry, which stressed out. I firmly believed the results of these tests would be unfavorable.

What else could I have expected? Looking back on the past five months, I'd done everything I was told by my medical support team to avoid. I hadn't been eating right, and I'd overly stressed and frustrated. My latest alcohol abuse was like lighting the fuse on a stick of dynamite.

Since being diagnosed HIV-positive in 1995, my nature had been not to dwell on the illness. This had always seemed a sound practice. Whatever was going to happen would happen, so why should I lessen the quality of my life with unnecessary stress?

About a week later, I went to see my doctor in regards to the results. What he told my was incredible—not to mention unexplainable.

"Your blood work came back and you're doing great," the doctor said. "Your liver is fine. Your CD counts are up, which is good. And most importantly, the virus still remains undetectable."

Needless to say, I didn't walk out of his office; I floated out on a cloud. I was exhilarated beyond belief. Even in view of losing such an incredible amount of weight, my immune system remained as strong as ever.

Wedding in Armstrong, B.C. 49

I had all but forgotten, but in March I'd committed myself to going to Armstrong, B.C, to attend the wedding of Brad's daughter. This caused me a tremendous amount of stress. On the one hand, out of loyalty and respect for my friend I knew I should go. On the other hand, I was felt guilty about it, like I was letting Debby down. I knew there would be no one to care for her the way I did. Everybody urged me to go; it would only be for four days, and they felt I needed some time away to clear my head. Explaining this to Debby was easier than I expected. Her immediate response was, "That's great, hon. When do we go?"

I knew she would say something like that, and I was prepared with a suitable answer. I told her I had spoken to her doctor about taking her with me (even though there was no possible way I could have taken her), and that he had said if it hadn't been for some upcoming tests, she could have gone. Sensing her sadness, I said, "Deb, maybe when I get back and you're done with those tests, you, Jayson, and I could go up to Chase and visit Wayne."

With a faraway look indicating she was in thought, she said, "That would be wonderful, as I need to take it easy for a while."

Everything was now in the works for me to go, but I still couldn't shake off the guilty feelings.

Since I would be passing through Kamloops, Jayson had made prior arrangements for me to drop him and a friend off at his dad's place for a couple of days.

Two days before I was to leave, my brother Tomo and his family showed up out of the blue. They'd been living in Chilliwack, about an hour's drive from me. He pedaled some story about back rent and some other bills. Their intentions were to eventually move back to Saskatchewan, but he needed to store his stuff somewhere till they got settled. In order to help him, I had to talk it over with Al, since he was living at the farmhouse, too. It was decided Tomo could store all of it in the barn out back. I didn't give it much thought, as supposedly they were leaving within days, and I had my own problems to contend with. I suggested that since I would be gone for part of the week, they could use the bedroom at the house. There was no need for them to sleep in their van at a campsite.

In the days prior to leaving, I spent an enormous amount of time with Debby. I reluctantly left on July 25, but not without spending most of the morning with her. I didn't really want to go; if she took a turn for the worse and something happened, the guilt would surely haunt me forever.

Well, it was too late to back out now. Jayson was looking forward to seeing his dad, and Brad was waiting for my arrival. Debby wished me well and told me to say hi to everyone for her.

After leaving the hospital, on the drive to pick up Jayson, I broke down and had a good cry. I said a silent prayer that she'd be fine till I got back.

Arriving at Donny's, Jayson and his friend were all packed and ready to go. When I look back on it, I laugh. I was going away for four days, and all I took was a plastic bag containing the stuff I needed. As was his nature, Jayson packed enough stuff to last him a month. It was a wonder we got it all in my car.

Having them both on this trip with me was a blessing, as they helped keep me preoccupied. I can't remember the last time I laughed as hard as I did then. We drove for a couple of hours and then came to the town of Hope, B.C. I asked if they wanted to stop and get something to eat, and maybe stretch their legs. I guess they must have been hungry, for Jayson said, "Mino, that would be a great idea." He went on to say he and his dad had always stopped there for a breather, before making the rest of the journey to Chase. I pulled into the downtown core, which wasn't much to begin with, maybe four or five blocks. I found a parking spot and we then went into a restaurant.

Jayson had the look of death on his face when we sat down. He appeared to be truly spooked! The waitress came over and I ordered, then asked them what they wanted. They replied, "Nothing!" They weren't hungry all of a sudden. This puzzled me to no end.

"What seems to be the problem?" I asked.

Jayson said, "Mino, I'm scared. I don't remember this part of the town. Me and my dad have never been here before."

"Jayson, it's no big deal. We didn't come here to socialize, just to get a bite to eat, and then we'll be on our way." He remained stubborn in his reluctance to eat. "Suit yourself. You can watch me eat, as I'm hungry."

He wouldn't even have a pop, but when my food arrived his tune quickly changed. It looked delicious. Before the waitress had a chance to leave, they both ordered something.

Coming back from the restroom later, something was up. They were laughing hysterically amongst themselves, and I knew they had played some kind of trick on me. I sat there and finished my meal. By now, the whole restaurant could hear them laughing. I got up to pay the bill, and now the boys were roaring with laughter.

I came back to finish my coffee, as they were still eating. Then it hit me. I saw that my seat was wet. Immediately, I felt the back of my pants, and sure enough, they were wet. Even the waitress got a laugh out of this.

The rest of the drive was pleasant, and the weather was gorgeous. Wayne had been living in Chase for a couple of years. He used to live in Vancouver, but he had a serious and costly drug dependency. Luckily for him, he was smart enough to know that if he didn't get out of town, it would have just been a matter of time before he would have found himself in a serious problem. He bought himself a two-bedroom trailer, and for the next year or so he had a tough time adjusting. However, he remained persistent in his goals and eventually things came together for him. He got a job driving a truck. It wasn't any big money or anything, but it was a steady paycheck. As his boss got to know him, his hours increased. Before long, he was doing great for himself.

Wayne had been expecting us, and I sat and had a coffee with him. He had many questions about Debby and invited me to spend the night. I graciously declined.

It took just over an hour before I pulled into the small town of Armstrong. Brad and his girlfriend Kristi welcomed me and we sat around catching up on gossip. Our friendship went back about eight years, when I worked for him as a tree-planting employee. I never made much money in that field; I'd been more concerned about running into bears than planting trees. It seemed like yesterday when his daughter Grace was just a pup. Now here she was, not only about to get married but the proud mother of a beautiful baby girl she named Hope.

Everyone, including myself, thought this whole marriage idea was going to be a disaster, for a number of valid reasons, the first being that Grace was only eighteen years old and the man she was marrying was in his forties. Understandably, if two people have a genuine love and respect for one another, the age difference shouldn't be an issue. However, looking at it realistically, what did the man have to offer such a young girl? Was he financially stable? Did he have steady employment? You have to be able to support your family. It's called being a man and stepping up to the plate. Regrettably, he didn't have a job, nor did one seem likely in his immediate future. I heard rumors that he made ends meet by selling marijuana cigarettes in town. Pretty nice profession. If this was true, then sooner or later the long arm of the law would descend upon him, and then the only time he'd have to spend quality time with his family would be on visiting days at the local prison. I had no respect for this dummy, and it was obvious by his actions that he had none for Grace or their daughter.

In my opinion, their baby had more brains than he did. Why would you jeopardize the well-being of your family, and at the same time place them in such a position of danger? As is my nature, and out of friendship and respect for Brad and Grace, I managed to privately speak to him did on their wedding day, letting him know exactly how I felt. I wished him luck, hoping he'd do the right thing. "I would hate to have to make a special trip all the way back on account of you," I said. I stated this as a direct threat. After fourteen years in prison, I'd dealt with his kind on countless occasions. There was only one way to make things clear, and that was to be precise and to the point. Don't take me for a bully. If anything, I consider myself a fair person.

I hoped Grace's family could extend to him certain courtesies, to give Grace some form of financial stability. Brad's family was heavily involved in the logging industry and owned a very successful company. I told the clown if he played his cards right, they could make a job available to him. This wasn't to say Brad should give him a position where all he'd be doing is pushing a broom or a pencil. That would never happen. To start out, he needed a labor job in the bush. If he had any intentions of bettering himself, he wouldn't be concerned about his position; rather he would welcome the opportunity in having true stability for once. Those were a lot of "ifs," but if it worked out, then maybe Grace's family's opinion of him could change. Also, they could pull the plug on him at any time, should things not work out. I knew for sure was that anyone, given a little direction, assistance, and support, can change. I did!

I'd met most of Brad's family over the years, and had certainly always enjoyed their company and hospitality. All of them were unique individuals in their own special ways, and it had been a pleasure knowing them. The first to show up were Jack, Sue, and their son Jordan. From the very first time I met them, four years prior, we'd gotten along. Next to arrive were his brother David and wife Julie, and if my memory serves me correctly this was our first meeting. The last to show was his dad and his wife Liz, two really interesting and wonderful people.

Brad had arranged for a beautiful wedding, conducted in a beautiful park, and we had a gorgeous day for it. Regardless of his personal opinions of this clown Grace was marrying, I knew Brad loved his daughter with all his heart and wished her nothing but happiness and success in life. We all did.

By far the most impressive part of the ceremony, which had been kept secret, was when a beautiful horse-drawn carriage showed up to pick up the newlyweds. I considered this a class act on Brad's part.

Afterwards everyone joined up at the hall for the reception. Many of Grace's friends had taken part in arranging and decorating the hall, which looked wonderful. Brad was in charge of the food and did a marvelous job preparing most of it. After everything was said and done, with all the congratulations and toasts, everybody enjoyed a great meal. Then nonstop music played as we all mingled and danced.

My days in Armstrong were fairly preoccupied. I enjoyed myself thoroughly, but I didn't forget about Debby for a minute. I phoned her at the hospital every day, sometimes twice. I vividly remember the first time. I told the nurse on shift who I was and she handed the phone to Debby without letting on who was calling.

"Hi, baby. I love you," I said.

From listening to her on the other end, I could tell she was overwhelmed by my call. I let her know that she was always in my thoughts.

"You didn't have to call," she humbly replied. "But thanks so much. I really miss you, too."

Before hanging up, I briefly spoke to the nurse about how Debby was doing. She said to me that it was unbelievable how so full of life Debby appeared to be. This lifted my spirits to the point that I was able to relax somewhat.

Time went by quickly, although I looked forward to getting back home. I said goodbye to my friends, as I had to make sure Jayson and his friend got back in time for school. I should have known; just as they played a prank on the way up, going back was no different. They were lying in wait. They had their ammunition: ten water balloons strategically placed around the trailer. All they needed was their target to show up. I felt as though I was in a war zone, with balloons coming from all directions. Their aim needed practice, as I never got hit, but the car got a good wash.

While the kids were loading their stuff in the car, I had coffee with Wayne. The drive back was pleasant. As prearranged, Donny was waiting for us at my place when we got back, to pick up the kids.

Final Moments in Sight 50

While my thoughts raced in a million directions, I failed to notice the thick cloud of deception unfolding all around me. I loved Tomo, but sometimes he could be such an idiot. When I pulled into the driveway, I wasn't too surprised to find him and his family still there. Even though he had assured me they would be gone by the time I returned, somehow in my heart I had just known it was a lie. They ended up staying another two and a half months. What the hell was he thinking? He had a family to support and wasn't making any progress in that area.

He was an upstanding member of the laborer's union; not only was he classified as an industrial first aid ticketholder, he was also registered as a safety officer. His credentials were impeccable and in high demand. For ten years he had worked for PCL, a construction company with branches all over the world. Yet he couldn't be bothered to find work.

At the moment, however, I had no time to unravel other people's problems; I had enough of my own. Don't get me wrong: I wouldn't turn my family away in their time of need, no matter what. I strongly believed taking care of family was a two-way street. However, the decision to take in Tomo wasn't mine to make alone; Al lived there, too. Those two and a half months were an inconvenience to both Al and me. Actually, I was surprised Al didn't just pack up and move out. But if it had gotten to that point, Al wouldn't have been the one to go.

I often asked Tomo or Kim if they wanted to come and see Debby with me, and they always came back with a respectful no. It wasn't that they didn't want to see her; their point was that wouldn't be able to handle seeing her. This was especially hard on the many people who knew her well. They pictured Debby a certain way. Seeing her in the final stages of her life would leave a devastating impact. In the last two months, she had lost over thirty pounds, weighing no more than seventy pounds.

Debby never ceased to amaze me. She often forgot things that had taken place within a matter of hours, so I believed she wouldn't remember that I had called while I was away. Was I ever surprised! When I exited the elevator, I started singing, hoping to surprise her. I didn't expect a response, but instead I heard her reply to me all the way down the hall. You couldn't mistake the pure joy in her voice; she chattered away like an adding machine gone crazy. My heart pounded with excitement over her happiness.

When I finally entered the room, the very first thing she did was give me a tender hug and kiss, telling me how thoughtful I was to call her from Brad's. Our love had become as inseparable as two giant oak trees standing side by side, deep within an untouched forest. We truly had a special bond which would forever remain alive in my heart.

I had been advised by many people that I should think about cutting back on my visits. They were worried I had become so attached that when she passed away, it would have a damaging effect on me. I remained relentless; I wouldn't abandon her, regardless of the consequences.

I was caught off-guard in the second week in August. Kim, while in idle conversation, asked, "Mino, if you're going to the hospital today, would you mind if I came along?"

Somewhat shocked, I replied, "Kim, you're welcome to tag along anytime you want."

She made me stop along the way, for she wanted to pick up a few things for Debby. What she purchased brought a tear to my eye. She got her a huge bottle of lavender powder, which Debby just loved. I would rub the powder on her hands and arms daily, spreading it around her head where she lay. Debby also had a cute little teddy bear, and occasionally I'd give him a good rub as well. Kim also bought a magnetized angel, which she positioned on the wall above Debby's bed. This was very thoughtful.

The visit went great, considering Kim's greatest fear was whether or not Debby would remember her. She did. Astonishingly, Debby not only remembered Kim, but asked about Sunny and their baby girl Saffron. I could see the effect Debby's state of deterioration had on Kim, though. Although she was a strong-willed person, it was hard on her. She did, however, find the courage to come visit a couple more times with me, and on those occasions she brought Sunny.

I remember the first time we all showed up. Debby was just thrilled at having Saffron cradled in her arms. Regretfully, Debby couldn't see a thing anything more than a foot away. Yet hearing her go on—"Oh Saffron, you're so beautiful, and I love you so much"— filled our hearts with enormous compassion. I was concerned about Sunny, but for a fifteen-year-old she handled the situation quite well.

Jerry came up whenever he could break away from the art gallery he owned. I was always delighted to see him. He was a great source of inspiration and support to me, and at this point I needed all I could get.

What really surprised me was that Tomo decided to join me one day. This, from the guy who would turn pale at the merest mention of coming along to the hospital. Maybe his curiosity got the best of him; no one really believed how badly the cancer had ravaged Debby's body. He was apprehensive, not knowing what to expect or even how he would react upon seeing her. We stayed about an hour and everything was fine, although I could sense his uneasiness with the whole situation.

Before leaving, I told Debby I would return in a little while, as I was going to take Tomo home. She kissed and hugged us both, saying, "No problem, Mino. I was thinking of taking a nap anyway."

Debby's make-believe world really scared Tomo. He just couldn't understand it. In the near future, he made this journey with me one final time. His support at that time was greatly appreciated.

Almost from the moment Debby was admitted to the hospital, once or twice a week I would bring one of our three dogs along. This had a high therapeutic value for Debby; she absolutely loved animals, and the other patients enjoyed it as well.

By early August, Debby had been hospitalized a total of five and a half months. You would think all these illnesses that attacked her would have taken their toll and crippled her mind, as they did her body. Debby had a will all of her own, as strong as a mountain. Through it all, she kept her dignity, held her head high. I can only begin to understand how unbearable her pain must have been, and yet not once did I see her cry out in pain—unless someone pulled her the wrong way. I sat in awe of her, trying to unravel the magical mystery behind those sightless eyes.

Other than now and then asking for something for either a headache or nausea, she never asked for serious pain medication. In her final days, she was against being placed on morphine. My only explanation is that it withdrew her from reality. I often asked myself how it was possible for one person to endure so much without losing their dignity or spirit along the way. Debby had always been so full of life, having an extraordinary sense of compassion. She was a true humanitarian with a genuine willingness to help anyone and everyone. My only theory is that God granted her the gift of enjoying her final days in relative peace.

I was constantly on the phone with her doctor, and I knew her time was almost at an end. Her doctor suggested that if I still felt strongly about bringing her home, all the necessary arrangements concerning home care would be taken care of. I now had to view the situation from a different perspective. How would such a move affect Debby and those around her, especially Jayson? This was the most important concern. I was positive I could attend to Debby's every need, as I had done a good job of it so far.

I talked this over at length with Jerry. After considering all the factors involved, we decided Debby was in good hands right where she was. She had the best care, and more importantly it came with around-the-clock monitoring. Jerry was excited about going to Paris the following week, however. The trip had been arranged a month earlier, and was for the most part a business trip, something to do with the art gallery.

Any time I spent with Debby I considered an intimate moment. I'll cherish one particular moment for the remainder of my life, as it showed just how much Debby trusted and loved me. She hadn't asked in the longest time about going out for a smoke, then suddenly, after routinely asking her if she wanted to go outside with me, I was somewhat shocked when she perked up and said, "You bet I do, Mino." I gave the matter a little thought; it wasn't as simple as it used to be. More than anyone, I understood that just touching or moving her the wrong way brought her considerable pain. We both laughed as I said, "Okay, Deb, I'll be back in a minute. I'm just going down the hall to get you a taxi (wheelchair)." I scrambled down the hall in excitement, looking for the Cadillac of wheelchairs. They were almost twice the size of a regular chair. Not only were they heavily padded, they reclined!

On my way back to Debby's room, the nurses couldn't help but notice my excitement. They inquired what was going on. When I informed them of Debby's willingness to venture outside, they too found this extraordinary. They offered to help get her ready.

When the nurses went to try and move her, though, Debby freaked out. "Mino, I only want you to touch and move me, no one else!" she shouted. I assured her it would only be me. The nurses backed off, wanting to see how I would handle the task. As always, I stopped at the heated oven and grabbed a couple of warm blankets. One would act as further padding on the chair; I would wrap her up in the other.

Once I got the wheelchair prepared just the way I wanted, knowing she'd be comfortable, I gently leaned over her and whispered in her ear, "Honey, when I say okay, I want you to carefully put your arms around me. I'm going to very gently pick you up and put you in your chair." As she put her arms around my neck, I put my arms underneath her. Surprisingly, she wasn't hanging on for dear life. We had been through this drill so many times before; she knew I would do everything possible to cause her the least amount of discomfort.

As I picked her up, I had tears in my eyes. The harsh reality of her deterioration hit me like a sledgehammer right between the eyes, and I staggered backwards for a moment. She was as light as a feather; there could not have been more than sixty pounds to her. Quickly shaking off my feelings of despondency, I decided to rejoice in the moment we were about to share.

Throughout the procedure of getting her in the chair, I continually talked to her, hoping to give her assurances that everything would be all right and make her feel like an active participant in the move. Her only moment of panic or confusion came as I lowered her into the chair. This was understandable. Debby, being sightless, was afraid of falling and possibly hurting herself. However, once I had her comfortable in the chair, her million-dollar smile brightened the room again, leaving the nurses in awe. What to them a few moments ago had seemed impossible was now a living reality.

I stood back and observed her, so vulnerable and yet so fragile. She sat proudly, holding her head high with dignity, as though she didn't have a care in the world. To her, this occasion was special—intimate, in its own way, as it was our moment. She was truly a joy to watch. As I wheeled her through the hospital maze, her smile never left her face. Even though she couldn't see anyone, whenever she felt as though someone was close by, she would tilt her head in that general direction and say hello.

Once outside, I positioned her in such a way that the sun shone on her. We didn't stay out too long. Even though the breeze wasn't very strong, I realized the weather could affect her health dramatically. This was, in fact, to be the last time we ventured outside together. This was not to my disappointment, since I knew her time was close. From the beginning of this ordeal, I had tried to ensure all our precious moments together were special. I truly believed this was the greatest gift anyone could give another person in the final stages of their life, a true gesture of unconditional love and affection. I stayed with Debby for another hour, just talking, laughing, and sharing our fondest memories together.

I had gotten Tomo a job landscaping with me. Our task was to water every tree and all the shrubbery on the grounds of the two college campuses we maintained. It was very time-consuming, but then again this was fine when you're paid by the hour. At one point we started working the graveyard shift, which lasted two weeks.

In my daily visits, I knew Debby's time was very near; her weight had dropped below sixty pounds. She adamantly refused any form of food. Though she would from time to time have a drink of her juice, this was minimal. In her final days, I knew she was content and at peace with herself. Through my observations, it seemed evident that she had started to cross over to whatever awaited her.

Listening to her talk always brought tears of wonderment and joy to my eyes. Debby acknowledged my presence right up until she passed away, even if only for a few brief moments a day. She always let me know how special and loved I was. I had started drinking heavily again, possibly to mask the emotions which now threatened to shatter my sanity. Many thought I was like stick of dynamite waiting to go off, and all it would take was Debby's final breath.

Inescapable Heartache 51

Around August 20, they moved Debby one last time, and I knew it was only a matter of days now. They took her upstairs and put her in a very small room at the end of the hall. She weighed fifty pounds and sometimes was strapped to the bed, or to her wheelchair. I understood that this was for her protection. I never deviated from my daily routine of visiting, even though it was really tough.

For the first time since she entered the hospital, I saw her cry. I was perplexed, not knowing what to do. She didn't like being manhandled, she never had, and she definitely didn't like being doped up. On most of these last visits, Debby played on my emotions. She often said, "Mino, they got me tied up. Every day they give me some kind of pills, and I don't remember a thing until I wake up."

As far as she was concerned, everyone had entered into some kind of vicious conspiracy against her. I saw the reality of the situation. The hospital viewed Debby as one of its more colorful patients, and they had grown to love her just as I did. The reason my girl had her head strapped while sitting in a wheelchair was that the nurses wanted to make her as comfortable as possible. Quite often, her head would awkwardly hang and come to rest on either shoulder. She had no strength to even hold her head up, poor thing. As she lay in bed, I explained the necessity of the straps while tenderly holding her hand. She came to terms with that, but continuously protested against the drugs. From her point of view, being drugged was like placing her in a bare isolation cell where she had no contact with other people. As the end was near, I would like to believe Debby was reflecting on her spirituality, whatever her beliefs may have been. God's response to her would have been in the words of this incredibly graceful poem:

> Debby, has your heart ever been broken?
> Soon you'll come be with me and
> I will heal it like no other can.
> Have you ever wanted to be with someone,
> But they wanted to be with another?
> Soon you'll come to me and there will be no other.
> Has your mind wanted to go one way,

> But your body wanted to go another?
> When you come to be with me,
> They'll both want to go the same way.
> Have you ever wanted to go past the stars,
> Where no man has ever been?
> When I come and take you by the hand,
> I'll take you to a place no one ever has.
> Have you ever seen your soul
> Through the eyes of another?
> Soon you'll come to be with me.
> You shall look into my eyes, and you will see.
> Have you ever seen your eyes shine
> With love for another?
> When I come and take you by the hand,
> You'll see how it's going to be.
> Just let go without fear.
> Come be with me and you shall see.

August 26, 2002 would come to haunt the deepest corridors of my mind. It was to be the saddest day of my life, yet it brought a wholesome sense of contentment as I never felt before.

Tomo and I had recently switched to watering the campus grounds on the night shift. We'd put in our twelve hours, starting at eight in the evening. After this particular shift, I was totally fatigued. The job wasn't demanding, as all it entailed was moving a probe—a fancy term to describe a hollow three-foot pole attached to a garden hose. It was a very dry time, so we needed to feed the roots directly. A hundred-foot cedar or oak usually took twenty minutes to thoroughly soak. Wedges had been welded on the probe about a foot from the bottom; I stuck it in the ground, turned the knob, and waited.

This night, most of my thoughts focused on all the armchair quarterbacks in my and Debby's life—those people who over the course of the last six months had sat idly on the sidelines, yelling instructions as to game strategy yet refusing to play the game themselves. I had driven myself many times past the point of physical, emotional, and mental exhaustion in my passion to care for Debby. I had stepped up to the plate when no one else could or would. Issues concerning my own health were brought into question, but I remained determined in my unconditional act of compassion.

For the longest time, I didn't quite understand it. Before this tragedy had begun, Debby had hung me out to dry! I had been thinking in terms of reconciliation, and doing my best to make it happen, when suddenly she discarded me and Bob moved in.

In recent weeks, I saw deceptiveness and treachery around me. I fought through it on a daily basis, keeping a harness on my anger and sanity. For the life of me, I couldn't understand the lack of appreciation and respect I was shown by some members of Debby's family. Even Jayson only saw her six times during her hospitalization. I know that ate at her more than the cancer ravaging her body. The only concern on people's minds should have been seeing to Jayson's needs. Even more than Debby herself, he needed our support and encouragement now, yet too often I felt the brutal harshness of indifference all around me.

As Tomo and I made the thirty-minute drive home from work, my thoughts briefly centered on him and his family. They had been living in my house for the past two months, yet there remained a distance which hovered around us like a thick cloud. For the moment, such thoughts seemed immaterial and irrelevant; I would soon be grinning from ear to ear, giving Debby a gentle hug and kiss. When I reflected on this extraordinary woman, my thoughts weighed heavily on the existence of a higher power, something far beyond ourselves.

Debby, in all her beauty, wasn't much more than a skeleton now. She knew about all her struggles, from multiple sclerosis relapse to cancer to blindness, yet they had no meaning to her. The most excruciating pain she felt wasn't physical but emotional. By far, her greatest pain was in the fact that there was nothing she could do to comfort Jayson, whom I know she loved more than life itself. But even as I write these words, I see the falsehood in them; she was far from helpless in guiding her son, although crippled and bedridden. In her greatest time of vulnerability, she still managed to leave her son the most precious gift a mother can in departing the world. Debby's parental instincts went far beyond protectiveness. As if guided by heavenly angels, Debby gave all she had left to give.

No one understands the mind of God, but I'd like to believe that as a result of the kindness Debby showed to complete strangers, God blessed her with a relatively painless journey in the final stages of life. What other conclusion could I draw? She adamantly refused pain medication. She spit out any pills they tried to feed her, ripped out any and all IVs. Possibly the reason she quit eating was that she believed the hospital was trying to trick her by placing medication in her food.

I had become very predictable in my daily movements. Once Tomo and I arrived home, I stayed only as long as it took to get changed. Sunny, Kim's daughter, expressed an interest in coming along. There was nothing odd in this, as she had been with me to visit on a few other occasions. Sunny took a great interest in Debby's well-being and always asked questions about her. I was somewhat apprehensive about Sunny's request, though, as she hadn't seen Debby in about a month. I wasn't sure if Debby's deterioration would leave its imprint on this fifteen-year-old.

During the trip to the hospital, I tried to prepare Sunny as to what she could expect. Mainly I was trying to judge her reactions; if she showed any signs of hesitancy, I would turn the car around and take her home. I definitely didn't need her getting emotional. I explained some simple procedures in dealing with Debby. For example, she was to always speak in a whisper. I went on to say that if she felt like giving Debby a hug, which I knew she'd welcome, Sunny was to think of her as a newborn baby; all her bones had become brittle. It was easy to cause Debby excruciating pain.

Lately, whenever I entered the hospital I was filled with an overwhelming state of distress. Part of me never knew just what to expect. I ever so briefly always envisioned the worst.

As Sunny and I approached the closed door of her room, a feeling of uneasiness embraced me. For months, it had been my constant companion.

Upon entering the quietness of Debby's room, I saw that she was very restless. While speaking softly to her, I bent over and kissed her lips. She tried to put her arms around my neck, to give me a hug, but the effort was just too great a strain on her. I could clearly see she was becoming weaker with each passing hour.

As was my nature, when speaking to her, my voice gave no indication that anything was out of the ordinary. I told her that Sunny was here as well. To my amazement, she not only perked up, but remembered her.

Regardless of others thought, Debby still had the capacity for rational thought. She and Sunny talked for a bit, and I was surprised at how well Sunny seemed to grasp the nature of what was going on. Never mind talking, the simple task of keeping her eyes open was an effort for Debby. While she focused her attention on me, Sunny sat in the nearby chair; I sat on the bed next to Debby. She was constantly slipping in and out of reality. Her exact words were, "Honey, I'm a little tired. When you go to work, I'll take a nap, then go out and do some shopping. But I'll have supper waiting by the time you get home!"

I glanced briefly in Sunny's direction, where she silently sat with tears in her eyes. Her expression showed how much she admired Debby for her courage.

I would not disillusion Debby in her make-believe perception of reality. Ever so gently, I wrapped myself around her in a hug, without actually touching her; in my heart, I knew she felt my closeness.

"Deb, I have a few minutes yet," I whispered. "I'll just sit with you for a bit. Your beauty overwhelms me. I hope it's a short day, so I can hurry back to you."

Her face lit up like the sun. She tried to squeeze my hand. It never changed; whether our visits were lengthy or short, even a few moments with Debby was emotionally draining. It was more demanding than any physical labor.

Within minutes, Debby drifted off to sleep. Or maybe she had just slipped out of consciousness, as she was prone to do.

Before we left, Sunny watched me in my parting ritual. It had almost become like a religion to me. I washed out her juice container thoroughly. Regardless of the fact that it was full, I made sure it was refreshed, with lots of ice and fresh orange juice. I closed the pop-up lid, then nestled it in her blanket where she would have easy access to it. Next, I lightly sprinkled the stuffed bear I had gotten her with lavender powder. I ever so gently sprinkled the powder on her hands and around the pillow, where her head lay. She adored the fragrance. I made sure she was properly covered and protected from any drafts. I slightly opened and left ajar the top half of the window in her room.

There was no hiding it; I was exhausted. My body was slowly but surely wearing itself out, and my recent pattern of drinking didn't help. It was bound to catch up with me sooner or later.

Sunny, for a fifteen-year-old, seemed to have a good understanding of things. She noticed my dreariness and tried to lift my spirits. She wanted me to know that regardless of Debby's present state, she found Debby to be no different now than the first time they had met. "Debby was always so full of life and kindness," Sunny said. "Always smiling, just as she was today." In Sunny's heart, Debby would forever be thought of with the fondest of memories.

Once home, I had a quick bite to eat, jumped in the shower, then headed straight to bed. While waiting for the sleeping pill to take effect, I focused briefly on the absurdity that had become my life.

Debby certainly owned many things, as she was a bit of a packrat. She would keep anything and everything. However, she didn't have many possessions with monetary value. Material things weren't too important to her. The way I saw it, everything she owned was now rightfully the property of Jayson. When her time came, no one other than Jayson —and I mean absolutely no one—would lay claim to her things.

When he was through deciding what to keep in memory of his mother, Darlene would be more than welcome to anything leftover that held sentimental value.

During the last couple of months, I had begun the laborious task of packing all her things. This had to be done rather meticulously. Each box had to be clearly marked. I had washed all her clothes and folded them neatly in boxes. In all this time, no one came offering to help. It seriously made me wonder where people's priorities were. I wasn't complaining, though; I wholeheartedly welcomed the privilege. I looked at it as a gift from the heavens above. In taking my time to do this, I realized how very special Debby really was. Over our years together, we had accumulated an assortment of things. In going through them, I came to truly understand who Debby had been for most of her life. She had countless boxes of photographs. While pondering each image, with them came cherished memories.

Darlene, in view of everything taking place, felt it a matter of great importance to claim Debby's car, the lawn mower, and an antique desk. Why didn't this surprise me? My final thoughts before drifting off to sleep were, *Here's Debby, hanging on by the final threads of her life, and all her sister can give any thought to is what she can take.*

Tomo awakened me at about 7:30 that evening. I must have fallen into a deep sleep, as his words seemed to come at me from somewhere off in the distance. It took me a few minutes to orient myself to my surroundings. Then, suddenly, as if a lightning bolt had struck me, I began to grasp the significance of his words. They tore at every fiber of my soul.

Looking very pale, he repeated himself for the third time: "Mino, the hospital called. They want you to come to the hospital now."

Only two possibilities existed. Either Debby was calling for me, as she had done so many times in the past… or that last breath had finally escaped her.

Tomo somewhat reluctantly offered to come along. He probably felt I needed support now more than ever. I truly appreciated this compassionate gesture.

We drove to the hospital in complete silence. My thoughts wandered aimlessly in reflection of Debby's probable passing. In all her trials, in the constant struggles she had endured, she had at all times held herself in a dignified manner. I was grateful for my own strength and perseverance in being able to walk with her through her time of greatest vulnerability.

I felt secure and content in the knowledge that she had not needlessly suffered. From the beginning, I had remained strong. I certainly hoped I would not crumble now.

It was eerie. As the elevator doors opened at her floor, I knew that the good Lord had come for Debby. The whole floor seemed to be masked in an aura of dimness. The air was suffused with hushed quiet. As I walked toward her room at the end of the hall, waiting there was a woman from the Hospice Society. She embraced me, offered heartfelt condolences, and asked if I wanted her to come in the room with me. I replied that her support and encouragement was to be commended, but I declined. I wanted to pay my final respects to Debby by myself.

As I opened the door, I felt the exhilarating rush of my trembling body. Never for a moment did I doubt what I might say or do. If not for the brightness of the full moon filtering in through the window, the room would have been in total darkness.

On unsteady feet, I approached Debby's bed. Her face was lit like a glowing rainbow. I was awestruck, for in her peacefulness she looked like the most beautiful angel I'd ever laid eyes on. I smiled. On her face was no indication to suggest that her crossing over had been painful. Her eyes were fully open, and their expression said that whatever she was looking at, it appeared to be the most beautiful thing she had ever witnessed. Her mouth was slightly ajar from her final breath. Even in death, her beauty would forever remain etched in my mind. I adored everything about this extraordinary woman.

I bent down and ever so tenderly kissed her on the side of the mouth, where her lips began to part. I lingered there before whispering, "Hello, my darling angel. All your trials and tribulations have come to rest. You're now at peace, and may God embrace you in the warmth you've given so many throughout your short life. I will always cherish your memory. To me, you will always remain a source of great inspiration. Through all your struggles, you showed absolutely no fear. Your head was always held high with pride and dignity. Your courage and strength has exceeded anything I have seen or had to endure through my own struggles in life."

Feeling more at ease, I knew in my heart she never wanted to be remembered in tears or sadness, but instead with fond memories. I took my coat off and carefully lay down beside her. For a few brief moments, I cradled her in my arms and gently brushed her hair back. Looking deep into those beautiful, captivating, sightless eyes, all the beauty that had been Debby was plain for all to see. My thoughts centered on the magic, the mystery of this special woman. Somehow she had managed to accomplish the impossible. At a time in my life when I needed a miracle to pull me away from the demons threatening to extinguish my life, Debby had stepped in. When no one else seemed to care or understand what was going on, she was there. She had succeeded in what no one else wanted to attempt. From the moment she entered my life, she filled me with constant hope, instilling in me the strength to carry on. Even in death, she would remain my guiding angel. Throughout all her struggles, her insurmountable display of strength and courage became my kindness and compassion.

Rocking her in my arms, with my eyes closed I let her know that for the rest of my days, I would cherish her in loving memory, and that she would forever remain alive in my heart. I silently prayed to God to warmly embrace her soul in everlasting peace.

Before exiting the room, again in my predictable custom, I spread that lavender scent she so much adored around her.

Jayson, on one of his visits, had brought his mother an imitation red rose. To me, that rose signified the love in his heart. His love for her would never die, and neither would her precious memory. On another day, Kim had brought along a beautiful angel figurine. Carefully, I placed these symbolic items on the pillow beside Debby's head.

Tomo was somewhat relieved to see me reappear in the hallway, for it was obvious he was very uncomfortable. However, in continued support, he didn't waver. He let me know that he'd stay as long as was necessary. I told him I just needed to make a few quick calls, and then we could go outside for a smoke break.

Now and then from the moment I arrived at the hospital, guilt tugged at me. Without any regrets, I chose not to call anyone regarding Debby. Yes, in this I was selfish. I desperately wanted more time, without interruption, to pay my final respects to her.

After a while, I phoned Debby's sister, then her mother. I called Donny next. Finally, almost as an afterthought, I called Jessie. For regardless of my opinion of her, she and Debby had been very close friends for a long time. I'm sure she appreciated the gesture, for it didn't take her long to make the forty-minute trip from Vancouver.

Darlene visited for twenty minutes, and then I called Donny again. Regrettably, they wouldn't be coming out. On the one hand, this surprised me. But in another way, I understood. With Jayson living with Donny and Sandy now, everyone had known Debby's final breath could come at any moment.

That's when Jessie showed up, and I was actually delighted to see her. She seemed to have a clear understanding of what was going on. Although she was all smiles at first, when we hugged I felt her body tremble. She was overjoyed that I had thought to call her, as she welcomed the opportunity to say goodbye to her dear friend.

You had to love Jessie; she showed no hesitation. She climbed right in bed with Debby, taking her in her arms and smothering her with kisses. Her tears were those of genuine friendship. In all this she displayed enormous empathy. Jessie stayed for close to two hours, and the only time she expressed any reluctance was when she had to leave. Seeing her happiness, I felt really good about having called her.

I knew that in staying any longer, all I was doing was tormenting myself. I wouldn't be going to work for a few days.

More than anything, I needed a couple good stiff drinks. On the way home, I stopped and got a bottle of whiskey and a case of beer. Trouble was on the horizon.

Relationships where there exists a deep emotional bond, especially those of a long-term nature, are similar to those of ducks. Yes, ducks! The mating rituals of ducks are unique in the animal kingdom. From the moment two ducks' relationship begins, their bond is cemented forever. When one dies, the other stays with its mate and dies as well.

The same pattern is documented in human relationships. My grandparents lived together for sixty years. When my grandfather passed away, even though my grandmother was considered to be in good health, within a matter of months she died. The only conclusion I can draw is that we establish inseparable bonds which even death cannot transcend. When our mates die, depending on the level of our emotional connectedness, a huge part of ourselves dies as well.

Without realizing it, I had created such a bond.

I was oblivious to the sheer destructiveness my recent drinking was having on me. There would be severe consequences. In my subsequent actions, it appeared as though I didn't care about anything anymore. My drinking escalated into a vicious cycle which continued for the next four months.

In fact, it almost extinguished my life.

SURVIVING THE AFTERMATH 52

Leaving the hospital, I had Tomo stop at the beer and wine store where I bought a bottle of Jack Daniel's whiskey and a case of cold beer. Once home, Tomo headed straight to bed; he somehow sensed I had my own agenda. I just wanted to be by myself. I thought, the drunker I got, the further my separation would be from the pain which now embraced my soul. However, instead of distantness, I found myself seriously pondering the invisible issues in my life.

Living on a five-acre property offered many of its own benefits and advantages, privacy being the number one consideration. Tonight I was free to play my music as long as I wanted in the backyard. Also, I could enjoy the beauty and magical mystery of a roaring fire.

By the time I had set everything up just right, I'd already had four or five drinks and was feeling quite relaxed. As the fire roared with its own mystical crackling, the songs of Roy Orbison echoed from the stereo through the stillness of the night. I got comfortable in one of the many old recliners around the fire pit. Gazing towards the heavens, I thought to myself, *What a beautiful night.* The sky was perfectly clear, aglow with the vastness of the stars, which all had their own special twinkle about them. I wondered to myself which of these stars right now represented Debby. I came to the conclusion that she was the biggest and brightest one.

In awe of the beauty and vastness of the universe above, my thoughts arrived at a spiritual level. In my slightly intoxicated state, I pondered how everyone is entitled to their own belief; some believe in fate, while others believe in the existence of God and that He is the divine creator of all things, knowing everything about us from birth to death. However, there's a huge difference between belief and faith.

Speaking truthfully, even while in reflection of all the complicated paradoxes of my life, I still hadn't embraced true faith. Although all the signs had been present in my life, it would take another three years before I grasped the significance of divine intervention and its role in my life.

Whether I was in search of faith, or inadvertently running away from it, this supernatural yet mystical force hadn't abandoned me. It had tenderly wrapped itself around me. I asked myself countless times, was it possible angels really existed here among us on earth? I had never put much faith in anything, let alone angels. However, on this particular night, in my final thoughts before peacefully drifting into a deep sleep, I unquestionably believed the heavens above had blessed me with an earthly angel, and Debby was her name.

When I woke up, all that remained of my roaring fire was a bed of hot coals. I was thankful for the blanket I found wrapped around me, although I didn't remember how it got there. Had I at some point gone in the house and brought one out? Perhaps Tomo or Kim had come out to check on me.

While collecting my thoughts, I nursed a couple of stiff drinks. I would have rather just stayed where I was, but I had volunteered to pick up Debby's belongings from the hospital. It would be my final trip there.

I went inside and washed up so I'd at least look somewhat presentable. When I arrived, I parked at the far end of the hospital's parking lot. I sat in complete silence while looking at this imposing fortress. It had been Debby's home these past five months. I drank three beers in the car; strangely enough, my thoughts weren't of a negative nature. Within these hospital walls there existed tremendous pain, unimaginable trials of recovery which told their own tales of sadness, strength, and courage. When viewed from a different perspective, there was overwhelming joy here also, as expecting mothers gave birth to new life. The bond between life and death is inseparable, a paradox of grandiose beauty; clearly, the boundaries of respect between the two would never be broken.

Through all of Debby's heartache and struggles, together we had shared many experiences. I would forever look back on this time with the fondest of memories. From the day Debby had entered my life to the time of her final breath, every moment we shared together was eternally engraved on my heart.

It's strange how two sets of unrelated circumstances can seem to be one and the same. Alone in the hospital room, while packing her things, my past prison experiences came to mind. It was as if I was once again in that lonely cell, the morning of my release. There seemed to be no difference. Whether you spent months or years confined in small quarters, it all amounts to the same thing. Everything you have seems to always fit into one small suitcase.

On the drive to Darlene's place, I hoped my relationship with her could change. It was probably wishful thinking on my part! I sat and had a few drinks with her and Toby, as I couldn't stomach much more stupidity than that. I liked Toby, as he was from the old school. He never had much to say, and I'm positive he knew Doll was in the wrong. That's what marriage is all about—right or wrong, you stand by your partner. In Toby's case, he took a back seat to the whole affair. I'd hoped we could all just have a few drinks in peaceful remembrance, but almost from my arrival Darlene started in with that one-track mind of hers about how she wanted to have Debby's car and the lawnmower. She made no mention of Debby's pictures, which in themselves were priceless.

It would take another two weeks, but I'd clearly see the full extent of Darlene's treachery and greed. When I use the term treacherous, I'm being kind. Her actions in the following weeks indicated that her plan had sprouted the day Jayson decided he would live with Donny and Sandy instead of with her.

Having enough of this familiar song and dance, I went home. I had a lengthy conversation with Jerry. As the executor of the will, he drafted a letter to Darlene regarding Debby's possessions. I received a copy, too. Basically the letter stated that her only entitlement was to Debby's clothing and personal items, if she wanted any. Other than that, she had no claim to anything else. She also only had until September 15 to collect those items. This left her three weeks in which to do this, an important fact to keep in mind.

Two days after Debby's passing, Jerry left for Paris. The plans had been made long ago and the airline tickets were nonrefundable nature. The trip could not be postponed. Darlene got her nose bent out of joint over this; she craved pointing her finger everywhere but at herself. She felt Jerry was in the wrong and that he should have more swiftly attended to issues of Debby's will. She adamantly stated the importance of having closure. If this was truly of concern to Darlene, why did it take almost a month before she came for her sister's things?

Jerry asked me to pick up Debby's ashes from the crematorium. Without hesitation, I said it would be an honor. My personal life was rapidly becoming unmanageable, but I looked forward to the opportunity to help out. I was suffering emotionally and physically, deteriorating day by day. I now faced my own trials in salvaging not only my own sanity, but my very life.

In May, because I had been doing so well, Dr. Montaner had decided to give my body a break from the toxic medications. I knew it was sound advice, but in light of everything now going on around me, it was no longer an opportune time to do so. I was under tremendous amounts of stress—the virus's best friend and my worst nightmare. On top of the stress, I wasn't eating properly or getting enough sleep. I was swiftly heading towards a mental breakdown, and the drinking certainly didn't help the situation.

The blame was all mine. I wasn't communicating with others or playing by the rules. I had been instructed from the beginning of my treatment about the importance of monthly blood tests, which allowed for close monitoring. It had been three months since my last test, and it would be another three months before I got one done. Drinking seemed like a great alternative to the painful void in my heart. In my self-imposed solitude, I felt like the loneliest man on the planet, yet I also found peaceful, contentment.

In the weeks following Debby's death, all the pieces of Darlene's treachery fell into place. All along she had been waiting for the right moment to strike, and Jerry's trip to Paris provided the perfect opportunity. Debby's mother had received a large sum of money from her sister's estate and had decided to give forty thousand dollars to each of her four children. She had made it known that Debby's portion would be put in a trust fund for Jayson. I always agreed this was the right thing to do.

It now made sense why Darlene had wanted to delay the drafting of Debby's will. Without a will, the inheritance could easily be contested. However, once Jayson made it clear that Donny and Sandy would become his legal guardians, her deceitfulness went to the highest level. Once Jerry left the country, Darlene went to work on their mother. By the time Jerry returned, it was too late. Debby's portion of the inheritance, and Jayson's rightful entitlement, had been divided up.

Jerry was furious at her deceptions and cold indifference. From that moment on, he refused to speak to his sisters, or even his mother. It's sad how the children are always the ones to suffer. Jayson's decision to live with Donny and Sandy was made to appear as abandonment, when in reality it was the wisest choice.

We decided to spread Debby's ashes at Queen Elizabeth Park, as she would have loved the idea of being surrounded by beautiful flowers. Darlene couldn't make it, which didn't surprise me.

Jessie made arrangements to have a service held by the women's auxiliary group from the Royal Canadian Legion, of which Debby had been a long-standing member. It was a great tribute to a wonderful woman, with about seventy people in attendance. I got up to say a few words, as did Donny and Wayne.

Darlene sat off to the side with her mother, declining to say anything on her sister's behalf. There were hints from Jessie that Bob might show up.

"Jessie, if he shows up," I said openly, "you had better make sure an ambulance is on standby. He'll definitely need one!"

Nothing further needed to be said. He never showed up.

Afterwards, I received the dreaded call from Darlene. "Hi, Mino. Is it okay if I come by tomorrow for Deb's things?"

She didn't even notice the coldness in my voice as I replied, "I'm looking forward to seeing you."

Al knew all too well that the confrontation could turn explosive, especially with me drinking so much whiskey. He tried to caution me. "Mino, do yourself a favor. Just for tomorrow, don't drink. Let her show up, grab Debby's things, and it will be over with. You won't have to ever see her again." His words were sound advice.

"Don't worry about it, Al. I'll be on my best behavior." I knew it was a lie. This being the last time I'd ever see the viper, I had a few things I wanted to say.

I got up early, grabbed a clean glass, and opened a fresh bottle of Jack Daniel's whiskey. We had some patio furniture out in the front yard. I sat down there and began drinking. By the time Darlene and Toby had showed up, I had gone through half the bottle. I was like a loaded machine gun, waiting to go off.

Al came out with a couple of glasses, hoping he might somehow diffuse what was about to happen. As I sat silently, filtering the garbage coming out of Darlene's mouth, I decided I couldn't contain my resentment anymore. "Darlene, first you abandoned your sister in her greatest time of need. Second, you robbed her son, your nephew, of his just entitlement. Third, when the dust has settled you come here with only one intention: to see what else you can rape and pillage from what little Debby owned. Not once have you given consideration to the fact that everything in this house, down to the erasers on the pencils, belongs to Jayson, not you. I packed all her clothes, which you can freely take, but until Jayson takes what he wishes, you're not getting anything else. If anything, you should be hanging your head in shame."

Without anything further being said, they loaded the boxes containing Debby's clothes in their truck and left.

HIV Shows its Ugly Teeth Once Again 53

Late in November, just a short three months after Debby's death, I once again found myself sitting in Dr. Webb's office, with that all too familiar feeling of helplessness. Three weeks prior to this appointment, I had gotten some blood work done. It had been six months since I last had any blood drawn.

My participation in the HIV antiviral studies had begun in 1997, and I always requested a copy of the results. I didn't understand most of it; my main interest was always the viral load, which is exactly what it implies. For five years now, the virus had consistently remained undetectable. Another indicator of the illness's progression was the CD4 helper count. This represented the strength of my immune system. A healthy range was between four hundred and thirteen hundred. As I scanned my current results, I knew that whatever the doctor was going to say, it wasn't going to be good.

The virus had definitely come out of remission. There were over a hundred thousand copies of the virus alive in every milliliter of my blood, and my helper counts had dropped to 280. This was frightening, as just nine months ago my counts had been at 760. Another clear sign of deterioration was my weight loss. Just before Debby's death, I had weighed 175 pounds, but now the scale stopped at 140.

When Dr. Webb entered the examination room, he didn't waste any time in idle conversation. For the second time in the seven years he had been my physician, he gave me a death sentence: "Mino, I'm sorry, but all the lab work suggests your HIV infection has once again come out of remission, and is going into the final stages." He briefly paused, studying my face for signs of my reaction. If it hadn't been for my breathing, I could have very easily been mistaken for a department store mannequin; I maintained a cold indifference. I really believed my body and brain just didn't care anymore. It was almost as if there was no fight left in me. I was very tired. Dr. Webb closed by saying, "Mino, my advice, and really your only option, is to go see Dr. Montaner again and see how he might possibly help."

Before leaving his office, I assured him I'd make the appointment. I didn't plan to, though. Clearly I was again giving up on myself and the world around me. Everything looked grim and hopeless.

There was one thing I never took into account: God didn't give up on me.

In 1997, when I was first told I was dying of AIDS, I invoked the greatest promise given to mankind. I ever so briefly stepped from the physical world into the spiritual and asked the sovereign God for His help. The Bible clearly states in Jeremiah 33:3, *"Call unto me, and I will answer thee, and shew thee great and mighty things, which thou knowest not."* God was showing me lots of things, but I just wasn't tuned into the same channel.

I loved my landscaping job and my boss Andy really appreciated me as a worker and friend. After work, I used to go to the Walnut Grove Pub, a hotel close to where I lived. It certainly wasn't out of the ordinary to see me at a corner table, nursing a jug of beer, hunched over, writing my memoirs in a notebook. I'm not sure how it was possible, but some of my best writing was done while drinking.

Since Debby's hospitalization, Bob had gone into hiding, not that I was looking for him. If by chance our paths were to cross, though, we definitely had a few issues to straighten out. What can I say about Bob? He was too lazy to work, and definitely too stupid to steal. He really wasn't the sharpest knife in the drawer.

In the middle of December, after popping into the pub for a quick beer, I heard a familiar, weasely voice and felt the hairs on the back of my neck stand up. That voice belonged to Bob. As soon as I turned around to face him, I saw he wasn't alone; he had a couple of friends with him. I immediately made my intentions known and told his friends that if they started mouthing off, they'd get a beating.

Most of the regulars knew the story and surrounded me. You could feel the electricity in the air. Within minutes, I had drunk three double whiskeys and had an assortment of choice words for Bob, all the while intentionally trying to provoke a situation.

Bob ordered some drinks. He passed by me on his way to the patio and said, "Do yourself a favor and get over it."

That was the last straw. He was referring to Debby as if she were a used pair of socks you'd throw away.

I looked towards the bartender, Randy, and told him, "Bud, do what you have to, but I'm going out to the car and I'm coming back with a pair of pliers. I'm going to pull every tooth out of the goof's head." At six-foot-four and weighing 260 pounds, you didn't mess with Randy the bartender.

I darted outside, found what I was looking for, and came back into the pub. Five of my friends blocking the way. I don't recall everything that was said, but they managed to talk me into going home.

I never saw Bob again after that. I heard he got the beating of his life and moved to Vancouver. Draw your own conclusions, but it wasn't me.

My good friend Brad called and invited me to spend Christmas with him and Kristi up in Armstrong. I told him I'd drive up on December 23. That was definitely another day I would have died, if God had not intervened.

ESCAPING CERTAIN DEATH IN CHILLIWACK 54

Two days before Christmas, I was in good spirits again. There was nothing in the air to suggest mayhem was right around the corner, though I was headed straight into it. Within hours, I would be taking on the six-hour drive into the interior, to the small town of Armstrong. Brad and Kristi were expecting me, and I'd been looking forward to getting away for quite some time.

I had just one stop to make. Andy called the day before and cheerfully said, "Mino, you've been with me a year now. In showing my appreciation of your dependability and hard work, I got you a little something for Christmas. Can you meet me tomorrow around noon at the college?"

Andy had been very good to me. Upon hearing about this bonus, I felt guilty, as I hadn't even thought of getting him anything. I countered with, "Andy, that's so considerate. You didn't have to do that. Certainly I'll be there. Thanks."

"Mino, it's my pleasure," he replied. "Don't worry about it."

I went out and got what I knew would hold the greatest significance to him: a card in which I expressed my gratitude. Andy knew most of my history, and had always been in awe of how far I'd progressed. He loved the way my mind worked and gave me a lot of respect and trust. He often said, "Mino, you've been to hell and back many times, and it's beyond me how you survived it all. I'd have absolutely no reservations about leaving for a week with you in charge." His friendship helped mold me in many ways. When looking at the bigger picture, I see that God knew what He was doing all along.

When I arrived at the college, Andy was already there with two of his sons, Josh and Sam. We talked for a bit, and then Andy gave me what I knew was a bottle of alcohol. It was perfectly gift-wrapped. I gave him the card, and as he read it I joked around with the boys. I could tell Andy was touched by what I had written, as he knew it came from the heart. His eyes watered a bit and he gave me a bear hug. "Mino, you're like one of the family," he said. "You have a safe trip and we'll see you when you get back." Before leaving, I wished him and his family a merry Christmas.

I had never been one for surprises. Three blocks away, I opened Andy's gift to find an expensive bottle of cognac. I already had a six-pack of beer on ice for the drive upcountry, but that voice in my head said, "Go for it. One for the road won't hurt you." I opened the bottle and made myself a good strong drink.

As I drove, I thought to myself, *Why not stop in and see Danny?* He lived off the highway in Abbottsford. That was mistake number two; I should have stuck to the original plan and drove straight through.

Danny was happy to see me and wouldn't let me go without having a drink with him first. One thing led to another and we not only polished off the bottle of cognac, but a whole second bottle. I considered myself very easygoing, although I could very quickly go into Jekyll-and-Hyde mode, especially under the influence of alcohol; this largely depended on the company and conversation. A friend of my brother's showed up—we called him "Newfie"—and it didn't take too long before all hell broke loose. Newfie was never one for drinking hard alcohol; he preferred his beer. I kept ragging on him to have a drink with us like a man. It didn't take him more than a few to get looped.

He started complaining about how life was so unfair. You definitely didn't want to go down that road with me. I'd had my share of hardships, but I was never a whiner. I gave him the classic Clint Eastwood look and said, "Newf, what are you, a little girl? Quit your crying before I give you something to cry about."

It's strange how quickly people develop liquid courage. A few drinks and suddenly they're Hercules. As Newfie's fist hit the table, he jumped to his feet and started yelling, "You think you're tough? You want to step outside?"

"Sit down before you trip and hurt yourself," I coldly replied.

Again he beat up on the table. As a result, Danny got mad; he ripped off his t-shirt and grabbed Newfie in a bear hug. Danny was a powerhouse of strength and cracked two of the guy's ribs.

Well, I'd had enough of this circus act and decided to leave. Mistake number three. There's no reason or rhyme to a drunk's logic. It was at least a five-hour drive to Armstrong and it was now seven o'clock in the evening. More importantly, the roads were treacherous. I should have just driven home and left in the morning.

Somehow I drove for an hour and made it to Chilliwack. Why I stopped, I'll never know. What follows is a reconstruction of exactly what took place.

I found myself off the highway in an industrial part of town, on an isolated stretch of road. All I remember is driving quite fast. I could see there was a main road of some sort up ahead, but I failed to see the stop sign. Next thing I know, something slammed into me with such force that it sent my car in a sideways skid, thirty feet down the road.

As I regained my senses, I noticed that my car resembled a crumpled accordion. I managed to open my door and climb out. I wasn't hurt. Not even a scratch! Keep in mind that I drove a Mercury Capri, a compact car.

I saw the other driver, who'd been in a big Dodge Dakota. Next, the police showed up. I knew I had jumped into the frying pan this time. I saw no way out. How or why I escaped an impaired driving charge remains unexplainable to this day.

Soon I was in the back seat of the police car. The officer asked if there was someone who could come pick me up. Who was I to argue? I gave him Danny's number.

"Good evening, Mr. Pavlic," the officer said into his phone. "This is Constable Logan. Your brother Mino has been involved in an accident. No, he's fine, but can you come to pick him up?" The constable gave him the address and added, "See you in twenty minutes."

He then wrote me a ticket for failing to stop at the stop sign, and issued me a twenty-four-hour driving suspension. I thanked the constable before leaving with Danny, who brought me back down to reality.

"Mino, do you realize you just beat death?" he asked. "There's a truck stop a mile down the road. Never mind the Dodge Dakota, it could have easily been an eighteen-wheel semi! If that had been the case, they wouldn't have called me but the morgue."

A semi would have flattened me like a pancake. What a sobering thought.

Four days later, my body was in convulsions from the alcohol. I looked in the mirror, frightened by the reflection staring back at me. My complexion was pale, my eyes were sunken, and at 132 pounds I looked like a refugee from a prison camp. I may have escaped a certain death sentence, but what good had it done me? It had just been replaced by another nightmare. The HIV was ravaging my body. Again I thought there was no hope. I needed more than a miracle—and it came three days later, in what can only be described as a divine restoration.

In reflecting on my life, nothing seemed to make sense. My life, with all its hardship and suffering, had played itself out by the gates of hell. There was a serious battle going on, yet to me it was unseen. On the one hand, some mysterious force was seeking my destruction, but something far more powerful had its hand upon me. No matter what came against me, it couldn't interfere or prevail. Jeremiah 1:5 states, *"Before I formed thee in the belly, I knew thee; and before thou camest forth out of the womb I sanctified thee, and I ordained thee a prophet unto the nations."* Very powerful words, which makes one wonder just how much we're really in control.

They say a cat has nine lives. Well, up to this point I'd had more lives than ten cats put together.

DIVINE RESTORATION 55

My life appeared to be coming to its final, devastating conclusion. While staring in the mirror, the reflection staring back at me was death itself. My eyes were sunken and shallow, and my complexion had taken on a pale tinge. Standing on the bathroom scale, I saw that I had dropped in weight again: just 132 pounds. I could see that full-blown AIDS was slowly extinguishing my life. Even the fiercest warrior would crumble in despair under such circumstances. Even my doctor had given up on me. My family and all those around me were distancing themselves. Why? They, too, were persuaded there was no hope.

At this particular point in my life, God was just a figment of someone's colorful imagination. In due time, many would try to convince me that the Bible actually speaks to us personally. My heart had been hardened by the brutalities of life. I was colder than the iceberg that sank the *Titanic*.

A week had passed since the car accident, and my future looked very bleak. My car had been totaled, and I was sure the insurance company would hold me liable, as well as for the damages to the Dodge Dakota. I had been drinking myself into the grave and was almost broke. Andy had said we wouldn't start up again until the middle of January, still a couple of weeks away. It seemed there was no way out.

Exactly the way God wanted it.

The world around us is continually trying to convince us that we're a hopeless case. It took seven years for me to figure this out, but the Bible, written over two thousand years ago, already told the story. Our situation, no matter how horrific, can be used to deceive us. Psalm 3:1–4 would later hit me like a sledgehammer right between the eyes; it clearly applied to the circumstances I was facing:

> *Lord, how are they increased that trouble me! many are they that rise up against me. Many there be which say of my soul, There is no help for him in God. Selah. But thou, O Lord, art a shield for me; my glory, and the lifter up of mine head. I cried unto the Lord with my voice, and he heard me out of his holy hill.*

In 1997, I had called upon the Lord in disbelief, and He heard my plea. From that time on, God kept calling me with many signs, wonders, and miracles. In my stubborn ignorance, I wouldn't even pick up the phone to thank Him.

I thought about weightlifting again, but even that seemed like a pathetic proposition. I saw a hollow empty shell in the mirror; my bicep was no bigger than my wrist. I flexed the muscle as hard as I could, but it still only measured eleven inches around. I needed some extra motivation to get me going, and none was in sight.

First miracle: I watched the mailman stop and put something in the mailbox out by the fence. I went out to retrieve whatever it was and found a letter from the insurance company. I expected the worst. After opening it, attached to the short note was a certified check in the amount of twelve hundred dollars. This puzzled me. As I read the letter, it seemed that I wasn't at fault, but rather the driver of the truck was. Legally, he shouldn't have been behind the wheel, as he was under a driving suspension, therefore making him liable. They estimated the book value of my car at twelve hundred dollars. I was just about broke, but here was an unexpected sum of money. The kicker? A month before the accident, I had paid just three hundred dollars for the car.

Second miracle: Danny called about an hour later and said, "Mino, I know you need a car. I've got one for you. It's a 1981 Cadillac Eldorado. You can have it for five hundred dollars, and just pay me when you're back at work."

He had no way of knowing I had any money! "Danny they just paid me out for the Capri," I said. "If you can bring it over, I'll pay you now."

Within the hour, it was a done deal. Even Danny, a strong atheist, was surprised when I showed him the letter. "Mino, the odds of this are astronomical. Especially seeing as you were falling-down drunk!"

Third miracle: no sooner had he left when Andy, of all people, called. "Mino, I'm glad to have caught you. Are you ready to go back to work?"

"Whenever you're ready, Andy," I said without hesitation.

"It's going to be hard work, though. There's a lot of shoveling involved, as both colleges want everything on the property to be bark-mulched. It could take a couple of months, but I don't have anyone else to spare. If you're up to it, I'll get you a truck. You could start within the next few days."

He had no way of seeing the huge smile on my face, but I was in absolute glory.

"I'm your man," I replied. "Let's do it."

Wow! If I'd been looking for motivation to spring me into weightlifting, I had just received it. The project ended up taking five months. We had to load and spread six hundred tons of bark mulch.

In the beginning of June 2003, just a ten months after Debby's death, I was finally able to breathe a little easier. I had certainly come a long way. Everyone in my inner circle began to look at me differently. It hadn't been that long ago when they all felt my days on this planet were numbered. My weight had bounced back to 170 pounds, and my arms now measured an impressive seventeen inches. Health-wise, I felt and looked fantastic, and my latest blood work showed that the virus had once again become undetectable. My helper CD4 counts read 780, and I wasn't even on any antiviral medications.

Before Debby's hospitalization, I had written a manuscript about my life. I now rewrote it and found what I was looking for: a small self-publishing company. How I came across them was a matter of blind luck… or was it? In my initial contact with them, I outlined my manuscript and their reply knocked me off my seat. In the past, I had many firms contact me, but it seemed their only interest was in securing a paycheck. The owner of this press took an immediate interest in me as an individual, and also in my story as a whole. She strongly felt it was workable and had potential. Just what I wanted and needed to hear!

From the moment I first began typing it, I had known of its potential for success. The story was about courage and surviving life's many obstacles, a moving and inspirational tale. But because this was a self-publishing company, there would be expenses. We entered into an agreement, and all I knew for sure was that my book would be published soon. Or so I thought.

What I didn't know was that a lot of hard work goes into bringing a book to publication. People around me said I should have applied pressure to speed up the process. Sure, I could have done this, as I had paid for services to be rendered. For one reason or another, these services were always postponed. I never complained. The idea was to have my work published in its best possible form. By applying pressure, this would not have been possible. As with most things in my life, it was a waiting game.

I needed a distraction. I was like a robot when it came to the weightlifting and had almost finished my second manuscript, a story about Debby's trials. However, I needed something else.

Slowly I was coming to terms with Debby's death. It had been so traumatic, leaving me emotionally drained. I felt an incredible need to replace this lost love in my life. I often thought of finding a new romance, although I was somewhat apprehensive.

In the past, at my brother's insistence, I had placed an ad on an internet dating site for HIV patients. I did get a few replies and corresponded, but nothing serious developed. I never cared for this method of meeting someone. From reading different profiles, everyone seemed to be shopping for a Ken or Barbie. This had me scratching my head. Anyway, I gave it some thought and reached the conclusion that I should try again, only this time try to write more than a sentence about myself in the ad!

Before I could put together a profile, I had to consider my expectations and priorities. In view of my medical condition, all replies had to be from women who shared my illness. That way, there'd be no confusion or regret. In fact, the shared illness could be the bond of establishing a serious relationship. Finding and establishing a relationship is involved process all on its own, with many factors determining its success. I put a lot of rational thought into this process and came to the conclusion that there were three major categories to be explored in looking for my soul mate.

The first category was the single crowd. Obviously, I wanted to meet someone who was single and unattached. Being single brings rise to unanswered questions, such as, "Why are you single?" Certainly there could be many reasons. Maybe someone just wishes to remain invisible. Maybe they're not ready for a commitment. An illness or disability can certainly add to someone's reluctance in entering a relationship. Illness like HIV can result in confusion and frustration, so why take the chance of being hurt further? On the other hand, being single can be the direct result of instability in a person's life. Heightened insecurities can sink even the best of relationships.

The second category to choose from was people who were either divorced or separated, which left me somewhat uneasy. With these types, there existed the strong possibility of unresolved issues, excess baggage being carried over from an old relationship. I wanted someone free and clear, with whom I could start and share a brand new life.

The third category was the recently widowed. They seemed to hold the most value for me, and were most suitable to my expectations. In this category, I would find the strongest bond of commonality. Sadly and unfortunately, only those who experience the death of a treasured love can fully appreciate it. When two people hold and cherish such a special intimacy, nothing can break its chain, not even death, which in its own peculiar way strengthens that bond to even greater levels.

Through my own grieving period, it was next to impossible for me to let anyone get close to me, nor did I really want anyone to. I pushed everyone away. After all, how could anyone really understand? The life Debby and I shared could never be lost. How could I make someone understand the bond we had established? The grieving period was painful, and in some ways crippling.

So what was I looking for? What did I want? In searching for these answers, I had to look within myself. This almost discouraged me altogether, as my ideal soul mate would be a reflection of myself. For the last seven years, I'd gone through a long process of self-discovery. All of my experiences, combined with my deeper understanding and acceptance of myself, made me into a unique person. I don't consider myself to be anything special, but I knew exactly what I was willing to give in a relationship and what I expected to receive. In all my relationships, I have given my love unconditionally, without question or reservation. I had always exhibited a strong attachment almost immediately. Commitment was very important to me, as I felt it created a bond through which two people could easily open up to one another.

I considered myself loyal, dependable, and faithful. I'd often been told that, with my many wonderful qualities, I would be a perfect partner. Apparently everyone but me could see these qualities. Where did they come from? How could I develop them? I now believe that the more pronounced our qualities are, the more likely they are to be the direct result of our personal suffering and hardship. At some point, we come to terms with our suffering, and in so doing get a clearer understanding of them. I have uniquely grasped the true meaning of compassion for myself and others.

On the other hand, I have many insecurities. Then again, we all do. In view of the life I've lived, and the lifestyle that went with it, who wouldn't have insecurities? A person like me could be controlling, manipulative, and deceptive. You'd have to be in order to survive and deal with the madness. Within a twenty-five-year period, I had spent fourteen in prison. On and off for over thirty years, I had continued in a suffocating cycle of alcoholism and drug addiction. With these facts in mind, understandably my insecurities were deeply ingrained in my nature.

In the next five months, I would clearly see and come to understand the extent and magnitude of my own fears. I felt that finding my ideal partner would prove to be tough proposition, yet somehow I believed that is someone out had very similar character traits to my own. The woman in my future would certainly have to be one of great strength and courage.

It took a couple of days, but when I had finished I was very impressed and satisfied with the profile I'd put together. I had described myself in as much detail as possible. I wasn't in the least bit deceptive about the life I had led, nor about my medical condition. To me, it was imperative to be totally honest. At this point in my life, I wanted no excess baggage, no loose ends, nothing that would come back to haunt me. If I established a new friendship or relationship, I wanted to be clear and free.

Now all I had to do was find the right site. This was easier said than done, for a number of reasons. When it came to computers, other than typing I was an illiterate!

Regardless of a person's illness or disability, everyone has his or her own views and opinions when it comes to disclosure. Right from the starting gate, I felt it was imperative to know who my true friends were and where my support lay. I had no time to play mind games. I needed a positive atmosphere around me. If anyone had a problem with my disability, it would be best that we parted company right away.

I've never been misleading or deceptive about my HIV, and I have never hid in fear. An unbelievable number of people hide in fear not of the illness itself but the stigma. Sadly, they've limited themselves to a lonely, unrealistic existence. My ad clearly indicated my medical condition; in this, there could never be any mistake.

After days of searching the internet, I almost gave a couple of times. I eventually stumbled upon a site that seemed right up my alley. It met all my needs. It was a dating site directly linking people with HIV, along with several other invisible disabilities. I placed my ad, and now it was just a matter of waiting.

My wait wasn't to be long. The following day, I received an email from a woman named Lisa. Little did I know that a wonderful relationship was about to blossom.

Then again appearances, can be so deceiving.

PART 3

LEAVES IN THE WIND

The Telephone Call 56

Lisa entered my life at a point filled with uncertainty. Into it, she brought all the sunshine and warmth that was in her heart. I never expected I'd love her more and more with each passing day, or that I'd build my entire life around her in a short period of time.

Did I know or understand the significance of what being in love meant? I don't think anyone could answer that with any certainty; we all have our own views and interpretations. I believe that love, in its simplest form, is the process in which we empty our innermost feelings and unconditionally give what's in our heart to one another. In these endless expressions of love, we are continuously reminded of the bond we have entered and established together.

Do I believe it's possible for two people, after a chance meeting, to fall in love and cherish each other forever? Certainly it's possible. From the beginning of time, countless stories have been written about this mystery. Although falling in love is truly an exhilarating experience, it can also be very scary. When we allow ourselves to fall in love quickly with a total stranger, we enter an unknown reality in which we become very vulnerable. This person somehow touches us deep within our heart and reawakens our joy of being needed and loved. While in this feeling of our heart's extreme exhilaration, we sometimes delude ourselves into believing our chance meeting is destiny at work. This is a misconception. We magically believe this is the person we want to spend the rest of our lives with, that our heart and soul has found a permanent mate and home.

I've always wondered, and probably forever will, what attracts two people to one another. What keeps them committed to each other, and what ultimately drives them apart? Six months from now, I'd have a much clearer understanding of this complicated game of love.

From Lisa's initial email, it took only one day for her to ask for my telephone number. Within ten days of that first call, we committed to each other. This should have raised many questions. I should have been forewarned, due not only to my recent loss but also my addictive tendencies. I was drawn like a magnet to this woman. We were on the phone constantly.

Through our letters and conversations, it was evident that Lisa was also a person who attached herself strongly, without question or reservation. I found this very appealing and welcomed her attachment with all my heart and soul. I knew I would attach myself to her as well. It was only a matter of time.

We talked about appearances at length. I considered myself to be in great shape, and not too hard on the eyes. My biggest worry was my tattoos, for I had many and they projected a certain stereotype. This didn't seem to bother Lisa at all; she adored me and the honesty in my heart.

When it came to herself, she needlessly worried about many things. She definitely needed her glasses, as without them she had trouble seeing. She was in the process of getting braces put on to straighten her teeth. I believe our true beauty comes from what's in our hearts, and it's just my opinion, but I think women tend to worry about their physical appearance more than men. We had exchanged numerous pictures, and from this I knew she was a beautiful woman, inside and out. She was religious, which I didn't seem to mind. She didn't smoke or drink, either. It just couldn't get any better. I couldn't believe I might have found the woman I would gladly spend the rest of my life with. She was an American, from a small town in Ohio, and was in her early thirties. She was a stunning, blue-eyed blonde, very easygoing, intelligent, and levelheaded.

She lived with her sister and worked full-time as a secretary. What I found odd, and never questioned, was that most of what she owned was in boxes in the garage. She didn't even have her own room. She slept on a cot. Her willingness to submit herself to such a lack of privacy for the better part of a year should have raised a few questions. What was really going on? Was she in the process of finding her own place, or was her arrangement a convenient way of saving money for a major move?

In the first few days, we talked extensively about ourselves. Lisa felt her life was rather dull, certainly in comparison to mine. I didn't think so. The extent of her compassion, understanding, and giving nature instilled in me exhilaration. I believe everyone's life is a story in itself; you just have to walk a mile in their shoes. From what she outlined, her life as a child was a struggle, as her family was very poor. I had never given much thought to how serious financial hardship could make life almost unbearable, especially if one's family was of a considerable size. I can also see and understand how being the oldest child put a greater pressure on her. I could tell through our conversations that she would much rather forget all about her childhood. In this, I empathized with her.

Lisa's previous relationships, from what I understood, were for the most part short-lived. I felt extremely adamant that whatever had happened up to this point in our lives was irrelevant. What mattered most were our intentions and desires for a brighter future together.

After she finished school, as a way of getting ahead in life she enlisted in the army, where she stayed for three and a half years. This said a lot about her. Once committed to something, she would see it through.

After the army, she returned home and almost immediately involved herself in a new relationship which proved disastrous from its beginning. Lisa was searching for something, yet in view of her own strong insecurities, any port in the storm would do. She ended up getting married, which only lasted a brief time, and due to continued abuse she walked out—or should I say, she ran away from it. She later got an annulment.

For about a year, she drifted in and out of several relationships, none of which went anywhere. Most of us, especially if things seem to be going sour, reach the conclusion that a change in environment is the answer, instead of looking within ourselves. Through the internet, she met someone from Florida. Although reluctant to make such a big move, the deciding factor was that she knew some people there; if things didn't work out, at least she wouldn't be stuck.

This said a lot about her. She was very analytical, very calculating in most of her decisions and actions. In light of this relationship and the others which followed, it's obvious that she had several serious issues needing to be addressed and resolved. There definitely appeared to be a pattern to all her relationships: they didn't thrive too long, and she steadily involved herself with men at least fifteen years older than herself. After Florida, she decided to make a dramatic change in life. This time, she enlisted in the Navy. Due to injuries in both legs, her enlistment was brief. She would have liked to return to Florida afterward, but instead she returned to her family in Ohio.

She only barely settled herself down before jumping into another relationship. Although everything seemed to be going well, there was one major hurdle: Lisa did not want children. As a result, the relationship ended.

During this period, she decided to make use of her GI bill and go to college. After a couple of years, she graduated with honors and obtained an associate's degree in computer digital media. I was impressed by her life, the choices she had made, and her persistent nature to see things through.

Lisa's calls and letters were overpowering. She remained firm in her belief in us as a couple, destined to be together forever. Within a week, she fully imprisoned my heart and soul. My greatest concern was that she didn't share in my illness. This was a major issue. As far as any kind of sexual relationship was concerned, it just wasn't going to happen. I had given this serious thought. Was it even possible for someone infected with HIV to have a normal heterosexual relationship?

The answers seemed to be both so complex and so simplistic. First and foremost, there's a huge difference between HIV and AIDS. HIV is an incurable disability, but it's manageable, whereas someone with AIDS is unfortunately in the final stages of their life. I don't know when or how I came to the realization, but it was definitely possible for me to sustain a normal and healthy intimate sexual relationship.

If someone in good health wants to enter into a relationship with someone with HIV, should their sanity be questioned? Such a relationship would be guaranteed to face immeasurable hardships. At first, I thought it had no choice but to fail. On top of this, don't forget that an uninfected person's family might display resentment, and possibly even hatred, toward the infected partner.

On the other side of this coin, should those suffering with a disability or life-threatening illness be forced to have an empty, lonely life? It's human nature to want to be loved, accepted, and needed. If two people, regardless of their condition, can find love and create happiness together, this togetherness would help them find peace from the madness within.

Even though Lisa had her own medical concerns, in terms of my own disability, I definitely didn't need any unnecessary stress in my life. In the first couple of weeks, I talked to her extensively about the HIV issue, sometimes strongly voicing my opinion. I wanted to know why a beautiful young woman in the prime of her life would want to put herself at considerable risk of contracting this incurable illness. It was a very real possibility.

Steps of Deception 57

As our relationship rapidly progressed from friendship to commitment, our conversations grew heated. Willingly subjecting herself to HIV didn't make any sense to me. I tried so many times to discourage her, as to me this was an issue of paramount importance. A relationship with me would be a decision she—and also her family and friends—would have to live with for the rest of their lives. She would have to disclose this information to them at some point.

However, her response assured me she had given this delicate issue, with all its surrounding implications, considerable thought. "Mino, the love and happiness I've always searched for… well, I believe I've found it."

One by one, we removed the barriers.

Countless times she told me about her fears of HIV illness. She purchased a number of books on the subject to gain a greater insight. She often said that in life, striving for the things you really want is all about taking risks. She was adamant that she wanted nothing else but to spend the rest of her life with me.

She tried to make me realize that up to this point, all that passed between us had been mere words, cheap and easily scattered, leaves in the wind. She believed that actions spoke best, so it really wasn't important whether her words seemed logical, or even believable; she intended through her actions to prove she was in this relationship for the long haul.

Her arguments seemed to outweigh my own, and she seemed willing to take on any and all obstacles that came our way. I sincerely thought about what she'd said regarding risks and sacrifices. In my opinion, sometimes people are so imprisoned by loneliness, emptiness, and infatuation that the emotions become crippling. Sometimes we don't think rationally.

I should also have concentrated more on Lisa's nature, which bordered on paranoia. From the beginning, she displayed a strong reluctance to tell her family more about me, especially about my medical condition. I should have insisted on it from the start. I'm positive everyone would have tried to convince her to leave me, and perhaps they would have critically questioned her sanity. This all would have been welcomed by me, for if she still felt the same way after her family's input, then surely there would be no question of her love for me. She rationalized that her family would have to know eventually, but her father was very critical and she wanted to hold off.

Lisa's letters continued on a daily basis. It was hard not to fall completely in love with her. She put me up on a pedestal. I just couldn't understand it! I'd be the first to admit my own faults, but I welcomed the attention. I hoped for everything to be rosy and perfect. Her words of commitment in all the letters engraved themselves on my heart. I had never experienced such pure devotion. It engulfed me.

Certainly I knew there existed a heavy void in my life, an emptiness filled with tremendous loneliness. I just never imagined how starved I was for the affections of a woman. The warmth, closeness, and tranquil love I received from Lisa expressed the deep and wonderful sweetness that seemed to be within her. I definitely wanted to be a part of it. To have found someone as special as Lisa was a dream. Developing such a strong attraction in such a short period of time complimented us both, didn't it?

I've suffered much throughout the course of my life. You would have thought I had realized by now that words have no meaning. I'd been let down so many times. Many people offer blind love, and infatuation is the most common reason. Lisa repeatedly assured me that infatuation played no part in her decisions. Throughout our conversations and letters, it was so evident to her that we were very much alike.

It only took a month before she became the most important person in my life. I finally jumped in with both feet, committing myself fully as well. Here I was, forty-seven years old, feeling and acting like a fourteen-year-old all over again. The first two months were full of that childish silliness.

From the beginning, we both agreed on the importance of communication, regardless of the issue. We talked about my book, my life, and the many obstacles I'd faced. As to her opinions on one day being a parent, she had never envisioned herself having kids. She seemed to be more focused on her own needs, goals, and career, which took most of her energy and concentration.

Within weeks, we even had a serious discussion on the possibilities of marriage. I had never been married, but held the vows to be a sacred bond in the unification of two people. We seemed to talk easily about anything and everything. We mutually understood that nothing could or would stand between us. It seemed as though we were perfect for one another.

But we still hadn't met in person. She was in Ohio, and I was in Canada. I waited patiently in anticipation of one day meeting this incredible woman who made me feel needed and desired. Words couldn't begin to express how I felt. We shared all our hopes and dreams in regards to a future together.

We already decided that she would come to Canada for a week in August.

Lisa praised me for having overcome so many obstacles, and for accomplishing so much. I explained to her how Debby's recent passing had been immensely hard on me. Naturally there was a grieving period, but at some point you just had to let go and get on with life. Letting go was never easy, but failing to let go could be even more damaging.

She was also impressed by how I seemed to be so full of drive and determination, with a positive outlook for what I wanted to accomplish in life. In just ten days, she made me feel like one. Her sophistication, charm, and elegance shone in her every word.

We loved sending questions back and forth. I felt that these questions revealed a lot about her, and the answers revealed much about me, and vice versa. What made her questions so interesting was they weren't no-brainers; they actually made me search the depths of my mind for answers. My favorite was, "If you could go to any period back in time, as you are now, with all your knowledge, where would it be?" After some thought, I answered, "I think it would be exhilarating to go back in time to follow and listen to the words Jesus spoke, as two thousand years later he's still the most charismatic and celebrated person of all time."

A question I asked: "Let's say you didn't have to work, that finances wouldn't be a problem, and health-wise you felt great… but you only had a year to live. What would you do?" I've given this considerable thought and asked it of many people. Lisa always felt strongly about traveling to different parts of the world and helping those less fortunate. My own answer would go like this: "Why would you wait until you only had a year left to live to do something that's obviously important to you?"

Our long-distance relationship was quickly gaining momentum as Lisa and I found compatibility in every area of exploration. We had in our communications knocked down many emotional walls which we'd spent most of our lives building. Next we ventured into an area neither of us as yet had gotten our feet wet: sexual intimacy. I felt very uneasy with such discussions, as some things in my life were of a private nature—and this was one of them. I hadn't yet met this woman, and even though we had decided that she would come for a weeklong visit in two months, there still remained the possibility of this never happening.

From our conversations, I pictured Lisa to be a very compassionate and giving person. However, sexual intimacy could only be gained through personal trust. To me, something so meaningful lost its specialness when freely discussed over the phone. And yet as our conversations got more intense, they also got steamy.

Lisa had already purchased her airline ticket. If I had only cared to look at things more realistically, instead of buying into the beautiful fantasy Lisa was spinning, I would have recognized that she had some very troubling issues. In the course of our discussions about the trip, she let it be known that she was prepared to just come and stay. That she would say this without ever having met me, that she would come three thousand miles and just move in, clearly indicated that whatever was going on in her life in Ohio, she just wanted to run from it—and it didn't really matter to where or to what! Only in looking back do I plainly see the signs of a deeply scarred and emotionally troubled young woman. In this, I must not only find compassion, but forgiveness as well.

When my birthday came close, Lisa mentioned that she had sent me a gift. I wondered what it could be. I had gotten to know her quite well and knew she wasn't one for trinkets. Never in my wildest imagination could I have guessed what she'd gotten me.

When the parcel arrived, upon opening it, my eyes began to water. It was an emotional thing for me, and it said much about her character and thoughtfulness. I had taught her to say "I love you lots" in Croatian: *Ja te volim puno*. Inside the box, I found an all-purpose knife with twenty-four different attachments. I liked it very much, but what made it incredibly special was the engraving. On one side of the knife was my name, and on the other, *Ja te volim puno*. It came with a beautiful keychain that also had my name engraved on one side.

One thing that really bothered me was her obsession with privacy. She was very uncomfortable with me calling her place if she wasn't home. She seemed to be afraid of me speaking to her sister. I often wondered why. Was it that I might say something about my HIV status? Or was it something she might say to me?

My biggest insecurity revolved around possibly losing Lisa. Understandably, having HIV played on my self-worth. Lisa and I talked at length about various forms of control and ways of manipulation.

The ones she felt most strongly about were power, sex, and money. In regards to those issues, I thought I was safe. I'd never longed or wanted power. I just wanted a simple life. As for money, it didn't govern or control me. Certainly if I had success from my book, it would offer me financial stability. Sex could in no way manipulate me, or so I thought, as my life had for the most part been a lonely one. My relationships had been too few and too far apart. However, the concept of love, of being wanted and accepted, definitely manipulated my thought process, becoming a controlling factor in my life. Until then, I hadn't noticed it.

An interesting subject we talked about extensively had to do with fear—those things in our lives we would like to completely erase from our minds as though they never existed. Although Lisa didn't voice her fears to me, there could be no mistake that she had several very real and troubling fears. She often brought up this topic.

Fear can imprison us. If we don't address our fears and let them go, they immobilize us. Something as simple as going to the store can become a scary thought. A glance from a stranger can be unbearable, allowing us to think, *They know!* For the moment, however, everything except our passionate desire for each other was lost in the crescendoing excitement of her imminent arrival.

When it came to my book, Lisa was always very encouraging and positive. She thought everyone would want a copy, that people around the world would know my name. Mino Pavlic, the man for whom no obstacle is too great! Not just a survivor, but a fighter conquering all life's trivialities! With vigor and unwavering determination! She felt that I was an amazing individual. I was the answer to all her troubles, and together we would not only face life's difficulties but conquer them all. Our future together, as seen through her eyes, would be extraordinary.

I'm far from that shining knight. I was just a lonely man with simple desires; if I could have those, I would have fulfillment. With Lisa, I felt positive that together we would make all our hopes and dreams a reality.

As the day of her scheduled arrival approached, so many pieces of the puzzle still had to be brought into focus. One remaining, nagging issue: sexual intimacy. Certainly the closeness Lisa and I shared was of rare quality. On the one hand, the intensity of my feelings towards her raged like an uncontrolled fire, always burning, forever growing, but I was fighting within myself for some deeper understanding of Lisa's motivations. She was about to make an overwhelming commitment and sacrifice.

I wanted more than anything for her to rationally comprehend the position she was placing herself in. I wanted Lisa to be a part of my life forever, but we hadn't yet passed the point of no return. I wanted her to know that she could still reconsider this relationship, without any hurt feelings. If she harbored any doubts, now was the time to voice them. I would definitely be very understanding. There would be no resentment whatsoever. We had firmly established a wonderful and solid friendship, and if it had gone no further that friendship still could have continued on forever.

We had discussed the issues surrounding precautions when it came to sexual intimacy. Her response was always the same: "Mino, whatever transpires between us will come naturally out of our love for one another. I have no doubts, reservations, or fears. I will love you forever." Her words and actions left no room for doubt, unless I wished to question her sanity—and if I were to jump to such an assumption, there really would have been no point in going any further. We had talked about the idea of marriage; all our conversations seemed to be headed in that general direction.

While in thoughts of marriage, I conscientiously decided that Lisa should absolutely know everything about me. There could be no secrets whatsoever. I had nothing to hide, nor was I ashamed about anything. I had written a book about my life, so you could literally say my life was an open book.

In my previous life of criminality and prison survival, where cold deceptions and calculated manipulations were commonplace, I always had a sense of what was going on around me. This had saved me many times, yet now I failed to see the important clues. Then again, even if I had suspected something was out of the ordinary, would it have been possible for me to walk away?

Just a week before her arrival, many things still needed to be done. I certainly wanted to make a lasting first impression, and this went well beyond my personal appearance, grooming, and hygiene. It had been a long time since I'd had a woman in my life, and now I had to take a closer look at the little things I took for granted. I wanted Lisa to feel comfortable in my home. I was far from being a slob, but the farmhouse definitely needed a thorough cleaning. It took me a few days.

In those final days, I found myself seriously reflecting and reevaluating everything between Lisa and myself. Could all this really be possible? Or was it all an illusion, a cleverly devised smokescreen? Lisa, in reading my book, knew just about everything about me. She wasn't from the lifestyle I had grown up in, nor could she related to such an existence. Maybe it was my inbred way of not letting people get close, but right from the starting gate I let her know that I was bound to have lots of insecurity. Realistically, it would be next to impossible for none to exist. She repeatedly assured me, "Mino, I'm sure there won't be any issue we can't resolve together."

Our final phone conversations left me with a delirious joy and excitement, but I was still leery. Unexplained uneasiness embraced me. The painful healing process following Debby's passing had been an extraordinary transition period, yet my own self-protective nature seemed to be telling me, "Don't set yourself up for failure," and I just wasn't listening.

In the weeks leading up to this visit, numerous times I strongly voiced my concerns regarding the need in practicing safe sex. The implications of not doing so were astronomical; failing to use precautions could haunt us the rest of our lives. My mind threatened to snap as I sought to justify her lack of concern. The explanation I kept feeding myself was that sexual intimacy wasn't high on her priority list. How could I really be sure?

That she would travel three thousand miles to be with me for a week said a lot. We were both certain that everything between us was love in its purest form. We seemed to be so compatible—mentally, intellectually, and emotionally. But if sexual intimacy was to play any role in the progression of our relationship, then surely we would have to be insistent on the practice of safe sex—at least for this one week.

Sex did not seem to be an issue between us. I could draw many conclusions and assumptions in this regard, and I found myself looking at three possible reasons.

Firstly, considering the site we had met on and Lisa's very guarded nature, perhaps she had actually been HIV-positive all along, or suspected that she was. At no time during our relationship did she tell anyone about my medical condition, but why not? Lisa professed that she was prepared to make the ultimate sacrifice, as she wanted us to be connected in every way, to be united forever. But was it really a sacrifice, or an act of manipulation?

Secondly, could she have an ulterior motive in this love affair of ours? Taking everything into consideration, this was out of the question. It made absolutely no sense. I was not yet a success, so what could she gain from me? My book was still six months from being published, and any thoughts of its success were pure speculation. Since we had discussed marriage many times, I would have willingly given her anything I had. But maybe she was running away from her own medical issues.

Lastly, when putting everything into perspective, I had to question her state of mind. Since I'd known Lisa, she had shown herself to be rational, intelligent, and highly organized. She was meticulous in everything she did. Understanding these things about her, it wouldn't be wrong to say she was very calculating. Many times, through our letters and conversations, I experienced the depth of her analytical nature. No matter the topic, she would break it down and explore each segment from different perspectives.

With two days to go, I still wasn't sure of many things. This uncertainty should have been my greatest warning.

Lisa's Arrival 58

The day before Lisa's arrival, I still had some last-minute preparations to take care of. I bought myself a new tracksuit and runners. While in the department store, I picked up some scented candles, air fresheners, and flowers for the house. For the bathroom, I got a variety of different bath lotions and soaps. I also bought a wicker basket with three different compartments and a beautiful bouquet of flowers with a card. I then got a couple of cute little stuffed animals. Since she liked fruit, I bought various exotic kinds, along with a half-dozen bottles of root beer. I picked out a couple of t-shirts for her that had "Vancouver, Canada" on them. Before calling it a day and heading home, I got a haircut.

Her plane was scheduled to touch down at 10:40 a.m. the next morning. Lisa was very determined and nothing was going to prevent her arrival. Lisa and I were in constant communication.

It had been a restless night for me, as I only got three hours of sleep. I had figured on an hour-and-a-half trip to the airport, so I got up at 6:30 and left shortly after 8:00. Airports can be busy, but for some reason there was an unbelievable amount of people in the terminal this day. Once inside, it was pandemonium. No happy campers in sight. I went to the arrivals screen and was shocked to see that Lisa's flight had been cancelled.

About an hour went by before I was able to get through to the information desk. Due to the blackout, all inbound eastern flights had been cancelled, as well as those going east. From Toledo, Lisa's plane had landed in Chicago, where she'd planned to catch her connecting flight to Vancouver. From what I was told, all flights leaving Chicago had been cancelled. For how long? The friendly diplomatic airport response was, "Until further notice!" It could be anywhere from a couple of hours to a few days. Overlooking my own confusion and frustration, my thoughts drifted to Lisa and how she might be taking all this. Nothing was moving this way. Even if she wanted to, she couldn't even return home; everything had been grounded. What to do?

There were only a few options open to me. I could hang out and hope for the best, but this would have been irritating and pointless. No matter what, she was stuck in Chicago. Even if her plane were to leave immediately, it would still take several hours to arrive.

My nerves were starting to get the better of me, so I quickly decided to go back home. I'm sure Lisa had tried calling there. Besides, I could always check on the computer for changes in her flight's status.

On the drive back, I worried about the severity of the blackout. Maybe all flights for the next week would be cancelled. I just kept telling myself, *If it's meant to be, she'll get here.*

When I made it home, there were ten messages from Lisa on my answering machine. This setback showed a lot about her character; she didn't seem to be in a panic. She was obviously was one of those people who can think on their feet. I could imagine her disappointment in discovering that all flights westward were cancelled.

Listening to her first couple of messages, I could feel her hopelessness and frustration, and was almost in tears myself. Instead of allowing panic to set in, she seized an unbelievable opportunity, and this was all done within the first hour of her landing in Chicago. There just happened to be a flight leaving for San Francisco she could get on, and from there she'd catch a connecting flight to Vancouver. She did this, to hell with her luggage—if it caught up with her, fine; if not, eventually it would. Lisa was determined. We were going to meet, even if it was just with the clothes on her back. Nothing was going to get in the way of that.

The only drawback was that she would have to spend a couple of hours in San Francisco, but she said she'd call as soon as the plane landed. I received her call seven hours later, although her mood was one of pure joy. In just a few short hours, we'd be in each other's arms. I could tell from the sound of her voice she was literally exhausted, as she was now close to thirty hours without sleep. We chatted for a while, but understandably she was eager to remain close to the departure gate. Until she was on that plane to Vancouver, she would carry that fear of being stranded. Who could blame her at this point? Several times throughout this conversation, we shared tears of happiness. She told me that her plane was scheduled to arrive at 10:20 p.m., and that I shouldn't get there too early, as she would still have to clear customs. It was anybody's guess how long that would take. When we said goodbye, I left for the airport. I now knew for sure that barring anything short of a hijacking, she was on her way. It wasn't that I didn't want to take her advice about not getting there early, I just couldn't. I was so full of adrenaline that I didn't know if I was coming or going.

On the drive, I thought about how tired and weary Lisa would be I'd make the return drive as quickly as possible, let her get settled, and then just to hold her until she fell asleep. That's how I thought this exhausting day would play out.

I got there an hour early, which was fine by me since the airport had quieted considerably. I imagined that most of the crowd had gone home to wait by the phone. I immediately went to the incoming flight board and was delighted to see that Flight 745 from San Francisco had departed on schedule and would arrive on time. With plenty of time to spare, I decided to pace about outside, smoking like a chimney.

Lisa neither smoked nor drank, which endeared me to her all the more. I had decided that I wouldn't smoke while she was here. When I mentioned this to those in my inner circle, they just raised their eyebrows as if to say, "Yeah, sure, we believe you." I could understand their lack of confidence, as I had been a smoker for thirty-six years. As with many things throughout my life, people always underestimated me. I did not, in fact, smoke from the moment her plane landed until it was flying overhead on her return trip home.

While patiently waiting with a couple hundred other people, I felt out of place. I could count those bearing gifts of welcome on one hand. It would seem people are in such a rush nowadays that they take the little things for granted. Somehow I managed to position myself at the railing which barricaded the waiting area from walkway all incoming visitors would have to exit from.

It was a long hour-and-a-half wait, but I felt really good about myself. I must have had fifty different arriving women ask if the wicker basket full of goodies was for them. At one point, I started to wonder if it were possible Lisa had walked right past me. Worse yet, a paralyzing thought: had there been another unforeseeable problem on her end? Had she even managed to get on the plane? Doubts began to fill my thoughts, as there were only ten other people around, and those exiting were few and far between.

I asked one of the security guards if there were more people still to come from customs. She asked me to describe whom I was waiting for. I gave her Lisa's description and she went in to have a look. After a few minutes, she returned and said, "There was no one there matching that description." She went as far to suggest I might have gotten the flight mixed up. Did she think I was going to second-guess myself? Not a chance. I wandered over with her to the arrivals board and pointed out Lisa's flight, which according to the board had landed two hours ago.

Almost like magic, from right behind me, I heard my name and I knew it was Lisa. For the first twenty seconds, it was as though Lisa and I were alone in the airport, and the security guard and everyone else ceased to exist. It happened quickly, but I remember it so vividly. I put the basket down and slowly turned around.

There before me stood, even in her tiredness, an amazingly beautiful woman. I gazed upon her beauty, then tenderly took her in my arms. We shared in our first passionate kiss, something we had only dreamed of up to that point. The initial embrace, the first shared kiss between a couple, is the ultimate expression of love. A kiss ignites one's desire and passion. Although our embrace was only brief, it seemed like an eternity.

Before letting her go, I softly whispered in her ear, "Honey, let's go home."

Knowing that she despised the cold, I wrapped my coat around her and picked up the basket and her carry-on luggage. This was all she had for the moment. Her baggage somehow along the way got rerouted to who knows where. It took three days to catch up to her. If memory serves, in the car while waiting for the heat to kick in we shared a few more warm hugs and kisses. She got herself comfortable, and other than holding hands and listening to soft music, the drive home was quiet. Not that we didn't have anything to say; it was just that she'd had a hectic day and needed some peace to unwind from the madness of the past twenty-four hours.

I didn't know what the coming seven days held in store, but I was sure it would be positive. We had no reservations; there was no nervousness between us. It was like we were a long-term couple just returning home. We were very comfortable and relaxed in each other's company, which was rather mystifying as we'd never met. You'd think there would be some instinctive nervousness, some apprehension between us.

I wondered how I would do when it came to sexual intimacy between us, as I was still nervous and insecure in that regard. It had been a little over a year since I'd last shared in any female companionship of this nature. The more I dwelt on this, the worse I made it.

There wasn't much too getting Lisa settled. She was more interested in using the washroom and going to bed. Resting her head on my chest, with her arms wrapped around me, we fell asleep.

For the first few days, the bond we established was priceless. Through our sexual intimacy, we passed the point of no return. Lisa at no time exhibited any concern or regret regarding my HIV. In her mind, regardless of the obstacles to our future, we would be united forever. The togetherness we shared was unique; most new couples find one another new and exciting. It seemed totally different between Lisa and me, as our relationship had already transcended the highest levels of intimacy. We were in harmony with one another.

In our brief but treasured moments together, I was to discover many wonderful things about Lisa's inner beauty. She very much appreciated and cherished the closeness that came with physical intimacy. From the moment she got off the plane, she made me feel completely wanted and desired. I had no doubts anymore. She filled me with an excitement driven by wild, passionate desire, like nothing I'd ever felt before. I was in total ecstasy of her sweet breath and those deep, passionate kisses that seemed to linger forever. Even now, seven years later, the thought of them leaves me trembling in rapture. Before she arrived, I often wondered whether she truly knew just how lonely and empty my life had been this past year. How my body and soul had longed for someone as special as her to enter my life. I discovered Lisa had the same burning desire for complete togetherness.

As you could well imagine, seven days didn't really give us the time to do much of anything, nor did we really have a desire to do much. Understandably, we were both lost in the excitement of having finally met. All sense of time escaped us. Together we explored Vancouver, and I could see she was captivated by its beauty. I had planned for us to take the six-hour journey into the interior, driving the Coquihala highway, so she could experience why British Columbia is so widely known and appreciated around the world. I'm sure this would have been a treasured memory for Lisa. Regrettably, we didn't make the trip; from her arrival, we were under an imposed state of confusion, lasting several days, regarding her missing luggage.

In regards to my soon to be published book, I had hoped it would launch before Lisa's arrival. It would have been an honor to share my joy with her. As most everyone else in my inner circle, she expressed tremendous excitement in this event. However, everyone's anticipation soon began to border on impatience. Until my publisher explained to me how the industry works, I myself felt impatient. In the publishing arena, there's no room for impatience, as that's the quickest way to bury the best of stories.

With firm conviction, Lisa and I spoke about many things—and the topic of marriage came up several times. We both welcomed the prospect of getting married in the near future. We expressed our views and opinions regarding marriage, and we shared with each other what such a bond meant to and instilled in us.

Another touchy issue we discussed had to do with her return trip. Simply put, she didn't want to go. Don't get me wrong; I didn't want her to leave, either. Now I had to think in logical, unemotional terms. I knew the decisions now rendered could in many ways come back to haunt us. Nothing in my thoughts or actions could be construed as controlling, manipulative, or deceptive behavior. Had I simply said, "Lisa, I want you to stay," eventually this would have caused me unimaginable anguish and stress. At some point, her family would have to be told about me, and if they were against our relationship I would have been viewed as the bad guy, the guilty one. As a result of my illness, they would say I took advantage of Lisa. More than anything, I would guard against this outcome. From the moment I was diagnosed with HIV, I had always made it a point to disclose my condition. I believe in knowing from the starting gate where I stand with people.

Therefore Lisa would definitely return home, and this decision weighed heavily on many important issues that needed to be addressed by her. In proceeding this way, we could demonstrate that both had given everything full consideration and were progressing in a responsible manner. I was thinking in realistic terms. This move in Lisa's life was enormous. It wasn't like she was just moving across town.

The first consideration of paramount importance had to do with her family and friends. Full disclosure was foremost in my mind. They needed—*deserved*—to understand and accept the fact that she was moving to Canada and that the man she had promised to marry and start a new life with was HIV-positive. What was going on in her mind? Why was she so unwilling to share these facts? She couldn't blink and forget these people had ever existed, could she? Their views, opinions, and input were relevant! Everything they had to say was extremely important. She tried to explain to me that her family wasn't a close-knit group, but that eventually she would tell them.

Another issue was her pending medical treatments. She was in the process of obtaining braces and was about to progress to the next level of this lengthy procedure. It was imperative that she follow through with these appointments for a number of reasons. She would have to make her orthodontist aware that in four months she would be moving to Canada. On this end, I would have to find her a suitable dentist who would be willing to continue her treatment. Her files, along with all x-rays, would then have to be transferred. I would have to find her a family doctor as well.

The list of things to be done was endless and would take the better part of three months to complete. Although she was eager to stay, I should have realized that all was not as it appeared at her home, some three thousand miles away. Instead of facing and dealing with her issues, she would have rather just distanced herself from them. I wish she could have found the courage to be open and honest, as we would have worked through it. But when it came to her personal affairs, she had a very guarded nature.

Can long-distance relationships, specifically those established through the internet, work? Regardless of the distance between two people, they can find happiness and love by sharing what's truly in their hearts with one another. This is the fundamental component of all healthy and lasting relationships. We had established a unique connection, a genuine friendship full of love. During our time together, we fully explored sexual intimacy on many levels. There were no restrictions whatsoever in the progression of our relationship.

I should have hung on to her and never let go.

59 LISA DEPARTS AND GOES FOR THE JUGULAR

The days before her departure were the toughest. Although we didn't brood over it, there was definitely some sadness in the air. The night before her departure we fought against sleep, wanting to treasure the remaining time we had left together. Eventually exhaustion set in and we fell asleep in each other's arms.

I awoke about an hour later to find that Lisa had managed to comfortably wrap herself around me. Her arms and legs embraced me, her head rested on my chest, and her soft blond hair and warm breath offered its own gentle caress. In the quiet solitude, her beauty overwhelmed me.

From the moment Lisa had become part of my life, although it only been two months, the changes within me had been extraordinary. We normally don't notice these changes until those in our inner circle draw our attention to them. For the longest time, I had restricted myself to self-imposed reclusiveness; my nature had become very guarded, making it tough for people to get close to me and enjoy my company. When looking at it in its proper perspective, I think it's understandable.

An unpredictable volcano threatened to erupt within any moment, as a result of Debby's passing. I had allowed my health to decline, almost to the point of no return. The stress I felt was insurmountable. In meeting Lisa, I did a complete one-eighty. Now I had an air of strengthened self-confidence and assurance. I was more outgoing and displayed friendliness and interest towards the people I came in contact with. This lends considerable weight to the mystical yet natural healing power of love!

My thoughts drifted to my own personal achievements. In the last seven years, I had detached myself from the tormented and unpredictable lifestyle of addiction which had shut me up in a suffocating prison. My principles and values, along with my ethics and morals, had changed. It was as though I stepped into a different dimension.

As a result of who I am today, I'd have to say that positive and constructive change is always possible. However, it doesn't come easy. As in everything you want from life, there's a price to pay. The underlying question is, are you prepared to do whatever is necessary to succeed? Are you willing to go the whole nine yards?

Change is a lengthy process that takes a tremendous amount of strength and courage, determination and persistence. Above all else, it begins with passionate desire. Lacking this essential requirement, you need not proceed any further. Whatever you want from life, without desire your chances of achieving and fulfilling your goals and dreams are greatly diminished.

Until recently, I hadn't truly enjoyed the wondrous experience of a healthy and meaningful relationship. When it came to romantic involvements, I was a dinosaur, a relic from the distant past. The love and warmth I held for Lisa really had no beginning or end. I gave to her with a passion and conviction, and I did it unconditionally. My love had no limits, no boundaries. Everything that was part of me was hers for the taking. Regardless of any storm Lisa and I may have encountered together, I committed to remaining firm in my convictions.

Feeling her stir beside me, my thoughts returned to the present. I didn't want the night to end. With each passing hour, my uneasiness grew. An empty feeling filtered in, and I knew from the moment she boarded her plane I would miss her immensely.

If there was one thing in all my life I was sure of, it was in the fact that Lisa would always remain a part of my life. Everything about her perfectly entwined itself around me. The qualities we offered one another were matchless. Our hopes and dreams were in harmony and balance.

Any disbelief I'd harbored about us being a couple were completely broken by the events of this week. I had attached myself to her in every way. So strong was this attachment that the thought of her leaving filled my body with a painful ache.

Lisa stirred and I could clearly see she was waking up. She displayed the gracefulness of a cat awakening from deep sleep. Slowly and gently her body stretched next to mine, familiarizing itself with her surroundings. She wrapped herself even tighter around me, an expression of love.

When she finally looked up at me, the inviting smile on her face told its own story.

"Hello," she said. "It's so good to see you."

Her blue eyes sparkled with the promise of treasured tomorrows. With heightened passion, we explored one another relentlessly. Afterwards, in each other's arms, in gentle caress, we talked about the future and how the next four months would quickly pass. Our biggest source of strength would come from the continued support we gave each other. As to Lisa's coming back to me, I had no doubt. She even decided to leave a good portion of her things behind, because it made no sense to lug them back and forth.

Just as I had predicted, a feeling of emptiness was already beginning to take hold of my emotions. In its firm grip of slow strangulation, I knew the pain and longing would be enormous. Above all else, it was imperative that I show no sign of emotional weakness in her departure, or exhibit the slightest hint of insecurity; it would only make our time apart that much more difficult to deal with. Lisa had remained unfalteringly consistent in showering me with her affection from day one.

While driving to the airport, just hours from her departure, her fingers softly ran through my hair, massaging my scalp. She expressed how deeply she loved me and that our future together was firmly cemented. Nothing would ever come between us.

In these final moments together, I realized we were both feeling a lot of stress in wishing for the atmosphere to remain positive, full of strength and encouragement. This was essential to our continued growth.

At the airport, as we still had time, I set the camera on the roof of the car and adjusted the timer. In each other's arms, we posed for some awesome pictures. While in a tender embrace, I whispered my pledge of love in her ear. I wanted her to know and feel it in her heart. As long as her love for me remained alive, with unrivalled passion, I would wholeheartedly love her for the rest of my days.

We had arrived several hours before her scheduled departure, as was requested by the airport staff. Our actions made it abundantly clear, however, that we were reluctant to venture into the terminal. We understandably assumed that whatever awaited us inside was nothing short of chaos, filled with frustration and confusion. Almost as if tempting fate, we wished that somehow her plane would leave without her. Still in the parking lot and oblivious to the people around us, we danced in each other's arms a little while longer.

Realizing that the process of registering her luggage and clearing customs would be a lengthy process, we entered the airport and almost immediately felt like running away. Words can't describe the pandemonium that surrounded us as literally thousands of people scrambled about in all directions in a hurried panic. It seemed as though the lineup for international flights was two blocks long. Regardless how many check-in counters they had, I couldn't see how it was going to be possible for Lisa, even with two hours, to clear them. Amid my impatience, I learned a valuable lesson that day. I managed to maneuver myself and Lisa to the back of the line. Slowly, every couple of minutes, we moved ahead a few feet.

Always on the alert as to what was going on, airport attendants kept popping up near the front of the line. Finally, with fifteen minutes before her flight left and about a hundred people still ahead of us, I flew into a panic. I cornered one attendant and explained the situation. The response made us feel idiotic, like the sheep we really were. Lisa was taken to her departure counter, with me right behind her. The reason they had been appearing periodically was to ensure passengers made their international flights. They would ask if anyone was waiting for particular flights; passengers were then supposed to identify themselves and follow them through the swarm of people right to the check-in counter, where they would be processed within minutes and ushered through. So basically, showing up hours in advance was only meant to test your patience to extraordinary limits. If I ever happen to find myself travelling in the future, I'll arrive fifteen minutes before the flight, then head directly to the front of the line, all the while looking completely baffled and in a panic. I'll latch onto an attendant, telling them my flight is about to leave!

Lisa and I were committed to our promising future, as well as marriage. I'm sure she realized that returning home to do things in the proper way was the right thing to do, but the process of it was so frustrating. My understanding and helpful nature greatly took a lot of the pressure off her shoulders.

The following three months flew by, as there were many preparations to be dealt with before Lisa could return. In the first month, we both did a lot of research. It's quite a process for a U.S. resident to move to Canada, presenting many complications. One has to apply for residency, and this can take up to a couple of years to get final approval. However, I knew that if she came as a tourist, a visitor, she could legally stay for six months. During that time, if we were to get married, she would automatically be granted residency; the only drawback was that if she left the country in the following two years, immigration could refuse her reentry. We had decided to proceed this way.

We explored many avenues of getting her things shipped to Canada. A freight company was out of the question, as it was very costly, and everything would have to be processed through customs. It was the same with a moving company. Another option was to go through an independent trucker, but to me this seemed very touch and go; a trucker wouldn't risk his license for a couple hundred dollars. There was only one way to ship her things, and that was through the postal service. Everything would have to be packed into small boxes and sent as gifts. We decided that the best time to send them would be thirty days prior to her return.

In Lisa's first six weeks home, she suffered severely from some type of flu, and daily fought off irritability. My only explanation was that it came about due to the sudden climate change, which is not uncommon. She also got braces put on her teeth.

The month of October was also hectic for Lisa. After I sent her the money, she looked into purchasing her airline ticket. We discussed it together and decided on Sunday, December 15, for the date of her return. Once she purchased the ticket, everything would be official. At that time, she would give her workplace notice of her intention to leave. During this time, she also opened a bank account in Vancouver and got herself a family doctor and dentist. Everything was going well, although as of yet she still hadn't informed anyone of my medical condition

In one of her letters, I sensed deceptiveness from her. She had taken care of everything in its proper order, but it had seemed to be more of a hurried need, as though she was saying, "Time to get out of Dodge." Lisa found no privacy where she lived, which I found really strange. She lived with her sister, and if everything were aboveboard, why did she suddenly need guarded privacy? Lisa no longer used her sister's computer to email me, and started going to work an hour earlier, so she could email me from there. As the date of her scheduled departure grew near, her personality took on a paranoid nature.

In November, Lisa began the slow process of packing everything neatly into boxes. By the time the last box arrived, which consisted of her brand-new computer, I had received a total of thirty of them, all different sizes. In total, it cost close to fifteen hundred dollars to send it all.

Due to the constant pressure, she was like a walking stick of dynamite. All that was needed was for someone, or something, to light the fuse. Her mind was working overtime to desperately wrap everything up in Ohio, and there was no one to help her there. On top of all her bills, she still had to pay thousands of dollars for the braces and save money for the trip.

Then there were the steady stream of questions, which seemed to come at her as if fired from a machine gun. People at work were trying to find out what was going on, and her sister and family were plying her for answers.

Even though she was three thousand miles away and dealing with pandemonium on the homefront, Lisa still found the time to be a great source of encouragement for me. I was about to have my first meeting with my publisher, and there was talk of a radio interview. Lisa was adamant about the importance of appearance in leaving a good first impression. After all, one of the best statements of a changed life is personal hygiene. She had no reservations about the impact my testimony would leave. I knew this to be true, as everyone I came in contact with was left in awe upon hearing my story.

It was strange to have such influence, yet disappointingly my own family members failed to acknowledge my transformations. I never projected myself as better than them, but always looked to them for support, which never came. Possibly they did acknowledge my accomplishments, but if so it left them with condemnation, as they still couldn't shake their own demons. I would never find a better manager than my brother Mike, however. Lisa felt that once the world at large became familiar with me as an author, they would see that Mino Pavlic was someone who could help make a difference to those who needed hope most.

Finally, Lisa presented her resignation letter at work, and everyone was happy for her.

Lisa had said I should feel free to open the shipping boxes as they came, in a sense helping her to unpack. While she was here, we had taken a tremendous number of pictures, enough to fill a photo album. No sooner did I unpack it than she asked for me to send it back to her, though I didn't understand why at the time. She also went ahead and bought her ticket.

So far, so good. Thirty days to go. What could possibly go wrong?

Nearing the end of November, two weeks before Lisa's scheduled return, for some reason everything began falling apart. I had already received all of Lisa's personal belongings, and she was appreciative that I had unpacked her things as they arrived. It would be that much less for her to do.

I knew Lisa was exhausted. These past two months hadn't been easy on her, but now, with everything out of the way, she could just relax and spend some quality time with her family. However, now I started to notice a slight change. I'm sure it had to do with telling her family about me. In this idle time, instead of knocking down the final barriers, we slowly began creating *new* barriers.

As her departure date neared, a deep fear engulfed her: the fear of disclosure. One day everything was fine, and the next day she was talking to me about possibly rescheduling her flight to a later date. In our brief telephone conversation, she said, "Mino, I just think I need some more time to think!"

It felt as though she had sucker-punched me. "Lisa, from the beginning of our relationship we discussed all things imaginable. Our most important asset has been our ability to openly communicate. That seemed be the cement that held us together."

I decided to give her respect and space. A few days later, instead of calling me, she sent me an email saying that she had thought things through, and suddenly felt we would face far too many struggles. She decided that coming to Canada in December was out of the question. She further suggested that she might not be ready for such a drastic move, and honestly didn't know if she ever would be.

This hit me like a sledgehammer between the eyes, delivered without any warning or concern as to how it would affect me.

I tried calling for the next couple of days, but no one answered the phone.

Nothing made any sense. From the beginning, she had initiated the progression of our relationship, to the stage it was now in, on the threshold of marriage, and now she wasn't sure of such a move? Why then had she come three thousand miles and spent a week with me? Why had all her letters led to the topic of marriage? Why had she set up a bank account, a dentist, a doctor, and meticulously sent everything she owned? She obviously had known exactly what she was doing and couldn't wait to get away.

Finally, after repeated calls, on the third day she found the courage to call back, and her words were cold.

"Could you please just send my things back?" she said before hanging up. "I'm not coming!"

In the next few days, while I was trying to figure things out, she emailed me again. She basically stated that she saw no point in remaining in a relationship that was so controlling, manipulative, and which had no hope of success.

Nothing made any sense. For some reason, instead of talking it through, she was going straight for the jugular. Whatever her reasoning, there was no gentle way of saying we'd come to an end, without any possibility of reconciliation at a later date.

I'd be lying if I said I wasn't disturbed by her decision. I was emotionally crippled. It took a while, but I did come to terms with it, as it showed Lisa's genuine level of commitment. All along she had professed undying loyalty through thick and thin, yet at the first sign of difficulty she ran, as had been her hidden nature all along.

Even though it left my head spinning, the aftermath wasn't as bad as I expected. At first, it wasn't easy to moving on with my life. It took about a year to finally erase all the haunting memories of her.

It took me many more years to understand the motives behind her actions. Had I addressed my own lifestyle more clearly, I would have seen her own addictive personality. I had foolishly accepted her intensity as intimacy, when in fact it was nothing more than a smokescreen to cover her own unresolved addiction issues. In reality, Lisa loved the process of falling in love. However, when it came to commitment, the paralyzing fears she harbored would tighten like a noose around her neck.

My first thought was to start a fire out back and throw all her stuff in it, to just cut my losses. It would cost lots of money to send everything back. Besides, there was still the issue of the nonrefundable airline ticket I had purchased. Nine hundred dollars wasn't a loss I was prepared to accept.

There had been many clear signs in most of her letters. Looking back, they were like bells going off, but I refused to take notice of them. In the beginning, she continuously expressed a need for togetherness, and how she looked forward to doing things for me, little things such as preparing home-cooked meals. Then, as her departure date neared, she began with subtle questions that slowly turned into expectations. She came up with things that I would have to accept without question, and privacy was at the top of her long list. If this had been a big issue for her, why had she told me to unpack her things? What could be more private than one's personal belongings? Suddenly she became a vegetarian and hated the smell of food, so cooking was a concern.

I had tried to reason with her. "Lisa, if I'm to be a partner in your life, it would only make sense that I'd like to establish a comfortable balance between your goals in life and the things you have a hard time with. Although I couldn't even begin this process if I don't know what's involved."

"Mino, you just wouldn't understand," she replied.

This was about as idiotic as her demands. I was beginning to see that I was like a seal jumping through hoops. These statements had me scratching my head. My gut reaction was that something was very wrong. She had given herself to me unconditionally in every way and had been convinced of the success and happiness of our long future together. In the blink of an eye, she had gone from a person who exhibited full control of her actions to one who seemed feebleminded. Obviously something drastic had taken place.

Realistically, looking at things from her side of the fence, the move itself had become a scary proposition. She'd lose her independence and rely on me for many things. She couldn't work once she moved here, as that would require a work permit issued by the government.

I let her know that any barriers that now seemed to come between us were of her own creation. "Lisa, I myself have never run away just because the light went out in the tunnel. All my life, the people I've trusted most have abandoned me. Not many have had the courage, patience, and strength to weather the storms of life, but I'm hoping you do."

I started drinking heavily in hopes of escaping the issues now eating away at me like a cancer. Deep down, I knew she had already made up her mind, but like a department store mannequin, I refused to admit it. When I thought about it, too much had been said between us. It would have been tough to forgive, let alone forget.

I was devastated and heartbroken. One day I'd come to understand that it had nothing to do with her decision. We had spent a week together, had shared in a dream, an illusion conjured from deep within our own imaginations. Like an enchanted storybook fairy tale, it had almost became a reality.

Like all the shipwrecks of my life, I would rebound from this one. I just needed a distraction. My publisher had arranged for me to speak to the John Howard Society about my life. It was an opportunity of enormous magnitude, to market both my book and myself. I had just over a month to prepare a speech.

Escaping the Madness 60

A dominant characteristic in my life is my uncanny nature for resilience. Anytime I remain uninfluenced by emotions, or when my judgment isn't clouded by those suffocating nooses of addiction, I possess a unique ability for deep rational understanding. I somehow view things empathetically and compassionately. In the first couple of weeks following Lisa's crippling decision, which seemed to threaten my sanity, I knew I quickly needed to step out of my pit of depression before I got buried in it. If I had gone ahead with my first reaction, which had been to burn all her things, I would have put myself on her level in many ways. I, too, could be as cold as an iceberg. Clearly that reaction would have come out of anger and resentment.

Without question, at first my thoughts were governed by anger, although this wasn't so much a product of the events but rather her cold indifference. Her decision crushed the life from my heart. Without allowing me a chance to recover, she wanted to know if I could quickly repack and send her things back to Ohio. Lisa wasn't playing with a full deck. She expected me to just put aside my feelings as though nothing had happened between us.

I finally did come to terms with it. In a brief telephone conversation with her, I said, "Lisa, I'll repack and send all your things to you. I'll do this as quickly as possible. You may not like my packing, but the sooner your stuff is gone, the sooner I'll be able to let go and get on with my life. However, because this was your decision, you bear the weight of all expenses, and I'd like to be reimbursed for the airline ticket."

She agreed.

However, my first priority was a speaking engagement my publisher had arranged with the John Howard Society, a highly respected organization known around the world for dealing with criminal offenders of all ages and leading them towards rehabilitation. I would be speaking to fourteen board members, and the regional director would also be in attendance. This meeting would take place in Nanaimo, a city located on Vancouver Island. I feverishly drafted a seven-thousand-word speech entitled "Escaping the Madness" which held a message that needed to be told.

As I spoke, the room around me remained in complete silence. The look on the faces of these men and women seated at the huge oval table was that of deep interest. I was nervous as I spoke from my notes, but in continuing I grew more confident, soon realizing that I didn't need notes, as I had lived and survived the nightmare I now presented to them.

After listening to me for forty-five minutes, the first to get to his feet was Tony White, the regional director. Without a word being said, he began clapping. One by one, the men and women around the table joined him in this standing ovation, the first I had ever received. After they all congratulated me, Mr. White referred to me as a diamond in the rough.

They wanted me to speak to five hundred kids at various high schools, twice a week. However, as I was still wet behind the ears, they offered to groom me. When I sat down with them, they told me that my willingness in sharing the experiences of my life had only one purpose: hopefully my words would leave a lasting impact on someone's life and somehow make a difference.

They suggested I come over in the future and watch the more experienced speakers in action. I even signed twelve copies of my book, which I had presented as a gift to everyone in attendance.

Leaving their office, I was drunk on attention rather than alcohol. The glitter and hype of everything, including the book signing, went right to my head. My publisher gave me a ride back to the ferry. On the two-hour ferry ride back to the mainland, I managed to sign and sell ten more copies.

Once back in the comfort of my Toyota van, my first stop was the beer store. I needed a drink in celebration, and besides, it was a long drive home. I thought about their proposal. What an awesome opportunity! Unfortunately, due to my stubbornness, it was short-lived. I mistook grooming to mean I would be made into a puppet. I hated any and all restrictions.

Alcohol was still a major problem for me, as I was about to find out. Arriving home in Langley, I headed to my favorite drinking spot. Everyone there was excited for me. I signed seven more copies of my book—and drank seven pints of beer before moving on. I made another stop down the street, and the scenario seemed to duplicate itself.

My last stop was the Langley Hotel. As it was getting late, before leaving I had three pints, each with a double scotch chaser. I had the easiest route home mapped out in my head. The problem was, I was drunk. I still felt I could make the ten-minute drive.

As I approached the train tracks, I saw that the preventive arms were down. I recklessly drove into the arm, breaking it. Instead of stopping, I gunned my motor to get home as quickly as possible. No sooner had I found myself in the comforts of my home than three police officers knocked on my door.

I was in one of those moods. After opening the door and inviting them in, I asked no one in particular, "It's pretty late for you boys to be out soliciting for your annual get-together."

They found no humor in my words and proceeded to write me a ticket for the broken arm bar. Without looking at it, I let the ticket drop to the ground. I wasn't going to pay for it. One of the officers picked it up and again handed it to me. This time I decided to look at it, and saw that it was for $465.00.

I again threw it on the floor. "That's a mighty expensive piece of two-by-four."

They really tried to be nice about everything, but now, with firmness in his voice, one of the officers handed me back the ticket and said, "Listen, we're willing to overlook everything else, which will save you a lot of headaches, if you do the right thing and sign the ticket. No more will be said, but if you throw it on the floor again, we'll be leaving. And so will you."

I signed the ticket and carefully placed it in my shirt pocket, then thanked them for their patience and wished them a good shift. I learned a valuable lesson that night: fame and fortune certainly have a destructive side.

PART 4

JOURNEY INTO GOD'S PRESENCE

An Appointment with God 61

Looking back on my life, I can only imagine how the heavens above must have thundered in frustration at my persistent stubbornness in failing to grasp the significance of God's continued intervention in my life. Make no mistake about it: God has had His hand on me for a long time, but I wasn't getting with the program. God certainly could just think of something and make it happen, but if He interfered in such a way, He wouldn't be a loving God anymore, but instead a dictator. He gave us free will to either follow Him or get sucked in by the world around us. We have to decide what the world around us has really done for us. Absolutely nothing!

In view of my stubbornness, God decided it was time to step in and build a relational bridge between us that would slowly introduce His heavenly kingdom to me. However, again He left the decision up to me whether I wanted to cross that bridge. Just remember that where God intends for you to end up isn't necessarily where He first puts you. My heart was spiritually deadened. Had God placed me anywhere other than Creekside Church, I definitely wouldn't be writing this part of the story.

Regardless of whether you're in search of faith or running away from it, once you invite God into your life, He will never abandon you. In my case, He decided it was time that I got with the program and scheduled an appointment with me. Yes, you heard correctly: the Almighty, for the benefit of His special lost sheep, was about to make me an appointment! In His cleverness, He not only ensured I would run across the bridge, but I would come early.

My younger brother Mike had been missing in action for the last couple of years, and no one had seen or heard from him. This wasn't out of the ordinary for him. When immersed in his horrific drug addiction, he often disappeared for long periods of time. Without a phone call, he would remain underground for two years or more before resurfacing.

In 1975, after my parents divorced, my father remarried and began the gradual process of distancing himself from us. The last time I saw him was in 1982. At that point, he'd had two more daughters, Milan and Milanka. He would go on to have a third daughter, whom I didn't even know existed for years.

Twenty-one years later, in February 2004, this mystery sister was to play a crucial role in God's plan. My brothers and I were genuinely concerned about Mike. Even when he found himself in prison, he'd call to let us know he was okay. But this time, nothing. One day, my thirteen-year-old niece took it upon herself to look for a "Mike Pavlic" listing in the local telephone book. To our puzzlement, she found one. Could it be that he'd been living under our very nose all this time?

I dialed the number and a woman answered. After explaining the reason for the call, the woman said she was sorry, but there was no *guy* there by that name. *She* was Mike Pavlic. After being a little inquisitive, I learned that this was my father's third and youngest daughter. I spoke to her several times on the phone after this, and we both expressed an interest in meeting for the first time. However, after hearing all kinds of stories about us, she felt the need for safe, neutral ground. We could have gone for coffee, or we could have met in a dozen other places; instead she picked her church. I hadn't been in a church in over forty years, though the suggestion didn't throw me off.

On the scheduled day, as was my nature, I arrived early. Going to church brought its own sense of apprehensiveness, but nothing was to prepare me for what followed. I was a complete stranger to these people, yet this church seemed to embrace me in a blanket of complete friendliness, despite my gruff appearance. This took me by surprise. Being suspicious by nature, I felt like a lamb on the verge of being devoured by a pack of wolves. Everyone I met had a lot of questions for me, and I politely explained that I was there to meet my sister, whom I had never met. This certainly puzzled them, as Creekside consisted of a small congregation, and they all knew each other quite well. As soon as I mentioned my sister's name, I found myself shaking hands with Pastor Jim. He then introduced me to his family, who was very good friends with Mike. I found out she liked to be called Mikey.

While waiting for my sister to arrive, I nervously paced back and forth in the tiny foyer. I believe this apprehension was to be expected. Having grown up in a family of males, I wasn't prepared for the kind of feelings I felt at learning of my sister.

Watching her walk towards me from across the parking lot dispelled any such notion. Instead a deep warmth embraced me. I felt proud as only a big brother could, and immediately understood the protectiveness such a relationship implanted. At twenty years of age, she was a beautiful young woman who took pride in her appearance and carried herself with dignity.

We openly welcomed one another's warm embrace, but a touch of distance existed between us. In the twenty minutes prior to the service, we briefly shared the history of our lives. My book had just been published and I had three signed copies with me—one for each of my sisters.

Despite having never met, we certainly were cut from the same cloth, as we thought alike. We were both considerate in bringing photographs to exchange. In 1982, I'd lost twenty large photo albums that my mother had meticulously put together, so I didn't have a picture of my father. Mikey had brought one that was taken within a year of his death from cancer in 1998.

The reunion was fantastic, although short-lived. This had nothing to do with my sister, but rather her mother, Milka. When I learned that my father had passed away six years ago, my resentment against Milka was uncontainable. She hadn't even made an attempt to inform us! It would have been nice to pay my last respects. I could understand her desire to distance herself from us while my father was still alive, but I now felt no more important than a bug on a windshield.

Well, God had succeeded in bringing me to His kingdom, but how was He to keep me on that side of the bridge?

In God's eye, I was a lost sheep. Now that He had gracefully drawn me to His flock, an anchor was needed to prevent me from straying. To this task, God brought Pastor Jim into my life. He would momentarily become a small spark of influence. In essence, he became my "bell sheep."[7] I sat through the pastor's message and found myself uniquely drawn to it. It wasn't so much what he said, but how he said it. This was like no church I could remember. There was no pressure of membership or direct demand upon my finances. The church entertained a simple logic: if you were in the process of checking out God and felt uncomfortable about the collection plate, you were supposed to let it pass you by and consider the service a gift to you.

Pastor Jim's role was more than one of offering spiritual guidance and interpretation. It took me about a year to grasp the importance he played in my life, which in itself held a holy symbolism. In 1980, while in Wilkinson Road Prison, I had befriended a career criminal by the name of J.P., who represented evil in its rawest form. Pastor Jim, more often known as P.J., represented pure goodness. This distinction between good and evil played an important role in my life.

God was about to turn up the heat.

---

[7] Shepherds with a great number of sheep always have one sheep in particular that obeys the shepherd's commands. Not wishing to lose any of his flock, he puts a bell around its neck. The sheep that strays always returns to the ringing of the bell.

God Turns Up the Heat 62

When it came to writing, especially in terms of unraveling the roller coaster ride of my experiences, it never mattered how long I found myself sitting in front of my computer. In my darkened sanctuary, in the stillness of the night, as I ventured deep in the unexplored corridors of my mind, I often heard the thunderous roar of that unexplainable yet real voice inside my head dictating the very words I was compelled to write. I would find myself shaking my head, as if I might somehow awaken from a dream which at times seemed to border on fantasy. Many times, I would momentarily step from the visible into the unknown, and everything that had previously seemed to be nothing more than a concept suddenly became living reality. How or why any of this seemed possible, or even rational, could only be understood in reflection of the miraculous transformations in my life.

Hopefully, within the boundaries of my writing, I hoped to explain with a clearer understanding of Matthew 22:14—*"For many are called, but few are chosen"*—and how it applied to my life. No one ever schooled me as to the presence of God in my life—rightfully so, as no man could reveal to me that which was from above. If they had tried, it would have remained a colorful interpretation of someone else's imagination, as stale as yesterday's bread. This isn't an interpretation, but rather undeniable fact. As to God directing the steps of my life, the only thing missing would have been for Him to give me a stick, just as He gave Moses. Then again, maybe in my case He already had: a pen. I truly believe this book was part of God's direction for my life. Without my testimony being declared to the world, all my sorrows, hardships, and tribulations would have been wasted.

The first six months of attending Creekside passed quickly, with no significant changes in my life. I'd show up at the church every Saturday, head straight for the front row, and sit throughout the service like a department store mannequin. I wouldn't raise my hand, wouldn't clap or sing, and for the longest time I wouldn't even stand up with the congregation in worship. One almost had to question why I bothered showing up, especially if I wasn't willing to be part of the service. Only now, seeing it from a different perspective, I see that the congregation may have known they were to deal with me very delicately, as if I were a fragile piece of crystal.

Obviously my cold indifference originated from my complex nature. Above all else, I valued sincerity and commitment. When in my old nature, I was what I was; I jumped in wholeheartedly with both feet. All my life it had been that way. There were no half measures. It had always been all or nothing. I wasn't prepared to buy into this religious stuff just yet. Unbelievably, I needed more convincing. Having never embraced true faith, I wasn't even sure if I was capable of doing so. Even if I had been willing to grab hold of something that resembled faith, would it have been enough to hold back the constant spears of discouragement in my life?

There's a great distinction between those who are brought up with a religious background and those who one day see the light and decide to become followers of Jesus Christ. It's quite another thing to be chosen by God, to be plucked from the unimaginable depths of darkness to become the miraculous. At a time when I seriously considered taking my own life, I inadvertently called upon God to step in, and He did just that. With hammer and chisel, God began the wonderful molding process of restoring my shattered life. He knew it would be no easy task, as my heart had become hardened to everything but basic survival.

An article I once read was adamant that miracles are always associated with the certification of those who give us God's revelation. In further consideration, as I reread the piece, a deeper appreciation embraced me. According to this author, miracles authenticated the messengers of revelation. The breath of this statement thundered at me from the page, for nothing about my life could be considered anything less than a miracle of divine nature. Before anyone could become a spokesman for God, they first had to be authenticated as such. Only then would the people know that this man was of God and spoke the truth. God always manifests Himself through miracles, as they're designed to call attention to certain spiritual revelations.

However, before anyone could even be willing to listen to what God might have to say, they first need to be convinced of His existence. The transformation of an impossibility into a living reality has always been a sign for those who don't believe. Basically, before I could tell anybody about heavenly things, I needed to first convince them of the things I knew about. In a million years, I couldn't have changed the direction of my life with my own resources. Only something from beyond the walls of this earthly dimension could have done it, and that's what my life's journey is all about—the testimony of Jesus Christ stepping into my life.

Many people today teach that the era of miracles is long past. In my opinion, those teaching such nonsense wouldn't know God if they happened to trip over Him.

The supernatural event about to take place in this world should be every Christian's blessed hope—the second coming of Jesus Christ. Maybe I'm mistaken, but my Bible tells me that Jesus was a miracle worker extraordinaire. He didn't say, "Wait until I come back and I'll fix all the hell and crud in your life." The only reason He's coming back is for His church. Until His return, He wants us to have life here on earth, and to have it in abundance. Nowhere is this clearer than in John 14:12–14:

> *Verily, verily, I say unto you, He that believeth on me, the works that I do shall he do also; and greater works than these shall he do; because I go unto my Father. And whatsoever ye shall ask in my name, that will I do, that the Father may be glorified in the Son. If ye shall ask any thing in my name, I will do it.*

Let no man on the face of the planet ever deceive you. From the moment Jesus ascended to heaven, with the outpouring of the Holy Ghost on the day of Pentecost some two thousand years ago, miracles are for today. Ever since I called upon Him, God has been stirring the pot, but the flavor wasn't yet to my liking when I first started to attend at Creekside. God was about to add a special touch of spice to the pot. He had already erased twenty-five years of criminality from my life. My ever coming to church had been a long shot, but now, for six months under extraordinary circumstances, I not only found myself sitting in one, I was in the front row.

I had been steadily working for a landscaping company for two years, which I failed to recognize or even acknowledge as being a miracle. My medical condition suddenly recovered to heights previously unattainable, but I still failed to answer God's telephone calls to me.

It wouldn't be long now before I started to realize one undeniable truth: each and every time I placed my hopes on things of this world, I was disappointed. The world thus far had done nothing for me, nor could it. Only the promises of God were guaranteed. Sooner or later, the bitterness which embraces us in disillusionment will awaken and lead us into the unexplored dimension of spirituality. God had already given me many revelations, yet my hardened heart remained indifferent to His truth.

My eyes were about to be opened. For the third time, I was told that I was dying of AIDS.

In being able to capture and express the experience of my life in words, I've come to understand that I've truly been entrusted with a gift which is not of this world. Because of this, I find myself assuming an even greater measure of accountability. The truths, convictions, and beauty found in my powerful testimony can only be measured by the extent of its influence on other people's lives

The heart of today's society is quickly becoming cold, especially when it comes to the things of God. Two thousand years ago, Jesus came and taught us what true Christianity is all about. He continually prayed for unity and openly rebuked all division, yet today there are literally hundreds of denominations, doctrines, and who knows how many different Bibles in existence. An unbeliever could go to ten different churches and listen to a hundred different messages, yet nothing would seem to pierce their hardened unbelief. In today's society, many people openly argue over the validity of Christianity, and there's good reason: the presence of God is not there. Remember what I said: when God steps in, the miraculous takes place. It's all about lives that have been transformed by grace. When God steps into your life, you're a new creature; the old things pass away. Those who have read the Bible, or parts of it, can agree that anytime God steps in, the extraordinary happens. God has and always will be in the midst of the miraculous.

What is the miraculous? Is it about good works, or transformation? Personally, I would rather be part of a church that's full of transformed lives than one that's governed by good works. As long as the means are provided, anyone can dish out soup and a sandwich, but only the Spirit of Jesus Christ can transform lives!

After twenty-five years of battling for my life, I could be considered a long-term HIV survivor. I offer expert testimony. Anyone who gets through the kaleidoscope of torture this horrifying illness inflicts upon the body has to then contend with a multitude of frightening side effects. According to scientific researchers, the transition from HIV to AIDS is a death sentence. Statistics prove this. And according to the results of recent blood work, I was once again told I was staring death in the face.

When I first entered the drug trials in 1997, I had to take a dozen pills daily. Believe me, it was unbelievably hard on the body. The second time I went on the drugs, the fight against HIV/AIDS was a little further advanced; I only had to take a half-dozen pills per day. In the near future, I was to be placed on the toxic medications once more, and this time I took just one pill per day

There was no point in placing any expectations on the world around me. The world had already done all it could for me. I'm not even sure why I consented to becoming a human guinea pig, especially when there was no hope. Hadn't I suffered enough already? In entering these trials, all the doctors could hope for was that their toxic cocktails might prolong the inevitable.

The circumstances I found myself in reminded me of story found in 1 Kings 18:20–39. The story takes place in the land of Judah, where God's chosen prophet Elijah was about to have a spectacular showdown on Mount Carmel with four hundred and fifty false prophets. Everyone wanted to discredit Elijah and the God he served, as he was stirring up the people. These false prophets could represent the educated elite of our society today, who outwardly express a form of spirituality yet wouldn't know God if they tripped over Him.

Two identical altars had been prepared with a sacrifice. Whichever sacrifice God set on fire would reveal which prophet the people should follow. The odds seemed insurmountable, yet Elijah said to the four hundred and fifty, "Knock yourselves out." After a day of pleading, nothing happened. Not even a spark. When it was Elijah's turn, to make sure everything was fair, he dug a trench around his altar. Then he had four barrels filled with water brought up and poured on the wood. This was done three times. As everybody stepped out of the way, Elijah began to pray a simple prayer of faith, and God Almighty consumed Elijah's altar in fire. Even the water in the trench was gone.

Just as in Elijah's day, we need irrefutable evidence of God's presence today. In my fortieth year, I called out in a feeble plea to God. Could those barrels of water represent the hardships of my forty years of struggles? Before Elijah called unto the Lord, his altar had to be irreparable, meaning it would need more than a match to set on fire. Three times the wood was drenched. Three different car accidents should have taken my life, but I walked away without a scratch. Three times the doctors assured me of certain death, yet God stepped in. He had always restored me to greater heights.

We need to understand that an invisible presence of darkness stands against us. It's not just at work in the heart of society; it's everywhere. Turn on any radio or television and you'll hear about cities around the globe blanketed in total wickedness and corruption. Nations are full of poverty, sickness, oppression, and suffering. Every week, like falling dominoes, disasters hammer away at humanity. This darkness is the wickedness of Satan as described in the opening chapters of the Bible.

Once this darkness attaches itself to our lives, it becomes like an electrical current, and it has taken many of us to unimaginable limits of desperation. Through dysfunctional lifestyles, we enter the very gates of hell, where helplessness, addiction, madness, and suicide become frightening realities. Somewhere along the road of our lives, we have allowed the darkness in, and it has hardened our hearts to the things of God. As tough as it may be to believe in the unseen, no one can ever deny someone's personal transformation from the unimaginable to the extraordinary. Throughout the Bible, in all those people whom God worked the miraculous, their severest trials and sufferings were part of God's obstacle course, creating an atmosphere for deliverance.

I am just another voice crying out in the wilderness. When the struggles of life hammer away at you, it's easy to forget that the stranger who just brought you a coffee or gave you a tract to read could be someone God purposely sent your way. Time is running out. Try to see these people not as interruptions, but divine appointments. The darkness of sin has lured many of us into captivity, and Satan continues to rob you of your Christian heritage. His greatest fear is that you should realize the greatness you were destined for. Always remember one thing: we were all created in the image of God. As the world around us slowly shuts down, it cries out to God for a miracle of deliverance.

Faith has always been in our grasp, and the key to unlocking its mystery lies in these very words: in order to have a faith, you first must have a belief, and to have a belief, you must acknowledge a higher power, a supernatural force greater than yourself which has been guiding the steps of your life. Our most painful journey will be one of internal reflection, as that's where the foundations of change and growth begin. Once fully explored, the possibilities of the unknown will be awakened and you'll begin to realize the unlimited realities of the world of the impossible. It's there that you'll find undeniable faith.

A True Testimony Is Making a Difference 63

From the moment I walked through the doors of Creekside Church, I knew something wasn't quite right. I kept hearing powerful sermons about miraculous transformations of men and women of past generations—of what they had dared, suffered, and accomplished—yet in the newness of my Christian curiosity, something was missing. These biblical testimonies were extraordinary, but without present-day physical evidences of the miraculous, they were no more than stories.

To me, a testimony is a personal revelation, a witness of what one has seen and endured, what one knows of crippling impossibilities and intolerable suffering. Could these experiences testify of amazing transformations from the unimaginable to the extraordinary? As I listened to Pastor Jim, I was almost convinced that he himself had crossed through the parted Red Sea. I really struggled with this. Shouldn't there have been an abundance of present-day supernatural transformations, especially since the world around us seems to be falling apart? How are we to experience unprecedented revival if all we're getting is colorful stories?

I don't care how many books someone has read or written. I put very little faith in degrees or certificates. There is nothing more powerful than a personal experience. God did deliver me. Miracles happen each and every day. As long as preachers would rather preach textbook theology than introduce God's living testimonies, we'll never know about them. Here's the bottom line: in this day and age, we need more than principles.

As each new page of my life unfolded, I left my hideous past farther behind and ventured closer to my destination. What had seemed to be a hope beyond hope was in reality a journey to the glory of God.

Even though God was now in the driver's seat of my life, I wouldn't acknowledge His presence for another sixteen months. However, when it comes to the reality of God, always remember that you can't give anyone the keys to your car if the keys aren't yours to give. This is pretty straightforward, and God finds Himself in the same situation. He cannot give you cancer, suffocating addictions, or other illnesses. He can only give you what's His to give.

The proof of this is found in the book of Job. All his life, Job was blessed of God; he had a perfect life, for he was in the will of God. One day Satan showed up in heaven, and God asked him, "Where have you been?"

"I've been roaming about, seeking whom I might devour," Satan replied.

You have to understand that Satan's greatest passion is the destruction of humanity, God's creation. Satan at one time was God's highest angel. Lucifer led a third of heaven in rebellion against God, and got thrown out.

"Have you considered my servant, Job?" God asked.

In reading the story for yourself, it's easy to experience the hatred in Satan's response: "I have, but you've got a hedge of protection around him. If you take that protection away and let me at him, Job will certainly curse your name."

God always knows the beginning from the end, so He confidently replied to Satan, "Fine, do your thing, but you can't kill him."

God knew that when the dust settled, His faithful servant Job would still be standing.

Like falling dominos, disaster upon disaster came against Job. He lost his wealth, family, friends, and even his health. His suffering became intolerable. But Job knew something we often take for granted: God was in control. Even though Job welcomed death over his suffering, he never questioned the sovereignty of God. Because of this, God stepped back into his life and restored everything Satan had destroyed. He restored Job's life to even greater heights.

God can only give you what's His to give, and He will give it in abundance. When we get past our own self-pride and ask for God's intervention, that's when it seems as though all of hell breaks loose in your life. Just remember that the only reason this happens is that hell is persuaded that it's on the way out. Our problem is we need to persuade ourselves.

We certainly need preachers, both men and women who will bring us into a clearer understanding of biblical principles. I've said it before and I'll continue to say it; there are tens of thousands of churches around the planet today who believe in God and His supernatural reality, yet no physical evidence of such a God exists in their lives or in their midst.

Let's momentarily assume that the Bible was only now going to be written, and we were to be its main characters. The underlying question is this: would your journey through the kaleidoscope of life's obstacle course inspire, encourage, or impact anyone? I believe mine has, and this will be my greatest reward.

Anytime someone says to me that they know God, warning lights flash in my head, for you cannot get to God without first coming through Jesus. There is no other way. He is the only door. The first four books of the New Testament clearly illustrate this. Lastly, and more importantly, anytime someone says to you that they know Jesus, expect to see physical evidences of divine intervention, deliverance, healing, and restoration in their lives. Anything less is a smokescreen of deception. Whenever Jesus steps into anyone's life, it is transformed by signs, wonders, and miracles.

So my HIV infection came out of remission for the third time. The horrifying symptoms seemed to indicate I was on death's doorsteps. Satan really thought he was going to hit a home run this time. Nonetheless, I'm positive God has always been so very good to me. I had repeatedly been delivered from the burning pits of hell, though I had never given Him even a "Thank you" in return. In spite of this, His blessings continued. One way or another, God was determined to get my attention. The Bible is full of extraordinary accounts of where God has used men and women, apparent nobodies. My journey had been a rocky road. God allowed Satan to go the extra mile in order to make my circumstances seem irreversible. Sometimes the price of being chosen of God can be astronomical, but the reward is far greater.

After self-publishing my book, the Langley newspaper did a book review. I also did a book signing, which I greatly enjoyed. My book was also in twenty different libraries. When it came to computers, a kindergarten student knew more than I did, yet I somehow managed to create a personal website which attracted incredible responses from around the world.

I soon entered into a beautiful online friendship with a woman named Tammy. From the beginning, I noticed there was something different about her, something special. Even now, I'm convinced it was no chance meeting. I personally have never met her in person, or any of her family, yet in ways beyond measure they were instrumental in my recovery.

Tammy had read everything I wrote, and she was hooked. She strongly felt that my story was an exceptional work of a transformed life. At first, her fascination was in whether I was the genuine article. My emails to her didn't seem to cut the mustard for Tammy. Truthfully, I could be whatever and whoever I wanted to be on paper. We quickly exchanged telephone numbers and were in constant communication with one another. She asked me to buy a webcam for my computer so we could see each other while we spoke on the phone. This is how she introduced me to her daughters, Billie and Shelia.

My symptoms started slowly. First it was the night sweats, followed by chronic stomach cramps, which often had me doubled over in excruciating pain for days on end as my belly swelled up like a beach ball. Then it was as if I had moved into the bathroom; the episodes of diarrhea became severe and frequent. Every bone in my body started to ache, and it literally felt as though a steamroller had run me over. My weight rapidly dropped. No matter how much I ate, I couldn't keep anything down. My body rejected everything I tried to put in it. I had long periods of insomnia, and when I finally did manage to fall asleep, I'd often wake up in a cold sweat.

Dr. Webb thought it was either an ulcer or viral stomach flu. The poor diagnosis really wasn't his fault; he was a family physician, not an HIV specialist. Doctors often aren't sure of the problem, or the remedy. "Let's try this and see you in two weeks." If the problem persists, they'll simply try something else.

Finally, after months of deterioration, a blood test seemed appropriate and the results weakened me in the knees. When I finally went in to see the doctor, he asked me, "How are you feeling, Mino?"

I responded rather aggressively. "You know how I'm feeling. You've given me one prescription after another, and nothing seems to work. Whatever is going on is interfering with my work. I only seem to only be able to put in six or seven hours a day."

He looked at me, dumbfounded. "Mino, I can't believe you're out of bed, never mind working."

The blood work revealed that my white blood cell count had dropped to a dangerous level, and trying to get a straight answer from the doctor was like pulling teeth. Basically, even in healthy people, our white blood cell count shouldn't go below 4.2. Mine had dropped to 2.9. The lower it goes, the closer you get to organ failure. This definitely seemed to be the direction I was headed in.

You would think that by now I would get some kind of message, but sometimes we don't want to give anybody control of our lives, not even God. It wouldn't be long now before I started to realize one unquestionable truth: the world thus far had done nothing for me. Only the promises of God are sure.

Twice now, I have overcome insurmountable odds, literally battling for my life as the HIV progressed to its final stages. I basically ran to Dr. Montaner's office. Upon seeing him, I requested to be placed on the toxic antiviral drugs again. In his unique way, he explained the hazards and pitfalls. He said that as a result of my system being resistant to the first drugs I'd been put on, we would have to try a new combination, which might not even work. He further said that it could take up to four or five months to see any kind of improvement, all the while I'd be dealing with side effects more horrifying than those of my original drugs. Without wavering, I asked him to once again spark me up.

The HIV in my blood had once again gone from undetectable to uncountable. The progression of HIV to AIDS is always measured by the detectable amounts of the virus in the bloodstream. "Uncountable" means that there were over one hundred thousand copies of the virus in one milliliter of my blood.

Imagine for a moment that your body has five liters of blood in it. That would be five thousand milliliters. Now visualize five hundred million parasites eating your body from the inside out. No wonder most of the bones in my body were brittle and ached; there was a banquet going on inside my body. There were a number of medications to try, but the problem was, which combination? It was imperative that we hit the nail on the head on our first try, as there would be no second chances.

I still pride myself in going that extra mile. In view of the circumstances, it would have been easy to just give up. The following three months were a struggle, and I spent many a night on the phone with Tammy. Often her tears freely flowed as we spoke. She was a tremendous source of encouragement in my time of need. Some would call our meeting blind luck, but Tammy and I know different.

Suddenly, the HIV once again returned to its undetectable state, and for the first time ever my white blood cells went up to 6.2. Tammy was so mesmerized by my recovery that she wrote the following poems to me:

The Demon Within

There is this man, Mino is his name,
who came out of the pits of hell with
a demon on his tail to claim God's fame.
Though most people run from his name,
Mino looked deep into his eyes day after day
with his spirit high and an angel by his side,
saying, "Even though we might have to grow old together
you will never be seen by anyone,
for I'm am strong and you are weak,
and that is how it will always be."
And the war was on, with Mino ahead,
saying, "Try and beat me if you can. You won't get far.
I beat you twice already and I'll do it again."
So day after day, the war rages on.
Armed with weapons, and his angel by his side,

Mino lives on with more battles left to come.
One day a battle will be fought, the war will be
over with the demon in his plot,
and Mino saving the lot.

Our Friendship
Every single day, you're the one who brings joy to my heart
Just by knowing you will be there waiting for me to wake.
Who you became makes me want to be more then I am.
No matter what I say and do, you are there to get me through.
You make me believe there is no obstacle too great to bear
Because of what you went through and you're still here to share.
You let me know in so many ways that our friendship is for real
And that makes me feel that it will always be no matter what.
My friends may come and go, but I know you are here to stay
Because I know you would never let me down or make me cry.
You are my writer, and right now mine alone, though one day I know
I will have to share you with the world, but for now I'm glad I don't.
I know you get lonely and sad some days, but always remember
I will always be here to show you the way.
So I wrote this poem to make all your days and nights,
For I will be your friend, forever and a day.

Having battled and overcome the odds of defeating HIV in its final stages for the third time, I now focused my attention on preparing for my upcoming speaking engagement at a local high school. Josh, my employer's son, had convinced his criminology professor to have me come to his class in December as a guest speaker. I was very nervous, as I would be speaking to a Grade Twelve class. I felt that they wouldn't be able to relate to the hardships I had endured. Even though I put together ten thousand words in notes to draw from, I was still nervous. Mr. Abrams, the teacher who had extended this invitation, was very confident that I had so much to contribute.

I arrived at Mission Secondary School early, as suggested by the teacher. Mr. Abrams and I talked over lunch and I welcomed his continued encouragement. Along with the twenty students in attendance, there would be a few of the other teachers present, along with the school's principal, which added to my inclination to just run away.

I knew the key to my success was in immediately capturing their attention. My opening statements, therefore, had to be of a powerful nature. I had a few ideas, though I used none of them. Instead my first couple of sentences came right out of left field. When I walked into the classroom and saw these young men and women about to go out into the world on their own and face unexpected challenges, I began, "I have faced many obstacles throughout my life, but none of it really mattered. Not the twenty-five years of criminality or the fourteen years I spent in prison. For thirty years I was a drug addict, battling chronic alcoholism. As a result of my lifestyle of sharing needles, I contracted HIV, which came out of remission three times, threatening to extinguish my life. I struggled to understand specifically what had for most of my life left me colder than an iceberg. However, in being here today, I guess I should be thankful for the coldness, as without it I don't think I could have survived."

I knew I had their attention, as all eyes were fixed on me. "What happened to me could very easily happen to anyone in this room. Many might say, 'Oh I'll never be like that.' Don't ever fool yourself in this false perception. I never imagined myself going to prison, let alone spending a third of my life there. I was deathly afraid of needles, and still am, yet I became an intravenous drug addict. I didn't think HIV could ever happen to me, but it did. Believe me, it can very easily happen to anyone. It's all got to do with choices."

Throughout the hour in which I spoke, you could have heard a pin drop. When I was finished, these high school kids had tears welled in their eyes. They gave me a standing ovation. Before leaving the class, many came up to shake my hand. The teachers were mesmerized, and I was invited to return in a week to speak again, partly because of the following endorsement from Mr. Abrams:

In the spring of 2005, Mr. Pavlic addressed my Criminology 12 class at Mission Secondary. For an hour, Mino wound through his personal story of choices and consequences, drug addiction and crime, failure and success, and then answered difficult questions with candor and sincerity. I was pleased my students had the opportunity to share his experiences and hear his message. Mino puts a face to the dark stranger, the East End addict, and the HIV-infected patient facing and struggling with the results of his choices. He offers himself as an example and speaks with passion against substance abuse of all kinds. He does not minimize the small steps in the beginning, but links each step, each choice, to outcomes and possible tragedy.

He is an effective anti-drug spokesperson. Mino's message is also about hope, the will to succeed, and the ability to meet challenges. [His book] contains an important message of what can be achieved if one has the will and confidence. The writing of the book stands as an example to young adults facing graduation and wondering if they are capable of fulfilling their dreams.

I am pleased to support Mino's quest to tell his story. He is passionate about helping others and I believe he has a significant contribution to make.

Within weeks, I received a totally unexpected package in the mail from Tammy's daughter Sheila. Tammy had tried on many occasions to get her to read my book, but as her letter explained, she was very career-minded and had only read three autobiographies in her life, mine being the third. As I slowly took the two items out of the box, tears ran down my face; I knew an invisible force had to be working in my life. The first treasure was a gold-rimmed picture frame. Enclosed within its glass enclosure was a poem Sheila had written. It was no ordinary poem, as she had used every letter of my name to begin each verse.

Mino Pavlic
Making amends with your past.
Insisting on a better path.
Now knowing all you've missed, you're
Opening your heart to other lost kids.
Pleased with how far you've come,
An angel in heaven is smiling above.
Violence and drugs no longer your choice,
Love and laughter now have a voice.
In your heart your angel now lives.
Courage and goodness in you the Lord saw
when He sent you an angel to help with your
flaws. Slowly but surely you have learned from
your mistakes. Now the world is yours to take.

Also in the package was something her grandmother had made for me, and I cherish it with all my heart. It was a small plaster-cast figurine, about eight inches high, of Jesus carrying the cross on His shoulder. I will forever carry it, never letting go.

A Proven Statistic and New Inroads 64

The evidence of a changed life is found in miraculous transformations. Sharing one's experiences in humility exerts a positive influence. But we can only give sound counsel, instruction, and recommendations based on the storms we ourselves have weathered. When our hearts have truly been refined, it becomes natural for us to bless those less fortunate. It took me many years to learn this.

One day, I picked up the *Vancouver Sun* and was shocked by an article I read in it. A local HIV-infected man, who by all appearances was fighting for his life, had put his hope in a new, highly toxic antiviral therapy offered by Dr. Montaner. The problem was that the pill cost forty dollars each and needed to be taken every day. The man couldn't afford such a cost, and when he applied to the government for assistance, they refused his petition without due consideration.

As a result, I wrote the following letters to the reporter who wrote the story, and then gave Dr. Montaner's office a copy.

Dear Sir:
My name is Mino Pavlic and I've taken it upon myself to write to you, in response to your article written in today's newspaper, regarding Tiko Kerr, the B.C. artist who it seems is being denied financial support for antiviral drugs which could save his life. I find the government's lack of compassion in this matter to be incomprehensible and inexcusable, for I am definitely a proven statistic. Tiko Kerr has committed no offence, yet it seems by Health Canada's decision that they are condemning him to a horrifying death, without the possibility of appeal. For Mr. Kerr, time is a crucial factor, and in his case, it's quickly running out. I have been HIV-positive since 1991, almost fifteen years now, and have been directly involved with the highly respected HIV/AIDS researcher Dr. Julio Montaner and his award-winning antiviral drug trials since 1997. Unquestionably they have not only prolonged my life, but greatly improved the quality of my very existence.

The comments within this letter are not so much a defense of Dr. Montaner as a testimony to my complete belief in the unlimited miracles associated with what the government, in their ignorance, describes as unproven clinical therapies. In 1997, when I first met Dr. Montaner, as blunt as could be put, I was in the process of slowly dying. I was asked if I'd care to participate in a worldwide study involving one hundred participants. The specialist was clear regarding all the factors which needed to be taken into careful consideration. When confronted by someone whose life is on the verge of being extinguished, why should he skirt around the facts?

I was told in a very professional and informative way that the drugs of the trial had thus far only been used on monkeys, with no favorable results. If I could get past this frightening reality, I then had to seriously consider the unimaginable side effects. In clear thought, I signed a waiver of responsibility and entered the study, where I was meticulously monitored over the following four years. It turned out to be one of the best decisions of my life, as within this period of time the HIV in my blood became undetectable. Due to their toxic state, we agreed to give my body a break. I have seen people actually cry at the prospect of taking their medications. With me, it was the opposite; if I didn't have them, I'd cry. They've done wonders for me.

I have overcome insurmountable odds. My HIV infection came out of remission for the third time last year. I literally ran to Dr. Montaner's office requesting to be placed on the toxic antiviral drugs again. In his unique way, he explained the hazards or pitfalls. He said that as a result of my system now being resistant to the first drugs I was on, we would have to try a new combination, which in fact might not even work. He further went on to say that it could take up to four or five months to see any kind of improvement, all the while I'd be dealing with side effects which were more horrifying than those of my original drugs. Without wavering, I boldly asked him to once again spark me up. Remarkably, within thirty days, there was no HIV in my blood, and the side effects have been minimal. A year later, I'm now in excellent health and still undetectable.

In my opinion, the government's reluctance to grant Mr. Kerr the treatment outlined by Dr. Montaner is unacceptable. In essence, you are condemning him. Make no mistake about it, people such as myself, Tiko Kerr, and countless others around the world are willing to be used as human guinea pigs. This is where the foundation of all scientific research must begin, especially in the struggle to hopefully one day find a cure for HIV.

The way I saw it in 1997, my life was definitely coming to an end. There were no promises, just a glimmer of hope. It was easy for me to make my decision, to accept the harsh realities of the study involved. Was I to do nothing and die a horrifying death? No, I entered the study. At least in dying, it would be with dignity and a sense of participation. Dr. Montaner, in my opinion, is beyond reproach with his research, which I'm sure is collaborated by scientific geniuses around the world. Inasmuch as he would like to take a gigantic step forward, it seems his hands are tied in government procedure and policy. In my most diplomatic voice, I say to the government, it's time to act or get off the pot. The hell with policy or procedure; it's time to throw them both in the wind. Take a look around you. I'm not sure of the exact figures, but the people dying on a daily basis are steadfastly growing out of proportion.

In closing, I'm in the trenches, so to speak. In my willingness and courage, I'm prepared to do whatever is necessary in combating this illness. Are you? Don't suffocate us in the noose of procedure and policy. In the boardroom, bureaucrats always have the luxury of time on their hands. Down here, on the front lines, time is running out.

This is the second letter:

As is my entitlement, having succeeded beyond my wildest expectations, what follows could be the ravings of a delusional man—or, in layman's terms, have I hit the nail on the head? When I think of the devastation of the HIV/AIDS plague and the countless lives it's taken since its existence, I'm stunned and sit in complete bewilderment as to any government's reluctance to sponsor the clinical drug trials.

It should never be a matter of dollars and cents, as this epidemic has reached astronomical proportions internationally. I believe that even if a possibility exists to prolong a human life, especially in cases where that suffering individual is willing and courageous enough to accept the risks involved, there should be no barriers to treatment. This raises a question we must all ask ourselves. In view of all the experimentation and research to date, isn't it time to stand united and move to a new level in combating this illness?

As to our government's position, that these antiviral trials are unproven, since my association and willing participation with Dr. Montaner, my life has been prolonged. Due to the unique relationship I have with his office, and my persistence to follow the rigorous treatment outlined, the quality of my life has improved tenfold since 1997. I'm certainly a proven statistic. However, it goes far beyond taking medications, which is basically what this letter is about. Involving oneself in these unique clinical trials is about a person's determination, persistence, and desire to stand fast against destructive behaviors which invite failure with each new day. One must be willing to rise above one's own illusions of insurmountable odds. The greatest obstacle any of us will ever face in life is underestimating our ability to succeed.

Victory is all about being prepared to step up to the plate. Are you prepared to go the whole nine yards? Again, I understand that not all of us have the ability to overcome our own haunting yet inescapable demons. Not everyone has the luxury of a stable environment, or the means to maintain a proper balanced nutritional plan. As a long-term survivor, I can tell you that the above requirements are essential factors, crucial for success. I'm not saying that the government is wrong in their position; when they look at the balance sheet, they see a very small percentage rate of success. That's a harsh reality.

Awareness and personal accountability are a must in containing this crippling monster. When one's immune system is compromised, everything is detrimental to one's health. However, anyone in such a position *must* realize that life as they once knew it has ceased to exist. Those of us fighting HIV are on a different playing field where the rules are alien to us. Our own selfish wants and needs become a thing of the past. Instead of wallowing in self-pity, which breeds irresponsibility, we must stand firm in our reality and accept total responsibility. Especially when it's on the government's nickel, irresponsibility gets pretty expensive. I see so many necessary changes within personal accountability, as that's where most of the battle begins.

If there were ever a poster boy for the viability, manageability, and remarkable success of these extraordinary medications, it would be me. The facts of my journey are indisputable. I have lived a life which gives insurmountable weight and credibility to combating HIV/AIDS. In terms of medical research, the pursuit of excellence has thus far been relentless, to the point of exceeding my wildest expectations. From my own perspective, we must now venture in a new direction with the fight.

When I think of people such as myself, Tiko Kerr, and the countless men and women who have willingly and courageously put their lives on the chopping block in the continuing hopes of overcoming this serious global threat, the government seems to take our unfortunate yet assumed responsibility lightly. We are like modern-day explorers, or astronauts. They are going where no man has gone before, in hopes of discovering new benefits for mankind, putting their very lives on the line. We are not given an iota of the concessions given to astronauts.

Bear with me, however, as I'm about to drive this nail home. My proposal is simple. We have drug and alcohol treatment centers, so why not a first-of-its-kind an HIV/AIDS drug rehabilitation/research center? We would invite one hundred people from all over the world, in different stages of the illness, to participate in a three-month structured program to be monitored daily, under constant supervision. My own success with the very toxic medications speaks to closely following the strict parameters of the treatment prescribed. All the prospective participants would, in essence, be ambassadors from their respective countries.

Why would such a concept work? Build an environment not representing a hospital background, but rather a rehabilitative setting. They build seventy-million-dollar prisons, state of the art, but thus far all I've seen for those struggling within HIV/AIDS is a paper bag containing three months of meds with instructions. Why not a unique facility with all the benefits of education, nutrition, and counseling available around the clock? Dr. Montaner, in my opinion is beyond reproach with his research, which I'm sure is collaborated by scientific geniuses around the world. Inasmuch as he would like to make a gigantic step forward, it seems his hands are tied by government procedure and policy.

If an HIV-infected person isn't willing to go the extra mile, there's no sense in the government wasting time and money, as the pills won't work for them. That's a million dollars per day flushed down the toilet, because they're not willing to let go of addictive behaviors. I also see mandatory urine samples as a necessity. We're not playing games here; it's life and death. It's said that the life expectancy of an infected person is five to six years. Well, I've been infected since 1991. The choice is yours.

I never got a response to either letter.

THIRTY-THREE YEARS OF ALCOHOLISM ERASED 65

The spirit of God is similar to an airplane; it's always looking for a place to land. From the moment you've been targeted as a landing strip, you come under His express protection, as He gives His angels charge over you. It is said that from the moment you call upon the name of the Lord, He will never abandon or forsake you. However, before He can land, the strip must first be cleared of all its garbage.

In the Bible, Mary Magdalene had seven demons cast out of her. These demons could easily represent all those critical things which have negative effects in our lives. Jesus said that He had come to restore all that was taken away by the devil. To many people, this may seem like a fabrication, and believe me, at one time, I was one of them. Slowly my eyes were opened to the truth. My feeble plea of unbelief had been uttered almost eight years ago. Up to that point, my life was bound by many suffocating and inescapable nooses. One by one, the landing strip was being cleared and the following obstacles were removed from my life. In total, there were seven. Once they were removed, I never went back.

1. Twenty-five years of drug addiction.
2. Twenty-five years of criminality, the ingrained spirit of criminality.
3. Fourteen years of imprisonment, enslavement to sin.
4. Lust of the flesh. Since Lisa's departure, I have remained in abstinence.
5. Thirty-three years of chronic alcoholism.
6. Forty years of smoking, gone in the blink of an eye.
7. Healing and deliverance from HIV.

One would almost think I was related to Houdini, as I also escaped three car accidents which should have by rights taken my life. I walked away without a scratch.

The one I thought would be almost impossible to shake was my thirty-three years of chronic alcoholism, but that too was about to go. Strangely enough, once I decided to quit drinking, I never gave it another thought. It was wiped out, as though it never existed.

I've certainly had angels watching over me, but on one particular night they must have gone out for pizza. As the bar closed, I staggered to my Toyota van and slowly made my way home through quiet back streets. I found myself half a block from my house, waiting for the light to change, with a car in front of me. Having made it thus far, I didn't think the next fifty yards would be a problem. The light changed, and the car ahead of me started to cross the intersection. For whatever reason, halfway through the intersection, the car stopped and I banged into it.

I got out, saying, "I'm sorry." There was absolutely no damage, but the person was bent on making an issue of it. "Here are my insurance papers," I said. That wasn't good enough. They wanted to involve the police. The reason? Well, her insurance company would have told her to take a walk, but by involving the police, who eventually tagged me with an impaired driving charge, she got to claim whatever she wanted, as I was at fault. I even told her I would have given her a couple hundred dollars just for walking away. I ended up paying a heavy price, but I paid it, accepting the consequences. God knew when the dust settled that I, not Satan, would still be standing. My license was suspended for three months, and the court fees ended up costing me five thousand dollars.

Luckily, my boss Andy liked me a lot. This placed a definite hardship on him, but we made it work. I now had to drive my ten-speed bicycle ten miles back and forth, each day. I wanted to throw in the towel and say, "I'll see you when I get my license back." However, I'm sure had I done so, there would have been no job waiting for me.

I continued to drink, but I haven't had a drop since the moment my license was reinstated. Anyone caught in the vicious cycle of drug or alcohol addiction knows that the battle can seem next to impossible. Without the benefit of treatment centers or counseling, I did it. Believe me, I didn't do it in my own strength. This was demon number five. How was it possible?

The Old Testament contains the greatest promise ever given to mankind from God, by far:

Call unto me, and I will answer thee, and shew thee great and mighty things, which thou knowest not. (Jeremiah 33:3)

Notice how the promise is given in three distinct parts. We must ask, He will answer, and then we will do what no one else could. In the New Testament, we basically have the same three-part promise given by Jesus. Many of us continue to live beneath our privileged glory simply because we fail to ask and then follow through, and nowhere is this clearer than in John 16:24:

Hitherto [up until now] have ye asked nothing in my name: ask, and ye shall receive, that your joy may be full.

Wow! Here we have Jesus, who was God manifested in the flesh, telling us that we don't receive because we simply don't ask. It couldn't get any more straightforward. God is waiting for us to start asking Him for things. Secondly, just as important, God will answer us with clear instruction. Expect nothing less. If you're looking to use His stuff, it'll only be on His terms.

John 15:7 says,

If ye abide in me, and my words abide in you, ye shall ask what ye will, and it shall be done unto you.

Lastly, why would God want to do anything, especially in a life such as mine, full of open rebellion and ungratefulness, unworthy of any such consideration? The answer is found in John 14:13:

And whatsoever ye shall ask in my name, that will I do, that the Father may be glorified in the Son.

Regardless of who you are or what you've done, and no matter how bad things appear to be, God will step in for the simple reason that He is to be glorified for what only He can do in your life. However, given our human nature, we all have a dark side. When a miracle of divine intervention does take place, and wipes out that crippling addiction or intolerable illness as though it never existed, our greatest transgression isn't so much in our failure to give thanks to God, but rather in our refusal to even acknowledge His existence.

We are all repeat offenders, which raises an issue demanding serious consideration. Have you ever stopped and wondered why it is that when crippling obstacles are removed, we often find ourselves not only missing them, but in many instances turning back to the same destructive patterns? The answer is quite simple. When anything of the physical world attaches itself to us, its presence becomes like an inescapable electrical current. It only stands to reason that if we've never experienced the reality of God in our lives, we won't recognize His presence, nor will we miss it.

In order to better understand this, we need look no further than the example of an incarcerated prisoner. For twenty years before his incarceration, he was a chronic alcoholic who also smoked two packs of cigarettes a day. Suddenly, he finds himself serving a two-year sentence and there's no drinking or smoking allowed in the institution. After the completion of his sentence, his abstinence is irrefutable evidence that he has overcome what was once a crippling addition, yet upon his release he heads for the nearest pub, while smoking a cigarette. This is not a fabrication; it's reality. I've done it myself a number of times.

Never mind treatment centers or counseling. At their best, they're no more than a crutch, a band aid. When that crutch is kicked out from under you, you will fall. The Bible tells us that in our own power, we would be able to move mountains. At one time, this was the most idiotic thing I had ever heard of. I'm a living testimony that it's a fact, and here's how it works. The mountain is that overpowering fear or crippling addiction in your life.

I've faced many such mountains. For thirty years, I've tried climbing them only to fall each and every time. I've tried to go around them, only to discover that the base of the mountain is never-ending. So what's the answer? For the longest time, I thought that when we're willing to overcome something, each day while in abstinence either the mountain takes a step away from you, or you from it. This in actuality is untrue, as you could always step back into the nightmare at another time. What actually happens is this: after each day of abstinence, the mountain literally becomes smaller and smaller, eventually disappearing from sight.

In our own lives, we can all experience the amazing phenomenon of walking on water. Metaphorically speaking, the boat in the raging storm is us ensnared in the inescapable addiction. When we decide to get out of that boat and leave the demon behind, as long as we have our eyes on Jesus, the storm immediately becomes calm. Each day that we remain abstinent is another step away from the boat. Imagine what was once a crippling impossibility suddenly becoming a living reality.

But if you ever turn back, the journey gets tougher. Never mind being back in the boat again, you'll find yourself five hundred miles inland. You'll have to make your way back to the boat, and unfortunately for many of us it's a journey we can never complete.

Finally, the Acknowledgement of God 66

A year of many new beginnings, 2006 would prove to be very significant in my life. What was about to take place was a revelation from God. I had been attending Creekside Church for roughly two years. In all honesty, there seemed to be an unexplained emptiness continually embracing me. One would think some form of spiritual maturity would have exhibited itself by now, but that was about to change.

In view of all the tribulations and accomplishments in my life, it's unbelievable that I still never acknowledged God, and really wasn't sure if I ever would. Many of us need to cross through our own parted Red Sea experience before we are fully persuaded to the presence of an unseen God in our lives. This is understandable, for if all you ever experienced amounted to nothing more than a procession of crippling failure, then even a small spark of hope can appear as a cruel joke just waiting to be snatched away.

Our belief and faith in God can only be strengthened as a result of our personal victories. Before my moment of complete brokenness, there never existed in me a hope that could have been extinguished. Only God Himself could have delivered me from that cesspool, yet from the time He stepped in and transformed my life, it still took me ten years to be convinced of His existence.

When God steps in and wants to introduce Himself personally into your life, there will be no mistaking such a revelation. For me, it was in the solitude of my car on the way to the airport. I was listening to a gospel CD by Elvis Presley. The songs were familiar, as I'd heard them sung many times in church, but now they seemed to take on greater reverence. One song in particular, "Where Would I Be Had it Not Been for the Lord," seemed to literally wrap itself around me. I had never experienced such an outpouring of emotion! I had to pull over on the side of the highway. The floodgates of my soul were opened and unquenchable tears streamed down my face. I sat there for a good half-hour, thinking, *Where would I be had it not been for the grace of Jesus Christ in my life?*

In that half-hour, my life flashed before me and all the horrendous events took my breath away— the childhood abuse, parental abandonment, criminality, and years of imprisonment. My thoughts were invaded by the nightmare of near-death escapes from three car accidents. Then the thirty-plus years of inescapable drug and alcohol addiction, followed by the drug trials and what should have clearly been the brick wall at the end of the road. As I sat on that dark highway, one unavoidable thought crossed my mind:

all those things were gone, as though they had never existed. Where would I be had not God stepped in so many times? Either dead or in prison. From that moment on, I wanted to learn all I could about God.

However, be careful of what you ask for, as it may come in waves. It did for me.

When I regained my composure, I reentered traffic and headed in the direction of the airport in silence. I wondered about what had just taken place, but I found no rational answers, nor at the moment could I see its significance. God had just given me a touch of anointing for protection, as a reminder of who was controlling my every step.

I was on my way to Brockville, Ontario, where I would spend the next two weeks visiting with my brother Mike, whom I hadn't seen in almost four years. I was looking forward to this reunion, but I did so with a guarded apprehension.

Mike's life hadn't been a bed of roses, either. At forty-seven years of age, he'd also faced brutal hardships. His greatest battle was with a chronic thirty-year addiction to narcotics. After serving his latest six-month sentence for fraud, he was transferred to the Brockville Recovery House. While there, he befriended a wonderful woman named Sheila, who had a heart of gold. Even though she was happily married and highly successful in the community, she and Mike had become inseparable.

It had taken them the better part of a year to persuade me to make this trip. I had sent them my book. I knew they were overwhelmed by my achievements and miraculous transformations. For the longest time, they wanted me to move out there. What nobody understood, least of all me, was that the freedoms I now enjoyed had nothing to do with anything I had done. Many red flags continued to surface during the course of our long-distance conversations, as the character traits of addiction clearly exhibited themselves. God allowed this reunion to take place, which was not for my benefit—nor was it going to be by anyone's rules except His, as I was about to find out.

For the first hour on the plane, I enjoyed what you would call my first taste of celebrity status. I signed and gave away ten copies of my revised book. It still takes my breath away to think that when those people caught their connecting flights, my book was headed in different directions all over the world, hopefully in some way leaving its impact.

The last leg of the flight was spent in thoughts of my mother. Mike hadn't seen or spoken to her in over thirty years. I had given her his number, so she would call in the next day or so. I already knew Mike's point of view on this issue. To him, she had been dead all these years, and I knew he wasn't ready or willing to resurrect her. His heart was full of resentment, anger, and deep pain, as she had abandoned her children to satisfy her own needs and wants. She'd often say to me, "I can't believe what you kids have done with your lives," and I would reply, "I can, for we had good teachers."

I was in great health, but on the second day I fell deathly ill with pneumonia and was bedridden for the next twelve days, with a fever of one hundred and three. Just before my scheduled return, the fever disappeared. Mike was rather disappointed, but I think it was for the best. In reality, I don't think he was struggling so much with addiction as he was hiding it from me. And no, he never did resurrect dear old mom.

I had prearranged to meet Mom on my return flight, during my two-hour stopover in Toronto. Somehow our wires got crossed, though, and we missed one another. I reboarded the plane, but there seemed to be a delay with the takeoff. Little did I know that it all had to do with me. Somehow my mother got to talk to the pilot, and next thing I know the pilot was apologizing for the delay but saying there was an emergency situation which would only take a few minutes to resolve before we were on our way. All of a sudden everybody was clapping. I looked up to see my mother coming down the aisle, with the pilot behind her carrying a duffel bag. She gave me a hug, said she loved me, and then left the plane.

This was the last time I saw my mother, so it most definitely proved to be a reunion only God could have arranged. In the bag, amongst other things, were a few of bottles of expensive wine, and six bars of European chocolate. It took a little persuasion, but eventually the stewardesses accepted these not as gifts but rather tokens of my appreciation.

Once on familiar ground, I started reading more about God. In a very real sense, it was almost as if I was scared of what I might discover. I was standing in the midst of the miraculous, and I didn't even know it. It's one thing to say you believe in God, but quite another to step into His presence.

Through the following week, I was filled with childlike excitement about attending church. I was eager to share with Pastor Jim what I thought had been the unveiling of God in my life. When I finally approached him, it proved to be a huge disappointment. For all the enthusiastic encouragement I had expected, I would have done better sharing my revelation with the monkeys in the local zoo.

For the moment, I didn't understand the significance behind Pastor Jim's indifference. His statements and actions would prove to be a major turning point in my life. In the near future, I would cut all ties with is church. Believe me, it was the will of God.

God Moves in for the Baptism Checkmate 67

One of my favorite books of the Bible has always been Exodus. Undoubtedly, the Israelites would have to be considered one of the greatest underdogs in history. Imagine a couple of million people held captive in what amounted to nothing more than forced labor. I have many times likened the story of the Israelites' four hundred years of horrific Egyptian bondage, and their miraculous deliverance, to my own journey through life.

Only God's supernatural intervention could have persuaded Pharaoh, the ruler of Egypt, to let the Israelites go, and also give them untold riches. God delivered His people safely through the Red Sea, where they roamed in the wilderness for the next forty years. Have you ever asked yourself why they wandered all those years through the wilderness? Think about this. Not once in four hundred years of bondage did the Israelites dare complain to the Egyptians. As a result of their miraculous deliverance, they were a nation favored by God. Yet almost immediately upon achieving their freedom, they developed a bold self-arrogance of complaining, which led to open rebellion, even against God. That's why only Joshua and Caleb crossed the Jordan River into the Promised Land. Believe what you will, but before any of us can enter our own Promised Land, we must first be emptied of all worldliness and self-pride.

Our wilderness experience is supposed to be our personal revelation from God. Look at it this way. When God delivers us out of the unimaginable and places us in the wilderness, there we find a bridge built between us and God. Before any of us can cross that bridge, we are left in the wilderness to look at where we just came from. We must understand that our deliverance was in and of itself an improbability that could have only come from beyond the walls of this world. Only when we acknowledge the existence and sovereignty of God can our journey into the miraculous become an enjoyable experience. Creekside Church was my wilderness experience. However, God didn't want me to remain stuck in the wilderness. God was about to bring me into the Promised Land.

A one-in-a-billion chance meeting was about to take place—or rather, it was divine intervention. One day I was driving on the other side of town when I decided to pull into a mini-mall parking lot. A big pet store sign caught my attention. I had recently been given a beautiful husky/wolf cross pup and I needed to get him some food and treats. This was as good a place as any. Before leaving the mall, I was craving a coffee, so I pulled into a coffeehouse.

Entering the store, I saw there was a line-up. I decided to wait it out, and in doing so my life was about to forever change. While waiting, I looked out the big picture window and saw a car pull into a parking spot out front. A young woman got out of the car and I was immediately mesmerized by her appearance. She looked as though she had just stepped out of the 1800s. Everything about her suggested a sophisticated elegance. She wore a long skirt which ever so lightly caressed the pavement as she walked, and her tucked-in white blouse was buttoned to the collar. She wore her hair up in a bun. She could have easily passed for a librarian, except for her stylish hat which suggested otherwise. She came into the store and stood directly behind me. Almost immediately, I engaged her in idle conversation.

I complimented her appearance, and she briefly explained that this was how she dressed for church. This intrigued me all the more, as Creekside's dress code was very casual. I told her that I, too, went to church, which sparked her deeper interest. As I began explaining the journeys of my life, I bought her a coffee and we ended up talking for hours in that coffee shop, mainly about religion. I didn't know this woman, nor had we ever met before—or so we both believed. Her name was Bonnie. As I was to later learn, she was thirty-seven years old, an important fact in God's plan. In all honesty, she taught me more about God in those first three hours than Creekside had in three years. She was full of knowledge and insightful understanding, and the more I hungered, the more she unconditionally gave of her time.

For the next two weeks, in this same coffeehouse, while spending hours just talking about God, a true friendship blossomed. At times, she would read parts of the New Testament to me, and then we'd have a discussion. In essence, she was giving me my own private Bible study. Our relationship, from its infancy, was always of a spiritual nature. I just couldn't understand her fixation with me, but it unquestionably proved to be God's will, as I was almost ready to be brought out of the wilderness. Bonnie and I frequently discussed the significance of baptism.

Neither of us was aware of it, but Bonnie was to become one of the most influential night-and-day differences of my life. We quickly established a cemented bond, and for the next several months met every evening. Without her continued encouragement and spiritual guidance, I would still be walking around aimlessly in the wilderness. However, when God is in control of your life, only in the fullness of time will He move you in His orchestrated direction, like a pawn in a chess game.

In light of what had already transpired in my life, and what was about to take place, I truly believe God had chosen me with a specific purpose in mind. I understand that to suggest such a thing seems like a trumped-up fantasy. Believe me, the outcome in this unfolding story will have you scratching your own head for answers, but there can be no denying the facts. Read your Bible and know that the Holy Spirit of God will confirm any such calling by signs, wonders, and miracles.

Anyone can believe in God, but those whom He chooses will definitely be schooled. They will fall down again and again and again, until every part of them knows beyond a doubt that God alone is in complete control. Their training will be the toughest, most excruciating regime to be endured anywhere in the universe.

In the particular game of my life, when the unsuspecting checkmate came, looking back at the moves to its execution, there is no mistaking the supremacy of God. This unknown and invisible game of chess had been playing itself out for fifty years. It would seem that Satan had launched an attack, and there seemed to be no avenue of escape. The game appeared to be one-sided.

Bonnie was the second most valuable piece in the game—the Queen—yet until now she had never been moved. In the best of times, I'm not the easiest person to be around; therefore, her unwavering loyalty lent our friendship divine definition. She truly left an everlasting trail of footprints deep in my heart. Throughout our many sessions together, while we retraced the weathered steps of my life, searching the depths of my soul, it seemed as though she called in her own personal excavation crew. I'm not sure when or exactly how it happened, but she alone melted the coldness inside me. I always wanted her to know that if there were no tomorrow, I would consider our friendship, after our Lord Jesus, the greatest gift of my life.

We talked a lot about God, and we seemed to be on the same page. However, when she started in on me about Jesus being God, I started to develop headaches. She made it so simple that a child could understand. Over and over again, we'd go over the same issues, with no clear resolution on my part. I would argue with her, sometimes just storming out the door, but I would always return the next evening.

After a solid month of studying the book of John, I began to understand her point of view. It was all there, in the first fourteen verses of John 1.

Our next battle had to do with actual baptism. Even though she took me through John 3, step by step, and I knew she had many valid points, I continued to play the dummy. In my three years at Creekside, only two baptisms had been held, and I just assumed this was because it was a sacred ritual. One day, during an annual camp meeting going on, I read through Romans several times, and something definitely pierced my heart. I immediately drove up to the campground near Hope, B.C., and sat down with Pastor Jim. I told him I wanted to get baptized. Coming from me, this should have knocked him off his chair. His only response was that they'd have a meeting about it. What did I know? As far as I was concerned, that's how these things were done.

For the moment, I didn't mention my decision to Bonnie, as I wanted to surprise her. I still had a lot to learn about the ways of God, but like a newborn baby, you don't feed it steak until it's weaned off the bottle. Finally, after three months of waiting, I decided to share with Bonnie my desire to be baptized. She was ecstatic at my willingness to accept Jesus into my life, and wished to know when the baptism would take place. To put it mildly, she was appalled by my answer. I stated that I had approached the pastor of my church three months ago, and was told they would have a meeting about it; her bottom jaw hit the floor. I listened to her arguments for over an hour, and instead of entering into a debate with her, as had so far been my stubborn nature, I remained silent and deep in thought. In a very simplistic manner, Bonnie explained the significance behind such a decision, and the importance of its urgent fulfillment. I just knew she was right. In my own reasoning, it was now perfectly clear to me that church membership was never meant to be a prerequisite obstructing the path of baptism. In such cases where someone's heart has been softened and opened to desire baptism, God's servants should understand the urgency. A church's hesitation, unwillingness, or neglect regarding baptism weighs heavily on the balancing scale towards successful conversion.

The God I read about in my Bible is a God of complete order. Simply put, confusion is not of God. In reading John 1:1–14, it's made clear that Jesus is God:

In the beginning was the Word, and the Word was with God, and the Word was God... And the Word was made flesh, and dwelt amongst us, (and we beheld his glory, the glory as of the only begotten of the Father,) full of grace and truth. (John 1:1,14)

Jesus came as an example to proclaim the good news of the kingdom of heaven, which had always been our rightful inheritance, as we were created in the image of God. Jesus came to let us know there is only one God and only one method of entrance into His kingdom. In this regard, we should be in one accord. Jesus willfully went to the cross for three reasons.

1. He was persuaded that His shed blood would take away the sins of the world.
2. He was persuaded that death itself could not and would not hold Him.
3. He was persuaded that after His accession, He would pour His spirit upon all flesh.

Have you ever wondered why there's such a cold indifference in society today in regards to religion? Have we really asked ourselves why there's such a falling away within the church? Jesus came to build a church, continually prayed for unity, and strongly rebuked division. Yet there are literally hundreds of different denominations in existence today, each preaching their own contradictory doctrine. This definitely doesn't represent the unity Jesus prayed for; it's division of the highest order. Instead of one Bible, there are lots of different interpretations on the bookshelves. A classic reason many don't read the King James Version is that they don't understand it. Here's the answer: get right with God and you will! The watered-down versions just don't cut the mustard with me. As a classic example, I'll use myself. If you were to feed my prior alcoholic self 190-proof whiskey, rest assured I wouldn't water it down. I'd want the potency of the real deal to saturate my body in its fullest force.

Regarding repentance and baptism, Acts 2:38 clearly states,

Repent, and be baptized every one of you in the name of Jesus Christ for the remission of sins, and ye shall receive the gift of the Holy Ghost.

Nowhere does it say, "Go home while we have a meeting about it." A church's hesitation regarding baptism clearly shows me that they have put themselves above God. In my opinion, to be properly baptized, we must be immersed in water as Jesus was. John the Baptist paved the way, and Jesus confirmed it. In John 3:5, Jesus said, *"Except a man be born of water and of the Spirit, he cannot enter into the kingdom of God."*

I don't wish to offend anyone, but ministers aren't to dictate how one is to be saved from eternal death. The Bible, for those who believe it, tells us who saves us and how it's to be done. If I should happen to breathe my last breath while you're having a meeting about my salvation, I'm going to miss out on heaven and spend an eternity in hell.

Let's say I've been a chronic alcoholic for thirty years and wish to get baptized. I've seen it with my own eyes; some ministers will say that they'll baptize you when you quit drinking for three weeks. This is very wrong, for if I could quit the drugs, alcohol, or smoking on my own steam for three weeks, what would

I need Jesus for? John the Baptist introduced a radical form of repentance, which by its very nature was violent. Jesus offered repentance through grace, and it was all about the blood of Jesus. Once that baptism takes place, we will find ourselves in a continual state of separation from the world. Anything less means you're still dancing with the devil.

A preacher who has never tasted life from my side of the fence cannot become a full-time thief, alcoholic, and heroin addict overnight; he can only reach those limits of desperation, line upon line. It shouldn't make any difference what side of the bridge you're on; the journey is the same, line upon line, precept upon precept. As I understand it, we are all running a *continual* race towards the perfection of Christ. Everyone is different; some are born on a smooth track, while others on one full of speed bumps. I was put on a terrifying obstacle course.

I believe the greatest hurdle we must first overcome in this race is to accept Jesus Christ as our Lord and Savior. This is the first hurdle, which enables the grace of Jesus to step in. Then we actually begin our transformational journey. With Jesus on our side, we can overcome each coming hurdle one by one. The blood of Jesus removes each off the track, making each step easier.

It is often recited like a broken record that many go into the baptismal tank a dry sinner and come out a wet one. Well, if the grace of God is truly upon someone, the cleansing process of transformation will begin almost immediately. Only God gives the increase, but how could He possibly give the increase if you don't even know Him? It's simply won't happen. If you bypass the grace of Jesus and expect to do it John the Baptist's way, then just like him you will end up beheaded. Repentance takes place the moment we realize our helplessness and ask for baptism. That's when Jesus steps in with grace, not violence, and slowly begins to transforms us.

However, I still had a lot to learn.

Baptism at Emmanuel Pentecostal Church 68

After hearing Bonnie out, she indicated that her church would baptize me. Without a second thought, I asked her to set it up. Within a week, I was having lunch with David Jobson, an associate pastor of Emmanuel Pentecostal Church. When it came to churches, I was still wet behind the ears. To me, they all represented the same thing. Was I in for a surprise! Dave and I spent an hour together talking, and then he said they would baptize me in two weeks' time. I was fired up like a rocket ship.

The following Saturday, while speaking to Pastor Jim, I told him of my decision. He was strongly opposed and had quite a lot to say about the Pentecostal movement. A lot of crazy stuff was said, which I found to be strange, as Bonnie at no time had ever put Pastor Jim or Creekside's beliefs down, nor for that matter did David Jobson. I found it quite comical. Suddenly, Creekside wanted to baptize me the following week.

"Pastor Jim, I've been waiting on you guys for the past five months, and I never heard a peep about anything from you," I said. "I stand firm in my decision. However, I welcome anyone in this church to attend my baptism in support."

No one came. Their loss.

To say the least, I felt a little apprehensive about my upcoming baptism at Emmanuel Pentecostal Church. I couldn't help but be affected by the bitter sting of unsubstantiated rumors Pastor Jim had thrown out as a ploy to hinder my decision. My home church was slamming the Pentecostal Movement as a cult, based on their opinions rather than personal experiences. I guess they were trying to prepare me for what was to come. What Creekside Church failed to grasp was that just as God Himself had brought me to them, He was now directing my steps to the next level: the Pentecostal church.

I had been a smoker for forty years and had no reason or desire to quit, yet three days before my scheduled baptism I decided to quit cold turkey.

When I showed up for that week's service at Creekside, I was literally vibrating. I sought out he pastor. "Pastor Jim, in the three years I've been here, I've never asked anyone for anything. I quit smoking a few days ago and I'm having a really hard time of it. Could you please pray for me."

I'll never forget what he did. It was still early and there were only twelve people there. Pastor Jim had us all gather together in a circle. While kneeling down, we all joined hands as the pastor prayed. I'm very secure in saying that what I felt had absolutely nothing to do with my nicotine withdrawal. When we joined hands, I felt as though I'd been hit by a Taser gun. When the prayer was finished, I definitely had peace about me. The vibrating had stopped. Miracle number six. I haven't had a cigarette since.

The night before my baptism, before leaving the coffee shop, Bonnie wanted to know if I would allow her to pray for me. I consented. However, I wasn't fully prepared for what was to come. It was dark in the parking lot, and she just asked that I close my eyes and receive her prayers. She placed one of her hands on my shoulder, the other on my forehead.

Her opening prayer was clear and beautiful in its nature: she prayed that I would be cured of HIV. Then, without warning, she broke out in a language which I thought was Hungarian. However, after she finished, to my surprise I learned she spoke no other language except English. Keeping my thoughts to myself, I felt she was very naive in suggesting that God would heal and remove my HIV. Little did I know she had just made a prophetic statement. A prophecy is a prediction about something that will happen in the future. I found her prediction beyond staggering. For the moment, the virus was undetectable, but that could change at any time. To me, it was never a question of *if* but *when* I would hit the cement wall for the final time.

Before we went our separate ways, we sat in her car and talked for a couple of minutes. At every opportunity, she reminded me of how proud she was of me for not backing out, in spite of hearing all kinds of garbage about the Pentecostal Church. I often joked with her, and this time I said, "Bonnie, my life has played itself out in the devil's backyard. If there's any truth to those rumors, I guess I'm finally going to meet him." From the time I met her to this moment, she had never exerted any pressure at all regarding baptism.

It definitely wasn't by accident that in exactly my fiftieth year I found myself on the steps of Emmanuel Pentecostal Church in New Westminster, B.C. I remember the night quite vividly. It was the second Sunday of November 2006, and I had arrived early. There was a slight chill in the evening breeze, but the spine-wrenching chills that penetrated the depths of my soul had nothing to do with the weather

Although I was still trying, with difficulty, to grasp the significance of divine intervention and its role in my life, I was about to jump my greatest hurdle and accept Jesus Christ as my personal savior, and be baptized in His name. While waiting for Bonnie to show up, I paced back and forth in restless apprehension in the church's inner courtyard, my thoughts racing frantically. I was gripped within a combination of fear and reverent awe.

I had carefully studied this church, which was well over a hundred years old, from many angles. I noticed that it had not only weathered many of its own storms, but it had resisted and overcome many obstacles. Suddenly, as if touched by lightning, I received all the clarification I needed regarding the hardships of my own life and what it all meant. My answers seemed to be found in the rustic nature of the church's appearance. I saw my own persistence and determination in its rugged beauty. In these precious moments, I somehow grasped with a firm conviction that Christ all along had known the circumstances of my life and was now drawing me to Himself. I broke out into a cold sweat. It had nothing to do with being nervous; the devil was mad, and he wasn't about to give up without a fight.

When Bonnie showed up, I entered the church with her for the first time, and was immediately embraced by its beauty. There was something very different about this church, as I could actually feel electricity in the air. I was embraced by an atmosphere of unbridled excitement. Looking at the people around me, I felt as though I had stepped onto the set of a Victorian movie; they were all dressed so regally.

The church could easily seat six hundred people, and just my luck, they all seemed to be in attendance tonight. My first impulse was to run. However, in overcoming this fear, I suggested to Bonnie that we sit close to the front. My reasoning was that I wouldn't have to worry what—or who—was behind me.

Dave Jobson was up on the platform, behind the pulpit, and clutched in his hand was a copy of my book. I just hoped there wasn't going to be a big production about me. More than anything else, I couldn't stand to be centered out.

A visiting evangelist was speaking that night, and his message—"Just keep on walking"—was powerful compared to anything I had previously heard at Creekside. Six years later, his message bears the same impact as when it was first given, for I'm still walking strong in that unmovable and unshakable faith.

I noticed that these Pentecostals had a way of getting into the spirit. Call it what you want, but they actually believed that the presence of God was in their midst, and they sure showed it. So far, it was like nothing I had expected. After the evangelist preached his sermon, I figured on an easy exit. No such luck. An altar call was given, and Bonnie pushed me out of the pew, leading me up to the front. Until this moment, I had never witnessed, let alone participated in, this biblical ritual.

Ten people circled me and started praying. One by one, they all lay their hands on me. I closed my eyes and tried to concentrate on what Dave Jobson was saying, but I found it very difficult and distracting, as many voices around me were giving advice. Maybe that was part of the problem. I was too busy paying attention to the physical to notice the spiritual. As long as you're following the direction of another, your focus moves away from God.

After twenty minutes, I was led upstairs to a room where I changed into a pair of sweats and a t-shirt. The baptismal tank was located in the floor behind the pulpit.

Within five minutes, I was baptized and back in my clothes.

Now came the moment of truth.

The Moment of Truth 69

Had there been a progressive, positive change in me leading to the baptism? More importantly, was there a noticeable change in me after coming out of the water? Many venture into the ritual of baptism clueless, and unfortunately leave in the same manner. It only stands to reason that if all you had getting into the tank was the smallest measure of hunger, then unquestionably that indescribable heartbeat of the universe would plug itself into your life, and one way or another, you'd know about it. Jesus told His disciples before His ascension to heaven that He would pour out His spirit upon all flesh. The pulse of God is in no way confusing; it's the greatest gift in the universe, and it's not about a feeling or an emotion, it's an unforgettable experience.

As I said, there must have been six hundred people at my baptism, and I really hated crowds. Before leaving that night, though, I'm pretty sure I shook hands with almost every person in the building. Another remarkable change I noticed was the swearing. Before my baptism, I had a foul mouth. I would use a curse word in every other sentence. After coming out of the water, I'm telling you, it was almost three months before I uttered the next curse word. When God steps into your life, you'll know it.

In life, there's two sides to every coin. Eventually we'll either become followers of Christ or continue to be servants of Satan. Following someone's baptism, you'll know what side of the coin they're on. If the spirit of God truly touched them, immediate transformation must take place. Those once covered by sin slowly begin to separate themselves from the things of the world, and their greatest desire turns to studying the Bible. Yet those who claim to have a strong relationship with God are often the very ones you never see with a Bible in church. I will always question such people's their relationship with God, as well as their sincerity.

But what could I possibly know of God? Writing about my experiences has in no way been meant to glorify myself. I have nothing to be proud of in my sorrowful past. In the world today, there are many whose hearts are full of unbelief toward the reality of God. They remain satisfied within their indifferent and unchanging rejection of His written Word. In this, the enemy of righteousness continues to imprison and blind them within his deceptive cloak of darkness, which extinguishes hope of their true glory.

Bitter words of discouragement are often hurled at those who have given their lives to God, by those who have never tasted the dynamic, cleansing power of the Holy Spirit. I often hear in their chronic complaining how hard it is to do the right thing. I challenge anyone on the face of the planet to put their trust in Jesus, who is mighty enough to restore a soul from any circumstance. Try it wholeheartedly for thirty days, for unquestionably you'll have a different story to tell.

There are a million reasons for people's continued resistance of God's promised light, but not one stands higher than our ignorance and defiance in the face of that which is unseen. As true Christians, we will encounter many who remain blinded to the light. Just as a lightning bolt stops you dead in your tracks, sometimes a warning just as powerful is needed. As born-again Christians, we must be willing to give expression to the enchantments surrounding our own faith, speaking directly about those unbridled blessings in our own deliverance, which we are persuaded have come from the throne of God.

According to 2 Corinthians 4:3, *"But if our gospel be hid, it is hid to them that are lost."* Something can only remain hidden until it is brought out of concealment. Those who have been blinded by darkness must have their eyes opened to the fact that there is a way out. They gather at a church in search of answers. However, those who know the difference continue to embrace the darkness of sin without exploring the possibilities of deliverance. They openly reject the message of salvation, as they would rather be servants of Satan. I wonder if such people think they'll get in twenty minutes before the rapture of the church. Their only hope of escaping the pits of hell is through the salvation found in the written word, which is the breath of our Almighty God! However, you cannot live a wholesome Christian life by exercising the strength of your faith alone, and those who try to run this race alone know nothing. Sustaining grace is mercifully given to us by a redeeming God who alone has freed us from the temptations and captivity of Satan.

When you accept Jesus into your life, contrary to what many would have you believe, you're not on a cruise ship. Instead you're on a battleship which is continually headed into the eye of the storm. This must always be a present reality, as we're now on our way to the Promised Land. You'll never get there without a constant battle. We must crucify our flesh, not weekly or monthly, but *daily*. No matter what anybody tries to tell you, believing in or accepting Jesus as your personal savior and being baptized in His name will never in a million years get you into the kingdom of heaven. The entrance requirements to heaven are the baptism of the water and the spirit, but this is only the bottom rung of the ladder. Anyone can receive the Holy Ghost, as it's a free gift; keeping it is where the problem arises. The storm is the continual separation from all aspects of unrighteousness. It's a brutal battle between the fleshly desires of the physical and the spiritual mantle of righteousness!

As is evident throughout my life, before coming to know God I played by the rules of the world, even making up some of my own along the way. Now that I've crossed over to the right side of the fence, the only rules I need to follow are those found in the King James Bible, God's inspired Word to us. This needs to be an extraordinary revelation to every so-called Christian.

Without any doubt, the sovereign God who many claim to worship is one of separation, and I will prove this. If anyone, from any denomination, can't grasp this straightforward principle of separation, which is an undeniable characteristic of God's nature, they will never know Him. The following words are an interpretation of what God said to Moses in regards to creation itself, and there's no mistaking God's frame of mind. In the beginning, God separated light from darkness, water from land, Eden from the rest of the world. He put Adam and Eve in Eden, demonstrating that He wanted them to be separated. What did God say once He had finished separating everything? Genesis 1:31 tells us, *"And God saw every thing that he had made, and behold, it was very good."*

Separation wasn't just good through the eyes of God, sovereign of the universe; it delighted Him. There's an enormous distinction between stepping into the presence of God and inviting His Holy Spirit to live inside you, which is what the baptism of the Holy Ghost is all about. It's no longer a matter of separation; it becomes the commanding issue of death to sin, as His righteousness *cannot* and *will not* indwell in unrighteousness. Simply put, they don't belong together. Many will find their own irrational interpretations in an attempt to discredit this, but it's an exercise in futility as there's no greater authority than the Bible. When it comes to God, there are no exceptions. Not one.

The first step in the process to receiving the Holy Ghost is one of separation. We first need to be convinced that God exists, giving us a doorway of escape from any situation. For us to actually step into the presence of God, we must first be willing to separate ourselves from those things which are unpleasant to Him. It only stands to reason that just as stepping into God's presence requires separation, death to all sin is the absolute prerequisite of His Holy Spirit coming to live within you. The Bible clearly tells us that *no one* is righteous.

Most of what I say isn't an interpretation. It's fact, as it comes directly out of the King James Bible. Churches all around the world need a drastic wake-up call, especially now, in what I am convinced are the last days. Given my extraordinary journey, I'm entitled to my opinion and ask in the deepest form of humility that anyone reading these words to not take them as arrogance. These are words of encouragement when it comes to receiving the Holy Ghost, the greatest gift in the universe.

In Matthew 24:4–5, Jesus clearly states, *"Take heed that no man deceive you. For many shall come in my name, saying, I am Christ; and shall deceive many."* He was talking about anyone who claims to be a minister or ambassador of Christ. The Bible also tells us that God will not be mocked. Don't be fooled by anyone's agenda or motive; there's only one opinion that has complete authority over you, and that's the inspired Word of God—your Bible.

Many people come to the altar fresh off the street, and after a few words from a self-glorified man of God—a few unintelligent phrases which are nothing more than a counterfeit of the truth—they claim that they really want to know God, but they haven't got a clue as to the process involved. The man of God nods, affirming that this clueless person has just received the Holy Ghost. Give me a break. This is as deceptive as a three-dollar bill. This person just received the spirit of God in him, the greatest gift in the universe, but as soon as he steps out of the church he lights up a cigarette, drinks, and does drugs. I guess we're now taking the express elevator to the top, bypassing the essential requirements of separation.

Without separation, you can't step into the presence of God, which is acknowledging His very existence. Without this recognition, you can't receive the Holy Ghost, and rest assured, you will never enter the kingdom of God without it. That's a fact. Don't fool yourself. Receiving the baptism of God's righteous Spirit dwelling in you requires nothing less than the greatest battle you've ever had to fight. Anything less is about as dry as a peanut butter sandwich in the hot sun. Take it from a voice of experience.

The Footprints of God 70

I'm convinced that each and every one of us has experienced the footprints of God many times throughout our lives, yet many would find themselves hard-pressed to give even one example. In the Old Testament, God gives us the clear instruction for recognizing those footprints, and in the same scripture it becomes self-explanatory why we miss them.

Psalms 46:10 says, *"Be still, and know that I am God."*

Our lives, for the most part, are like major airport terminals. Twenty-four hours a day, seven days a week, they're in a state of constant pandemonium, as they never shut down and never have time to be still. This is so true of our lives, especially in the world we live in, where no matter which way we turn, things seem to be spinning out of control at breakneck speed. We also must contend with what I call the deliberate technological distractions that keep us not only occupied, but continually hypnotized, if not desensitized.

When we look at the hundreds of prophecies (predictions) surrounding the coming of Jesus Christ, who was the fullness of God manifested in the flesh, we see that any ten of them went beyond mathematical improbability. Looking then at the journey of our own conversion experiences, expect to see similar patterns of improbability. Had someone given my parents an exact road map, it would have been discarded long before its fulfilment. Not only were the miraculous transformations of my life improbable, they clearly had the footprints of God all over them.

To begin with, one must first understand that the beginning stages of any conversion are twofold. First comes the revelation of who God is. When God introduces Himself to us, He does so in such a way that there can be no denying you've heard from God. Also, in whatever manner He decides to manifest Himself to you, He will continue to do so in the same fashion. He won't talk to you in ten different ways, as that could get pretty confusing, and as the Bible tells us, God is not the author of confusion. Secondly, there must come the revelation of Jesus Christ, as without recognizing His lordship over our lives, we can never understand the true nature of God.

People continually come to the Lord in many different ways. Most have been blessed by being raised in a Christian atmosphere. I never had that privilege. Considering the history of my family, religion was something from another planet. If there ever were a family whose heart was hardened, it was mine. Many find spiritual guidance and direction through close friends; again, this was a dead end for me, as I never had religious friends, and any I may have known were kept at a guarded distance. Lastly, many attend church and find God through an invitation. None of these were influences in my life, and for the most part they were viewed as weakness.

In some cases, God has to reach down and pluck someone out of the unimaginable. The steps of my conversion were nothing short of a marvel, preordained by God Himself. Please understand this conclusion is made from a spirit of humility. Even now I consider myself undeserving. As I unravel my road map, though, my conversion experience is as clear as when Jesus stopped the Apostle Paul on the road to Damascus. The only difference is that I didn't become convinced of it until my fiftieth year.

When I first began writing the story of my life, without realizing it I documented the miraculous footprints of God. However, it took seven years before I acknowledged them as such. My intention has never been to try convincing anyone of anything. We all have God's footprints in our lives, it's just a matter of thinking about our own journeys and then writing down all those extraordinary and unexplainable events.

The Bible clearly tells us that no one comes to the Father (God) except through the Son (Jesus). Therefore, in pinpointing the footprints of God upon my life, I'll concentrate on the life and death of Jesus Christ.

Jesus Christ was God manifested in the flesh. Two thousand years ago, He was born of a virgin, and for exactly thirty-three and a half years He dwelt among us. After He was crucified, as was predicted, He was resurrected from the grave and spent forty days with His chosen disciples. Before ascending to heaven, Jesus instructed His disciples to wait in Jerusalem, as He had no intention of leaving them comfortless. He then sent His Holy Spirit to empower them to carry out the great commission, which was to take the good news of the kingdom to all the world, but His Spirit would indwell each and every believer. They prayed together in one accord, and ten days later they were all baptized with the Holy Ghost and fire.

Exactly fifty days after the resurrection of our Lord Jesus Christ, the New Testament church was born, yet Pentecost was never an afterthought with God; it was a divinely orchestrated event in God's three-part salvation plan.

When in careful study, you can see that Pentecostalism has a colorful history. It is sovereign in nature. Twelve hundred years before the supernatural birth of Jesus Christ, God's chosen people, the Israelites, went into their predetermined slavery under Egyptian rule. After four hundred years of complete silence to their prayers, God sent Moses to bring all the Israelites out of captivity. I find it fascinating that Moses, who at one time was being groomed for the throne of Egypt, spent forty years on the backside of the desert in hiding as a murderer. Before being given this mission by God, Moses definitely had the anointing presence of God's Spirit upon him.

Before Pharaoh agreed to release the Israelites, God first had to inflict ten plagues on Egypt, and the tenth plague—death to all firstborn—was the worst. Clear instruction was given to the Israelites that they were to mark the doorposts of their homes with the blood of a spring lamb. When the Spirit of the Lord came that night and saw the blood, it immediately knew to pass over the firstborn in those homes. As a result, Pharaoh let a nation of slaves go free. From that moment on, the feast of Passover became a time-honored celebration by the Israelites, in remembrance of what God had done for them.

Symbolically, this could well be considered the birth of Pentecostalism, of things yet to come. Moses's forty years in the desert and the ten plagues represent the number fifty. Also, from the time the Israelites left Egypt to the time Moses received the Ten Commandments on Mount Sinai, fifty days went by, and in this began the Feast of Pentecost, a celebration of the Law which Moses received from God.

Given the nightmare of my trials and tribulations, the odds of my ever coming to Christ were very slim, yet as if it were an appointed time, in exactly my fortieth year, for the first time ever, I found myself asking for God's help. I never really expected anything to happen, yet within three days, God answered my insincere plea. Could it be that I'm just looking for coincidences? Then explain how it was possible that on exactly the third day, when I was at rock bottom, with no way out, Debby miraculously stepped into my life. From that moment on, like falling dominoes, it seemed as though my life was blessed with one miracle after another.

Shortly after Debby's death, almost seven years to the day of first meeting her, God decided to enroll me in my Christian kindergarten experience. I know how all this might sound, but understand that my conversion was totally dependent upon the progression of these events. The number seven represents completion. Just read the opening verses of Genesis. God created the universe in six days and rested on the seventh. I—and that is the key word—could have gone to any church at any time I so desired, but then it would make it my will, not God's.

The Bible says that signs, wonders, and miracles shall follow them that believe. Since the utterance of my feeble plea, one could easily question my belief, but let's look at it from another perspective. Jeremiah 33:3 says, *"Call unto me, and I shall answer thee, and shew thee great and mighty things, which thou knowest not."*

When one cries out to God, He *will* answer. It's got nothing to do with a verbal response; God will direct the path in which you are to go, and He'll make a way where just a moment ago none existed. As long as you're willing to go in that direction, whether you believe in God or not, your compliance adds to or strengthens your unrecognized faith.

My parents divorced in 1974, and my father quickly remarried. The last time I was to see him alive was in 1982. Twenty-two years later, I spoke on the telephone to a young woman whose name strangely happened to be Mike Pavlic, the same as my younger brother. I learned that she was my father's third and youngest daughter; until that phone call, I hadn't known she even existed. We could have met in any number of places, yet she wanted to meet at her church. We met there a couple of times before she disappeared, yet for the next three years I attended that church regularly. Clearly, God never intended for me to build a condominium at Creekside Church; realistically, it was only a place of preparation for what was yet to come, God's ultimate design for my life.

After three years, one day while running around doing errands I stopped to get a coffee, where I met Bonnie. Our conversation ventured into areas of spirituality I had not yet experienced. Over the course of five months, we formed a unique friendship. Her teaching gave me a much clearer understanding of the Bible.I found myself researching and reading all I could on baptism and finally decided I needed to make a decision. From an ignorant understanding, this much even I could figure out. If Jesus Christ decided He was coming back tonight, I'd find myself on the wrong side of eternity in the morning. In the words of

Jesus Himself, John 3:3 says, *"Except a man be born again, he cannot see the kingdom of God."* Then again, in John 3:5, it says, *"Except a man be born of water and of the Spirit, he cannot enter into the kingdom of God."* After speaking about baptism with David Jobson, an elder from her church, he agreed to baptize me the following Sunday.

The night before my baptism, Bonnie prophesied as she prayed for me. Just as I read in my Bible, Bonnie anointed me with oil, then laid her hands on my shoulders and began praying in tongues. She asked Jesus to heal me of HIV, and I was moved by her compassion.

The number forty is mentioned many times throughout the Bible. It's clearly a number God attributes major importance to, especially when preparing to use someone for His glory. In exactly my fortieth year, I called out to God. As we already know, Pentecost represents the number fifty, yet in exactly my fiftieth year I was baptized in Jesus's name in a Pentecostal church. As I said, God always leaves His signature.

Seventy-three was the year of my gradual descent into the cesspool of hell on earth. When Bonnie stepped into my life, I find it uncanny that she was thirty-seven years old. The numbers are inverted. Not convinced? Buckle your seatbelt. As far as I or Bonnie were concerned, we had never known or met each other prior to meeting at the coffeehouse. Two months after my baptism, I gave her a copy of my book to read. When she gave the book to her mother, imagine our surprise to learn that when Bonnie was born, she lived three houses away from ours, and I was actually friends with her brother. The reason I never knew her is that she was just a baby in a crib!

At the beginning of this chapter, in recalling the life of Jesus, I stated that He was God manifested in the flesh, who dwelt with us on earth for thirty-three and a half years. When my book was first published in 2004, in no way had I yet acknowledged God in my life. In May 1973, my life turned itself upside-down and the chances of my ever coming out of the pit were slim to none. In November 2006, I was baptized in Jesus's name. Now you tell me, is it really a coincidence that between the two dates exactly thirty-three and a half years elapsed?

A year and a half after Bonnie prayed for me, someone from Dr. Montaner's office spoke these words: "As a result of your blood work continually being undetectable to traces of the virus, and since you have absolutely no side effects, it's safe to say there is no HIV in your body." To me, those words were the next best thing to a healing. To date, seven years later, I remain undetectable, with no side effects. Praise the name of Jesus.

However, accepting Jesus as your personal savior and taking on His name through baptism is just the beginning. Through gradual steps of separation, your life in all areas will experience a transformation you never thought possible. God will use you for His glory as well. All of us, in one form or another, through our trials, have been groomed for a specific calling or ministry. Looking at the nightmare of my life, what ministry could I possibly fulfill? Three years after my baptism, when I was approached and asked to become part of the prison ministry group with the church, I thought that these people were very naïve. Someone with my background could never step into such a position. Behind me there's a trail of sixty-six adult convictions, for a multitude of offences. Having spent fourteen years of my life in prisons across Canada, I assumed this immediately disqualified me as a suitable candidate. I expected an outright denial from the prison administration, based on my record. Not wanting to discourage the good intentions of those in the church, I filed the necessary documents with the local RCMP detachment. Well, the birthplace of the miraculous has always found itself in the pregnancy of expectation.

The church never for a moment doubted my participation in the prison ministry. As if orchestrated by divine appointment, for the past five years I've been regularly ministering behind the walls to incarcerated inmates. My testimony has chipped away at what were once considered hardened and unreachable hearts.

Sometimes you have to break the thick layer of ice before you can go fishing. On my last visit, I started out this way: "I'm aware that many different groups come in throughout the month, and each undoubtedly brings with them a kind word of encouragement, telling you how much they know about God." I looked at each man individually. "Well that won't be me here today, and I'll tell you why. I'm looking into the faces of men who need something far greater than mere encouragement. All your lives, you've received from judges, probation officers, parole officers, and guards the same old encouraging rhetoric. By all appearances, it's done absolutely nothing for you."

When you pile up all the tribulations, heartaches, and disappointments these men had been through, all the encouragement in the world couldn't begin to erase the nightmare of their journeys. Every time I go into the prison, I find myself staring into the faces of men who are searching for a hope beyond hope, and that's why I believe our coming together was ordained by divine appointment. Having once been hardened to everything but survival, I tell the men there's only one reason they should carefully consider every word I say. Their only question should be, "What does this person know of what I've been through, am presently going through, or how I feel?" I've definitely walked a mile or two in their shoes, and then some. My purpose is not to tell them about God, but rather to serve as a living testimony, to tell them what God will do for them. Whatever He's done for me, if they're sincere and truly desire a change, He will do the same for them.

Just as a spiritual road map exists, which reveals the steps of our conversion experience, a similar road map clearly outlines the return of Jesus Christ. As the present period of grace nears its closing moments, rest assured that the instant this door closes, nothing will delay the return of Jesus—and I personally believe we are on that very doorstep. Are you ready, and do you know in which direction you're headed?

Conlusion: The Final Hour

Since coming to the Lord, I've heard countless messages and theories from men and women who have more degrees behind their name than a thermometer, predicting end-time doom and gloom. Their elegant rhetoric could win Academy Awards, but they're missing the point, and their antics are very deceptive. Firstly, as born-again Christians, we're not supposed to be in the entertainment industry. I thought it was all about soul-winning. Prophecy really has nothing to do with what might happen next month, next year, or years from now; it's all already in the Bible and it's going to happen. For born-again Christians, that should never be our concern. We should be more worried about what might happen tomorrow.

Tomorrow as of yet doesn't exist. A sad fact of life is that many around the planet will never get to see it. We were given the great commission by Jesus Himself, to go into all the world and preach the good news of the kingdom to all people. But we aren't supposed to stop there. Any time there's a sermon or message given, any time the opportunity presents itself for an evangelistic outreach, any time we open our mouths to witness to someone, if we don't tell them how to get into the kingdom, along with an open invitation, we might as well close the doors of the church. My Bible tells me exactly that: *"If I do not the works of my Father, believe me not"* (John 10:37).

When you meet a first-time visitor to church, or have a chance encounter on the street, it may be a divine appointment orchestrated by God. It may be that person's only (or final) opportunity to hear about the kingdom. How sad and neglectful should that person happen to wake up tomorrow on the wrong side of eternity! They're eternal question should be ringing in all our ears: "Why didn't they tell me?"

My Bible tells me that God will send the foolish things of the world to confuse the wise. Truthfully, as you've read my story, you couldn't get more foolish than me. As it says in Hebrews 13:8, Jesus Christ is the same yesterday, today, and forever. In light of this eternal promise, religion must demand an experience from its declarations; truths without facts—or more importantly, declarations without actual experiences behind them—are more dangerous and far more deceptive than a lie.

In closing, until we meet again in another book, my greatest reward will be that in some way, the story of my life has dropped its seed upon your life and inspired you to reach for greater heights than you ever imagined.

Remember, you are never defeated until you choose to accept defeat as your reality.

To contact the author, visit
http://www.fanstory.com/minopavlic